essays are the work of Swedish, German, Polish, Italian, English, South African and American scientists.

Some of the various aspects of the race question discussed in the essays are:

◆ The anthropological history and racial systematics of the races of man.

◆ The history of racial classification and the principles underlying the morphological approach to racial systematics.

◆ The relation between race, heredity and the rise and fall of peoples and civilizations.

◆ A review of past research on interracial and subracial crosses and results of studies of the offspring of Italian mothers and colored fathers in postwar Italy.

◆ The basic principles of population genetics and the genetic basis of racial differences.

◆ The interrelationships between race, genetics, history and the structure of society, and the interaction between culture and biology throughout the evolutionary history of man.

◆ The concept of race in contemporary social theory and the roots of racial preference and group identity.

◆ The relation between race and culture with works of art as a guide to racial differences in psychological traits.

◆ The difference between Negroes and Whites in psychological test scores.

◆ The problem of measuring mental differences between primitive or non-literate racial and ethnic groups.

Race and Modern Science contains a mine of information on the history of the races of man and how they differ. These sixteen scientific studies, free from all political orientation, will prove rewarding to the thoughtful reader.

RACE AND MODERN SCIENCE

RACE
AND
MODERN
SCIENCE

*A Collection of Essays by Biologists,
Anthropologists, Sociologists and Psychologists*

EDITED, WITH AN INTRODUCTION, BY

ROBERT E. KUTTNER

SOCIAL SCIENCE PRESS

NEW YORK · 1967

COPYRIGHT © 1967 BY SOCIAL SCIENCE PRESS
LIBRARY OF CONGRESS CATALOG CARD NUMBER 67–22036
Manufactured in the United States of America by
Kingsport Press, Inc., Kingsport,Tennessee

TO

THE MEMORY OF THE LATE

R. RUGGLES GATES

WHO PROPOSED AND HELPED PLAN THIS BOOK

CONTENTS

INTRODUCTION   xiii

PART I   ANTHROPOLOGY

RACE AND ANTHROPOLOGY, by BERTIL LUNDMAN   3
> THE EUROPIDS; BLOND INDO-EUROPEAN TRIBES; RACIAL TYPES IN MODERN EUROPE; RACIAL CHARACTER OF INDIA; THE MONGOLIDS; AMERICAN INDIANS AND ESKIMOS; THE NEGRIDS AND OCEANIC PEOPLES; RACES AND CLIMATE; LITERATURE; LITERATURE SURVEY

MORPHOLOGY AND THE CLASSIFICATION OF RACE, by JAN CZEKANOWSKI   29
> RACIAL CLASSIFICATIONS OF MANKIND; CONTRIBUTION OF RUDOLF VIRCHOW; EVIDENCE OF THE BIOLOGICAL REALITY OF RACES; TYPOLOGICAL ANALYSIS OF OBSERVATIONS ON THE LIVING; WANKE'S METHOD OF APPROXIMATION; ANALYSIS OF THE DEFINITION OF RACE; CRITICISM OF MORPHOLOGICAL APPROACH TO ANTHROPOLOGY; RACIAL TYPES AND MIGRATION; LITERATURE

RACIAL BIOLOGY OF THE BANTU OF SOUTH AFRICA, by J. D. J. HOFMEYR   69
> POPULATION GENETICS AND FORMATION OF RACES; GENES AND INTELLIGENCE; RACIAL ORIGINS OF THE BANTU POPULATION; ETHNOGENESIS AND ETHNOLOGY OF THE BANTU; SOCIAL ORGANIZATION OF THE BANTU; PHYSICAL ANTHROPOLOGY OF THE BANTU; AN OPPORTUNITY FOR STUDY OF GENETIC DRIFT; LITERATURE

RACE AND THE BIOLOGICAL HISTORY OF PEOPLES, by Ilse Schwidetzky   95
> ANTHROPOLOGICAL THEORIES OF HISTORY; THE GENETICS OF RACE MIXTURE; PHYSICAL ANTHROPOLOGY AND RACIAL HISTORY; POPULATION STRUCTURE AND CULTURAL GROWTH; RACE MIXTURE AND THE DECLINE OF CIVILIZATION; THE IMMIGRATION FACTOR IN SOCIAL SYSTEMS; LITERATURE

PART II   BIOLOGY

A STUDY OF RACIAL AND SUBRACIAL CROSSING, by Luigi Gedda   123
> THE CROSSING OF SUBRACES; WHITE AND COLORED MISCEGENATION; AN INCREASE IN HYBRIDIZATION; LITERATURE

RACE AND HEREDITY, by David C. Rife   141
> POPULATIONS AND GENETIC VARIATIONS; THE OCCURRENCE OF KURU AMONG A NEW GUINEA TRIBE; THE PROPORTION OF SPECIFIC GENES CAUSE POPULATION DIFFERENCES; DEFINITION OF RACES OF MAN; GENETIC FACTORS IN POPULATION RELATIONSHIP; INTERACTION OF HEREDITY AND ENVIRONMENT PRODUCES CULTURE; THE INFLUENCE OF CULTURAL BARRIERS; THE RESULT OF RACIAL AMALGAMATION; HYBRID VIGOR AND MISCEGENATION; TALENTED ETHNIC GROUPS WHO HAVE ABSTAINED FROM INTERRACIAL MARRIAGES; LITERATURE

THE RACES OF MAN AND HUMAN GENETICS, by C. P. Oliver   171
> THE PROBLEM OF RACE AND SPECIES DEFINITIONS; DIVERSITY WITHIN A POPULATION UNIT; DIVERSITY AMONG POPULATION UNITS; STUDY OF GENIC CONSTITUTION; ORIGIN OF GENETIC DIVERSITY; SIMILAR PHENOTYPES WITH DIFFERENT GENES; NATURAL SELECTION AND ADAPTATION; PLEIOTROPISM AND GENETIC UNBALANCE; THE EFFECTS OF INTERACTION; MAN AND EVOLUTIONARY PROCESSES; MORE KNOWLEDGE OF GENES AND HUMAN RACES NEEDED; LITERATURE

BIOCHEMICAL ANTHROPOLOGY, by ROBERT E. KUTTNER   197

    BIOCHEMICAL METHODS AND TECHNIQUES; NUTRITIONAL SUBSTANCES; CHOLESTEROL; SERUM PROTEINS; BIOCHEMISTRY FINDINGS AND RACIAL VARIATIONS; SERUM ELECTROLYTES AND PEPSINOGEN; SALIVARY AMYLASE AND URIC ACID; HEMOGLOBINS; MISCELLANEOUS FACTORS; AN AID TO THE STUDY OF RACES; LITERATURE

PART III SOCIOLOGY

HUMAN SOCIETY AND GENETICS, by C. D. DARLINGTON   225

    EARLY MAN; INBREEDING AND OUTBREEDING; THE LAST PALEOLITHIC EXPANSION; THE ORIGIN OF AGRICULTURE; THE NEOLITHIC EXPANSION; INVENTIONS, TRIBES AND CASTES; THE CITY AND THE NATION; THE LINGUISTIC EXPANSIONS; THE NEW PEOPLES; POPULATION CONTROL; DESTRUCTION OF HABITAT AND MIGRATION; THE CARRYING OF CIVILIZATION; RELIGION, RACE AND CULTURE; MENTAL TRAITS AND EVOLUTION; LITERATURE

RACE AND SOCIOLOGY, by CORRADO GINI   261

    RACE CONSCIOUSNESS IN CIVILIZED SOCIETIES; THE QUESTION OF "PURE" RACES; RACE, PEOPLE AND NATION; THE RACIAL COMPOSITION OF VARIOUS NATIONS; GROUP SENTIMENT AND RACE FORMATION; THE INFLUENCE OF GEOGRAPHIC FACTORS; RACISM AND EVOLUTION

EVOLUTIONARY THEORY, RACE AND SOCIETY, by A. JAMES GREGOR   277

    ETHNOCENTRISM AND HUMAN BEHAVIOR; DEVELOPMENT OF GUMPLOWICZ THEORY; PHYSICAL ANTHROPOLOGY AND RACE; MODERN CONCEPTION OF RACE; DYNAMICS OF MATE SELECTION; CONSCIOUSNESS OF KIND; "DEVELOPMENTAL IDENTIFICATION"; SIMILARITY AND PREFERENCE; ADULT RESPONSE MORE VARIABLE; THE BASIS OF RACIAL PREJUDICE; NOTES

SELECTIVE ASSOCIATION OF ETHNIC GROUPS,
by George A. Lundberg 305
> THE SUBJECTS AND METHOD OF STUDY; FREQUENCY AND OVERLAPPING OF CHOICES; THE CHOICES OF THE DIFFERENT ETHNIC GROUPS; COMPARISON OF IN-GROUP AND OUT-GROUP CHOOSING; CHARACTERISTICS OF THE NON-JEWISH WHITES WHO MADE OUT-GROUP CHOICES; OUT-GROUP CHOICES BY THE MINORITIES; APPLICATION OF THE FINDINGS TO LARGE POPULATIONS; THE ABOLITION OF FREEDOM OF CHOICE; NOTES

PART IV   PSYCHOLOGY

RACE AND CULTURE, by Friedrich Keiter 333
> PHYSICAL APPEARANCE AND CULTURAL HISTORICAL PROCESSES; THE BEHAVIORAL EFFECTS OF RACIAL MORPHOLOGY; WORKS OF ART AS A GUIDE TO RACE AND CULTURE; THE IMPORTANCE OF SOCIAL BEHAVIORAL DIFFERENCES OF THE SEXES; RACE AND GROUP BEHAVIORAL PHENOTYPES; AREAS OF RESEARCH IN THE STUDY OF NATIONAL CHARACTER; HAPTIC AND OPTIC HISTORICAL WORKS OF ART; PREHISTORIC CULTURES REVEALED IN ART FORMS; RESULTS OF ANALYSIS OF AFRICAN AND POLYNESIAN LYRIC POETRY; LITERATURE

THE CULTURAL HYPOTHESIS AND PSYCHOLOGICAL TESTS, by Frank C. J. McGurk 367
> THE PSYCHOLOGICAL STUDY OF DRAFTEES IN WORLD WAR I; RESEARCH PUBLISHED BETWEEN 1935 AND 1950; THE TANSER STUDY—1939; THE BRUCE STUDY—1940; THE SHUEY STUDY—1942; THE BROWN STUDY—1944; THE RHOADS STUDY—1945; THE MCGURK STUDY—1951; FINDINGS FAIL TO SUPPORT "CULTURAL HYPOTHESIS"; CULTURAL CLIMATE AND TEST-SCORE DIFFERENCES; VALUE JUDGMENTS AND SCIENTIFIC EVIDENCE; LITERATURE

RACIAL DIFFERENCES IN SCHOOL ACHIEVEMENT, by R. Travis Osborne 383
> CANNOT KEEP PACE; I.Q. REGRESSION; RACES AND SEXES PAIRED; PROBLEMS FOR EDUCATORS

ETHNIC GROUPS AND THE MAZE TEST, by S. D. PORTEUS   409
>THE RESPONSE OF ABORIGINES; BUSHMEN SHOW KEEN INTEREST; RESULTS OF TEST IN AN AIR FORCE UNIT; TEST PERFORMANCE OF AMERICAN INDIAN; RESULTS AMONG VARIOUS ASIATIC GROUPS; DIFFERENCES IN TEST ACHIEVEMENT; THE QUESTION OF MENTAL ALERTNESS; MAN THE ANIMAL AND MAN THE THINKER; LITERATURE

INDEX   i

INTRODUCTION

To attempt an exhaustive treatment of the race concept within the confines of a single volume, however large, would be unrealistic. The present volume entertains no such intention. What it does intend is to be stimulating and informative. In being informative it is expected to contribute to the analysis of the concept "race." In this subsidiary sense this volume constitutes a contribution to concept analysis.

For a collection of essays to be stimulating requires at least that the contributions deliver themselves of something more than commonplaces, that the several essayists have, in fact, something to say. And for what is said to be informative requires that the contributions be competent.

The original essays collected in this volume certainly meet these minimum qualifications. The participating authors, who are eminently competent, were invited to contribute to this symposium because their ideas were known to be original, provocative, and even controversial. Their essays are here collected in the conviction that science thrives on originality, stimulation and the conflict of ideas.

Nothing is more stultifying to science than unthinking unanimity of opinion. But the essayists who have contributed to this volume have something of significance to say and they say it with competence which qualifies this collection as a serious contribution to the contemporary literature devoted to the race concept. That this is so recommends this work to the specialist and the intelligent layman alike.

The subsidiary concern of this collection is to provide material for an analysis of the concept "race." Like so much of its vocabulary, science inherited the term "race" from ordinary language. Of obscure etymological derivation, the term has an awesome constellation of meanings in ordinary discourse—and, unfortunately, a very high affect potential. Among the many "meanings" a term can have, emotive "meaning" is not the least significant. In ordinary language we refer to the emotive "connotations" of a term, that indeterminate collection of sometimes highly volatile sentiments that a word invokes.

Throughout its history, the term "race" has been a word capable of generating enormous heat. This has been particularly true in the twentieth century. As a consequence there has been a concerted effort on the part of a not inconsiderable number of research scientists and scholars to abandon the use of the term entirely. In its place complex nouns like "ethnic group" or neologisms like "genogroup" were to be substituted. Such a substitution recommends itself only as a device to urge what every competent scientist knows, i.e., that the cognitive meaning of a term must be distinguished from its emotive connotations.

That scientists should have to be reminded of such a consideration is indeed curious. But such terminological substitutions are of little concern in the serious treatment of a scientific concept. Whatever can be said of "genogroup" can be said without qualification of "race." On occasion, however, the suggestion has been made that the term "race" literally has no reference, that there are no natural entities that could be characterized as races. Scientists are counseled not to find alternate expressions for the term, but to abandon the concept. This is a much more ambitious claim.

But that Laplanders have more in common with each other than any of them have in common with Negroes seems so evidently the case that such a contention borders on the absurd. However mankind is studied subspecific distinctions are made and the several constituent aggregates meet the minimal nominal definition of "race": a population sharing a common gene pool which differs from that of other populations in gene frequency, i.e., in the relative commonness of certain hereditary characteristics. It is simple imposture to identify, without qualification, the concept "race" as a "myth."

Introduction

Whatever cognitive significance a term has can be explicated by nominal and real definition. The basic requirement of a nominal definition is that it enable us to eliminate the *definiendum*, the term to be defined, in favor of the *definiens*, a term or phrase whose meaning is already determined. Since this is the case, there is almost universal recognition of a nominal definition of "race" which meets this requirement. The real definition of "race," on the other hand, involves matters of empirical fact, the observation in nature of phenomena that characterize the concept. If a term is not to be solely a linguistic device it must satisfy the minimum conditions for real definition. It must have empirical reference. "Race" has just such reference.

Thus the concept "race" is not simply a "classificatory device." It supports more than simply nominal definition. It exemplifies the recognition of a natural fact, that human populations can be distinguished on the basis of the frequency and incidence of hereditary traits. What these differences are, in fact, can only be answered by the specialized sciences, and improved research techniques and increasing technological sophistication have indicated that these differences are more numerous than might have been suspected as recently as a decade ago.

The cognitive import of the concept "race" can be studied most effectively by determining the conditions under which the members of the scientific community are disposed to employ it. To ascertain the cognitive meaning of the term it is necessary to determine to what sorts of objects it is effectively applied. The essays in this collection, in which specialists address themselves to the problem of race, is a contribution to just that kind of concept analysis.

Whether the term "race" has a relatively specific intention, or refers to a set of approximating meanings, is a problem which cannot be fully resolved here, but it is clear the concept serves the major objectives of empirical science: to assist us to adequately and parsimoniously describe particular phenomena in the world of our experience and to provide insight into the general principles by virtue of which they can be explained and predicted.

Thus some of our authors will concentrate on the descriptive while others will focus on its explanatory function of the concept.

This distinction seems to characterize the differences in general anthropology between what has been sometimes called the taxonomic or morphological conception and the populationist conception of race. The former seems more concerned with description while the latter seems more preoccupied with explanation. The former is essentially the concern of descriptive or classificatory sciences like zoology, anatomy and physical anthropology while the latter is the product of explanatory sciences like genetics, psychology and sociology.

Whether these emphases and techniques can be synthesized into one overarching cognitive meaning that can be assigned to the term "race" is a question that cannot be dealt with here with any finality. But these essays do provide a contribution to the on-going attempts at resolution. However the issues are resolved it can hardly be gainsaid that the concept "race" has cognitive significance and scientific importance.

II

There is an extensive body of analytic and expository literature devoted to the race concept. Of that literature the material published under the auspices of Unesco merits some discussion. In 1950 the director general of Unesco was instructed to study and collect materials concerning questions of race; to give wide diffusion to the information so collected and to prepare an educational program based on such information. As part of this substantive and analytic program, Unesco issued what purported to be a definitive "Statement on Race" as well as a series of pamphlets devoted to various aspects of the race question. Fourteen of these pamphlets were later collected and reprinted in a single volume entitled *Race and Science*.[1]

This material met with such wide-ranging and searching objections from the scientific community that Unesco was forced to significantly modify the original "Statement" and to publish a booklet surveying these many comments and criticisms.[2] Among the scholars who expressed their views in *The Race Concept* and criticized, in whole or in part, the Unesco manifesto were such

[1] *Race and Science*. New York, 1961.
[2] *The Race Concept: Results of an Inquiry*. Paris: Unesco, 1952.

Introduction

international notables as Professors C. D. Darlington, C. S. Coon, R. Fisher, E. Fischer, G. Genna, F. Lenz, K. Saller, W. Scheidt, H. Weinert, K. Mather, H. J. Muller, A. H. Sturtevant, W. Landauer and T. Kemp.[3]

Similar criticism has been leveled against the series of Unesco pamphlets by other scientists. Professor Georges A. Heuse, the eminent French biologist and director of the department of ethnopsychology of the Institute of Applied Social Psychology of the Social Science Section of Unesco, critically reviewed a number of the pamphlets, and in one article remarked:

"Unesco's first venture into anthropology was an unhappy one and we recall the protests which greeted its first declaration on race—a veritable Bible for egalitarians—conceived chiefly by Ashley Montagu, an anthropologist who identifies race as a social myth, and by a group of sociologists substantially ignorant of anthropology."[4]

Dr. Henry E. Garrett, professor emeritus of psychology at Columbia University and past president of the American Psychological Association, in a review of Otto Klineberg's Unesco pamphlet, *Race and Psychology*, found serious omissions and misinterpretations.[5]

Dr. A. James Gregor, in a review of the Unesco pamphlet by Juan Comas, *Racial Myths*, characterized it as a work of "incredibly poor scholarship."[6]

In a review of another of Unesco's inspired publications, Marie Jahoda's *Race Relations and Mental Health*, Professor Gregor cited "instances of general confusion, the introduction of value predicates in discussion of fact, the gratuitous employment of elaborate psychoanalytic machinery (of dubious serviceability)," as well as the "seeming occurrence of elementary logical errors."[7]

---

[3] In view of the high standing of these scientists, excerpts from their criticism of the Unesco pronouncement on race have been appended to the introduction.

[4] Georges A. Heuse, "Race, Racismes et Antiracismes," *Revue de Psychologie des Peuples*, X (1955), 368–381.

[5] Henry E. Garrett, "Klineberg's Chapter on Race and Psychology: A Review," *The Mankind Quarterly*, Vol. I, No. 1 (1960), 15–22.

[6] A. James Gregor, "Comas' Chapter on *Racial Myths*: A Review," *The Mankind Quarterly*, Vol. II, No. 1 (1961) 30–34.

[7] A. James Gregor, "Race Relations and Mental Health: A Review," *The Mankind Quarterly*, Vol. I, No. 4 (1961), 248–252.

The Unesco series of publications on race which, to say the least, leave much to be to desired, suggested that what was needed was a new collection of essays devoted to the relationship of race and anthropology, heredity, sociology and psychology, such as are brought together in the present volume. The idea was originally conceived by the late Professor R. Ruggles Gates, a pioneer in the science of human genetics. It contains sixteen essays by outstanding scientists from seven nations and attempts to survey contemporary empirical research in the area of race and race relations and in so doing evidence the scientific import of the race concept.

The essays make possible an analysis of trends in the scientific study of race, a consideration of some of the problems, both analytic and empirical, encountered by researchers in the various fields and an indication of areas for future research.

In the field of anthropology, the concept of "race" has been employed primarily for classifying subgroups of man, for comparing the characteristics of diverse peoples, and for tracing the biological relationships between populations and ethnic units. Despite the shift in emphasis and orientation that has resulted from the application of genetic principles to anthropological studies of race, much work continues to be done along these traditional lines.

As a taxonomic unit, race is used to denote different levels of classification. Some workers restrict the term to the larger geographical unit or subspecies—i.e., Europid, Mongolid, Negrid—whose members possess a large number of traits in common and inhabit or originate from a specific geographic area. Below the level of geographical race, classical morphological anthropologists seek to identify anthropological elements or nuclear racial types defined by centers of concentration of anthropological traits.

On the other hand, population geneticists define race as a Mendelian or breeding population and concentrate on traits with a known mode of inheritance. While this has greatly advanced our understanding of the dynamic processes of race formation in man, there are apparent limitations in its applications. The anthropological traits whose exact mode of inheritance is known are few.

Classical morphological anthropology, therefore, still has its place in studies of race. It is the best method for investigations of racial history and for determining the affinity between living and historic populations. The application of newer mathematical techniques, such as multivariate analysis, and the availability of computer facilities enable workers to accommodate a large number of morphological variables in an accurate and objective research program. The development of these techniques has also made possible the greater utilization of the considerable body of data obtained in osteological researches in the past.

Future work in this field should be directed toward detailed longitudinal studies of specific historic and prehistoric peoples and the collection of data on the morphological traits of the lesser known living populations. Above all, an effort should be undertaken to bring about a synthesis of the older classical morphological anthropology with the newer population genetics.

III

From the standpoint of biological science, the term "race" is equivalent by definition to "groups (in a breeding community) that have in common certain genes which are lacking in other groups." This genetic definition of race views race as a "process" and emphasizes the dynamic aspects of evolutionary change in man. The racial population, not the individual, is regarded as the basic unit of inheritance and evolutionary change. Thus, recent genetic studies of race have been directed toward understanding the biological mechanisms of race formation in man—mutation, isolation, selection, and hybridization. Evidence has been produced of the operation of selective forces within living populations and of the adaptative significance of racial trait differences between populations.

The operation of these evolutionary forces over many thousands of years has differentiated man into various genetic populations with characteristic hereditary trait complexes. Considerable information has been gathered on the biochemical and serological variability of living races which has resulted as a consequence of the impact of these forces on man. Further research in this field is needed. There is also an uneven distribution of knowledge on the genetic characteristics of living populations, so that far more is known about the physical anthropology and serology of the inhabitants of West Europe than of East Asia. There is also a dearth of detailed investigations of the biological effects of race mixture.

From the perspective of the social sciences, race has been employed in the effort to understand the behavior and interaction of human groups. Thus groups of people who are characterized by high social visibility or whose members are conscious of their group affinity are often regarded as "races." These groups may be anthropological races, national or ethnic units, or even language and religious groups.

Empirical studies have demonstrated the existence of preferential association along racial and ethnic lines throughout the world. A fuller understanding of "race preference" or "race prejudice" has been provided through the integration of evolutionary theory and an adequate appraisal of race formation into the analysis of inter-group relations. This biosocial interpretation of race relations views race preference as an isolating mechanism favoring group survival and genetic variability; with the specific patterns of race relations, however, being shaped by historical and socioeconomic forces.

More empirical studies are needed on the racial aspects of preferential association in nations and societies other than the United States. These should be supplemented by longitudinal studies on the genesis of interracial attitudes.

Studies in the field of social biology have explored the role of race and heredity in the development of social stratification and historical change. Anthropometric and genetic differences have been found between social classes and occupational groups. Research is being conducted on the effects of assortative mating and the differential fertility of races and classes on the structure of society. However, much work still remains to be done on the genetic aspects of social phenomena.

In the field of psychology, race has been employed to define a unit series in the study of behavioral traits. Since mental and psychic behavior is subject to inheritance, the operation of raciogenic forces such as genetic isolation and differential selective pressure should have brought about mensurable differences in

Introduction

psychical as well as physical traits. Differences between races have, in fact, been demonstrated and described in the size, shape, and structure of the brain and endocrine system, in performance on tests of psychometric intelligence, educational achievement, personality and temperament.

Yet much work remains to be done in this field. The bulk of racial psychological studies have compared American Whites with American Negroes, Indians, or other national groups and African Negroes with European Whites or European norms. There are many racial and population groups throughout the world (particularly in Asia) for whom there is virtually no information on the distribution of mental and behavioral characteristics.

Progress in race psychology depends on the development of differential psychological methods and techniques. There is need for further research on the genetic basis of psychological traits, particularly the genetics of personality and temperament. Genetic linkage studies on the association between physical and psychical traits have been suggested as a means of investigating mental differences between populations. Factor analytic and longitudinal studies should provide much useful information on the nature of observed racial differences on tests of psychometric intelligence.

There is also a need for more work on the neurological foundation of race psychology, in particular studies of racial differences in the electrophysiology and chemical activity of the brain. All these approaches afford opportunities for much fruitful research in the future.

The editor is grateful to all the participants in this symposium for their assistance in this project of analyzing the role of race in modern science. The essays by the late Dr. Gini and Dr. Gedda have been translated from Italian and those by Professors Lundman, Czekanowski, Schwidetzky and Keiter have been translated from German. It is hoped that this symposium volume will contribute toward an understanding of current scientific work on the subject of race and in encouraging further research in this field.

ROBERT E. KUTTNER

ADDENDUM

The following excerpts from the criticism by eminent anthropologists and geneticists of the Unesco "Statement on the Nature of Race and Race Differences" are taken from The Race Concept: Results of an Inquiry, *published by Unesco in 1952. The page references are from the 1958 issue of the booklet whose pagination differs from the first issue.*

CARLETON S. COON: "[W]hile races may not have affected culture, as far as we know, culture *has* affected race. . . . Culture, by making it possible for people to live in given environments and to attain certain numbers in these places, has subjected man to the force of such natural laws as those of Bergmann, Allen and Gloger, along with the rest of the fauna." (p. 57)

C. D. DARLINGTON: "Are we to suppose that the difference between 'the common historical and sociological background,' for example of the Patahna and the Bengali, has no genetic component? Are we to suppose that the intellectual and temperamental differences between the Brahmin and the Untouchable, or between Moslem, Jewish and Christian inhabitants of Palestine, living together in the same country for centuries, have no genetic basis and nothing to do with race?" (p. 55)

"By trying to prove that races do not differ in these respects we do no service to mankind. We conceal the greatest problem which confronts mankind . . . namely how to use the diverse, the ineradicably diverse, gifts, talents, capacities of each race for the benefit of all races." (p. 26)

SIR RONALD FISHER: "Available scientific knowledge provides a firm basis for believing that the groups of mankind differ in their innate capacity for intellectual and emotional development, seeing that such groups do differ undoubtedly in a very large number of their genes." (p. 61)

EUGEN FISCHER: "The present Statement . . . puts forward certain scientific doctrines as the only correct ones, and quite obviously expects them to receive general endorsement as such. . . . The experiences of the past have strengthened my conviction that freedom of scientific inquiry is imperilled when any scientific findings or opinions are elevated, by an authoritative body, into the position of doctrines." (pp. 30–31)

GUISEPPE GENNA: "Knowledge of the psychological differences between human races is at present fluid and it would seem impossible to deny altogether the existence of these differences—at any rate as regards certain psychological aptitudes of the major groups." (p. 27)

"Although it is true that biological differences between human beings within a single race may be of the same nature as differences between our race and another, it is also true that differences between races are usually greater than those which may exist between individuals of the same race." (p. 62)

FRITZ LENZ: "In my opinion one of the dangers of the present Statement is that it disregards not only the enormous hereditary differences between men, but also absence of selection as the decisive cause of the decline of civilization, and it therefore runs counter to the science of eugenics." (p. 29)

"In my opinion, the Linnaean theory that all men belong to a single species is inaccurate. Moreover, it is by no means true that this theory is accepted by scientists in general. . . .

"If an unprejudiced scientist were confronted with a West-African Negro, an Eskimo and a North-West European, he could hardly consider them to belong to the same 'species.' Numerous 'good' species by no means reveal such considerable differences. Only one thing is certain: all men belong to the same genus." (pp. 34–35)

"[E]very attempt to restrict racial differences to physical differences is both arbitrary and scientifically unjustifiable. Linnaeus expressly included psychical differences in his diagnoses. Psychical hereditary differences are much more important than physical differences." (p. 47)

"Contrary to what is stated . . . it seems to me that there is very strong evidence to show that genetic differences are a 'major factor' in producing differences between cultural groups." (p. 57)

KARL SALLER: "Coming down to more specific details, I feel that there is a certain danger in the Statement, especially in so far as the drafts hitherto evolved have utterly disregarded or even flatly denied the existence of mental (psychic) differences between certain groups of peoples. We may or may not give the name of race to such groups of human beings, who differ in their inherited psychic characteristics, but the whole science of eugenics is based on the existence of such hereditary psychic differences." (p. 32)

WALTER SCHEIDT: "I can have no part in attempts to solve scientific questions by political manifestoes, as is the practice in Soviet Russia, and now at Unesco as well." (p. 31)

HANS WEINERT: "In my opinion, some of the statements made in Section 3 do not correspond to the facts. Many of the groups mentioned do actually coincide with racial groups. . . . In defense of prohibiting marriage between persons of different races, I should like to ask which of the gentlemen who signed the Statement would be prepared to marry his daughter for example to an Australian aboriginal. In regard to Section 9 (b), if it is true that all races have the same innate capacity for intellectual development, then why is it that so far only members of the white race have built up any scientific knowledge?" (p. 33)

KENNETH MATHER: "The aim of the document was not always clear to me, perhaps in part because of the somewhat loose terminology and partly, I suspect, because of its political implications. I felt that at times it was bending over backwards to deny the existence of race in the sense that this term has been used for political purposes in the recent past. I, of course, entirely agree in condemning Nazi race theory, but I do not think that the case against it is strengthened by playing down the possibility of statistical differences in, for example, the mental capacities of different human groups." (p. 25)

H. J. MULLER: "To the great majority of geneticists it seems absurd to suppose that psychological characteristics are subject to entirely different laws of heredity or development than other biological characteristics. . . . Since now there are these very abundant *individual* differences affecting psychological traits it would be extremely strange if there were not also differences, in the frequencies of such genes, between one major race and another, in view of the fact that there are such pronounced differences in the frequencies of genes affecting physically and chemically expressed traits. That would surely be the attitude of the great majority of geneticists. . . .

"[W]e do have every reason to infer that genetic differences, and even important ones, probably do exist between one living racial group of men and another, and our statement should not imply the contrary." (pp. 49–50)

A. H. STURTEVANT: "I have felt for some time that some of the arguments for racial equality were so obviously contrary to genetical experience as to be positively harmful. . . . There is excellent evidence for the existence of individual differences in mental characteristics—all the way from purely sensory differences such as color-blindness to severe mental derangements such as phenylketonuria. On general grounds there can be little question that less easily analyzed genetic differences occur in all sorts of mental properties. There can also be little question that there are at least statistical differences between races in such genes." (p. 51)

"The consequences of race mixture seem to me to be stated badly. . . . It is the general experience of those who have studied the results . . . of crosses between distinctly different strains of many kinds of organisms . . . that there is a strong tendency towards the production of physiologically inefficient individuals. The geneticist understands why this is so—and that understanding gives no grounds for expecting man to be an exception to the general rule. . . . The result of these considerations is that, even on a purely physiological level, crosses between quite different races are not free of danger." (p. 64)

WALTER LANDAUER: "It seems to me that the Unesco document was written on the assumption that from a certain body of scientific facts *necessarily* flowed certain ethical commandments. Perhaps because of this there was, I feel, some yielding to the temptation to treat *terra incognita* as *terra nullius*. . . . The declaration that all men are created equal was a fine one and remains so, even though and in the best sense *because* it is untrue in the biological sphere." (p. 19)

"What makes it unreasonable to expect that genes for mental and emotional traits have distribution patterns similar to those of physical traits, e.g., blood groups?" (p. 61)

TAGE KEMP: "If the races that have existed through several centuries can be supposed to have improved by selection, and therefore, have a particular harmonious and well-balanced constitution, race mixture can in certain cases be expected to lead to production of less harmonious and well-balanced types." (pp. 64–65)

PART I
ANTHROPOLOGY

BIOGRAPHICAL NOTE

BERTIL J. LUNDMAN, *Ph.D., is Professor of Physical Anthropology at the University of Uppsala (Sweden) and one of the foremost anthropologists in the Scandinavian countries.*

Professor Lundman has conducted extensive field studies of the physical anthropology of central Sweden and in the course of his broad-scale research personally took anthropometric measurements of more than 15,000 persons in the Swedish province of Dalecarlia. He has carried out investigations in several other Swedish provinces, which have added considerably to the present-day knowledge of the biology and physical anthropology of the Swedes, Lapps and Swedish Gypsies.

Dr. Lundman is a member of various scientific societies in Sweden and an honorary member of such groups in Germany, Italy and the United States. He is the author of more than a hundred and fifty articles and monographs and many books. Among the latter are Nordens Rastyper (*The Racial Types of the Nordic Countries*), *published in 1940;* Jordens Människoraser och Folkstammer (*The Physical Races and Ethnic Groups of the World*), *1943;* Nutidens Manniskoraser (*The Living Races of Man*), *1946; and* Stammeskunde des Menschen in Geschichtlicher Zeit (*The Physical, Linguistic, and Ethnic Races of Man in Historical Times*), *1961.*

RACE AND ANTHROPOLOGY

Bertil Lundman

IN CONTINENTAL European terminology, "anthropology" means only "physical anthropology." What is termed "cultural anthropology" in British and American usage is described here by the term "ethnography" or, if dealing with general questions, "ethnology." The term "race" is also used on the continent of Europe only in the physical sense. Consequently, names such as "Germanic," "Romanic," or "Slavic" races are entirely incorrect as designations for human groups who are defined by their languages.

Race, therefore, is a term that can be applied only to a reasonably homogeneous human group that has preserved its hereditary characteristics almost unchanged through a long succession of generations. Such a group differs from other races by a more or less specific organic type. This type is defined by a series of racial traits. These traits are also genetically determined. However, individual physical traits may be altered to some extent by different environments without losing their constant genetic basis. For example, the population of Sweden, whether Swedish or Lapp, has increased in stature as a consequence of the rising level of civilization. At the same time, however, the difference in height between Swedes and Lapps has remained completely unchanged.

The anthropologist must learn to distinguish not only whole types, but also to verify his findings statistically and repeatedly on sufficiently large groups. He should also employ pictorial material, distribution maps and diagrams, and clearly arranged tables in his presentations.

Experience has gradually taught us which racial characteristics are particularly suitable as sorting criteria. These anthropological traits exhibit little intra-group but large inter-group variability. They are easily determined and their heritability is fairly well established. These traits include head shape,[1] facial form, nasal form, skin color, hair color, eye color, etc.

In addition, there are several physiological group differences which have come to light mostly during the last few decades. The most important of these characteristics is the distribution of so-called "blood groups," such as the ABO system. This system has the advantage of being easily determined, even with large numbers of subjects. Its mode of inheritance is very accurately known and it is practically mutation-proof. The ABO blood-group system is only one characteristic among many and its significance for racial diagnosis should not be overemphasized. As a result of the operation of other biological processes such as genetic drift, blood-group distributions are often not very useful for determining more distant biological affinity.

This caveat applies with even greater force to some "micro-attributes" introduced by eager innovators. These include hairiness of the phalange of the middle finger in males and ability to taste phenylthiocarbamide (PTC). Neither the heritability nor the mode of inheritance of these traits has been firmly established. Furthermore, they lack any significance in determining the morphological-physiological total picture of a particular human population.

The above discussion applies to the classification of the living races of man. As we go further back into time we must realize that the genetic structure of human populations may, or rather must, undergo gradual change. For even races did, after all, "originate" somewhere, sometime. A particularly striking example of such an evolutionary trend is the genetically-determined broadening and shortening of the cranium, which has appeared in many population groups of the "White," "Yellow," and "Red" races during the

---

[1] The cephalic index, or more correctly the breadth-length index, expresses the breadth of the head as a percentage of its length. The height-length index expresses the height of the skull as a percentage of the length. Unfortunately, the latter can be calculated only on crania.

last few millennia. However, this trend has scarcely at all been very evident among the "Black" race.

What, then is the best criterion for classifying the races of man? For a rough division into major or primary races, the old classification based originally, but no longer exclusively, on skin color is still serviceable. On this basis we can divide mankind into "White" (or better "Europid"), "Black," "Yellow," and "Red" primary races. We must, of course, bear in mind that quite a few groups fall "in between" or "outside" these categories.

As far as the intermediate groups are concerned, they are quite often "hybrid" or "mixed" races that arose relatively late and do not invalidate the classificatory system. Others, as for example some groups in the interior of India, are evidently quite old. Luckily, they are rather rare. As regards the "outside" groups, they probably represent very ancient remnants or splinters of an as yet undifferentiated human species. The Australian aborigines fall into this category.

The more detailed system according to which European anthropologists classify the races of Europe originated with J. Deniker, who was born in Odessa, Russia, and worked mainly in Paris. For the classification of non-European races the system of the German anthropologist, Professor Egon von Eickstedt, is the most widely used.

With regard to race mixture it must be emphasized that the metric values of most anthropological traits will fall approximately midway between those of the parent races. Dominance and recession may occur in the case of single physical traits. Of course, this is especially marked in the first generation.

In mixtures of races with large and small noses, the larger and narrower forms often predominate, through polygenic dominance, in a surprisingly forceful way. Even more remarkable is that in a great many cases the progeny of race mixture have on the average longer faces than either of the parent races. This is partly but not wholly related to a general asthenization of the body build. The result is that the average facial morphology found in an area of race mixture is often quite unsuited for calculating the approximate proportions of the two parent races.

Even without such difficulties, race classification can never be put on an entirely firm and secure basis. On the other hand, it is by no means as insecure and subjective as claimed by many so-called modern investigators.

The Europids

IN THIS BRIEF survey we shall begin with the end of the last Glacial age, approximately ten thousand years ago. Too little is known about the temporal and spatial distribution of modern racial types in earlier periods. As far as we can determine, the geographical distribution of Europid, or at least pre-Europid, types at the beginning of the period to be considered here was much wider than it is today.

On the other hand, the distribution of the other primary races is sparse even in the archaeological finds made in their present homelands, except in the rather thoroughly explored Western Hemisphere. From all present-day Eurasia, as far east as the Altai mountains and northern India and as far south as northern, eastern and even southern Africa, almost only Europid types have been found. The cradle-land of the Europids, which must have been much smaller than the distribution indicated by archaeology, is still a matter of conjecture. Perhaps it was located in the steppe-like areas of northeastern Africa and southwestern Asia.

Here, however, we must introduce a distinction. The oldest known Europids had low-vaulted or chamaecephalic crania, a characteristic that was even more pronounced in the still earlier human remains from this region. Toward the end of the last glaciation, the first high-vaulted or hypsicephalic crania are found, first in southern Asia and soon after in eastern Europe as well as in Egypt. Since the chamaecephalic type has survived almost unchanged to the present day in western Europe, these eastern European high-vaulted crania are considered not to have originated directly from low-vaulted crania in Europe, but to represent a later migration from southern Asia. This theory agrees with historico-cultural considerations.

The present boundary between the high-vaulted crania in the east and the low-vaulted crania in the west runs approximately through the Baltic Sea, along the German-Slav language border as far as the Danube, skirting the Alps as far as eastern France, and reaching the Mediterranean near the west coast of Italy. Central and southern Spain are also regions of "high-vaulted" crania, while there are "low-vaulted" islands in the Atlas mountains of Morocco and almost the entire interior of Arabia.

The B blood group is much more common on the eastern side of this boundary. However, this applies only north of the Danube. South of that river the dividing line between blood groups runs to the Adriatic. Low B values are also common in the western portion of the Caucasus, which remained almost free of Mongol and other invasions, and in Inner Arabia. It may be said that in Europe and the Near East there is a general coincidence of high-vaulted crania and a higher percentage of blood group B. This does not hold for Mongolid northern and central Asia, where a prevalence of very low-vaulted crania coincides with that of blood group B. This indicates that the prevalence of B blood in eastern Europe is only to a small extent caused by late Mongolid admixture.

An entirely different set of factors conditions the contrast between long-headedness or dolichocephaly and round-headedness or brachycephaly in Europe. As we mentioned earlier, there was a strong prevalence of dolichocephalics in ancient Europe right up to the beginning of the Middle Ages. At that time there began a trend toward shorter and broader crania, without, however, affecting to any significant degree the shape of the face and body. This trend toward brachycephaly took place in a wide zone throughout all of Central Europe, from southwestern France deep into the heart of eastern Europe, being especially noticeable in mountainous regions. It occurred both in areas of low-vaulted and high-vaulted crania. Relatively unaffected by this brachycephalization were the lands around the Baltic and the North Seas, as well as Spain and the coasts of the Mediterranean.

The causes of this process are still being debated. It is certain, however, that the migration of peoples from Asia, such as the Huns and the Mongols, played no major role. The trend toward brachycephaly seems to have started in poor mountainous regions. It appears that during the Late Middle Ages such mountain dwellers descended into the richer plains, after these areas had been ravaged by such catastrophes as war and the Great Plague (ca. 1350 A.D.).

Thus there came into existence the Alpine race—occasional, rare precursors of which are found in earlier times—and, in the southeast, the Dinaric race. This, however, cannot explain the whole picture. Similar changes in head shape have taken place in many other areas of the world. It is evident that we are dealing here with a general evolutionary trend in mankind. Only among the Negrids and semi-Negrids is this trend almost unknown.

Blond Indo-European Tribes

AS FAR AS color of skin, hair, and eyes is concerned, northern Europe presents a unique picture which seems to have existed since the end of the Glacial age. The modern areas of light pigmentation coincide approximately with the extent of the last glaciation and its fringe. From these border regions came the populations which settled the areas left free by the melting ice. This change in pigmentation is partly an adaptation to a cold and damp climate. This, however, does not entirely explain the phenomenon.

Whole bodies, with skin and hair, of undoubtedly light-colored individuals have been preserved in deep moors in Denmark and northern Germany from as far back as 1000 B.C. The racial ideal of at least the majority of the Indo-European tribes which began to spread out from southeastern Central Europe and adjacent eastern Europe around 2000 B.C. was certainly blond. The upper social classes at least must have been blond from the very beginning.

It was the Indo-Europeans, not the Mongol late-comers, who first tamed the horse. The words for horse and for all parts of the chariot are common to almost all Indo-European languages. The chariot was developed by the Indo-Europeans from older Near Eastern prototypes, while the practices of horseback riding arose later. We now know also that Indo-European culture, even during the earliest period when it was still held in common by the

Race and Anthropology

various tribes, was by no means "barbaric." The Indo-Europeans possessed a highly developed mythology and great epic compositions that were common to most groups, though they later developed in separate ways.

We have thus come to the "reversion" of the migrations of peoples and races in Europe and western Asia. The current which formerly ran from south to north now began to run from north to south. In later times there were migrations of various Indo-European tribes, among others the then still blond Celts from southwestern Germany toward the west, south, and east. Then came the Germanic tribes and, later still, the southward and eastward migrations of the Slavs.

The movements of other tribes were less significant for European racial history. In the first century A.D. Finnish tribes migrated from central Russia to the Baltic Sea. Later on the Mongols began their preliminary occupation of the steppes in southeastern Europe. At present they have almost disappeared, mostly through intermixture with the earlier and more numerous populations.

Small groups of chiefly Armenid East Mediterranean traders and metal-workers arrived in southern and western Europe a few millennia before Christ, often traveling by sea. Their genetic traces can still be found as far north as the coastal areas of the North Sea. Other such groups reached the ore-bearing districts of southeastern Europe, northern Hungary, as well as Etruria (Tuscany).

Racial Types in Modern Europe

LET US NOW take a brief and schematic look at the racial geography of modern Europe. The tall, light-colored, dolichocephalic Nordic race now inhabits most countries around the Baltic Sea and the North Sea. It also forms an element of the Irish population, together with the North-Atlantic race, characterized by light eye color, dark hair, and a strong prevalence of blood group O. The Scandinavian Lapps are not at all Mongolid, but dwarfed Europids. In southern central Europe, the short, brunet, round-faced, brachycephalic Alpine race is predominant. In the western Balkans, however, there is a prevalence of the tall, brunet, hooked-nosed, hypsicephalic, planoccipital Dinaric race. The short, brunet, dolichocephalic Mediterranean race occupies in somewhat different forms most of the coastal areas around the Mediterranean Sea.

In westernmost Russia and other regions near the Baltic Sea we find the extremely blond East Baltic race with rather high-vaulted and brachycephalic crania and a high frequency of blood group B. The East Baltic race is also characterized by somewhat slanted and flat eyes, straight hair, and a thicker and less porous skin. Further within Russia there is a mixed area of a small proportion of Mongolid remnants along with East Baltic, Nordic, Dinaric, Alpine, Mediterranean, and many other elements, including a primitive Europid element.

The southern Europid area comprises northern Africa and especially western and southern Asia, extending as far as the Deccan and the Brahmaputra and southern Turkestan. It is inhabited mainly by races with hypsicephalic crania, a fairly high incidence of blood group B, and partial brachycephalization. The dolichocephalic races include the well-built East Mediterraneans in southern Russia, Iran, and northern Syria, who are morphologically similar to the Europid Hindus. The brachycephalic races include the Armenids in Armenia and large parts of Asia Minor. They are characterized by large noses and are related to the European Dinarics.

The present anthropo-geographic picture in the Near East is the result of migrations of peoples and races which we cannot as yet analyze completely, in spite of our fairly extensive knowledge of the ancient world. Thus we do not know at what time the Armenid race came into being. The Armenid type is already portrayed on very ancient sculptures and resembles that of the Dinarics even though their body build is more compact. However, we have hardly any Armenid crania dating from that era. It seems certain nonetheless that the Armenid race arose in the Near East from an East Mediterranean variant with large noses. The East Mediterraneans of today are partly mixed with Nordic elements which entered the Near East in the course of the Indo-European migrations in the second millennium B.C.

Of interest is the obviously ancient but still noticeable difference between two important Near Eastern groups speaking related languages—the Jews and the Arabs. The Jews originated in northern and northeastern Syria and exhibited a mixed racial character from the earliest times. The Arabs are often typical representatives of the race that has been named after them, with their almond eyes, "Semitic smile," narrow, receding forehead, etc. In most other physical traits they resemble the Mediterraneans.

Dolichocephalic Europid northern Africa ("White Africa") possesses an ancient and reasonably pure Cro-Magnid stratum in the Atlas mountains of Morocco and on the Canary Islands. The Cro-Magnids are characterized by a stocky body build, low-vaulted crania, and occasional blondness. The Sahara desert is inhabited by East Mediterraneans with high-vaulted crania, who are now often mixed with Negroes. They are closely related to the population of southern Spain.

In Egypt we still meet Mediterraneans with decidedly "eastern" characteristics such as a prevalence of blood group B, while Nubia and the area farther south are inhabited by Europid-Negrid mixed races of widely differing ages. The consequences of the Arab conquest of northern Africa from 700 A.D. onward were more religious than racial. The conquerors brought along few of their women and were rather quickly absorbed by the local population.

Racial Character of India

INDIA IS MORE or less a world of its own, despite frequent incursions from the northwest. It is still difficult to determine the racial character of the oldest population stratum. Perhaps it was Veddid. Important remnants of that race are still found among the primitive tribes in remote districts and among the lower castes. This pre-Europid race, so to speak, can be recognized quite easily even after intermixture, owing particularly to its very broad zygomatic arch, together with a very narrow and small skull. The Veddids are also characterized by high-vaulted and dolichocephalic crania, short and gracile body-build, dark brown skin color, and curly hair. This Veddid type can still sometimes be found among the Gypsies, who of course originated in India. On the whole, however, the Gypsies are unmistakably Europid.

The Veddid race seems to represent the basic southern Asiatic stock of the older post-Glacial era. Its distribution reached from the Sunda Islands to southern Arabia. The Veddids even penetrated, in very remote times, into North Africa as far as Egypt. Some of its different local variants probably developed into the East Mediterraneans. To judge by the archaeological evidence and skeletal remains, the Veddids were still fairly numerous during the oldest pre-Indo-European flowering of culture in northwestern India, even though there already existed East Mediterranean types. Whether the latter had migrated from other areas or whether they had arisen from Veddids in the more attractive portions of India is open to conjecture. In southern India there are also some rather small unassimilated Negrid elements.

We do not know whether the Indo-Europeans who entered India from the northwest around 1000 B.C. were the first to use this avenue into the rich sub-continent. Probably not. They were, of course, of a lighter color than the rest of the population, including the Europid element. The Indo-European invaders consisted of lighter-pigmented East Mediterraneans from southeastern Europe, mixed to some extent with Nordics. Since the East Mediterranean race had obviously existed in India before that time, it is hard to say what proportion of the modern Indian population is derived from the Aryan invasion.

Later migrations brought into India some Armenid types from the Near East and, from the northeast into Bengal, a great number of Mongolids. The latter can be sub-divided into several different subtypes. In the northwest the Mongolid element is remarkably small, considering the large number of Mongol conquerors who passed that way during the Middle Ages and more recent times. It seems that the local population was too numerous to be biologically altered, and many of the conquerors probably died out through intemperance.

This completes our admittedly rather cursory survey of the

Europid area, both in ancient and modern times, from Scandinavia to the Brahmaputra.

The Mongolids

TURNING NOW TO another primary race, the Mongolids, we see that this race can be sub-divided into two sharply distinct racial stocks—the North Mongolids and the Southeast Mongolids. One striking anatomical difference between these two Mongolid sub-groups is the difference in cranial height, which is low in the north, and high in the south. This difference, however, is substantial. The lowest mean length-height indices in the north are also the lowest found anywhere in the world. The highest means in the north do not even approach the lowest means found in the southeast. In fact, the highest southeast Asian means are also the highest in the world. Another difference is the much stockier body build of the North Mongolids.

It is noteworthy that well-defined Mongolids are found only relatively late in history. Their cradle-land seems to have been the interior of eastern and northeastern Asia, with the Southeast Mongolids dwelling to the south of the modern Gobi Desert, and the North Mongolids to the north of it. At the end of the Glacial age, the Gobi Desert was made almost impassable by a number of salt swamps. This geographic barrier is probably the cause of the sharp racial border between the two Mongolid sub-groups.

Let us consider the northern Mongolid group first. Up to 1000 B.C. the whole western part of Central Asia as far as the Altai was in the possession of Europid tribes speaking Indo-European languages. At that time the North Mongolids inhabited the areas farther eastward and northward. When the deteriorating climate caused the Indo-European tribes to move southward, the Central Asiatic Mongols gradually came into their own. Being better adapted to the new, arid climate with its cold winters and hot summers, the North Mongolids spread outward.

Acquiring, only at that time, the horse economy from the Indo-Europeans, they soon became widely feared horse-breeding nomads. Some of them attempted to overrun China but were stopped in part by the Chinese Wall which was built at that time. Most moved westward through the broad zone of desert steppes which stretches into southeastern Europe. First came the Huns, then the various Turkic peoples (Tatars), and lastly the terrible "proper" Mongols under Genghis Khan and Tamerlane.

Anthropological and genetic evidence of their progress can still be traced by a prevalence of low-vaulted crania and B blood, even among those western populations where the characteristic Mongolid type has more or less disappeared. The Siberian Forest or Taiga nomads, who are racially not so well defined, do not possess such an impressive history. Their migrations, however, cover an area stretching from the White Sea and the Kola peninsula to the Bering Sea and beyond into northwest America.

The Southeast Mongolids were not as late in leaving their homeland in northern China to migrate southward. Before their arrival in southern Asia, the area had been settled by Europid and pre-Europid Veddid races. There are also some traces of Negrids. The present population, though chiefly Mongolid, is the result of a mixture of these diverse racial elements.

Another migratory wave of southeast Mongolids traveled across Formosa to the Philippine Islands and Borneo at the end of the Stone Age. Their modern descendants, the Dyakid race, are typologically very similar to the American Indians, especially those living in the tropics. The mass of the coastal-dwelling Malays seem to have arrived later. They resemble the southern Chinese in many ways, but their eye-folds are not as narrow and slanted.

China has become the center of the Southeast Mongolids, following their migration from the northwest. With its great size, the country is far from racially homogeneous, even if we exclude the more distinctly non-Mongolid elements. The tall North Chinese, for instance, differ morphologically in many respects from the small round-faced South Chinese. As for the Japanese, those who live in the central rice-growing districts on the main island are of South Chinese type, as distinct from the mountain dwellers further to the north. The role of possible Ainu intermixture in the present Japanese population is still a source of dispute.

American Indians and Eskimos

THE AMERICAN INDIANS whose ancestors crossed the Bering Strait represent another primary race, rather homogeneous on the whole, despite very many variations. The Eskimos are an intermediate group between the Indians and East Siberians. As a result of Carbon-14 dating, we now know that man penetrated far into the Western Hemisphere more than twenty thousand years ago. This is not after but rather before the end of the Glacial age. Some of the oldest crania found in America, dating back some ten thousand years, have a remarkably "Indian" look about them. These crania are relatively high-vaulted.

Shell piles from later strata along the coasts have yielded primitive low-vaulted dolichocephalic crania. They resemble those of some modern though almost extinct Amerindian coastal populations from Tierra del Fuego and from Southern California. This American Indian type, however, is not found in the interior of the twin continents. Here, with the exception of northwest America and also some coastal areas, there are found only high-vaulted crania. This characteristic still marks the vast majority of Indian populations, with all their different types—the tall Patagonians, the old Redskins in the eastern United States (Silvids), the very short tribes around the Panamanian isthmus (Isthmids), etc.

All types, including those with high-vaulted and those with low-vaulted crania, seem to be exclusively of blood group O. This peculiarity sets the American Indians apart from all other human groups. Although other populations may occasionally lack blood group B, they will always have some blood group A. In the American northwest, however, blood group A is found, and in western Alaska B as well. Crania here are again low-vaulted, but more definitely Mongolid. However, according to recent studies, there is also evidence of some Ainu elements in the northwestern areas of America.

The Eskimos, though they are not usually classified with the American Indians, also seem to belong to the last migration of people with chamaecephalic crania. The external sagittal crest, which supports the enormous masticatory muscles, gives the spurious appearance of a hypsicephalic skull.

It seems to me that the racial relationships in the Americas can be explained in the following manner. Northwestern Asia has been Mongolid for a long time, and increasingly so. The chamaecephalic North Mongolids inhabited the north, the Southeast Mongolids, being adapted to a more moderate climate, settled further south. The boundary between these two groups shifted in accordance with post-Glacial climatic fluctuations, moving north during warm periods and south during cold periods.

The oldest known inhabitants of the Western Hemisphere appear to have been Southeast Mongolids who arrived during the somewhat warmer climate accompanying the outgoing Glacial age (Alleröd). The old chamaecephalic coastal dwellers arrived during the following relatively brief deterioration in the climate. During the lengthy warm period that followed, the main mass of the ancestors of the modern Indians migrated to America, apparently in several waves. It may be assumed that they were not entirely homogeneous.

It is unlikely, however, that the present diversity of types among the Amerindians is a direct consequence of this slight genetic variability. Their modern constitutions are obviously too well adapted to their current habitats not to have been the result of local adaptation. The American Indians did, after all, inhabit the Western hemisphere long enough for selection and adaptation to have had some visible effect. I do not see much merit in an hypothesis that different anthropological types of Indians, often after having wandered through more than half the continent, should finally have sought out those habitats which suited biotypes acquired in Asia.

We can only touch here upon the question whether there existed, in pre-Columbian America, small but distinct traces of types other than the Indian-Mongolid. Some writers have suggested migrations of Melanesians or even Australians, East Indians, Mongolid South Chinese, etc. Apart from certain tribes in the northwest and the originally northwestern Apaches, the pre-European inhabitants appear to have had exclusively O blood.

The presence of elements such as those just listed seems highly unlikely, despite some remarkable pictures of "Melanesian-looking" jungle dwellers from the interior of South America.

And, if we may step outside the field of physical anthropology for a moment, we may note that there existed even at that time a few Asiatic domestic plants and virus diseases and parasitic worms. There is also certain cultural evidence from Central America, including ancient sculptures portraying what looks like obvious Southeast Asiatic racial types. All this (though not necessarily the specific individuals of modern times, who may be descendants, after all, of late mixtures) points to ancient transoceanic cultural contacts between America and Southeast Asia. It is possible, however, that the number of these immigrant purveyors of culture was so small that their descendants escape all scientific detection and enumeration.

The Negrids and Oceanic Peoples

THE NEGRID primary race seems to have developed late, even later than the Mongolids. In any case, no truly ancient Negrid skulls have been found anywhere. The Negrid race, however, is a jungle race, not so much of the interior as of the fringe. And in that environment bones rot away quickly. Even in the presently more or less Negrid grass plains of South and East Africa nearly all ancient crania are of primitive Europid type. It is possible, however, that true Negroes may even at that time have lived farther within the jungle. Negro tribes from Southeast Africa—the Kaffirs—differ somewhat from the Negroes of Guinea and the Sudan by their lower-vaulted crania and different blood-group relationships, as well as certain Europid characteristics. However, truly striking differences between the different African Negro populations are not evident.

Apart from this, Africa is also inhabited by two races of shorter stature and lighter complexion, who appear only partly Negrid— the Congo Pygmies and the Bushmen. According to the latest views, the Pygmies were forced into the interior of the jungle fairly late, after which they underwent cultural impoverishment and dwarfing. The Bushmen, on the other hand, formerly inhabited most of the African, and possibly even the South Spanish, grass plains. The Bushmen are Negrid in some respects, but otherwise are a very unique race. They have been biologically adapted to a specific biotype. The Hottentots are a mixed race of Bushmen and Europids, as is evident from their appearance, blood groups, culture and language.

Finally, we come to the southern oceans, together with Madagascar. Some writers describe this part of the earth as the world's "dead end street," not only for humans but also for other forms of life, such as marsupials. The oldest, though *not* Neanderthalian, stratum is that of the Australian aborigines. They are also found, along with other races, on New Guinea and the larger neighboring islands. The southeastern and even more the southwestern tribes of the Australian continent are racially and culturally even more primitive than the northern and central ones. The difference, however, is not very great.

On New Guinea and the larger islands we also find Negrids. Their racial characteristics have not been disguised by intermixture with the Australian aborigines. This view is reinforced by the wholly Negrid, even if dwarfed, character of the inhabitants of the Andaman Islands in the Bengal Sea. Although these islands are farther west than New Guinea, they are still at a great distance from Africa. This also holds for certain dwarf tribes in the Malay Peninsula and the Philippine Islands.

Dwarfism, which also occurs in the interior of New Guinea, is probably conditioned both by selective, i.e., hereditary, as well as environmental factors. The relative strength of the two factors varies in the different population isolates. Whereas New Guinean dwarfism is mainly a result of undernourishment, the well-proportioned Andaman dwarfs owe their build largely to genetic factors. The above-mentioned but small Negrid elements in the interior of Deccan are also of interest.

The great resemblance between these Oceanic Negrids and the African Negroes provides strong evidence against a "tropical parallel development" theory, despite some small differences between the different Negrid populations. Thus, the palms of the New Guinea "Negroes" are said to be black as well as the rest of the skin. This emigration from Africa took place, no doubt, in the very distant past. On the other hand, it appears unlikely that the Negrid cradle-land could have been in southeast Asia.

Along certain coasts as well as in some of the mountains of New Guinea and some of the Solomon Islands there are dark Europid elements. This type seems to have constituted the basic stock of the original Polynesians who emigrated shortly before Christ from India or southern China. These areas were then less Mongolid than now. Nonetheless, the Polynesian population contained even at that time a good deal of Mongolid elements.

In the course of their migration past New Guinea and during subsequent piratical expeditions to that island, these capable seafarers carried off and absorbed a considerable degree of Australid-Negrid admixture. Later on they seem to have introduced some American Indian blood in the form of slaves into the eastern islands. However, this does not mean, as Heyerdahl asserts, that the mass of the Polynesians emigrated from America.

Madagascar was settled somewhat later by South Mongolid Malays mixed with pre-Europid Veddid, primitive races from the Sunda Islands. It is still a matter of debate whether Madagascar already possessed a sparse original population of Negrids, although I am inclined to favor this hypothesis. The numerous more or less Negrid types in western Madagascar are probably descended from imported slaves.

Races and Climate

EVEN IN THIS brief survey of the anthropogeography of the world, we cannot fail to be impressed by the large differences in environments, peoples, and races. Is it possible that it is nothing but an illusion, a fantasy concocted in ivory towers, that these racial differences, including the psychological, are not entirely accidental and that they go beyond our present generation? Is it not rather more plausible that racial differences in mental and behavioral traits, just as in morphological and physiological traits, are the result of selective and hereditary adaptations to diverse environments over thousands of years?

Finally, let us review the basic types of the different primary races of man, both physically and psychically.

First of all, we must remember that the so-called "rules of climate" which govern physical variation in animal populations also play a role in human evolution and raciation. According to "Bergmann's Rule," races belonging to the same animal species become larger in cold environments and smaller in warmer ones. According to "Allen's Rule," races or subspecies become stockier in cold areas, and slimmer in warm ones. These two processes together facilitate the conservation of body warmth in cold areas and they provide protection against overheating in warm areas. According to "Gloger's rule"—or, more exactly, "Gloger-Görnitz's rule"—plumage and hair color tend to become lighter in cold and dry areas.

The human race does not adhere to these rules as closely as the animal world. Thus, an increase in body volume in cold areas tends to be counteracted by a dwarfing process due to lack of proper nourishment. Also, man obeys an additional rule, that of Thomson-Buxton, according to which the external part of the nose and the nostrils become wider in hot and damp areas and narrower in cold and wet areas.

These selective adaptations take place gradually over a long period of time. They may be roughly considered as original adaptations of the primary races of man in their cradle-lands. These adaptations then become stable and quite resistant to change in new homelands and environments. Smaller changes characterize sub-races of the primary race in their new environments. The last-mentioned changes are much more likely to follow Bergmann's Rule than any of the others.

Such processes are especially noticeable in the Western Hemisphere. This is probably due to the direct influence of different environments on an "original race" that was once fairly homogeneous. This applies especially to the third wave of immigration. Such rather drily schematic and only approximately accurate rules must of course be used with caution in the explanation of the diversity of the modern races of man. Otherwise the entire science of man is in danger of deteriorating into sterile dogmatism.

The Mongolid race, especially its northern half, is a typical

Race and Anthropology 21

cold-area race. Physically, the Mongolids are short of stature, stocky, with thick and impermeable skin, a small, flat nose that does not freeze easily, and narrow eye-slits that protect against driving snow and desert sand. Psychically, the Mongolids are tenacious, self-disciplined, industrious, solicitous of the needs of others, and animated by community spirit.

An entirely different picture is presented by the tropical Negrid race. Physically, the Negrids are long-legged, with large nostrils, and very dark, loose skin which can easily be cooled through perspiration. Psychically, the Negrids are cheerful and passionate, with little foresight.

An intermediate position is occupied by the Europid primary race. The Europids are considerably more variable than the other primary races. The Europids are characterized by general rather than specialized adaptation, since they were not molded by such extreme environments as the other two primary races. Perhaps because of this, they exhibit a more mobile spirit.

The American Indians are obviously cold-area people. They are also stocky, with thick skin. Psychically, the Amerindians are taciturn and exhibit little joy in their everyday life. This holds even for the Indians of the tropics, who, even after thousands of years, have not become entirely accustomed to tropical heat. This is also one of the reasons why Negro slaves had to be imported for the settlement and development of the warmer regions of the Western hemisphere.

The members of strikingly diverse races are also individually more or less distinct as a whole type—in skin and hair color, in head shape and body form, in mental and behavioral traits, and in body movements. Pictures and especially motion pictures are usually much better suited to demonstrate such characteristics than numerical tables. Vivid descriptions are often better than arid definitions. But even such an organic view (*"Ganzheitsschau"*) fails to capture the totality of racial features, since it takes account mainly of external characteristics. The inner psycho-physical essence is apprehended but slightly, if at all. In this connection, the importance of collecting research data from individuals who inhabit regions similar to the homeland of the ancestors should be emphasized. For it was this homeland to which their genotype had been adapted through many generations of biological selection.

Chemical and physical measurements and calculations, carried out in laboratories and computing centers, are often good controls for exclusively visual observations. They can also correct or confirm anthropological hypotheses and assumptions. However, little truly new and significant is likely to be added to anthropological science in this manner. There is also the danger in our age of technology of becoming too immersed in details of technique and of amassing data of little worth.

Finally, no one method of anthropological investigation can claim to possess exclusive authority. It is necessary to understand and utilize modern anthropometric techniques. Yet, the modern researcher must employ all possible methods—intuitive and technical, synthetic and analytic—in order to arrive at a true picture of human racial diversity.

Literature

von Barloewen, Wolf-Dietrich (Editor). *Abriss der Vorgeschichte*. München, 1957.
Battaglia, Raffaello. *Africa: Genti e Culture*. Rome, 1954.
Baumann, Hans, Westermann, Dieter, and Thurnwald, Richard. *Völkerkunde von Afrika*. Essen, 1940.
Baur, Erwin, Fischer, Eugen, and Lenz, Fritz. *Erblichkeitslehre und Rassenhygiene*. München, 1940.
Bernatzik, H. A. (Editor). *Die grosse Völkerkunde* (3 volumes). Leipzig, 1939.
Biasutti, Renato. *Le Razze e i Popoli della Terra* (4 volumes). Torino, Italy, 1959.
Birket-Smith, Kaj. *The Paths of Culture*. Madison, 1964.
Bosch-Gimpera, P. *Las Razas Humanas*. Barcelona, 1956.
———. *Los Indo-Europeos*. Mexico City, 1960.
Boyd, William C. Blood Groups. *Tabulae Biologicae*, 17, 113–240, 1939.
———. *Genetics and the Races of Man*. Boston, 1952.
Buschan, G. (Editor). *Illustrierte Völkerkunde* (3 volumes). Stuttgart, 1922–1926.

Carothers, J. C. *The African Mind in Health and Disease: A Study in Ethnopsychiatry*. Monograph No. 17, Geneva, 1953.
Clark, Grahame. *World Prehistory: An Outline*. New York, 1961.
Coon, Carleton S. *The Races of Europe*. New York, 1939.
———. *The Story of Man*. New York, 1962.
———. *The Origin of Races*. New York, 1962.

von Eickstedt, Egon. *Rassenkunde und Rassengeschichte der Menschheit*. Stuttgart, 1933–1934.
———. *Die Forschung am Menschen*. Stuttgart, 1937–1944.

Freudenfeld, B. *Völkerkunde*. München, 1960.

Heberer, Gerhard, Kurth, Gottfried, and Schwidetzky, Ilse. *Anthropologie: A zu Z*. Frankfurt, 1959.
Heuse, Georges A. *Biologie du Noir*. Brussels, 1957.
Hirzfeld, L. *Konstitutionsserologie und Blutgruppenforschung*. Berlin, 1928.
Hooton, Earnest A. *Up From The Ape*. New York, 1946.

Keiter, Friedrich. *Rasse und Kultur* (3 volumes). Stuttgart, 1938–1940.

Linton, Ralph. *The Tree of Culture*. New York, 1955.
Lowie, Robert H. *Culture and Ethnology*. New York, 1929.
———. *The History of Ethnological Theory*. New York, 1937.
Lundman, Bertil. *Umriss der Rassenkunde des Menschen in Geschichtlicher Zeit*. Copenhagen, 1952.
———. *Stammeskunde der Völker*. Uppsala, 1961.

Mourant, A. E. *The Distribution of the Human Blood Groups*. Springfield, 1954.
———. *The ABO Blood Groups*. Oxford, 1958.

Piggott, Stuart. *The Dawn of Civilization*. New York, 1961.

Reuter, E. B. *Race Mixture*. New York, 1931.

Sauer, C. O. *Agricultural Origins and Dispersals*. New York, 1952.
Schwidetzky, Ilse. *Das Menschenbild der Biologie*. Stuttgart, 1959.
———. *Die neue Rassenkunde*. Stuttgart, 1962.
Shuey, Audrey M. *The Testing of Negro Intelligence*. Lynchburg, 1958.
Stern, Curt. *Principles of Human Genetics*. San Francisco, 1960.
Streng, O. *Blutgruppenforschung und Anthropologie*. Helsinski, 1935. *Zeitschrift für Rassenphysiologie*. Vol. 9, pp. 97–111, 1937.

Tischner, Herbert. *Völkerkunde*. Frankfurt, 1959.

von Verschuer, Otmar. *Genetik des Menschen*. Berlin, 1959.

Literature Survey

ONLY BOOKS AND symposia are discussed here, some of them going beyond the subject of this essay. Articles in journals and transactions of learned societies cannot be taken into account.

In a class by itself is the still unexcelled work by R. Biasutti (edited and two-thirds written by that author) *Razze e Popoli della Terra*. This four-volume work with about 3,000 pages in large octavo gives equal attention to anthropology and ethnography, and contains exceedingly detailed and knowledgeable sections on archaeology, as well as bibliographies, indices, illustrations, maps, everything of the highest caliber. There is nothing like this work in any language (except, perhaps, as far as pictures are concerned—P. Bosch-Gimpera, *Las Razas Humanas,* two thick volumes of large format). Biasutti's work ought to be translated at least into English as soon as possible. Only for Africa do we possess a small, but valuable book by R. Battaglia, *Africa: Genti e Culture.*

This writer has himself published smaller chiefly anthropological works, such as *Umriss der Rassenkunde* (an extensively revised and expanded edition is in preparation, to be followed, perhaps, by an English edition); everything in it is purely scientific. Also by this writer, *Stammeskunde der Völker* (areas of transition between anthropology and ethnography). Both books contain many original maps; the second also has an extensive analytical bibliography. A larger work, embracing the contents of both books is in preparation.

An excellent and comprehensive textbook of medium size has been published by I. Schwidetzky, *Das Menschenbild der Biologie* (the title is somewhat misleading), 218 closely printed pages, good bibliography. It, too, deserves to be translated. The *Fischer Lexikon der Anthropologie,* 360 pp., contains twenty mostly long articles of a strictly scientific nature by I. Schwidetzky, G. Heberer, and G. Kurth. [The book has been published in a much altered version as *Anthropology A to Z*, ed. by C. S. Coon and E. E. Hunt, Grosset & Dunlap, New York 1963.—Transl.] There are also several formally brilliant and in some respects pioneering works by E. v. Eickstedt. E. A. Hooton's well-known textbook *Up From the Ape,* last edition 1946, seems to me largely outdated. More modern, if rather popularized, is C. S. Coon's *The Story of Man,* 2nd edition 1962. As concerns the anthropology of Europe and the Near East, there is Coon, *The Races of Europe*, comprehensive, well planned and documented, but suffering from arbitrary and outdated conclusions. The chapters about the Near East are the best, and in some respects they break new ground.

In regard to ethnography, I should like to point—apart from the pertinent chapters in Biasutti—to several well-known and still very good descriptive works, which do not, however, deal with general questions. These are Z. Buschan, ed., *Völkerkunde*, 3rd edition 1923–6, three heavy volumes, and H. Bernatzik, editor, *Völkerkunde*, three volumes, two editions, 1939 (better) and 1954. Further, the small but imaginative book by K. Dittmer, *Allgemeine Völkerkunde*. It ought to be read by every ethnologist and all those interested in this branch of research. There is a good American book—R. Linton, *The Tree of Culture*. There is also the excellent *Fischer Lexikon der Völkerkunde*, edited by H. Tischner, in the same series as the volume on anthropology mentioned earlier; it confines itself to the ethnography of countries.

A small but thoughtful introduction to general problems is available in *Völkerkunde*, edited by B. Freudenfeld. A more extensive one is that of K. Birket-Smith, *Primitive Man and His Ways*, 1960 (translation from the Danish); a concentrated medium-size introduction is the well-known scientific textbook by R. Lowie, *Introduction to Cultural Anthropology*. Fundamental for African ethnography is Baumann et. al., *Völkerkunde* (French translation 1948).

The modern luxury work in the field of archaeology is that of S. Piggott (Editor), *The Dawn of Civilization*, followed by E. Bacon (Editor), *Vanished Cultures*. These volumes deal almost exclusively with the advanced civilizations, not with primitive peoples, past and present, or with domestic plants and animals. For the latter categories see C. Sauer, *Agricultural Origins and Dispersals*, and later essays of the famous German cultural geographer H. von Wissmann; also the very exact and well-documented *Abriss der Vorgeschichte*, edited by H.-H. von Barloewen, with an exceptionally comprehensive bibliography. There are also O. Menghin's unexcelled survey of America, and K. Narr's survey of Europe and Northern Asia. Much smaller is the survey by G. Clark, *World Prehistory*.

In the field of linguistic geography there hardly exists an appropriate work, unless we count my own *Stammeskunde*. One special work deserves to be noted—P. Bosch-Gimpera *Les Indoeuropéens,* 1961 (French translation from the Spanish) in which the linguistic problem is viewed from the standpoint of archaeology under broad scientific aspects—even though the author's anthropological judgment is decidedly negative.

For the racial psychology of the primitive peoples we have almost nothing apart from F. Keiter, *Rasse und Kultur,* Vol. II, and even here it is mainly the compendia of older works that are of interest. The rest of the volume, as well as the other two making up the trilogy, are of lesser interest. Negro psychology has been dealt with by J. C. Carothers, *The African Mind in Health and Disease,* and A. Shuey, *The Testing of Negro Intelligence,* and in many older but not necessarily outdated works by E. B. Reuter. On Negro physiology there is G. A. Heuse, *Biologie du Noir,* etc.

Human heredity is the subject of Curt Stern's in many respects unexcelled textbook *Principles of Human Genetics*. In a pedagogic strain there is the beautifully done work by O. von Verschner, *Genetik des Menschen*. There are many other works, some of them American, and in the last few years again a large number of good German ones. There are also some very valuable sections in the older standard work by Baur-Fischer-Lenz, not to be found in the newer books. As regards blood groups—genetics and geography—there are several well-known works by A. E. Mourant, 1954 and 1958, by W. Boyd in *Tabulae Biologicae,* Vol. 17, 1939, and the older pioneering works by L. Hirszfeld and O. Streng, both in German.

BIOGRAPHICAL NOTE

JAN CZEKANOWSKI, Ph.D., *is Professor Emeritus of Anthropology at the State University in Poznań, Poland, and an authority on the brachycephalic Neolithic population of Switzerland. He was born in 1882 in Gluchów, Poland, and educated in Warsaw and at the University of Zürich, Switzerland.*

From 1906 to 1910 he was research assistant at the Königliches Museum für Völkerkunde in Berlin, and was a member of the German Central African Expedition in 1907–1909. From 1910 to 1913 Professor Czekanowski was Scientific Custodian of the Ethnographic Museum of the Imperial Academy of Sciences in St. Petersburg. He was named Professor of Anthropology and Ethnology at the University of Lwów (Poland) in 1913, where he also served as Dean and Rector Magnificus. He remained at the University of Lwów for twenty-seven years, leaving in 1941 to become Professor of Anthropology and Ethnology at the Catholic University in Lublin (Poland). In 1946 he became Professor of Anthropology at Poznań.

Professor Czekanowski has been a member of the Polish Academy of Sciences since 1924 and was made an Honorary Fellow of the Royal Anthropological Institute of Great Britain and Ireland in 1961.

His writing covers Ugro-Finns and Slavic peoples, and the physical anthropology of the peoples of equatorial Africa. Among Dr. Czekanowski's many books are the five-volume work Forschungen im Nil-Kongo-Zwischengebiet *(Research in the Lake Regions Between the Nile and Congo Rivers), 1911–1927.*

MORPHOLOGY AND THE CLASSIFICATION OF RACE

Jan Czekanowski

Racial Classifications of Mankind

SINCE THE TIME of Linnaeus (1707–1778), natural scientists have been accustomed to take recourse to geography in order to avoid the difficulties caused by the classification of the human species. When Linnaeus found difficulty in distinguishing the races of man, he associated them with the four continents of the earth known at that time. That is evidenced by the terms introduced by him: *Homo Americanus, Home Europaeus, Homo Asiaticus,* and *Homo Afer* (in the sense of the African Negro). Only in the thirteenth edition of Linnaeus' work, which was edited ten years after his death by J. F. Gmelin in Leipzig (in the year 1788), was the classification of the human species into five races advanced. This was in a footnote added by Gmelin. Their designations were based upon the color of the skin, and read: *Homo albus, Homo badius, Homo niger, Homo cupreus,* and *Homo fuscus* (i.e., White, Yellow, Black, Copper, and Brown).

The distinction of five human races is derived from J. F. Blumenbach (1776). He spoke of Caucasians, Negroes, Mongols, Indians, and Malayans. The use of designations such as Mongols and Malayans shows that even the leading morphologists did not hesitate to enlist the aid of ethnography (or rather linguistics) in addition to geography. Systematic morphological classification was first realized by Georges Cuvier (1800). Cuvier limited himself to the major races (*Hauptrassen*): the White, the Yellow, and the Black. His synthesis forms the basis of the current morphological viewpoint in the field of racial systematics.

The ethnographic-linguistic viewpoint moved to the foreground in the first half of the nineteenth century, when identification of the anthropological components of the European population was attempted. Thenceforward ethnic groups (*Voelker*) and linguistic groups were considered human races. The first synthesis of the population of Europe was already realized in the year 1824 by the Polish philologist W. Surowiecki. On the basis of linguistic and anthropological (morphological) characteristics, Surowiecki distinguished five components, four of which are considered, at present, as principal racial elements (*Hauptrassen*) in the European population. Only in the year 1882 did J. Kollmann add the fifth component, whereby the morphological synthesis of the population of Europe received its definitive form. However, this has only been recognized and accurately demonstrated in this past decade.

With the triumph of evolutionary thought, interest in the problems of racial systematics diminished. Furthermore, the view became widespread that races exist only in books and are not to be sought in reality. Prominent anthropologists—such as Rudolf Virchow (1821–1902), for example, for whom the biological reality of the races of man was indisputable—were characterized as antiquated reactionaries. Julius Kollmann, who certainly was not alone in his belief in the biological reality of the races of man, was treated the most severely. For Kollmann separated completely the concept of race from that of the geographic and ethnic group, and even dared to defend the thesis of the stability of anthropological (morphological) types. He was branded as a man who, because of senility, was no longer in condition to appreciate the advance of modern science. Nevertheless, Kollmann was regarded as the most important representative of the allegedly completely antiquated morphological orientation. This is shown by the fact that Karl Pearson (1857–1936) continued the discussion relating to this question with the notorious opponents of the evolutionary plasticity of the present components of the human species—just as had been done earlier with Kollmann.

Thus, there gradually developed the two currently opposed

approaches in racial anthropology: (1) the classical *morphological* approach, in which the biological reality of the races of man is defended; and (2) the erroneously labeled *populationist* approach. One dares to say "erroneously," because human groups have been regarded as biological populations by the morphologists since the time of Kollmann. Furthermore, as a result of their closer acquaintance with the achievements of Gregor Mendel (1822–1884), the morphologists explained the fact that the component elements of a population did not blend into an amorphous new organism (local race) when crossed, to be a consequence of the Mendelian Law of Segregation. In this manner the stability of the morphological type, which was defended by Kollmann, has received a corroborating explanation in terms of the present status of our knowledge of the inheritance of anthropological characteristics.

The so-called populationist concept of race is in an analogous manner a continuation of the viewpoint of those anthropologists, who have regarded geographically and ethnically comprised human groups as anthropological races. This approach attempts to prove that the crossing of different human races leads to the formation of an allegedly countless number of local races. The originality of the populationist concept of race consists on the one hand in its concern with the evolutionary processes of race formation and on the other hand in its emphasis on the direct influences of the environment on racial characteristics.

For a critical natural scientist, who is not predisposed to either approach, his attitude toward two polemicizing scientific schools of thought is determined by the answer to the question: which leads to the more accurate and more elementary compilation and classification of the observed data? The valuation of their principal assumptions can be difficult, especially in the case of the so-called populationist concept of race, where the methodological premises form a complex of inaccurately defined elements unsuitable for analysis.

The advantage of the morphological concept of race is based on the fact that it bases the comparison of the human groups described on a few components considered as constants and investigated thoroughly. On the other hand, its weakness lies in the "morphological" methods employed. Namely, the systematic determination of the typological affinity of the individual investigated is based upon the subjective general impression of the morphologist. This process often leads to entirely hopeless discussions.

This occurred, for example, in the case of the skull from Gibraltar. It could not be agreed whether the skull belonged to the Neandertal race or was alien to it. It was not possible to make a certain, sufficiently accurate, and objectively determined judgment. Furthermore, in the case of the Gibraltar skull, where the results of measurements relating to several characteristics had been produced, it was not yet understood how to summarize these measurements of the objectively determined differences other than on the basis of a general subjective impression.

Contribution of Rudolf Virchow

THE HOPELESS condition of anthropology, which was caused by the failure of the morphological methods so successfully used in zoology, was widely recognized after the death of Paul Broca (1880). This state of affairs motivated Rudolf Virchow to deliver an important speech in the year 1899 at the Congress of German Anthropologists held in Lindau—the last Congress in which he took part—which was recognized as the scientific legacy of this great scholar.

Virchow emphasized the fact that the future of anthropology was endangered to the highest degree by the failure of anthropologists to successfully collaborate with prehistorians. Moreover, anthropologists had not yet accomplished the rendering of such concrete data with reference to human osteological finds, as zoologists and botanists had been able to do with respect to their finds. In this manner the problem of anthropological systematics, and above all the determination of the typological affinity of the skull, was pushed into the foreground by Virchow. The solution of this problem was evaluated as a scientific accomplishment, upon which the future of anthropology depended.

Nevertheless, Kollmann had already succeeded in very accurately determining the anthropological components of the European population in the year 1882. However, geographical viewpoints played a much larger role in the syntheses of the nineteenth century, although the first (W. Surowiecki, 1824) was based on linguistic-morphological concepts.

The geographic method was employed in racial anthropology by Paul Broca (1860). Basing his analysis upon a cartogram, which showed the numbers of those disqualified as unfit for military service on account of their small stature, Broca distinguished three anthropological components in the population of France.

Joseph Deniker (1898) proceeded in a similar manner. However, he compared two cartograms. The first cartogram showed the average stature, while the second showed the average cephalic index. By this means Deniker arrived at a separation of the anthropological regions in Europe. These regions were then associated with the races of Europe.

The results relating to East Europe were corrected in part by the Russian enthusiast of the geographic method—Ethyme Tschepurkowsky (1903–1912). Tschepurkowsky showed that the uniqueness of the eastern south Great Russian region, where an area of dark pigmentation appears, is limited to components tending to dolichocephaly. This is to be associated with the pre-Slavic Kurgan population. Both these representatives of the geographic method based their conclusions upon the general subjective impressions provided by observation of the cartograms.

The results obtained by Deniker were very different from those which Broca had obtained about forty years earlier. Broca allowed for three races in France, while Deniker distinguished ten races—although, to be sure, his analysis covered all Europe. Deniker further divided these ten races into six primary major races (*Hauptrassen*) and four secondary subsidiary races (*Nebenrassen*). Two years after Deniker, W. Z. Ripley (1900) published a comprehensive summary of the same observed data as that analyzed by Deniker, in which the geographic method was likewise used. However, Ripley limited himself to the three races distinguished by Broca.

This controversy over the views of the leading anthropologists resulted in the wide circulation of the opinion that racial anthropology is not a very exact science and that it employs entirely unreliable methods. This disqualification of anthropology appeared to have received its definitive formulation on the occasion of the address delivered by Deniker at the Huxley Lecture (1904), when the discussion carried on with reference to his controversy with W. Z. Ripley failed to reach a conclusion.

The crisis in the anthropology of that time, which was so dramatically emphasized by Rudolf Virchow in Lindau (1899), had reached its climax. This occurred when it was realized that the employment of the geographic method, from which so much had been expected, could not resolve the most important controversies over the systems of race classification based upon it.

It had to be admitted that the old, allegedly proven, research methods in racial anthropology, which were based upon the subjective impressions of the investigator, had failed. They sufficed in zoology and botany, where attention was actually concentrated upon the differences between species. However, they were not satisfactory in anthropology, where the investigator was concerned exclusively with the classification of components of species.

Even the introduction of refined measuring techniques in the treatment of anthropological characteristics could not place the subjective method upon a sufficiently objective basis. This failure of the subjective method resulted in casting doubt upon the biological reality of the anthropological races.

In this manner the question of the *biological reality of the races of man* has become the cardinal problem of anthropology. Their biological reality is defended at present by the morphological approach and disputed by the so-called populationist approach. In this essay evidence will be produced, which will leave no doubt as to the biological reality of the races of man and will secure the basis of human systematics.

Evidence of the Biological Reality of Races

ALREADY IN the year 1909 the problem of the classificatory determination of the typological affinity of cranial finds, which had been advanced to the foreground by Rudolf Virchow at Lindau (1899), was systematically analyzed. At that time I demonstrated that this question did not assume a hopeless form, if it was considered in the perspective of analytical mechanics. If the subject individuals are considered as points of an n-dimensional space, whose location is determined by coordinates which correspond to their anthropological traits, these points form centers of crystallization that correspond to the races—or rather to the racial complexes—of the morphologist. The mutual relations of these points in n-dimensional space can be represented graphically. That was demonstrated in the example of the graphical separation of the skull belonging to the Neandertal race from the rest. The skull of *Pithecanthropus,* although completely isolated, nevertheless proved to be closer to the Neandertal than to the remaining more recent skulls. Thanks to the textbook of Rudolf Martin (1914) this example became generally known to anthropologists.

This result completely and decidedly supports the theory that the Neandertal race is indeed an anthropological, biologically real, race, which cannot be disqualified as a conventional creation of the morphologist. Much more important, however, is the quantitative evidence, which is not based upon visual impressions.

In the case of the treatment of series of anthropological observations, the concept of centers of concentration in n-dimensional space formed a solution to the problem of the anthropological typological analysis of individuals—that is to say of their classificatory determination. Moreover, it was proven that with the use of the old subjective methods even large morphological differences could be matters of dispute. However, with the use of even the crudest statistical techniques—calculation of non-normalized average differences in anthropological traits, which can even be made on damaged skulls—morphological differences are completely indisputable. Thus the differences among the races of man prove to be large and sharply pronounced, when they are considered quantitatively.

In the years 1921 and 1922 I showed that the quantitative results of the Biometric School of Karl Pearson relating to the hereditability of anthropological traits and the Regression Law of Francis Galton are merely deductive consequences of the two

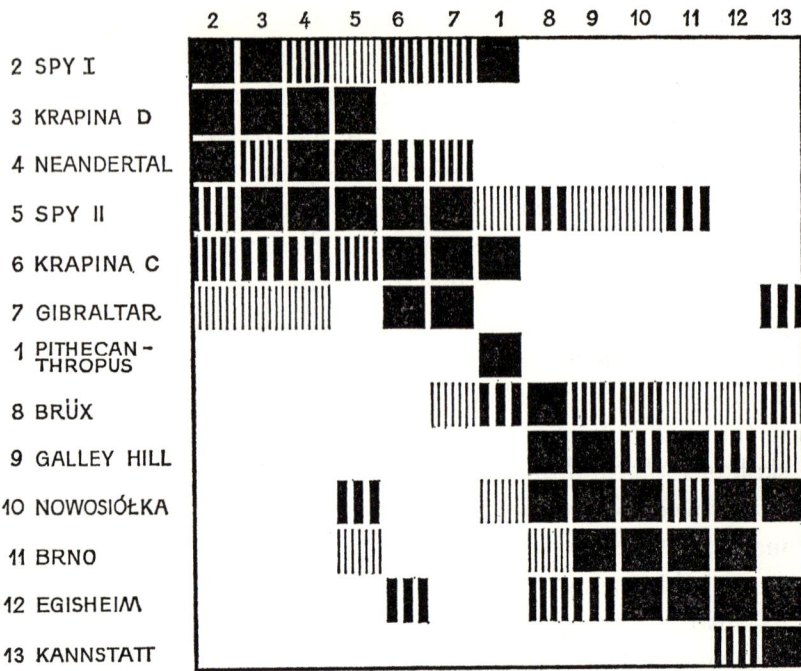

Fig. 1 Graphic representation of the morphological relation of the skulls of the Neandertal race to the more recent skulls and to *Pithecanthropus erectus*. After the calculation of the average differences for each combination of two skulls on the basis of the measurable differences between them (calculated for all possible anthropological traits), these were grouped together in a manner that corresponded to the diagraphic representation. In each column of the graphic representation the six smallest differences were illustrated: the null-value of the diagonal and the two smallest differences—by entirely black squares; the third smallest difference —by thick columns; the fourth smallest difference—by thick lines; and the fifth smallest difference—by thin lines. The complete isolation of *Pithecanthropus erectus* is revealed by the fact that it has no illustrated squares in its horizontal series (sequences)—apart from the null-value of the diagonal corresponding to it. The recent skull from Kannstadt, which had long been considered very ancient, is likewise very isolated. It only shows an affinity to the skull from Eggisheim. The remaining skulls are Upper Palaeolithic or Neolithic. The discussion concerning the affinity of the Gibraltar skull to the Neandertal race was reflected graphically by this means. The Gibraltar skull shows in its horizontal series only a sharply pronounced affinity to the Krapina skull, but otherwise conforms to the skulls of the Neandertal race in the fifth smallest difference (apart from the Spy II skull). This weak, but in other respects exclusive, connection to the skulls of the Neandertal race shows that the Gibraltar skull belongs to the Neandertal race, but is still very different from it, as has been shown in the discussion.

major Mendelian Laws—namely, the Law of Segregation and the Law of Dominance. It was thereby established that the variations in the coefficients of heredity for metrical traits are consequences of the Mendelian Law of Dominance. The magnitude of the coefficients of heredity—for parent and child—amounts to:

$$r = \frac{p}{1+p} \tag{1}$$

on the assumption that the proportion of the recessive genes p and the proportion of the dominant genes q amounts to:

$$p + q = 1 \tag{1a}$$

However, if the heredity is not complicated by dominance, if consequently $p = 1$ and $q = 0$, then the value of the coefficient of correlation obtained is:

$$r = 0.5 \tag{1b}$$

That is the first biological constant.

When calculating coefficients of heredity on the basis of the Fourfold Table, the value of the coefficient of heredity is not reduced by the factor of dominance. This does not occur in the case of the quantitative non-measurable anthropological traits. That is a consequence of the technique of calculation.

The variations in the value of the coefficients of heredity for the measurable traits are similarly a consequence of it. This proves that the inheritance of the traits in question is complicated by dominance. That is very important, because the direct observation of the phenomena of dominance in the metrical anthropological traits is inexact and difficult.

Pearson did not understand the explanation of why the coefficients of heredity are essentially lower in value for the metrical anthropological traits. Pearson was bound by his anti-Mendelian attitude. On this basis his repeated tests also failed to derive the "Law of Ancestral Heredity." In the year 1933 I demonstrated that this is likewise a deductive consequence of the Mendelian Laws and can be simply derived.

The assumption that the investigated human groups should be considered as statistical representations of intra-breeding populations has brought to light very important anthropological characteristics of these groups.

It is now no longer a matter of dispute that the frequencies of the separate serological categories correspond to the Mendelian expectation, that is given by the following formula:

$$(p + q + r)^2 = 1 \qquad (2)$$

The determination of the parameters p, q, and r gives a satisfactory description of the investigated human groups relative to the proportions of the serological components: AA, BB, and OO. Moreover, the first two are dominant in relation to the third, while these are mutually equivalent and yield an isolable hybrid form.

In a similar manner it has been proven that the results of the morphological typological analysis of central European craniological series can be summarized (as I demonstrated in the year 1928) with the help of the following formula:

$$(a + e + h + l)^2 = 1 \qquad (2a)$$

The parameters a, e, h, and l denote here the relative frequencies of the four races concerned in Central Europe—(1) the Nordic; (2) the Mediterranean; (3) the Armenoid; and (4) the Lapponoid. The equation (2a) was termed the *"Law of Frequency of Types"* (J. Czekanowski, 1928). The typological analysis (classificatory determination) was carried out on the basis of this law.

The mutual relations of the four principal anthropological components in the central European population and their six mixed-forms, which according to our hypothesis segregate out as a result of crossing, can be illustrated graphically in the following manner. The four principal racial elements are represented by points which form the corners of a square. The six lines, that can be drawn between these points, yield the corresponding mixed-forms.

If we have at our disposal at least ten (the more the better) central European craniological series, which have been classificatorily well-determined, the following system of i linear equations with 10 unknowns can be solved by use of the method of least squares:

$$\left. \begin{array}{l} a_i A + e_i E + h_i H + l_i L + k_{ae}a_i e_i (A - E) + \\ k_{ah}a_i h_i (A - H) + k_{al}a_i l_i (A - L) + k_{eh}e_i h_i (E - H) + \\ k_{el}e_i l_i (E - L) + k_{hl}h_i l_i (H - L) = M_i \end{array} \right\} \qquad (2b)$$

In the above equations the parameters A, E, H, and L denote the desired fundamental mean values of the cranial index of the

FIG. 2 MUTUAL RELATIONSHIP BETWEEN ANTHROPOLOGICAL TYPES

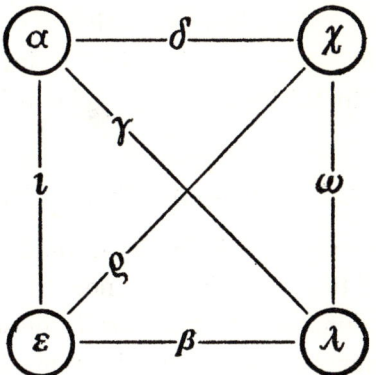

α—Nordic Type
χ—Armenoid Type
ι—Northwestern Mixed-Type
ω—Alpine Mixed-Type
β—Sublapponoid Mixed-Type
ε—Mediterranean Type
λ—Lapponoid Type
γ—Subnordic Mixed-Type
ρ—Litoral Mixed-Type
δ—Dinaric Mixed-Type

four races determined by formula (2a). The coefficients k_{ae}, k_{ah}, k_{al}, k_{eh}, k_{el}, k_{hl} similarly represent the consequences which are to be determined from the Mendelian Law of Dominance, while a_i, e_i, h_i, and l_i denote constants. Just as in formula (2a), they are the relative frequencies of the four races determined through typological analysis of the i-th. craniological series. Furthermore, the mean value of the cephalic index of this i-th. series was denoted by M_i.

The solution of the equations (2b) in the year 1930 allowed me to comprehend the relationships between the anthropological composition of the craniological series and their cranial index mean values in a satisfactorily accurate manner. For the series of recent crania (from the fourteenth to twentieth century inclusive) the corresponding empirical formula has the following form:

$$M_s = 76a + 68.5e + 88(h + l) + 7.5ae + 12a(h + l) \qquad (3)$$

(M_s denotes here the mean value of the cranial index).
This empirical formula establishes in an inductive manner that at present Armenoid and Lapponoid brachycephalic crania are dominant to the Nordic mesocephalic crania, while the latter is

dominant to the Mediterranean dolichocephalic crania. In the remaining combinations of races dominance was absent.

On the other hand, the analagous solution of equations (2b) for medieval central European craniological series (from approximately the fourth to thirteenth century inclusive) yielded the empirical formula:

$$M_s = 76a + 68.5e + 88(h+1) - 7.5ae - 12ah - 19.5eh \quad (3a)$$

In comparison this empirical inductive formula signifies that in the older periods of time the Mediterranean dolichocephalic crania was probably dominant to the Nordic mesocephalic crania and also to the Armenoid brachycephalic crania. At the same time the Nordic mesocephalic crania was probably dominant to the Armenoid brachycephalic crania. In the remaining three racial combinations dominance was absent.

Thus, we arrive at the following very important result: the empirically inductive formulas (3) and (3a) prove that the phenomena of dominance and recessiveness are racially-linked. This linkage (*Verknüpfung*) proves the *biological reality of the races of man*.

The formulas (3) and (3a) were published by me in 1930 and were termed "The Law of the Anthropological Mean Value of the Cranial Index." The conversion of the mean value of the cranial index to the cephalic index yields the "Law of the Mean Value of the Cephalic Index."

The "Law of the Anthropological Mean Value of the Cranial Index," or rather of the Cephalic Index, forms the control of *anthropological quantitative analysis*, which has been realized through the formulation of the "Law of Frequency of Types." Comparison of the two formulas of the "Law of the Mean Value" (3) and (3a) shows that the brachycephalization of the European population, which began approximately between the thirteenth and fourteenth centuries, can be simply explained through a reversal of the dominance phenomena.

In order to construct still further the circle of proofs of the biological reality of the races of man, the great accuracy of the "Law of the Mean Value of the Cephalic Index" was demonstrated on foreign observational material, which was statistically analyzed. Still later the accuracy of the analytical formulas was illustrated on the same observational material, which defined precisely the relation between the anthropological composition of the observational series and the relative frequency of the light-eyed.

Typological Analysis of Observations on the Living

IN CONTRAST to the satisfactory results obtained from typological analysis of the craniological series, which corresponded to formula (2a), the results of typological analysis of the living could not be brought into conformity with this formula. This circumstance led Adam Wanke to formulate the "Law of Frequency of Types" for use in typological analysis of the living in the following manner:

$$(a + e + h + l)^3 = 1 \qquad (2c)$$

The reason for such a modification of the "Law of Frequency of Types" is not difficult to explain. The craniological typological analysis is based upon two complexes of anthropological traits, which are independent of one another—the cranium and the face (Neurocranium and Splanchnocranium). Therefore, the form of the "Law of Frequency of Types" (2a) is quadratic. In the case of typological analysis of the living yet a third complex of anthropological traits is added, which is independent of the other two. That is pigmentation. Since we are concerned in this case with tri-hybrids, the form of the "Law of Frequency of Types" (2b) is, therefore, cubic.

However, if the typological analysis of the living is limited to two trait complexes—to physiognomy (photography) and pigmentation—the quadratic form of the "Law of Frequency of Types" is used. That has been demonstrated by the research of Jan Pavelčik (1948). Pavelčik determined the anthropological composition of the inhabitants of the small town of Nivnice in Moravia (Czechoslovakia) on the basis of the applications for the issue of passports. The application forms contained photographs and data relating to pigmentation. Pavelčik's study proved that racial differences in the heavily mixed European population are so large, that even such inexact observational material can be sufficient for the construction of a satisfactorily accurate anthropological analysis—if the material is handled by a good morphologist.

Pavelčik's conclusion shows that the use of the "Law of Frequency of Types" allows us to evaluate the *quality of the morphologist* in an accurate manner. It also explains why the noteworthy anthropologists from the year 1824 (W. Surowiecki) up until the present time arrived at the same racial components in the European population. This agreement of the research results is so much more important since one was not aware of this fact and it could only be demonstrated after the employment of more accurate methods of investigation.

TABLE 1
COMPARISON OF RESULTS OF TYPOLOGICAL ANALYSIS WITH THEORETICAL EXPECTATIONS BASED UPON THE "LAW OF FREQUENCY OF TYPES" (2b)

Terms of the Formula (2b)	Results of Typological Analysis	Theoretical Expectations	Differences	Square of the Differences	χ^2
a^3	33	26.3	− 6.7	44.89	1.71
$3a^2e$	34	30.3	− 3.7	13.69	0.45
$3a^2h$	32	31.9	− 0.1	0.01	0.00
$3a^2l$	29	35.4	+ 6.4	40.96	1.16
6aeh	31	24.4	− 6.6	43.56	1.79
6ael	32	26.9	− 5.1	26.01	0.97
6ahl	26	28.3	+ 2.3	5.29	0.19
6ehl	0	10.9	+10.9	118.81	10.90
e^3	0	1.5	+ 1.5	2.25	....
$3ae^2$	13	11.5	− 1.5	2.25	0.20
$3e^2h$	2	4.7	+ 2.7	7.29	1.55
$3e^2l$	3	5.1	+ 2.1	4.41	0.86
h^3	4	1.7	− 2.3	5.29	....
$3ah^2$	13	12.9	− 0.1	0.01	0.00
$3eh^2$	7	4.9	− 2.1	4.41	0.90
$3lh^2$	3	5.8	+ 2.8	7.84	0.31
l^3	3	2.3	− 0.7	0.49	....
$3al^2$	18	15.8	− 2.2	4.84	0.31
$3el^2$	7	6.0	− 1.0	1.00	0.17
$3hl^2$	3	6.4	+ 3.4	11.56	1.81
$e^3 + h^3 + l^3$	3	5.5	+ 2.5	6.25	1.14
Total	293	293	+32.1 −32.1	....	25.46

The fact that the results of typological analysis of the living indicate a completely satisfactory concordance with the "Law of Frequency of Types" (2b) was demonstrated by Bruno Miszkiewicz (1960) on a north Polish observational series. They are quoted in Table 1. Since the critical value of the sums of the χ^2 amounts to 27.6, as shown in Table 1, the concordance of the results of typological analysis with the theoretical expectations derived from the "Law of Frequency of Types" (2b) should be considered completely satisfactory.

The theoretical expectations were calculated after establishing that the population group (in north Poland) being investigated has the following composition: Nordic Race, 44.8%; Mediterranean Race, 17.1%; Armenoid Race, 18.1%; and Lapponoid Race, 20.0%.

The mean value of the cephalic index calculated from direct observation	82.60
The mean value of the cranial index calculated from formula (3)	81.90
Increase with conversion to the cephalic index	+0.58
Theoretical expectation relative to the cephalic index	82.48
The divergence of the theoretically expected and directly observed cephalic indexes amounts to:	−0.12

This study demonstrates that in the case of research on the living, Polish anthropology has attained a high level of scientific accuracy. That is attested to by the concordance obtained between the theoretical expectations and the results of direct observation.

The typological analysis of numerous series of observations, which have been based upon both the "Law of Frequency of Types" and also the "Law of the Anthropological Mean Value," has demonstrated that the noteworthy anthropologists of the nineteenth and twentieth centuries distinguished the same anthropological components in the population of Europe.

These racial elements were given different names by them since the earlier anthropologists were not aware of the concordance of their results. Little attention was paid to the investigations of Julius Kollmann (1882), who had already indicated several synonymous systems to his system of race classification. Our investigations have controlled this problem with the help of exact methods. We have thereby arrived at the comparative analysis of the classificatory systems of the anthropological components in the population of Europe as shown in Table 2.

TABLE 2
COMPARATIVE ANALYSIS OF THE CLASSIFICATORY SYSTEMS OF THE RACES OF EUROPE

	SUROWIECKI 1824	KOLLMANN 1882	DENIKER 1898	RIPLEY 1900	CZEKANOWSKI 1928	Von EICKSTEDT 1934	BIASUTTI 1959
1)	Blond	Leptoprosopic Dolichocephal	Nordique	Teutonic	Nordyczna	Nordische	Nordica
2)	Iberian	Chamaeprosopic Dolichocephal	Ibero-Insulaire	Mediterranean	Śródziemnomorska	Mediterranean	Mediterranean
a)	—	—	Nord-Occidentale	—	Północno-zachodnia (Hybrid-1 + 2)	—	Irlandese
b)	—	—	Litorale	—	Litoralna (Hybrid-2 + 3)	—	—
c)	—	—	{ Adriatique }	—	Dynarska (Hybrid-1 + 3)	Dinarische	Dinarica
3)	—	Leptoprosopic Brachycephal	—	—	Armenoidalna	Armenid	Anatolica
d)	—	—	Sub-Adriatique	—	Alpejska (Hybrid-3 + 4)	Alpine	Alpina
4)	Lappish	Chamaeprosopic Brachycephal	Occidentale ou Cévéniole	Alpine	Laponoidalna	Lappid	Lappone
e)	—	—	—	—	Sublaponoidalna (Hybrid-2 + 4)	—	—
f)	Slavic	—	Sub-Nordique	—	Subnordyczna (Hybrid-1 + 4)	Osteuropid	Baltica
5)	Finnish	Chamaeprosopic Mesocephal	Vistulienne Orientale	—	Paleoeuropidalna or Paleoazjatycka	Sibirid?	Europeidi Archaice

Races are designated by numbers and their hybrid-forms by small letters. In Czekanowski's system, the sums added in parentheses refer to the components of the hybrid-forms. In Deniker's system, the designation Adriatique was shifted in order to emphasize that in his classification the Armenoid race, which was not sorted out, was grouped together with the Dinaric hybrid-form. The Vistulienne race was shifted in order to indicate that it was so interpreted by Deniker and so that Otto Schlaginhaufen could identify this race with his Orientale race.

The mastery of the problem of the various systems of race classification (see Table 2) clarified the puzzling controversy over

Morphology and the Classification of Race

the systems of Deniker (1898) and Ripley (1900). It was found that both actually reached an agreement of results. However, Deniker and Ripley were completely unaware of it. So completely had they lost themselves in the chaos of anthropological systematics, that even the subsequent discussion (1904)—in which the prominent anthropologists of the time participated—did not comprehend the essence of the problem. Only after the formulation of the "Law of Frequency of Types" did it turn out that Ripley had restricted himself to the consideration of the principal racial elements. Moreover, the two round-headed and darkly pigmented races—the Lapponoid and the Armenoid—were combined in his "Alpine race." Thus, Ripley arrived at his three races, since the Paleo-Europid component lay outside of his field of vision.

On the other hand, Deniker did not consider the principal racial elements alone, but also their hybrid forms of the first degree. However, since he grouped the Armenoid race together with its Nordic hybrid-form into his Adriatic race, and in addition considered the Paleo-Europid component characteristic of northeast Europe as his Oriental race, Deniker arrived at his ten races. In this manner the Deniker-Ripley controversy, which had stimulated so much conflict, was definitively settled.

The fact that only five races are concerned in the population of Europe was proven by Adam Wanke in the year 1953. Furthermore, the fifth race—which is the Paleo-Europid component characteristic of northeast Europe—is very sparsely represented in central Europe, although it was supposed to be characteristic of the mesolithic population of Europe (W. Kóčka, 1958). The study made on 3,353 students at the College of Wroclaw (formerly Breslau), where many eastern Poles studied, demonstrated that those combinations of anthropological characteristics, in which the number of realizations exceed the theoretical expectations by at least 50 percent, correspond to the races taken into consideration in this case.

In this manner the foundations of the classification of the races in the population of Europe were secured. However, it was still necessary to demonstrate that the races have been determined in a satisfactorily accurate manner, or in other words that their definitions are satisfactorily accurate.

Wanke's Method of Approximation

IF THE INVESTIGATOR is not satisfied with determining the racial affinity of individuals on the basis of his general, subjective, morphological impressions, and uses the method of differential diagnosis (J. Czekanowski, 1909), the typological analysis of the series of anthropological observations requires a very great expenditure of mechanical labor. Even worse is the fact that this work increases very quickly with the enlargement of the series of observations. The increase occurs in accord with the formula: $W = \dfrac{n(n-1)}{2}$ (where W represents the expenditure of labor and n represents the number of individuals considered).

The introduction of this method of typological analysis, however, formed a great advance in the treatment of anthropological observations. It reduced the influence of subjective impressions. That is to say, this subjectivity was limited to the interpretation of the diagram of average differences, which illustrated the mutual relations of the individuals in the investigated group. However, this interpretation was controlled both by the "Law of Frequency of Types" and also by the "Law of the Anthropological Mean Value," which practically reduced the subjective motive to a minimum. In view of these successes the reduction of the necessary mechanical labor has become the most important problem of anthropological research techniques. However, this problem was solved by the introduction of Adam Wanke's "Method of Approximation."

This most important analytical instrument of Polish racial anthropology was first exhibited in the year 1952 at the Anthropological Congress in Wroclaw and published in the following year. Wanke's "Method of Approximation" permits the calculation of the percentages of the racial components, corresponding to the results of the typological analysis, for the population groups being investigated on the basis of their mean values. In this way even the older publications, which limited themselves to the quotation of the mean values of the morphological indices and the percentages of the pigmentation categories, were opened for analytical

Morphology and the Classification of Race

utilization. Up until the present time this material formed an archive that was principally used for cartographic compilations and with which nothing more reliable and more important could otherwise be constructed.

Wanke's "Method of Approximation" is based upon the assumption that concentrated masses of anthropological components remain in a state of equilibrium with respect to their centers of gravity, if the magnitudes of these masses are inversely proportional to the squares of the distances of their centers of gravity from the center of gravity of the entire system—that is to say of the mean values of the anthropological traits of the investigated population group. Thus, theoretical racial anthropology was linked even more closely to analytical mechanics by the work of Wanke. Quantitative anthropological analysis was now based upon the Law of Gravity. The fact that a pioneering, positive result is attained by this method, is demonstrated by the example given further below, of the anthropological survey of the Swiss army recruits.

The success attained by Adam Wanke should be evaluated even more highly, since the study made by Karl Pearson (1894) was a failure. Pearson only arrived at a solution for the special case of a population group consisting of two components. However, this special case still required very much work, since the solution involved a ninth degree equation. Pearson's method was not suitable for the anthropologist, whose investigation concerned several components. Wanke's "Method of Approximation" permits an unlimited number of components to be considered and yields more accurate results, the larger the series of observations analyzed.

The application of Wanke's "Method of Approximation" involves the calculation of the percentages of the individual racial elements in the population group on the basis of the following formulas:

$$i = \frac{k}{(A_1 - P_{i1})^2 + (A_2 - P_{i2})^2 + (A_3 - P_{i3})^2 + (A_4 - P_{i4})^2 + (A_5 - P_5)^2}$$

$$e_i = \frac{k}{(E_1 - P_{i1})^2 + (E_2 - P_{i2})^2 + (E_3 - P_{i3})^2 + (E_4 - P_{i4})^2 + (E_5 - P_{i5})^2}$$

$$h_i = \frac{k}{(H_1 - P_{i1})^2 + (H_2 - P_{i2})^2 + (H_3 - P_{i3})^2 + (H_4 - P_{i4})^2 + (H_5 - P_{i5})^2}$$

$$l_i = \frac{k}{(L_1 - P_{i1})^2 + (L_2 - P_{i2})^2 + (L_3 - P_{i3})^2 + (L_4 - P_{i4})^2 + (L_5 - P_{i5})^2}$$

where the factor k modifies the results obtained in a way which satisfies the condition:

$$a_i + e_i + h_i + l_i = 1 \quad \ldots\ldots\ldots\ldots (2c)$$

The parameters a_i, e_i, h_i, and l_i designate the percentages of the four racial components in the population group i—a) the Nordic; e) the Mediterranean; h) the Armenoid; and l) the Lapponoid. The magnitudes P_{i1}, P_{i2}, P_{i3}, P_{i4}, and P_{i5} are well-known and designate the mean values of the population group i relative to the anthropological traits considered in the classificatory determination: 1) Cephalic Index; 2) Morphological Facial Index; 3) Nasal Index; 4) Eye Color; and 5) Hair Color.

The application of Wanke's "Method of Approximation," which means the carrying out of the calculations on the basis of the above-mentioned four formulas, presupposes knowledge of the constants: $A_1, A_2, A_3, \ldots, E_1 \ldots, H_1 \ldots, L_4, L_5$. These are the indices of the position of the racial elements—in other words, the assumed descriptions of the races contained in the population group i. Professor Wanke demonstrated that fair approximations are attained if these unknowns are replaced by those combinations which indicate the maximal relative surpluses of the realized values in comparison to the theoretical expectations. However, I have succeeded (1954) in comprehending them more accurately—and in a manner which produces concordant results with the "Law of the Anthropological Mean Value" of the cephalic index. The racial elements in the population, defined in terms of anthropological traits, are given in Table 3.

The mean values for eye and hair color were expressed in units of the standard deviation (σ), in which the numbers indicated represent distances from the mean values of the totality of the Swiss army recruits. They were calculated on the assumption that the frequencies of the eye and hair color shades are distributed

TABLE 3
DEFINITIONS OF THE ANTHROPOLOGICAL ELEMENTS (RACES)

Anthropological Traits	Anthropological Elements (Races)			
	Nordic	Mediterranean	Armenoid	Lapponoid
Cephalic Index	78.0	71.5	89.0	89.0
Morphological Facial Index	89.5	88.0	86.0	80.0
Nasal Index	63.0	63.0	57.0	72.0
Eye Color	−1.252	0.984	2.170	0.944
Hair Color	−1.052	0.074	1.146	0.477

according to the normal (Gaussian) distribution. The mean values of the generality of the Swiss army recruits are in the case of eye color 0.670σ (sigma) from the boundary between Numbers 12 and 13 of the Martin scale and in the case of hair color 0.506σ (sigma) from the boundary of light hair, located between O-P and P in the Fischer-Saller scale.

In the case of the use of Wanke's "Method of Approximation," which means the carrying out of analytical calculations, the investigator must take into account the condition that the individual anthropological characteristics show great differences in their variability. The larger variables would influence the result of calculation according to their greater coefficient of variability. In order to eliminate the complications caused by this, the variables must be normalized. This means that their variations are expressed in their standard deviation (σ) units, in the same manner as those of the eye and hair color.

If it is considered that in the case of the Swiss army recruits the following standard deviations have been determined: Cephalic Index, 3.85; Morphological Facial Index, 5.40; Nasal Index, 6.98, the ascertained variations are reduced correspondingly. The calculation of the anthropological composition of the Swiss army recruits are shown in Table 4.

In order to control this analytical result with Formula (3) of the "Law of the Mean Value," the investigator must bear in mind that this yields the theoretical mean value of the skull. Therefore, this result must be converted into the mean value of the cephalic

TABLE 4
ANTHROPOLOGICAL ANALYSIS OF THE SWISS ARMY RECRUITS

Anthropological Trait	Mean Value	Deviations from the Indices of the Location of the Races							
		Nordic		Mediterranean		Armenoid		Lapponoid	
		Absolute Value	X/σ	Absolute Value	X/σ	Absolute Value	X/σ	Absolute Value	X/σ
Cephalic Index	81.31	3.31	0.860	9.81	2.548	7.69	1.997	7.69	1.997
Morphological Facial Index	89.45	0.05	0.009	1.45	0.269	3.45	0.639	9.45	1.750
Nasal Index	62.95	0.05	0.007	0.05	0.007	5.95	0.852	9.05	1.297
Eye Color	0.670	—	−1.252	—	0.984	—	2.170	—	0.944
Hair Color	0.506	—	−1.052	—	0.074	—	1.146	—	0.477

	Squares of the Deviations			
	Nordic	Mediterranean	Armenoid	Lapponoid
Cephalic Index	0.740	6.492	3.988	3.988
Morphological Facial Index	0.001	0.072	0.408	3.062
Nasal Index	0.000	0.000	0.726	1.682
Eye Color	1.568	0.968	4.709	0.891
Hair Color	1.107	0.005	1.313	0.228
Total	3.416	7.537	11.144	9.851
Reciprocal in %	29.37	13.27	8.97	10.15
Anthropological Composition	a = 47.5%	e = 21.5%	h = 14.5%	l = 16.5%

index (of the living subject). The empirical formula published by me in 1907 produces the conversion:

$$M_k = \frac{M_s + 8.6}{1.09721}$$

M_s designates here the theoretical mean value of the cranial index calculated on the basis of Formula (3) and M_k designates the corresponding mean value of the cephalic index of the living.

In this manner it is determined that the theoretical mean value of the cephalic index of the Swiss army recruits, in the case of 35,764 observations and of the precisely defined anthropological composition, amounts to 81.33, while the direct calculation yielded 81.31 (Table 5). The discrepancy between the theoretical and the directly observed mean, therefore, amounts to +0.02 index units, which means 0.00025 percent of the observed magnitude. That is an almost astronomical exactness.

In the case of smaller observational series larger discrepancies are observed. But that they are small is demonstrated by the analytical results obtained from the Swiss cantons, half-cantons, and districts of the Berne canton.

The concordance of the theoretically calculated mean value with the directly observed is remarkably good. That proves that the races have been comprehended in a satisfactorily accurate manner and that the "Law of the Mean Value" with the help of Formula (3) was formulated in a satisfactorily accurate manner.

In accord with this very important determination it shall be demonstrated that the racial definitions given here are valid for all Europe. In other words, the racial definitions are independent of the geographical environment. This is illustrated in Table 6.

The comparative analyses suffice to produce the conviction that, relative to the five anthropological traits considered here, identically constituted races are concerned for the entire present-day population of Europe.

Otherwise, the problem of the persistence of their external appearance in the course of time takes another form. The condition that the mean value of the cephalic index for recent populations be calculated on the basis of Formula (3) and the corresponding mean value of the cranial index for early medieval

TABLE 5

RESULTS OF THE QUANTITATIVE ANTHROPOLOGICAL ANALYSIS OF THE SWISS ARMY RECRUITS

Number of Observational Series	Anthropological Races in %				Cephalic Index Mean Value		
	Nordic	Mediterranean	Armenoid	Lapponoid	Observed	Theoretical	Divergence
1. Berner Oberland	59.8	18.2	9.9	12.0	80.70	80.44	−0.26
2. Obwalden	54.6	21.7	11.7	12.0	80.57	80.53	−0.04
3. Berne—entire Canton	53.3	19.7	12.2	14.8	81.16	81.00	−0.16
4. Berner Mittelland	53.1	19.5	12.3	15.0	81.24	81.05	−0.19
5. Aargau	52.0	20.4	13.0	14.6	81.16	81.02	−0.14
6. Basel—Rural	51.1	23.2	12.4	13.3	80.48	80.58	−0.10
7. Solothurn	50.2	20.9	13.5	15.4	81.17	81.14	−0.03
8. Nidwalden	50.0	21.2	14.3	14.5	81.32	81.03	−0.29
9. Schaffhausen	49.0	21.0	14.4	15.6	81.38	81.26	−0.12
10. Zürich	48.2	21.0	14.5	16.3	81.40	81.35	−0.05
11. Lucerne	48.2	20.9	14.4	16.5	81.44	81.37	−0.07
12. Basel—Urban	39.2	32.3	13.5	15.0	79.60	80.10	0.50
13. Geneva	39.6	30.8	14.2	15.4	79.75	80.35	0.60
14. Vaud	44.0	28.6	13.7	13.7	79.85	80.33	0.48
15. Fribourg	45.3	24.4	14.4	15.9	80.70	81.00	0.30
16. Neuchâtel	44.1	24.9	14.7	16.3	80.64	81.04	0.40
17. Zug	44.5	23.7	15.5	16.3	81.08	81.23	0.15
18. Glarus	43.7	22.8	16.0	17.5	81.29	81.49	0.20
19. Berner Jura	45.3	22.5	15.2	17.0	81.18	81.38	0.20
20. Appenzell—Outer Rhoden	46.4	20.8	15.5	17.3	81.60	81.59	−0.01
21. St. Gallen	45.4	19.8	16.0	18.8	82.01	81.92	−0.09
22. Uri	45.0	20.1	16.2	18.7	82.06	81.88	−0.18
23. Schwyz	44.1	20.4	16.7	18.8	81.81	81.92	0.11
24. Thurgau	43.4	19.7	16.6	20.3	82.14	82.13	−0.01
25. Graubünden	35.5	25.0	20.5	19.0	81.49	81.86	0.37
26. Valais	37.5	20.8	19.6	22.1	82.26	82.49	0.23
27. Appenzell—Inner Rhoden	37.7	19.0	20.6	22.7	82.85	82.82	−0.03
28. Ticino	27.7	18.0	28.5	25.8	83.66	83.80	0.14

TABLE 6
DIVERGENCES OF THE OBSERVED AND THEORETICALLY CALCULATED MEAN VALUES OF THE CEPHALIC INDEX IN EUROPE

Number of Observational Series	Anthropological Races in %				Observed	Theoretical	Divergence
	Nordic	Mediter-ranean	Armenoid	Lapponoid			
1. Iceland	87.7%	6.8%	2.6%	2.9%	78.10	78.18	+0.08
2. Pskow-Great Russia	53.4	14.7	9.5	22.4	81.90	81.99	+0.09
3. Hannover-Germany	55.7	16.6	11.8	15.9	81.40	81.32	−0.08
4. Kolo-Central Poland	54.7	16.7	11.0	17.6	81.42	81.44	+0.02
5. Kursk-South Great Russia	53.6	15.6	10.6	20.2	81.80	81.78	−0.02
6. Switzerland (Army Recruits)	47.5	21.5	14.5	16.5	81.31	81.33	+0.02
7. Pszczyna-South Poland	27.7	12.7	14.0	45.6	84.84	84.80	−0.04
8. Kalusz-Ukraine	21.9	13.7	29.7	34.8	84.94	84.96	+0.02
9. Keuper-Franken Bavaria-Germany	19.6	12.2	21.4	46.8	84.80	84.44	−0.36

craniological material be calculated on the basis of Formula (3a) proves that the external appearance of the races had assumed a different form in the early Middle Ages. In other words the location indices that are used with the employment of Wanke's "Method of Approximation" have to be defined differently. However, since the base constants of the races in Formulas (3) and (3a) are identical (they are not modified in the course of time), the conclusion is reached that the external form of the races has changed as a consequence of changes in the phenomena of dominance. The changes in the racial definitions are comprehensible, because these are identical with the constants in Wanke's "Method of Approximation."

Analysis of the Definition of Race

WANKE's "Method of Approximation" is especially important for racial systematics, because it permits a precise definition of the anthropological content of the races introduced into the professional literature by different authors. Of course that is only possible in those cases, where the investigators have taken care to define in a satisfactorily accurate manner the races introduced by them. Unfortunately that is often not the case.

In consideration of the circumstance that Deniker's synthesis has so strongly influenced the anthropologists of the twentieth century, as is evident from the above cited comparative analysis of the classificatory systems of the races of Europe, the results obtained from the analysis of Deniker's system of race classification with the help of Wanke's "Method of Approximation" will be described shortly. Not only can the substance of the interpretation of Deniker's (1904) "six races" given by Professor Otto Schlaginhaufen (1946) be made precise, but it can also be shown which modifications of the racial definitions bring us closer to the more accurate comprehension of the anthropological components on the basis of the assumptions of Polish racial anthropology. In the comparative analysis, illustrated in Table 7, the effects of the modifications introduced are inserted in parentheses.

It is seen here that the "Alpine race" becomes the Lapponoid

TABLE 7

RELATIONSHIP OF DENIKER'S SYSTEM OF RACE CLASSIFICATION TO THE RACIAL CLASSIFICATORY SYSTEM OF POLISH ANTHROPOLOGY

The "races" of Deniker according to the interpretation of Dr. Otto Schlaginhaufen on the basis of Swiss observational material.	Races of Polish Anthropology in %			
	Nordic	Mediterranean	Armenoid	Lapponoid
Nordic Race (Homo europaeus)	92.7	3.9	1.6	1.8
Ibero-Insular Race (Homo mediterraneus)	9.8	82.1	4.6	3.6
Alpine Race (Homo alpinus)	17.9 (2.6)	12.8 (2.4)	14.9 (6.6)	54.3 (88.3)
Dinaric Race (Homo adriaticus)	20.9 (4.0)	18.9 (3.9)	37.7 (79.4)	22.4 (12.8)
Litoral Race (Homo atlantomediterraneus)	16.1	39.8	27.1	17.0
East-Europid Race (Homo vistulensis)	51.1	16.2	9.7	23.0
Cro-Magnonoid Race (of I. Michalski)	50.8	24.8	8.6	15.8

race of Polish anthropology, if its definition is limited to: hyperbrachycephaly, europrosopy and hyper-europrosopy, and brown eyes.

In an analogous manner the "Dinaric race" becomes the Armenoid race of Polish anthropology, since its definition is restricted to: hyperbrachycephaly, leptoprosopy, very dark-colored eyes, and black hair.

The "Litoral race" is found to be a mixed-form, in which the Mediterranean and Armenoid races are represented considerably more strongly than the remaining. I have recognized it as such since the formulation of the "Law of Frequency of Types" in the year 1928. After the passage of almost 25 years this hypothesis was proved correct by Wanke's "Method of Approximation."

Furthermore, there is not the slightest doubt that the "Cro-Magnonoid race" of Michalski is identical to the "Oriental race" of Deniker, which is designated as the "East-European race" (*Homo vistulensis*) by Schlaginhaufen. It is also designated as the "Paleo-Europid race" by W. Kóčka. The use of Wanke's "Method of Approximation" provided the proof that different races are not concerned here, but only synonymous designations of the same anthropological components.

The first comparative analysis of the classificatory systems of the races of Europe was a direct consequence of the discovery of the "Law of Frequency of Types." However, its present formulation was only made possible as a result of Wanke's "Method of Approximation." It permitted an understanding of the relationships of the different racial definitions to the racial definitions of Polish anthropology, as was demonstrated above by the example of Deniker's system of race classification (according to Schlaginhaufen's interpretation).

In terms of the morphological concept of race, the fundamental biological reality of the races of man is decisively proven by establishing that the phenomena of dominance are closely linked to the race. That was already demonstrated in the case of the cephalic index (of living subjects). This proof has the defect that it presupposes a certain understanding of statistical methods. Much simpler is the establishment of the association of dominance with the race in the case of the inheritance of eye color. There direct observation is sufficient.

In order to determine precisely the theoretical expectations relative to the number of light-eyed on the basis of the anthropological composition of the population group, the cubic form of the "Law of Frequency of Types" is, of course, employed. We are concerned here with the result of the analysis of observations on the living, which was realized with regard to the three trait-complexes (skull, face, and pigmentation).

The results of the investigations of Professor Boleslaw Rosinski (1947–1948) have shown that the light eyes of the Nordic race (Martin Scale 16–13) are dominant to the dark eyes of the Lapponoid race in the case of mixture between these two races. For the central European observational series, which is composed of four racial elements, the theoretically expected percentages of light-eyed subjects can be calculated according to the formula,

Morphology and the Classification of Race

which I proposed in the year 1959 at the conference of Polish biometricians. This formula has the following form:

$$Y = 100\,[(a+1)^3 - 1^3] \qquad (4)$$

Y designates here the theoretically expected percentage of light eyes, if the proportion of the Nordic and Lapponoid races in the investigated population groups amount to a and l.

On the basis of this formula the percentages of the theoretically expected light-eyed subjects were calculated for the Swiss army recruits, since the magnitudes a and l were known. These magnitudes are found in the previously cited compilation of the analytical results of the anthropological study of the Swiss army recruits (Table 4). In this manner the tabulation in Table 8 was arrived at.

The concordance of the observed and the theoretically expected percentages of the Swiss army recruits with light eyes—calculated on the basis of the anthropological composition of the observational series—is remarkable. Only in five cantons, where the number of army recruits was greater than four hundred and one, was the divergence of the percentages greater than 3.0 percent. And in those cases the divergences ranged from 3.21 to 3.79 percent. Greater divergences occurred only in the half-cantons of Obwalden (+6.08 percent) and Nidwalden (+4.72 percent). And in those two places there were only two hundred and six and two hundred and nineteen army recruits, respectively. Therefore, there can be no doubt that the phenomena of dominance with respect to eye color, just as in the case of cranial form, is closely linked to the race. These are decisive proofs of the biological reality of the races of man.

The proof of this important fact does not depend upon eye color alone. Also very important is the previous proof that with regard to the three trait-complexes used in analysis of observations on the living, we must deal with tri-hybrids. This was demonstrated by the use of the cubic form of the "Law of Frequency of Types" (Formula 2c).

The establishment of the dominance of the blue eyes of the Nordic race to the dark eyes of the Lapponoid race is of great significance on practical grounds. It was earlier believed that dark

TABLE 8
CONCORDANCE OF THE OBSERVED AND THEORETICALLY EXPECTED PERCENTAGE OF LIGHT EYES AMONG THE SWISS ARMY RECRUITS

Number of the Observational Series	Observed %	Theoretically Expected %	Divergence %	Number of Army Recruits
1. Berner Oberland	34.02	36.84	2.82	—
2. Obwalden	23.29	29.37	6.08	206
3. Berne—entire canton	29.34	31.26	1.92	8,723
4. Berner Mittelland	28.79	31.24	2.45	—
5. Aargau	28.34	29.23	0.89	2,971
6. Basel—Rural	25.73	26.47	0.74	801
7. Solothurn	28.65	27.86	−0.79	1,139
8. Nidwalden	21.81	26.53	4.72	219
9. Schaffhausen	25.23	26.58	1.35	455
10. Zürich	25.79	26.40	0.61	3,454
11. Lucerne	23.09	26.63	3.54	1,971
12. Basel—Urban	16.15	15.58	−0.57	761
13. Geneva	19.64	16.27	−3.37	401
14. Vaud	22.74	18.95	−3.79	1,997
15. Fribourg	24.95	22.52	−2.43	1,467
16. Neuchâtel	23.41	21.60	−1.81	698
17. Zug	20.76	22.04	1.28	237
18. Glarus	22.02	22.39	0.37	346
19. Jura Bernois	27.19	23.69	−3.50	—
20. Appenzell—Outer Rhoden	24.25	25.33	1.08	670
21. St. Gallen	24.49	25.80	1.31	2,627
22. Uri	24.63	25.19	0.56	274
23. Schwyz	21.01	24.22	3.21	713
24. Thurgau	23.97	25.01	1.04	1,320
25. Graubünden	16.17	15.50	−0.57	1,092
26. Valais	23.82	20.09	−3.73	1,364
27. Appenzell—Inner Rhoden	18.71	20.87	2.16	259
28. Ticino	17.14	13.60	−3.54	1,209
Total	25.14	25.77	0.65	35,764

eyes were always consistently dominant to light eyes. At that time the paternity had to be doubted in all those cases where the children had darker eyes than their parents. However, in those regions where the Nordic and Lapponoid races were strongly represented, as is the case of the North Slavs and the Northeast Germans and even the Baltic peoples, children with darker eyes than their parents are very frequent.

This was demonstrated in the case of Poland by the investigations of Professor Rosinski on a very large observational series (1947–1948). In this instance the untenability of the generalization made by Professor C. B. Davenport in the year 1906 from his observations is evident. Almost half of the observations, which could be carried out in the immediate environment, contradict it.

Criticism of Morphological Approach to Anthropology

THE MORPHOLOGICAL approach in racial anthropology is criticized by young anthropologists, who have been bewitched by population genetics, as representing an antiquated point of view, because: (1) it believes in the biological reality of the races of man; (2) it does not consider changes in present-day Man caused by evolutionary processes; (3) it does not value the effects of selective processes; (4) it asserts the stability of morphological types not only with reference to historical times, but also for the prehistoric past; (5) it does not bring mutations into their system of thought; and (6) it operates with formulas that are absurd in terms of genetics, as is the case, for example, with the cubic form of the "Law of Frequency of Types" (2c).

The linkage (*Verknüpfung*) of dominance to the race, which has been proven exactly for the cephalic index and eye color, furnishes entirely sufficient proofs of the biological reality of the races of man. With analagous research on other anthropological traits the number of such proofs will increase. That is shown by the fact that the coefficients of heredity of all investigated traits show variations, if their lines of regression are equalized by use of the method of least squares.

In adopting a point of view with regard to the effects of the great evolutionary processes on Man, one should not leave out of consideration the fact that the science of anthropology considers Man in two different time perspectives—geological (biological) time and sociological time. In the perspective of geological time anthropology is concerned exclusively with morphological evidence of the evolutionary process, which takes the form of the scientific treatment of osteological finds. The conclusions are based on the assumption that morphological similarity is the measure of biological relationship.

This supposition is subject to dispute, because the distinction between homologies and analogies is often entirely hopeless. However, that is the only possible assumption of biological relationship which can be supported in palaeontology. What the geneticists can produce in this case are merely analogies, and these are no proofs. They merely remain suggestions, which in the best cases bring attention to new possibilities that remain to be proved.

However, if the anthropological phenomena are considered in the perspective of sociological time, it must be demonstrated in a satisfactorily accurate manner in each concrete case that the advance of the evolutionary process is evident. The process of evolution is no theoretical supposition, which arises from the belief in an inherent tendency to the perfectibility of the organisms. It is a biological fact, which is clearly evident in the perspective of comparative anatomy. However, in anthropology, if the investigator deals with facts that lie in the range of sociological time, the evolutionary phenomena should only then be spoken of if they have been proven in a satisfactorily exact manner for the particular case.

The investigator must also reckon on the circumstance that Man lives in an artificial milieu, which has been created by his own efforts. This was even emphasized by Benjamin Franklin (1706–1790). Consequently, the eventuality must be counted on, that in the perspective of sociological time and within the artificially created milieu, the process of evolution has a very weak effect or is generally not noticeable. Thus, for example, stimulated by my teacher—the famous German anatomist George Ruge—on the occasion of my sub-assistantship in the 1904–1905 winter semester, I conducted an investigation with reference to muscle variability in Man.

This investigation proved that in the perspective of comparative anatomy the indisputable process of evolution of musculature in a biological respect cannot be demonstrated in the case of central Europeans at the present time. Namely, there appeared no polarity of unbroken complexes of progressive and atavistic variations, although the observational material was treated accurately, with the use of statistical correlation methods. The result was such a great surprise to my evolutionary-minded teacher—a favored student of Karl Gegenbauer—that this student work appeared in the *Festschrift* in honor of Franz Boas (1906).

With respect to the process of selection the following remarks can be made. If the effects of the selection process are anthropologically investigated in the morgues of large hospitals and pathological institutes, it is established that the disharmonic couplings of anthropological traits occur in a disproportionate ratio, which makes the typological analysis of corpses very difficult. The constitutional types of the pathology appear to be disharmonic couplings of structural elements, which are interpreted as representing anthropological traits. That would explain why the attempts to correlate race and constitutional types resulted in such contradictory views.

The correlation of the disposition to cancer with disharmonic couplings of pigmentation traits even attracted the attention of old clinicists (Albert Neisser). J. F. Tocher (1906) drew attention to the disproportionately frequent occurrence of disharmonies in eye and hair color among the mentally ill. These observations were confirmed by Polish anthropology. Thus, the process of selection in the case of Man appears above all to be directed against disharmonic combinations of racial elements.

Our fragmentary investigations of the selection process have not yet resulted in a final conclusion which is free from contradictions. The investigations of Jacek Szmyt (1938) demonstrated that in the case of deaths from cancer, the Mediterranean racial component is represented almost twice as strongly as it is in the total population of south Poland, from whence the subject population originated. This tendency corresponded to the total reduction, which has continued since the Neolithic period, of the proportion of the Mediterranean race in the European population to the north of the Alps.

The observation relating to deaths belonging to the Armenoid race did not correspond to this result. The Armenoid race was almost as excessively represented among the deceased and there can hardly be a tendency to a reduction of this racial component. It is, therefore, questionable whether cancer can effectively influence the racial composition of the population.

Racial Types and Migration

THE OBSERVATION, made by Otto Ammon (1899), that in Baden the longer-headed individuals demonstrated a tendency to migrate to the cities, has had fatal consequences. In consideration of the fact that the city-dwellers would allegedly die out in a few generations, the thesis of the dying-out of the Nordic race was widely diffused by the German political-anthropological school—above all in the Teutonic lands. The Germans, especially, took the matter seriously and tried to remedy the evil by extermination of those regarded as anthropologically less worthy. The anthropological investigations carried out in Poland revealed the enormous superficiality of the German political-anthropological school.

Just as in the case of the migrants to the cities of Baden, the emigrants from Silesia and Poland Minor contained a disproportionately large percentage of the Nordic element. However, it was demonstrated that the *more mobile are a social formation the more their anthropological composition approaches the total average of the country*. The more mobile are more psychically disposed to wanderlust than the population bound to their soil. The migrants to the cities, like the emigrants to America from south Poland, must also be more Nordic, because they came closer to the German and Polish anthropological averages respectively. We are concerned here with a socially conditioned anthropological process, which has not influenced the biological basis—the permanent rural population.

It may be asserted that in recent centuries—in other words in the times for which satisfactorily accurate observations exist—the composition of the rural population has not been influenced in its anthropological relationship by the process of selection. F. Wokroj has demonstrated several cases of stability of this kind. The village of Podbereźce, which is situated approximately twenty kilometers east of Lwow, can be employed as an example. The farmers of this village were settled toward the end of the fourteenth century by Wladyslaw Opolczyk and have preserved their Silesian anthropological composition, despite their

Morphology and the Classification of Race

complete cultural Ukrainianization. However, they take care to marry exclusively among themselves, because they despise the neighboring Ukrainian farmers.

It was demonstrated earlier by Wokroj that the Germans originating from the Palatinate, who had been settled by the Austrians in the Carpathians after the partition of Poland, have, in the course of at least one century, preserved their Palatine anthropological composition in an entirely different geographical environment, as a result of their biological isolation. M. Gibowski, a student of F. Wokroj, showed that the individuals buried in the year 1710 in the epidemic cemetery of the village of Lowyń, possessed the same anthropological structure as the army recruits of the Nowy Tomysl district—according to the data of Jan Mydlarski (1928).

The comparison of the army recruits of the two Swiss half-cantons—Urban-Basel and Rural-Basel—still furnishes the most perfect illustration of the stability of anthropological structures. While the extremely exclusive, aristocratic city of Basel has preserved the character of a Gallo-Roman Municipium in anthropological relationship, rural-Basel, which is inhabited by Alemanni farmers, shows only a very weak influence on the part of the anthropologically alien city. In this case we have a racial distinction, which has been maintained since the last half of the previous millennium. That is the most perfect proof of the stability of anthropological structures. The two population groups have defied all selection processes that had to operate in the direction of anthropological equalization.

The association of the two population groups in the same geographical environment in the course of over a thousand years did not bring them anthropologically closer, just as the settlement of the Palatine Germans in the Carpathians did not alter their anthropological composition. In both cases they are the result of biological isolation. Only the anthropological traits which are directly influenced by nutrition—such as stature and body weight, for example—are greatly changed by the environment. On the other hand, the environmental influence on the racial-diagnostic traits is of little importance, as the above cited examples indirectly prove.

It is not likely that sexual selection could cause shifts in the anthropological composition of the population of central Europe. The statistical analysis of the observations collected by Galton and Pearson demonstrated that chance is decisive in the case of assortative mating. Furthermore, the allegedly established tendency toward homogamy has proven to be a sociological and not a biological phenomenon.

This problem was clarified by the investigations of Professor R. P. Rosinski. The investigation of the settled rural population of the Nasielsk region in the vicinity of Warsaw established a sharply pronounced tendency toward homogamy. The repetition of the investigation on the Polish settlers in Texas (U.S.A.) indicated no tendency toward homogamy. The same phenomenon was observed by K. Stolyhwo in Parana (Brazil) in the case of the Polish settlers there.

It is, therefore, clear that the quantitatively noticeable homogamy in Europe is a statistical consequence of the anthropological difference between social classes in the European society. The richer farmers marry richer and the poorer farmers marry poorer. With the destruction of the old social stratification on American soil the alleged "homogamy" also disappeared. The European observational material originating from different rural social strata was thrown together in order to calculate "reliable" mean values. Thus, "statistical homogamy" is produced if the richer and poorer farmers are anthropologically different. We are concerned here with analogous sociological effects, as that which had occurred in the case of the rural migration in Baden and in the case of the emigration from south Poland to America.

The mutation problem especially interests the morphologists. However, there is no known mutation phenomenon, which could influence the anthropological composition of the population. The well known change in the cephalic index around the turn of the thirteenth and fourteenth centuries can be explained in a satisfactorily accurate manner as a consequence of a change in the dominance phenomena. That is shown by a comparison of Formulas (3) and (3a), which was demonstrated earlier.

The assertion that many of the views of the morphologists are absurd from the viewpoint of genetics, as for example the cubic form of the "Law of Frequency of Types" (2c), is a concern of the geneticists. The morphological approach merely produces summarized observational facts with the help of mathematical formulas. If the morphological facts are summarized accurately, then the theories of genetics must be adjusted. Theories are adapted to the observational facts and not vice versa. The well-known scorn of the "population geneticists"—so much the worse for the facts—has no place in science, not even in genetics.

The proof of the biological reality of the races of man forms the most important result of the morphological-anthropological investigations.

The creation of a system of theoretical racial anthropology is of very great importance. It is based upon the hypothesis that the investigated human groups can be regarded as statistical representations of biological populations, which consist of a few racial elements that segregate out when crossed. In this manner the racial classification of the population of Europe has been brought into order.

Literature

Ammon, O., *Zur Anthropologie der Badener.* Jena, 1899.

Bernstein, F., Ergebnisse einer biostatistischen zusammenfassenden Betrachtung über die erblichen Blutstrukturen des Menschen. *Klinische Wochenschrift,* 3: 1495–1497, 1924.
Biasutti, R., *Le Razze e i Popoli della Terra.* Torino, 1959.
Broca, P., Recherches sur l'Ethnologie de la France. *Mémoires de la Société de Paris,* 1: 1–56, 1860.

Czekanowski, J., Untersuchung über das Verhältnis der Kopfmasse zu den Schädelmassen. *Archiv für Anthropologie,* N. F. 6: 42–89, 1907.
———, Zur Differentialdiagnose der Neandertalgruppe. *Korrespondenzblatt der Deutschen Ges. für Anthropologie,* 40: 44–47, 1908.
———, Les lois de Mendel et Galton et les coéfficients de l'hérédité de Pearson. *Révue Générale de Sciences,* 32: 671–675, 1921.
———, Prawa Mendla i Galtona i współczynniki dziedziczności Pearsona. *Archiwum Tow. Naukowego we Lwowie. Dział Matem. Przyrod.,* 1: 301–344, 1922.
———, Przybliżone mierniki współzależności przy założeniu praw Mendla. *Prace Komisji matem, przyrod. Poznańskie Tow. Przyjaciół Nauk,* 1: 244–273, 1922.

Czekanowski, J., Wyniki badań serologicznych Wojskowego Zdjęcia Antropologicznego. *Polska Gazeta Lekarska, 3:* 1–6, 1925.

———, Das Typenfrequenzgesetz. *Anthropologischer Anzeiger, 5:* 335–359, 1928.

———, "Coefficient of Racial Likeness" and "Durchschnittliche Differenz." *Anthropologischer Anzeiger, 9:* 227–249, 1932.

———, Das anthropologische Mittelwertgesetz. *Verhandlungen der Deutschen Ges. für physische Anthropologie, 4:* 15–20, 1930.

———, Mendelistisches "Law of Ancestral Heredity." *Zeitschr. für induktive Abstammungs-und Vererbungslehre, 44:* 154–158, 1933.

———, Die Schweizerische Anthropologische Aufnahme im Lichte der polnischen Untersuchungsmethoden. *Przeglad Antropologiczny, 20:* 218–314, 1954.

Deniker, J., Les races de l'Europe. *L'Anthropologie, 9:* 113–133, 1898. (Les six races composant la population actuelle de l'Europe.)

Eickstedt, E. von, *Rassenkunde und Rassengeschichte der Menschheit.* Stuttgart, 1934.

Gibowski, M., *Analiza antropologiczna ludności Łowynia z przełomu XVII–XVIII w. Dysertacja magisterska.* Poznań, 1921.

Kóčka, W., Zagadnienia etnogenezy ludów Europy. *Materiały i Prace Antropologiczne (Wrocław), 49:* 1–288, 1958.

Kollmann, J., Europäische Menschenrassen. *Mitteilungen der Anthropologischen Ges. in Wien, 11:* 1–8, 1882.

Michalski, I., Struktura antropologiczna Polski. *Acta Anthropologica Universitatis Lodziensis, XVII* 236 110, 1949.

Miszkiewicz, B., Struktura antropologiczna Autochtonicznej Ludności Warmoo. *Materiały i Prace Antropologiczne (Wrocław), 51:* 1–115, 1960.

Mydlarski, J., Przyczynek do poznania struktury antropologicznej Polski zagadnień doboru wojskowego. *Kosmos, 53:* 195–210, 1928.

Pavelčik, J., Mestys Nivnice. *Zpravy Anthropologicke Spolecnosti (Brno), 4:* 3–4, 1948.

Pearson, K., *The Grammar of Science,* London, 1900, 2nd edition.

———, Contributions to the Mathematical Theory of Evolution III. *Philosophical Transactions of the Royal Society (London), 185:* 71–110, 1894.

Ripley, W. Z., *The Races of Europe.* London, 1900.

Rosinski, B., Anthropogenetische Auslese. *Anthropologischer Anzeiger, 6:* 49–64, 1929.

———, Emigracja Polska w Stanach Zjednoczonych. *A. P. Zagadnienia Rasy, 5:* 89–100, 1931.

———, Emigracje Europejskie do Stanów Zjednoczonych pod względem antropologicznym. *Archiwum Lwowskiego Tow. Naukowego, 6:* 301–350, 1934.

Rosinski, B., O dziedziczeniu barwy oczu u człowieka. *Przegląd Antropologiczny,* *14:* 32–45, 1946–1947.

Schlaginhaufen, O., *Anthropologia Helvetica.* Zürich, 1946.
Surowiecki, W., Śledzenie początku narodów słowiańskich. *Roczniki Królewsko-Warszawskiego Tow. Przyjaciół Nauk, 12:* 1824.
Stołyhwo, K., Körpergrösse, ihre Vererbung und Abhängigkeit von dem neuen Milieu bei polnischen Emigranten in Parana (Brasilien). *Verhandlungen der Gesellschaft für physische Anthropologie, 5:* 94–106, 1931.

Wanke, A., Częstość zespołów cech antropologicznych. *Prace Wrocławskiego Tow. Naukowego (Seria B), 29:* 1–58, 1952.
———, Metoda badań częstości występowania zespołów cech, czyli metoda stochastycznej korelacji wielorakiej. *Przegląd Antropologiczny, 19:* 106–147, 1953.
Wokroj, F., Ludność ukraińska wsi Podbereźce pod względem antropologicznym. *Sprawozdania Polskiej Akademii Umiejętności, 49:* 458–463, 1948.
———, Charakterystyka demograficzno-antropologiczna ludności kolonii podkarpackich. *Przegląd Antropologiczny, 20:* 341–427, 1954.

BIOGRAPHICAL NOTE

J. D. J. HOFMEYR, M.Sc., Ph.D., *is Professor of Genetics and Chairman of the Department of Genetics at the University of Pretoria, South Africa. He was educated at the University of Stellenbosch, the University of South Africa and Cornell University.*

Professor Hofmeyr is the founder and president of the South African Genetic Society and served as president of the First and Second South African Genetic Congresses. He has done extensive research in the inheritance of various physical abnormalities by means of family pedigree studies.

Some of his findings in this field were summed up in a paper, "Chondrodystrophic Dwarfism in a Bantu Family," which he presented at the Second Congress of the South African Genetic Society, and in a paper on "Some Genetic and Non-Genetic Aspects of Blindness in the Republic of South Africa," delivered at the Third Human Genetics Congress at the University of Chicago.

In recent years Dr. Hofmeyr has been engaged in studies of the physical anthropology and population genetics of the Bantu peoples of South Africa. In the course of these investigations he has measured and compared differences in facial conformation between four Bantu ethnic groups.

RACIAL BIOLOGY OF THE BANTU OF SOUTH AFRICA

J. D. J. Hofmeyr

Population Genetics and Formation of Races

POPULATION genetics was another great step in the advance of genetics after the Mendelian and Chromosomal theory. It offers an explanation of the process of raciation and speciation. It is especially significant to view human races from this perspective—i.e., as larger or smaller population isolates, whose gene pools are being continually molded by bio-social selective forces. The consequent adaptation, over-specialization, and ultimate extinction of the breeding population form integral chapters of this fascinating study.

From the causes at work within the gene pool, which result in differences of gene frequencies between populations, we learn that raciation is a continuing process. And as far as human races are concerned, this molding and adaptation may affect the genetic composition of the population within a relatively brief period of time. This is due to the fact that each human being selects his own mate. There is no real panmixis within the human gene pool. Assortative mating is the rule. Furthermore, humans have consistently tended to determine the size of their families. This is especially true among the upper classes.

The prevailing social rules have a pronounced influence on the future of a race or nation. Numerous twin studies conducted in this century have demonstrated a genetic component in intelligence, temperament, and fertility. Social rules and customs governing family size, therefore, exercise a differential selective effect on the number and kind of able individuals within a population.

Furthermore, the rise of large, literate, urban civilizations has been accompanied by the development of specialized and differentiated social classes. The regulations and customs governing marriages within and between the social strata affect the balance of hybridity, recombination, and uniformity within the population. Indeed the modern science of population genetics has provided us with a genetic interpretation of the structure and history of society and furnished evidence of a genetic component in the survival of nations.

Three decades ago physical anthropology was a measuring, descriptive science. Today it is a dynamic, explanatory discipline, which has attained a high degree of agreement on most of its principles. Dynamic anthropology provides an integrative view of the process of raciation. Elements of this essentially biological process are plainly sociological in implication. A summary account of this process can be tendered by considering a hypothetical population—the result of the recent union of two diverse populations which had become modified in specific character through selection and genetic drift to a particular ecological milieu. Such a union can be the result of population pressure or forced migration.

Let us follow the genetic history of such a population. What are its characteristics? First, this population must show a high degree of polymorphism. This is usually due to a recent union with other races. In general such unions involve populations essentially similar in genetic character. This hypothetical union now resembles a pool containing hereditary traits of the populations involved. The analysis of this gene pool reveals a bewildering number of possible recombinations.

Such polymorphism, or intra-population differences, means that there is an increased number of genes pertaining to the trait. Such increased multiple allelomorphism makes possible a number of combinations hardly imaginable. Suppose there are in this gene pool 30 traits involving only two alleles. Then the possible number of different kinds of sperm and ova amount to 2^{30} or 1,073,741,824, so that the number of different genotypes theoretically possible is 3^{80} or 2,856,000,000,000,000 (16 integers). But in Drosophila more than 500 such gene-loci have been topographically mapped. The theoretical number of different genotypes now amounts to 3^{500} or 3,548 . . . for 239 integers.

Needless to say the number of different genotypes is a function of the actual number of ova produced, because fewer eggs are produced than sperm. In humans the female produces, during her 30–35 years of ovulation, approximately 400 fertilizable eggs. As a consequence it is impossible to realize all theoretically possible genotypes.

But even if we do not reckon with these astronomical values, the number of recombinations within the population is relatively great. The greater the size of the population the greater the number of ova to be fertilized. If the population consists of millions, then 400 times so many millions of fertilizable ova are produced. Random fertilization, however, never takes place. There are limiting factors, which taken together, function as isolating mechanisms. Among these factors, culture, tradition, religion, language, socio-economic status, and so forth, operate as isolating mechanisms with varying effectiveness.

Gregor (1961) commenting on Corrado Gini's book, *Corso di Sociologia*, writes as follows: " 'Racism' is understood as a generic term covering behavior which fosters the formation of endogamous isolates, inbreeding communities the extent of each determined by a 'common consciousness of spiritual unity, the product of a common historico-cultural patrimony and of a faith in common destiny.' *These isolates constitute the nuclei of races in formation.*"

And elsewhere Gregor (1962) writes: "Professor Gini's theory suggests an intimate connection between social or reproductive isolation and evolution—a connection rich in obvious sociological implications. The dynamics of mate selection, the factors involved in and determining the nature of breeding communities and breeding systems, are of critical importance in the attempt to understand the evolution of any species." Gregor then concludes: "Evolution proceeds through the agency of the natural associations in which men are to be found and that such associations are sustained by a disposition man shares with all social animals to associate with only select members of his own species."

Tobias (1961) studied specific anatomical features of the Bushmen and in a consideration of what factors led to their emergence makes the suggestion "that, under the peculiar conditions of human social and cultural life, evolution occurs most rapidly when natural selection and cultural or social or sexual selection pull in the same direction."

Let us once more give consideration to recombination possibilities for our hypothetical population. We have assumed only two contrasting pairs of genes or alleles. But with regard to the eye-color alleles of Drosophila, at least fifteen different colors exist in the pool, any two of which may form a pair. Multiple alleles of this size allow more than one hundred recombinations. So together with the number of gene loci, the occurrence of multiple alleles, at any locus, still further enlarges the possible number of genotypes, resulting in a rich gene pool or a highly polymorphic population.

In the meantime it must be kept in mind that in many cases, perhaps in most cases, a gene acts pleiotropically influencing more than one trait. Sometimes this may include both physical and psychical traits. Secondly, in many cases two or more genes at different loci, that is, non-allelic genes, may act together to produce a certain effect. Consider the following case, stated in very simplified manner. A person with the genetic make-up DDee, is deaf-mute. So is the genotype ddEE. But by mating these individuals the F_1 genotype is DdEe and hears normally. Consider that there are several of these genotypes so that the DdEe's may pair. Then one sixteenth of their children will be DDEE and therefore normal hearing pure genotypes. If they breed together a pure strain of normals will result.

Thirdly, traits may differ not in a contrasting manner, like brown eyes versus blue eyes, but quantitatively, like grades of color of skin and grade differences in height or intelligence. Here several pairs of genes, i.e., polymeric genes, act cumulatively to produce the extreme result. The greater the number of pairs involved, the smaller the graded differences within the population.

Genes and Intelligence

IN THE CASE of intelligence a relatively large number of such sets of polymeric genes are probably involved. For intelligence is a term of compound connotation, referring to several primary functions, for example, logic, abstract reasoning, learning ability, perceptual imagery, span of attention, perseverance of attending, inquisitiveness, memory, and so forth. Now for each of these primary functions a set of multiple or polymeric genes must be assumed.

This gives us some conception of the wealth of the gene pool. Such a population is a very variable one. It can survive radical environmental changes and can occupy almost any territory. Its degree of adaptability is in direct proportion to its degree of polymorphism.

Such a hypothetical population possessed of a high degree of polymorphism gradually becomes an organic community linked by national sentiment and common language and culture. This produces a breeding circle of reasonably well defined limits. National sentiment is an isolating factor of the first magnitude. Common sentiment and preferential breeding tend to produce, ultimately, a particular physiognomic phenotype. This, coupled with adaptation, which is the consequence of positive and negative selection by the environment of the inherent genetic potentialities of a people, leads to a reduction of polymorphism. This is especially true if the environment is of an exacting nature.

A population may, in the course of its history, meet one or another biological catastrophe. It may be cholera, pox, Spanish Flu, or some similar plague. Such contagious diseases may cause immense loss of life as did cholera in England from 1669–1672, and the Indian epidemic in the beginning of the nineteenth century. By 1813 the Indian epidemic extended into Asia Minor and Russia in Asia, and it continued to advance steadily, though slowly, westwards, spreading to England and reaching London in January, 1832. By 1835 it was general throughout North Africa.

Then it disappeared. But in 1841 another epidemic appeared in the East, which also reached Great Britain and France and was even more deadly than its predecessor. Similar affliction struck in Europe (Coon, Garn, and Birdsell, 1950) in 1865–1866, in 1884 (Haddon, 1925), and in 1892–1893.

What is the impact of such catastrophes from the point of view of population genetics? Thousands and thousands of people genetically prone to cholera were killed off, leaving a genetically resistant strain. But with this great decimation an enormous number of allelic genes have been lost to the gene pool—not only cholera irresistant genes, but many other genes possessed by those who perished. The gene pool has been impoverished. The population is now much less polymorphic, a greater outer resemblance being apparent.

Consider further, the two world wars we have witnessed during this century in which millions lost their lives. It is possible that a hardier race has emerged but at a price, namely, reduction in polymorphism.

Birth control devices, employed largely by the upper classes in any population, remove from the gene pool prime genes. The future stamp of the population will resemble more and more that of the lower classes. The reduced reproductive rate of intellectuals, when compared with relatively larger families among the less gifted, results in a population of reduced hereditary potential.

Professor Cyril Burt has suggested this may reduce by a few points per generation the level of intelligence of a particular population. As intelligence is the highest asset of a population, and the very best guarantee for adaptability, such a reduction means less adaptability, less resistance to pressures of nature, and less cultural creativity. Wars, plagues, and dysgenic breeding are more than enough to account for gradual transformation of populations within historic times.

The human species is further subject to natural adaptation (Dobzhansky, 1955). The more intelligent may gradually occupy territories by dint of natural ingenuity but the process is facilitated if they are physically adapted to the climate and environment. Depigmented peoples have proven more resistant to the cold and to the lack of ultra-violet light. As a consequence they have gradually settled in the northern parts of Europe. Drawn from the population they previously belonged to, they impoverished that gene pool as well as theirs. As a consequence of systematic endogamy they gradually became more similar. Doubtless they have become more adapted to that particular climate and environment. However, now a gene pool is left with a singular paucity of alleles. From such a gene pool few would be suitably adapted for tropical Africa. In this part of the world, the north Europeans are subject to the intense actinic rays of the sun and their fertility is impaired by the high temperatures of a humid climate.

During the seventeenth century approximately one thousand people of strong Nordic stamp were transferred to the Little Antilles with a temperature of 70°–80° F. in winter. They were unable to reproduce in sufficient number to maintain a viable population. They did not reproduce and have become extinct. The few remaining settlers moved to Saba Island with a milder climate. A similar difficulty was experienced by German and Dutch settlers in Dutch Guiana and Jamaica.

The Negro with his highly pigmented skin, large number of sweat glands, and respiratory system adapted to a hot climate, is very well adapted to his tropical environment, but easily contracts pulmonary disease in cold countries. His pigmented skin acts as a filter, reducing the amount of exposure to ultra-violet rays which, while necessary for healthy bone formation, is dangerous in overdoses (Boyd, 1950). Such a special and almost perfect adaptation to a specific environment arises from a gene pool of limited variability.

Now within the Negro race one has subraces having Negro traits but with still further adaptation to a subdivision of the environment, an ecological niche to which the subracial type becomes adapted. This represents a further reduction of polymorphism, a further reduction in adaptability to other, but different, environments.

The smaller the subdivision of a population the more specialized it becomes and the greater its uniformity. *This is a warning symptom.* It implies a relatively high degree of random pairing, possible in a small population. Eventually blood ties, as a result of inbreeding, mold the members of the population in the same matrix. Consequently one cannot easily distinguish the one from the other.

The Tasmanians all had a deeply sunken nose bridge, were either of blood group A or O, and had woolly hair which was golden brown when clean; 89.8 percent lacked the Inca bone (triangular bone) in the occipital region of the skull, while all had a mesatipellic pelvis. They were a primitive population, preserving a culture of Paleolithic type. When Europeans came in contact with them they numbered only a few thousand. They died rapidly on contact with civilization. Their gene pool was so deprived of alleles and they were consequently so monomorphic that they could not stand the slightest change in the environment.

The Bushmen are similarly circumstanced. Having been decimated by other races, their gene pool was greatly reduced. This process is enhanced by early death and small family size. Today the three groups, a few in the Cape Province, a central group in the Kalahari with Hottentot admixture, and the northwestern group of South West Africa (the purest but most primitive group) together, number perhaps ten thousand individuals.

The relatively large number of traits common to each one of them evidences a high degree of monomorphism. The average height of the males is 1.52 meters, with a normally proportioned body build. All have a striking brown-yellow skin. Their wrinkles form very early. All of them have a foetal cranial development and a typical head shape, with well-spaced peppercorns hair. All the women have the fatty buttocks of steatopygia, which shrink with age, the women possess labia minora of the external sex organs developed into a special supplement known as an apron (de Villers, 1961). The masculine sex organ is horizontal, with the scrotum contracted. They do not develop increased blood-pressure with age. Their fontanelle closes very early in life. Each Bushman has Negroid-Mongoloid features. Their voices are alike, and alas, they die relatively early (Schapera, 1930).

Although these traits, as such, may not be of sufficient importance for survival of the race, they do reflect homogeneity also of genes which could reduce the capacity of adaptation to gross changes in the environment (Tobias, 1956, 1961a, and 1961b).

Geneticists and anthropologists are of the opinion that the Bushmen may shortly become extinct. He certainly shows the symptoms of a very reduced degree of polymorphism and consequent specialized adaptability.

If a remedy is possible to keep this interesting primitive people propagating and maintaining itself, their breeding customs must be changed. First of all, absolute panmixis must be arranged between the three groups to increase genetic variability. Such large scale Hottentot-Bushmen intermixture could result in a more vigorous stock.

Racial Origins of the Bantu Population

THE WORD BANTU means "people" and refers to the different ethnic groups, and their subdivisions. Bushmen and Hottentots are included in the term Khoisan.

The northern boundary of these population groups extends from a point south of Nigeria at the big sweep southwards of the African coastline, eastward to Lake Albert, then in a southerly direction past Lake Victoria to the mouth of the Tana River on the East Coast.

To the south of this imaginary line live the Bantu, composed of about seventy million people, speaking two hundred different languages and dialects, and organized in a very large number of tribes (Seligman, 1957). The Khoisan peoples, on the contrary, are much fewer, numbered only in the thousands. They live in the central drier region and desert country.

Dart (in Schapera, 1956) observes that the distribution of races in Africa was very different two thousand years ago from what it is today. At that time very few Negroes were living in the eastern half of the continent, where the Bush and Brown (Hamitic) peoples were in direct contact, so that considerable mixing occurred between them. The Negro peoples occupied the west of Africa, the Hamites were concentrated in the northeast and the Bush peoples inhabited the east and the south.

The Sahara has been for thousands of years an effective barrier to restrict the free mixing of the Negro and Hamitic peoples and thus has been an important factor for the emergence of these two distinctive types. It is known that the Kalahari desert extended far beyond its present confines, in a northeasterly direction across the Victoria Falls and Rhodesia, in Pleistocene times. This also presented, for a protracted period, an effective barrier for the separation of the Bushmen from the Negroes to the west and from the Hamites to the north.

The presence of certain foreign elements in the indigenous peoples of Africa is described by Dart as follows: "The further you go up the eastern side of Africa, the greater is the number of Africans who have heads that are abnormally broad and high. They are western Asiatic or Armenoid in type. The further you go up the western side of Africa, the greater is the number of people whose heads are long and abnormally high. They are Western European or Nordic in type. These skull types are also found in the southernmost part of Africa and even among the Bush-Hottentots. This admixture happened a long time before Vasco da Gama."

At a later date Negroes migrated towards the East Coast where they came in contact with the other races resulting in considerable mixing. It is assumed that the Bantu originated mainly by the hybridization of Negroes with the Brown or Hamitic races which show affinity to the Mediterranean racial type of southern Europe. This is apparent from the physical traits expressed.

It appears that the Bantu migrated from the North to the South in successive waves mainly along the east coast of Africa between the Drakensberg Range and the sea. This brought them again in contact with the Hamitized Bushmen resulting in further hybridization. The Bantu is unquestionably of a highly mixed origin. According to Dart: "All types of breadth, length, and height combinations are to be found in skulls called Bantu; all types of cranial form, a wide variation of stature, skin color and face type are there. . . ."

Dart describes the three main parental types of the Bantu as follows:

The Negro Race: "tall and erect stature; well set up, athletic body of asthenic type, coal-black in color, and virtually hairless, save for the tightly-curled woolly mop protecting the oval head.

". . . The skull is infantile in form, being long and relatively narrow, of moderate height and ovoid in contour as seen from above. The eyebrow ridges are negligible or absent; the forehead is moderately wide and following the infantile form of the bone curves convexly, gently, and regularly to the crown of the head, whence it falls away with equal smoothness of curvature to the rounded occiput. The form of the orbits is almost square and their margins are strongly built. The cheeks are wide, and, with their supports (zygomatic arches), are bowed laterally in keeping with the powerful jaw musculature. The eyes are widely set apart by the broad and flattened nasal bones. The nose is flat and the nostrils widely expanded. The face is large and prominent. The jaws are prognathic . . . and are covered by full, fleshy lips, whose prominent mucosa is reddish-black or purple in color. . . ."

The Brown (Hamitic) Race: "They are short and slender, verging on the effeminate in bony structure and bodily physique. Their brunet bodies have scanty facial hair, except for a chin tuft; but their heads are covered with wavy, black locks. The skull is long and relatively narrow, of moderate height, and pentagonoid (coffin-shaped), when viewed from above; the eyebrow ridges are poorly developed, but the narrow forehead rises erect and full above them and the occiput is bulged out behind in marked prominence. The orbits are horizontal, ellipsoid and with thin margins. The cheeks are narrow, their bony supports flattened laterally. The nose is small and only moderately developed but has a definitely elevated ridge. The small jaws do not project and the chin is pointed. The face as a whole is straight, short, and narrow and of ovoid form."

The Bush Race: "Resemble the Negro in their broad, flat, and flaring nostrils and are even more specialized in respect to their loss of hair; its extremely rolled character and sparsity give origin to its peppercorn distribution. But here the resemblances end. Their bodies are shorter and more slender than those of the Brown race; while they are darker in color than the Brown they are not black like the Negro. The Negro skull we described as infantile in form; that of the Bushman is foetal. It is narrow relative to its length, but extremely low, and even more markedly pentagonal than the Brown skull when viewed from above. Eyebrow ridges are entirely absent and the forehead, instead of sloping backwards or rising vertically, bulges anteriorly as it rises towards the crown of the head and then falls abruptly, to the prominent occiput posteriorly. The horizontal orbits are small and circular and have thin margins.

"The face is short and straight and also pentagoid in form being widest opposite the cheek-bones and falling to a point in the chin region. It is flat and recessed in comparison with the Negro face, for the jaws project very little, while the bony parts below the lateral parts of the eyes bulge beyond the nose; this sub-ocular facial bellying emphasizes the width in this region. . . . The Bush retain primitive features in the lower jaw, the vertebral column, the structure of the feet, and the genitalia. . . . Thus while the Bush are in many points distinct and more primitive, the degree of affiliation between them and the Brown race is as great as, or even greater than between either of these races and the Negro. . . ."

Ethnogenesis and Ethnology of the Bantu

THE BANTU TRIBES of the Republic of South Africa and the British protectorates of Bechuanaland, Swaziland, and Basutoland are divided into four main ethnic groups on the basis of language and culture (see Schapera, 1956). These groups, whose population figures are taken from the 1957 Census and are shown in Table 1, consists of the following:

Nguni Ethnic Group: The Nguni, who make up 5.8 million or 63.0 percent of the Bantu population, are composed of four subgroups: Xhosa, Zulu, Swazi, and Ndebele.

The Xhosas, whose population is 2.8 million or 30.5 percent of the Nguni group, live in the Eastern Cape Province. They are composed of many tribes and may be divided into two main groups with respect to their arrival in the territory.

Under the name Zulu, some two hundred different tribes are included. They occupy Natal and bordering regions and their population is 2.5 million or 27.1 percent of the Nguni. The Zulus

TABLE 1
ETHNIC DISTRIBUTION OF THE BANTU POPULATION OF SOUTH AFRICA (1957)

Ethnic Group	Ethnic Subgroup	Population	Percent of Total
	Xhosa	2,800,000	30.5%
	Zulu	2,500,000	27.1
	Swazi	300,000	3.2
	Ndebele	200,000	2.2
Nguni		5,800,000	63.0%
	Southern	1,000,000	10.9
	Northern	1,000,000	10.9
	Tswana	800,000	8.7
Sotho		2,800,000	30.5%
Venda		200,000	2.2%
Tsonga		400,000	4.3%
Total Bantu Population		9,200,000	100.0%

were originally one of the smaller tribes of the Nguni. But under their warlike chief Shaka and his successors, they rose to supremacy.

The Swazis, with a population of 300,000 or 3.2 percent of the Nguni and who are concentrated mainly in Swaziland, were formed by the mixing of a few Sotho with Nguni tribes during the nineteenth century.

The Ndebele primarily inhabit the Transvaal Province. They number some 200,000, or 2.2 percent, of the total Bantu population. The Ndebele comprise a Southern and a Northern group which are differentiated by geographic location, language and custom.

The Nguni language with its noticeable Bush "clicks" indicates admixture with Bushmen and Hottentots.

Sotho Ethnic Group: This group, who account for 2.8 million or 30.5 percent of the Bantu population, is divided into three subgroups with a fair amount of distinctive features. These are the Southern Sotho (one million), the Northern Sotho (one million), and the Western Sotho or Tswana (800,000).

The Southern Sotho are made up of a large number of tribes. After the devastating Zulu wars, the remnants of the tribes that were left were reassembled and unified under the able leadship of the Sotho chief Mosjesj. Today the Southern Sotho constitute culturally, but not genetically, a homogeneous population. They mainly occupy the Basutoland territory, but some also inhabit the bordering districts of the Orange Free State and Cape Provinces.

The Western Sotho or Tswana are largely localized in Bechuanaland and the bordering districts of the Cape and Transvaal Provinces. The Tswana came southwards along the edge of the Kalahari desert in several migrations (van Warmelo in Schapera, 1956). There they came in contact with the Bushmen many centuries ago, resulting in considerable miscegenation.

The Northern Sotho show a greater ethnic diversity even than the Tswana, having made protracted contacts also with the Shangana-Tsonga and Venda. They are mainly centered in northern, northeastern and east-central Transvaal.

Venda Ethnic Group: The Venda tribes are a much smaller group than the Sotho or Nguni, and comprise only 200,000 or 2.2 percent of the Bantu population. They arrived comparatively late in their present domain in northeastern Transvaal. Those living in the far eastern area, in the mountains, are fairly isolated and comprise the purest form of the group. The rest show considerable admixture with the neighboring Sotho and Tsonga.

The Lemba is a very interesting, relatively small group that lives among the Venda. They have maintained their identity to a considerable extent. The Lemba do not intermarry with the neighboring tribes to whom they refer as "pagans." Their faces, although black, show semitic features. The semitic factor is further stressed by the fact that they do not eat pork, nor any animals which are not kosher-killed by slitting the throat. They also practice circumcision and it is quite probable that they were responsible for its introduction into the initiation ceremonies of Bantu adolescents. Finally, the Lemba are able craftsmen and live by bartering.

Tsonga Ethnic Group: The Tsonga, who make up 400,000 or 4.3 percent of the total Bantu population, migrated to the Republic of South Africa during the last hundred and fifty years from Portuguese East Africa (Mozambique). Their migration was another of the results of the Zulu wars. The Tsonga live among the Venda, but are culturally more closely related to the Nguni ethnic group, although their language shows marked differences.

Social Organization of the Bantu

ALTHOUGH THE various Bantu ethnic groups differ as to their languages, they show a basic cultural similarity. But according to Hoernle (in Schapera, 1956), there are more important differences with respect to social organization, economic life, political structure, etc.

The Bantu as represented by each separate tribal unit forms an integrated social entity. Their type of social organization is characterized by the underlying basis of relationships, the hierarchy according to seniority of age groups, the differentiation between sex groups, and the dominating status of specified relationship lines. These norms of social organization form the basis of social grouping as reflected in the tribal unit, the relationship group, and the family.

"The all-embracing traditional unit in the social organization is the tribe, based on a central group or nucleus of families descended from an ancestor or ancestors," Hoernle notes. "The latter are regarded as the founders of the tribe. The central group provides the man of authority in accordance with the principles of inherited status, and other elements are assimilated to this group. The binding factor upon which the survival of the tribe as a unit depends, is the chief.

"Another strong element holding the social fabric together is family relationship, based on the patrilineal system. Clear distinctions are made between the father's and the mother's line. Of great importance is the fact that every individual, in accordance with a classification of relationships, can have several 'fathers,' 'mothers,' 'brothers,' and 'sisters.' This fosters the formation of a large group of mutually dependent people, with mutual privileges and responsibilities.

"By following definite marriage rules, based on the system of family relationships or consanguinity, families come into being which, through their various marital relationships, act as a network holding the whole tribe together. There are forbidden as well as preferential marriages among certain groups and on certain grounds, but viewed from the social angle the outcome is the same in the end, namely the strengthening of mutual ties."

The Nguni is sharply distinguished from the Sotho and Venda groups with respect to marriage rules. Marriages between cousins having the same four grandparents are strictly prohibited. The broad relationship group represented by the sib forms an exogamous unit. Marriage or sexual relations between persons belonging to the same sib is strictly prohibited no matter the genealogical relationship, according to Hoernle. A sib in this respect is defined as a group of persons having the same heritable family name, with the assumption that they are descended from the same ancestor.

On the contrary in the case of the Sotho and Venda groups, marriages between cousins, with certain reservations, are not only allowed but are regarded as priority marriages. It is considered desirable for a man to marry the daughter of his mother's brother, the so-called cross-cousin marriage. Marriages between the children of two brothers are also allowed, but other types of cousin-marriages occur infrequently. For example, a marriage between a man and his mother's sister's daughter is regarded as undesirable since his mother's sister is a potential wife of his father under the system of polygamy which is in vogue among the Bantu. However, monogamous marriages occur far more frequently, Hoernle points out.

A fundamental requirement of marriage, according to the Bantu, is to beget children. Birth control of the European is unknown to them. However, a type of birth control is practiced, by spacing of births with two- to three-year intervals, since the Bantu child is weaned usually at an age of two to three years. For a woman to give birth to a child within that period is regarded as shameful.

Physical Anthropology of the Bantu

THE BUSHMAN is an example of a race with high visible uniformity in many traits. At the other extreme we have the Bantu showing a great genetic diversity in their make-up due to the ancestral admixture of Negro, Brown (Hamitic) and Bush races, and miscegenation with traders from the Orient, for centuries before Portuguese mariners rounded the Cape of Good Hope. Since historical processes have played an important part in the molding of the Bantu, as they are today, it is necessary to give them some attention (Theal, 1910).

History records that the wars of the Zulu Chief Shaka and his successors, during the first three or four decades of the previous century, were conducted on an unprecedented scale, probably unsurpassed in history. The land was laid waste far and wide and the inhabitants experienced famine and great hardship. Many tribes were massacred practically to the last man. Others fled in all directions leaving, also in their train, bloodshed and destruction. One such Sotho tribe, for example, trekked northwards for hundreds of miles through Bechuanaland and the Kalahari to the upper waters of the Zambezi where they are still today. The whole country occupied by the Bantu was in a turmoil. Extensive areas were depopulated to such an extent that the Voortrekkers who trekked inland and northward in 1836 found large regions uninhabited. They themselves, in turn, almost fell victim to the Zulu hordes. The Boers succeeded, however, in crushing the power of the Zulus in 1838. Before the Zulu wars the various Bantu tribes lived in comparative peace, which was restored upon the defeat of the Zulus.

Considering (a) the origin of the Bantu and (b) the mixing process resulting from the Zulu wars, we understand something of the processes which produce a very heterogeneous population showing a great deal of polymorphism. Upon this heterogeneity the mating patterns, such as the priority marriages of the Sotho tribes, and the converse of this of the Nguni, work their influence.

Some of the traits of the Bantu show considerable variation and merit a brief consideration. The parental Negro, Brown, and Bush races are long-headed and hence the Bantu are dolichomorphic. Dart (in Schapera, 1956) presents data obtained from Gear (1929) where eight of the nine possible types of dolichomorphs were recorded in the Bantu. In addition, he presents the preliminary cranial investigations de Saxe performed on seven hundred and fifty Southern Bantu, indicating a greater relationship between some tribes than between others. Hence he was able to classify them into five recognizable groups with respect to various cephalic traits.

Considerable variation is found in the facial features of the Bantu, ranging from the coarse flat-nosed, thick-lipped Negro face to delicately proportioned features with narrow high-bridged noses and thin lips. Dart (in Schapera, 1956) reports a study of facial types of nine hundred and seventy-seven Bantu representing various ethnic subgroups. The facial types were classified as Negroid, Bush, Caucasoid and Mongoloid according to the characteristics displayed. Throughout the series studied the Negroid face type accounts for 35–63 percent, the Bush for 15–44 percent, the Caucasoid for 10–35 percent and the Mongoloid for 0–5 percent.

In this study the subgroups were arranged in order of increasing percentages of Bush features. Similarly the subgroups were classified according to cephalic similarities in the previous study. It is of interest to note that when a comparison was made between the respective arrangements a fair agreement in the grouping was obtained.

Apparently there is also a relation between relative Bush admixture and skin color, which varies from yellowish to black. Subgroups with a high Bush component like the Tswana, Fingo, Bhaca, Mpondo, Sotho and Swazi are, on the whole, lighter skinned than the Xhosa, Zulu, Chopi, and Tsonga.

A significant difference in the distribution of blood-groups, especially of B, is observed when a comparison is made between the Bantu, Bushmen, Hottentots, and Koranas (related to Hottentots), as is indicated in Table 2.

TABLE 2

Source	Group	No. Examined	Blood Group (in %)			
			O	A	B	AB
Pyper (1930)	Bantu	880	53.2%	25.3%	19.2%	2.3%
Pyper (1932)	Bushmen	548	57.1	29.5	6.8	6.6
Pyper (1935)	Hottentots	505	34.8	30.6	29.2	5.3
Grobbelaar (1955)	Korana	377	22.0	39.8	31.7	6.7

TABLE 3

Sub-group	No. Examined	Blood Group (in %)			
		O	A	B	AB
Chopi	500	64.2%	17.8%	16.4%	1.6%
Inyombane	500	63.2	16.4	17.4	3.0
Swazi	500	61.2	19.8	17.4	1.2
N. Sotho	500	58.8	19.0	19.6	2.6
Shangaan	500	54.0	26.6	18.6	0.8
S. Sotho	500	53.8	25.0	17.4	3.8
Zulu	500	51.8	24.6	21.6	2.0
Angoni	325	51.7	24.3	23.9	0.9
Tswana	500	49.4	24.8	24.0	1.8
Xhosa	500	45.6	28.4	22.2	3.8
Mpondo	500	42.6	33.2	22.8	1.4
Achewa	574	50.7	20.9	26.0	2.4

It should be considered that the Bantu include different ethnic groups and are therefore more heterogeneous than either the Bush, Hottentots, or Koranas. A comparative study of Bantu sub-groups was conducted by Elsdon-Dew (1934) which is reported in Table 3.

Elsdon-Dew (1934) comments as follows on the above study: "The Bantu of Southern Africa are not homogeneous, and show a distribution in four main groups, the first—which we will call the ancient, consisting of Chopi, Inyambane, Swazi, and Northern Sotho. The second or intermediate group is composed of Tswana, Southern Sotho, Zulu, Shangaan, and Nyasaland Angoni. The third group consisting of Mpondo and Xhosa, from their proximity to the Caucasoid races, we may term the Caucasoid group. Finally the Achewa have a position separate from the remainder."

It has been known for many years that finger and palm patterns (dermatoglyphics) show significant variations from race to race. In a recent study by Tobias (1961c), he made use of the Cummins Pattern Index as an aid to express, by a single value, the intensity or complexity of the pattern formation in the groups investigated. He writes as follows: "This study provides the first evidence of differences in gene frequency between Northern and Central-Southern Bushmen and between Northern Bushmen and Eastern Pygmies. . . ." Central and Southern Bushmen apparently show a pattern approaching that of the Bantu more closely than that of the Northern Bushmen.

The different criteria enumerated may find a useful and ready application in the evaluation of tribal (clan) differences. Of special significance is the observation that a complex of traits, like cranial and facial features and skin color, may be associated with the different subgroups of the Bantu.

An Opportunity for Study of Genetic Drift

IT WAS INDICATED earlier that the tribe or clan is constituted around a nucleus with the same ancestor or ancestors so that the general picture is that of an interrelated community. This set-up would provide a favorable opportunity, initially, for the occurrence of genetic drift. In addition, the system of priority marriages, laid down by tradition, in the Sotho and Venda ethnic groups should be efficacious for selection and the fixing of genes. Hence it should be possible to record inter-tribal (inter-clan) differences in gene frequencies, and thus demonstrate incipient race formation.

As yet, this very interesting and very important aspect has not received the attention it deserves, since investigations, as a rule, are concentrated on larger groupings. The formation of mating groups in comparative isolation, within a population, should make evolution more effective, since this would allow primarily, intergroup competition and secondarily, individual competition within the group.

It is of interest to note that Darlington (1958) reported recently that cousin marriages in outbred communities are apparently at a disadvantage, compared to those of inbred communities. Hence, the fact that cross-cousin priority marriages are in vogue in the Sotho tribes may not be without a sound foundation.

It would be of considerable interest to compare the relative effectiveness of the Sotho and Nguni mating customs, with respect to the establishment of inter-tribal (clan) differences, within each ethnic group.

The author is of the opinion that the high degree of polymorphism and genetic diversity occurring in the Bantu should equip them, potentially, for adaptation to the demands of a changing world. The result would be that qualities of leadership in different directions may be realized in the different communities. On the other hand, the fostering of panmixia, as is apparently the aim in a classless state, would defeat the purpose of realizing to the fullest extent the genetic potentialities present in a population.

Finally, attention should be drawn to certain factors which may affect the genetic constitution of future generations of the indigenous races of the African Continent. Such factors are, among others, the improvement in the health and nutrition of the inhabitants.

Mackey (1953) observes that the Negro in the tropics has been harassed for centuries by a large number of parasites. It is more than likely that those who survived under the prevailing primitive living conditions were not the most intelligent.

Carothers (1953) suggests that the typical protein deficient diet of the Negro, since prehistoric times, could have acted selectively on his physiological and neuro-physiological development, "because those children that survived were often those who were better able to do with little protein."

The presence of a dominant gene causing a mild form of anemia in the heterozygous condition, known as sicklaemia, confers resistance to a serious form of malaria. The homozygous form, known as sickle-cell anemia, is frequently lethal. As a result of the resistance of the heterozygote, the frequency attained by this genotype may exceed 30 percent of the population in certain tropical regions of Africa (Allison, 1954). In recent years the large scale extermination of the mosquito, which acts as an intermediate host, has been so successfully pursued in South Africa that large regions were made available for settlement which previously were sparsely populated on account of malarial fever.

It would be of considerable interest to study the change in the gene frequency in a population with an initial high percentage of sicklaemia, since the selective advantage previously attached to the heterozygote would disappear where malaria is of no further consequence.

Man can determine his own evolution to a large extent if he is willing to apply his knowledge intelligently.

Literature

Allison, A. C., Protection afforded by sickle-cell trait against subtertian malarial infection. *Brit. Med. J.*, 6: 290–294, 1954.

Boyd, W. C., *Genetics and the Races of Man*. Boston, 1950.

Carothers, J. C., *The African Mind in Health and Disease: A Study of Ethnopsychiatry*. Geneva, 1953.
Coon, C. S., Garn, S. M., and Birdsell, J. B., *Races: a Study of the Problems of Race Formation in Man*. Springfield, 1950.

Darlington, C. D., Cousin marriages. *Triangle, Sandoz J. of Med. Sci.*, 2: 277–280, 1958.
Dart, R. A., Africa's place in the emergence of civilisation. S.A.B.C. Publication, Johannesburg, 1960.
de Villers, H., The tablier and steatopygia in Kalahari Bushwomen. *S. Afr. J. Sci.*, 57: 223–227, 1961.
Dobzhansky, T., *Genetics and the Origin of Species*. New York, 1951.
———, *Evolution, Genetics and Man*. New York, 1955.

Eloff, G., *Rasseen Rassevermenging*. Bloemfontein, 1942.
———, Die veramingsaspek van die genepot. *Tydskrif vir Natuurwetenskappe*. Pretoria, 1961.
Elsdon-Dew, R., Serological differences between various groups of Bantu of Southern Africa. *Bantu Studies*, 8: 361–366, 1934.
———, The application of blood grouping to South African ethnology. *S. Afr. J. Sci.*, 33: 976–992, 1936.
———, Bloodgroups. *Publ. S. Afr. Inst. Med. Res.*, 9: 29–94, 1939.

Fischer, Eugen, *Die Rehobothen Bastarden und das Bastardierungsproblem beim Menschen*. Jena, 1913.

Gates. R. R., *Human Genetics*. London, 1946.
Gayre, R., The place of anthroposcopy in ethnological and anthropological research. *Proceedings of the National Academy of Sciences (India)*, 1956.
Gear, J. H., Cranial form in native races of South Africa. *S. Afr. J. Sci.*, 26: 684–697, 1929.
Gregor, A. J., Book review of "Corso di Sociologia" by Corrado Gini. *Mankind Quarterly*, 1: 298–300. 1961.
———, On the nature of prejudice. *Eugenics Review*, 52: 217–225, 1961.

Gregor, A. J., The biosocial nature of prejudice. *Genus, 18:* 3–15, 1962.
Grobbelaar, C. S., The distribution of the blood groups of the Koranas. *S. Afr. J. Sci.,* 51: 323–326, 1955.

Haddon, A. C., *The Races of Man and Their Distribution.* Cambridge, 1925.

Junod, H. A., *Life of a South African Tribe.* London, 1927.

Lyde, L. W., *1st. Universal Race Congress.* London, 1911.

Mackey, G. P., *E. Afr. Med. J., 30:* 13, 1953.
Martin, R., *Lehrbuch der Anthropologie.* Stuttgart, 1957.
Mayr, E., Species concepts and definitions. The species problem. *Publ. No. 50, Am. Ass. for the Adv. of Sc.,* Washington, D.C., 1957.
Merrell, D. J., Selective mating as a cause of gene frequency changes in laboratory populations. *Evolution, 7:* 287–296, 1953.

Pyper, A., The blood groups of the Bantu. *Trans. Royal Society S. Africa, 18:* 311–315, 1930.
———, Bloodgroups of the Bushmen. *S. Afr. Med. J., 6:* 35, 1932.
———, Bloodgroups in Hottentots. *S. Afr. Med. J., 9:* 192–195, 1935.

Rensch, B., *Das Prinzip geographischen Rassenkreise und Problem der Artbildung.* Berlin, 1929.

Schapera, I., *The Khoisan Peoples of South Africa: the Bushmen and the Hottentots.* London, 1930.
———, *The Bantu-Speaking Tribes of South Africa.* Cape Town, 1956.
 a. Chapter I: Racial Origins, by R. A. Dart.
 b. Chapter III: Grouping and Ethnic History, by N. J. van Warmelo.
 c. Chapter IV: Social Organization, by A. W. Hoernle.
Seligman, C. G., *Races of Africa.* Oxford, 1957.
Singer, R., The origin of sickle-cell. *S. Afr. J. Sci., 50:* 287–291, 1954.
Sirks, M. J., Variability in the concept of species. *Acta Biotheoritica, 10:* 11–22, 1953.
Spengler, O., *Der Untergang des Abendlandes.* München, 1923.
Summary of the report of the Commission for the socio-economic development of the Bantu areas within the Union of South Africa. Pretoria, 1955.

Theal, G., *Geschiedenis van Zuid Afrika.* Pretoria, 1910.
Tobias, P. V., Les Boshiman Auen et Naron de Ghanzi. Contribution a l'etude des anciens jaunes Sud-Africains. *L'Anthropologie,* 59: 235–252, 429–461, 1955; 60: 22–52, 268–289, 1956.
———, New evidence and new views on the evolution of man in Africa. *S. Afr. J. Sci., 57:* 25–38, 1961a.

———, Study of Bushmen in the Kalahari. S. Afr. J. Sci., 57: 205–207, 1961b.
———, Fingerprints and palm prints: Kalahari Bushmen. S. Afr. J. Sci., 57: 333–355, 1961c.

Waddington, C. H., *The Strategy of the Genes*. London, 1957.
Westermann, D., *The African Today and Tomorrow*. London, 1939.

BIOGRAPHICAL NOTE

ILSE SCHWIDETZKY, *Ph.D., is Professor of Anthropology and Director of the Anthropological Institute at the University of Mainz, West Germany. She has done extensive research in the physical anthropology of prehistoric and living populations. Her first such work,* Rassenkunde der Altslawen *(Raciology of the Ancient Slavs) was published in 1938.*

Professor Schwidetzky studied under and later was a coworker of the noted German anthropologist Dr. Egon von Eickstedt at the University of Breslau. She assisted Dr. von Eickstedt in his classic study of the physical anthropology of the city of Breslau and, when the University of Breslau was destroyed at the end of World War II, she helped Dr. von Eickstedt establish a new Anthropological Institute at the University of Mainz in 1946. When he retired Professor Schwidetzky succeeded him as director of the new institute and as the editor of the institute's journal, Homo.

Dr. Schwidetzky is the author of ten books and more than eighty-five published articles. Among her books are Grundzüge der Völkerbiologie *(Basic Elements of Population Biology), 1950;* Das Menschenbild der Biologie *(Human Biology), 1959;* Anthropologie: A zu Z *(Anthropology: A to Z), 1959;* Die Neue Rassenkunde *(The New Science of Race), 1962; and* Die vorspanische Bevölkerung der Kanarischen Inseln *(The Pre-Spanish Population of the Canary Islands), 1963.*

Professor Schwidetzky's contribution to this symposium volume is based upon her book, Das Problem des Völkertodes *(The Problem of the Death of Peoples), published in 1954, an important pioneer work in its field.*

RACE AND THE BIOLOGICAL HISTORY OF PEOPLES

Ilse Schwidetzky

Anthropological Theories of History

THE NAME OF Comte de Gobineau is most frequently associated with any theory of history in which the loss of racial purity by a qualitatively superior race is conceived as the principal cause of the decline of a great culture-creating people. Less well known is the fact that Gobineau had not only predecessors but that he ascribed both positive and negative influence to racial intermixture. He ascribed, in part, the historic ascent of the Hellenic peoples to a Semitic admixture and he traced the artistic sensitivity of Europeans to a Negroid admixture.

Racial admixture is on one occasion construed to be the cause of cultural decline and on another an essential factor in cultural ascent. Both conceptions can be traced, sometimes in apparent contradiction and sometimes in separate ways, in later theories of history.

Herder and Meiners, who preceded de Gobineau, have been characterized as the "founders of the anthropological theory of history" (von Eickstedt, 1937). Herder (1744–1803) entertained the general conviction that the character of a people, and subsequently their history, is determined by their nature and heredity. With respect to race and race mixture and its significance for history, he expressed himself only rarely and then not without ambiguity. Herder speaks of the English-Norman conflict as an "infusion of peoples" as indispensable for the progress of mankind as cultivation is for the development of natural vegetative growth.

Yet in another place he rejects, with as much vigor as de Gobineau who was to follow him, the mixture of stocks, each of which he argues has adapted to a particular ecological niche.

Christoph Meiners (1747–1810), a contemporary of Herder's, was to inveigh against outbreeding, employing in his argument the ascription of value predicates. Meiners not only spoke of the "beauty and ugliness of the entire body and face" as "one of the most important characteristics of stocks and peoples" (a notion for which he would have found support in the strictly scientific Linnaeus, among others), but he referred to the spirit of an entire epoch as being "beautiful" or "ugly," "noble" or "ignoble."

"Only the Caucasian peoples deserve the designation beautiful. . . . The traits which distinguish (the peoples of the earth) are of native character and not the result of external circumstances. . . . Not all peoples in the family of mankind are men in the same measure. . . . There is a scale of humanity." Meiners went on to conceive the mixture of noble races with ignoble races as the cause of degeneration. De Gobineau was very much influenced by Meiners although he did not cite him with any regularity.

It is now common knowledge that de Gobineau's principal thesis, that certain races constitute culture-creating elites, was accepted and elaborated by later authors. One can trace the line of descent from de Gobineau through Lapouge, Ammon, Woltmann, Chamberlain, Madison Grant, and Hans F. K. Guenther to the racial teachings of German National Socialism and the American racial policies of the turn of the century which strenuously opposed racial miscegenation. The concepts of race and invidious qualitative distinctions were thus merged. Among the above named authors races were conceived as exhibiting significant distinctions of rank.

Along with enthusiasts, who advertised themselves as philosophers of history, there were those who not only earnestly and critically concerned themselves with history, particularly the history of the peoples who created the cultures of antiquity, but those who collected a significant body of anthropological data. Otto Ammon has, to a certain extent, been rehabilitated after the all too emphatic negative evaluation of his work in the recent past. His *Anthropologie der Badener,* in which he undertook the examination of thousands of military recruits and students, was a substantial work and even today constitutes an anthropological source book of importance.

As a consequence of his investigations, it was established that urban dwellers were more dolichocephalic and fairer pigmented than the rural population. No other conclusion was possible, given the knowledge of the time, than that the "Teutonic Race" was more significantly represented there and that "denordification" was the result of the continuing migration from the rural areas to the city (with respect to the so-called "Law of Ammon," see Schwidetzky, 1943). If such a process is conceived of as culturally and historically significant we have a continuation of the thesis of de Gobineau.

Less well known than this evident line of development is another which takes its departure from de Gobineau's contrary thesis. Even here de Gobineau had a predecessor, also a German historian, Gustav Klemm (1802–1867). From Klemm derives the expression, "the fruitful wedding of peoples," the consequence of his division of mankind into active and passive, male and female races. "Only through the admixture of the two races, the active and the passive, I might say through the wedding of peoples, can mankind be perfected." In the work of the somewhat younger de Gobineau the picture of the wedding of peoples sometimes makes its appearance, but it remained part of the background.

From him it was apparently taken up by Nietzsche who was familiar with de Gobineau's work with which he had been very much impressed. Nietzsche combined, as had Klemm whom he probably did not know, the conception of the sexual dimorphism of peoples with the dominance of barbaric strength and savagery which he thus characterized in his later works:

"Let us speak without euphemisms concerning the origin of every great culture! Men with a nature still uncultivated, barbarians in every frightful meaning of the word, predators, still possessed of an unbroken will and lust for power, threw themselves upon weaker, sedentary, peaceful races. . . . There are two types of genius: one which above all else creates and wishes to create, and another which rather allows itself to be fructified and bears forth. . . . There are also among creative peoples (both these kinds of genius) . . . peoples who are enamored of, and desire, alien races, those which allow themselves to be fructified. . . . These two types of genius seek themselves as do man and woman. . . ."

The historical literature in which one finds the broadcast notion of the fructifying and invigorating effect of the invasion of barbarians has, perhaps, Nietzsche as its principal source. Such ideas regularly appear in the discussion concerning the decline of the ancient world in which the "unspoiled" Germans are envisioned as having come into contact with the "decadent" society of the late Roman Empire. Such conceptions have frequently provided the explanatory hypotheses for world histories even if they no longer effect the same impact as the works of de Gobineau or Nietzsche. One work of this nature is the treatise by H. Schneider (1927–1932), *Die Kulturleistungen der Menschheit,* an essentially scientific work in which he attempts to establish the lawful, sequential relation between racial mixture and cultural ascent.

The Genetics of Race Mixture

WHAT CAN HUMAN biology say to all this? Should it dismiss such theories of history as uninteresting although they concern themselves with categories which fall legitimately within the confines of human biology? Should they be apprized incorrect or false even when the historical data are not sufficiently known to biology? From its own fund of knowledge human biology can, it appears, take a positive position with respect to two considerations. It can discuss the effects of race mixture and the peripheral racial history of peoples (even if such a discussion proves neither conclusive nor very satisfying). It can, above all, deliver physical data, something which, naturally, is of minor interest to historians but which can be important as a model. It can take a critical position with respect to the limits of its competence or the limits of our contemporary knowledge.

Beyond these limits historians can only operate speculatively employing concepts like race, the hereditary nature of men, the genius of peoples, and so forth. It must not be forgotten, however, that out of their special knowledge of the subject, historians and especially cultural historians might be able to identify the essential traits of a people (Schachermeyr, 1931). This could afford human biology access to considerations with which it would be occupied but with respect to which its own scientific methods have, to date, proven inadequate.

Since the results of racial mixture have been so differently assessed by anthropological theories of history, a preliminary distinction is here important. Those who are convinced of the positive effect of racial mixture think most regularly of the origins of peoples and cultures (as is the case with H. Schneider). A contrary appraisal of the influence of racial mixture is generally the result of consideration of the late period of a people's history—Rome being the favored and most thoroughly considered instance.

Such a distinction between the earlier periods with positive effects and the later periods with negative effects of race mixture is not explicitly developed in anthropological theories of history. It is rather to be drawn out of the examples of authors considered and finds echo in historico-philosophical observations. According to Le Bon racial mixture is a necessary prerequisite to the development of peoples while later mixture produces negative results.

To lend a certain order to the following discussion, it is necessary to pursue the distinction between the positive and negative effects of race mixture and the distinction between the early period and the late period in the history of peoples. With respect to the concept race and race mixture one need not restrict oneself to morphological, typological systematics (Coon, 1939; von Eickstedt, 1934, 1950), but must include the general definition of race afforded by population genetics. Generally, where changes in the frequency of traits and genes are the result of migrations and the mixture of populations, one can speak of race, racial changes, and the effects of racial mixture.

Positive effects of racial mixture are undoubtedly conceivable. Racial mixture increases the frequency of trait variation. In a population composed of mulattoes there are more variations in skin color and hair form, in nasal and lip width, than in a pure

Negro or a pure European population. In the conceptions of the modern genetics of evolution, the thought that polymorphism is valuable for selection and adaptation plays a role. Polymorphism provides the circumstances in which "fit" variations are made available for many different environmental situations. It must be, here, recalled that in animal breeding increased variation is systematically sought in the effort to effect greater adaptability. The effects of heterosis are of minor interest. For, although observed in the first filial generation in crosses, they are quickly dissipated (compare Stern, 1955; Garn, 1961; Schwidetzky, 1962).

Should one consider the effects of mixture even with respect to psychical traits? The terminology cannot be identical because we know of no single gene for psychical behavior. But the possible increment in the frequency of variation for behavioral patterns conditioned by heredity cannot be left out of consideration. The mixture of two breeding circles with differing hereditary potentials can therefore, conceivably, increase the distribution of talents and endowments.

The existence of talents to meet the multifold and multiform demands and tasks of an evolved culture can only increase the survival potential of such a society. A complex culture means an increasing division of labor and social differentiation demanding for specific tasks correspondingly specific talents.

E. Kretschmer, on the basis of research in constitutional types, believes that the number of gifted persons in Europe can be increased through mixture of diverse European types. He observed, with respect to one hundred and seventy married couples, that "opposites attract," that marriages between schizothyme-cyclothyme variations are more frequent than homogamy in which both marriage partners display the same psychic constitutional type. Kretschmer contends, further, that genius arises out of a profound inner tension that could be the result of the difference between the parents, the result, therefore, of "heterogamy." Racial intermixture can be conceived of as the sum of such "heterogamies."

Notably similar to the description of the gifted individual out of the basis of inner tension by Kretschmer is the description of a gifted people, the Hellenes, by the cultural historian Schweitzer. He speaks of the "multitude of hidden antinomies in the Greek essence which constitute its breadth and universality, its tension and productivity, strength of feeling and strength of thought, theocentric world feeling and anthropocentric world form, passion and measure."

In our own time (even if the position is no longer held so intransigently) it has been the mode to deny the existence of psychical racial differences. Were this the case then all the discussions of the kind undertaken by Kretschmer or Schweitzer would be pointless. It would be more correct to say that rather than there being no psychical racial differences, we know practically nothing definitive about them—that we stand in relative methodological helplessness before this complex of questions. Certainly no one will deny that there are intra-racial differences of behavior, talent, and character—that is to say, not all individual differences can be reduced to differences in the milieu. There are those who "by nature" are clever or dumb, musical or unmusical, bold or timid, and so forth.

It appears to the present writer unlikely that at least a part of such traits are not differentially distributed between populations. It seems equally unlikely that in the evolution of men—who actively, through creative cultural achievements adapt themselves to different circumstances—that specific behavioral dispositions and special talents have not proved themselves especially suited to a definite milieu.

Apparently one cannot progress any further in this area employing the general intelligence tests which have until this time afforded the bulk of data for racial psychological investigations. In general it would seem that the diverse human populations enjoy comparable levels of intelligence since all master, through active response, the "challenge" (Toynbee) of the environment. It is more conceivable that there are qualitatively different talents, engendered by different environmental circumstances and that selection operates on special dispositions.

It is thus certainly not out of the question that the spectrum of talent of an ethnic group is broadened through racial mixture—

that the differentiation of talents of a cultural community is thus fostered and a greater selection of diversified talent made available.

Physical Anthropology and Racial History

WHILE THE judgments concerning the effects of racial mixture can only provide the historian an assist, human biology can add to the sum of material relevant to the racial history of a people. Wherever the ascent or decline of a cultural community is related to the process of racial mixture, this mixture must be carefully considered before one can seriously contend that we are really dealing with an historical causal factor. If a racial history is reconstructed from human skeletal evidence then human biology operates with its own established methods. Although one is occupied in these considerations of skeletal remains with the classic preoccupation of human biology, it must be admitted that the results for the history of peoples and for the anthropological theory of history have been minimal.

This is true probably not only, and certainly not primarily, through the fault of anthropologists who cannot at will increase available data and thereby render racial history more precise. They are restricted to that which is found in excavations. But the general indifference to human remains which characterized the time have provided little in the way of prehistoric remains. Even today it often happens that while large scale human interments are carefully scrutinized for the smallest remnants serviceable for a cultural inventory, human remains are reinterred thereby abandoning priceless source material.

With respect to the relationship between racial mixture and the ascent and decline of peoples it is necessary to graph the racial history of a specific ethnic entity with the greatest possible number of index points. This constitutes a further restriction on the possibilities. This is true not only because it is difficult to deliver more rather than fewer series for the same population, but also because it is often difficult, with respect to peoples whose life history we can survey, to decide whether we are dealing with the same ethnic unit over specific time intervals.

Thus it is only to be expected that there are but unfortunately few instances in which the outlines of the racial history of a *determinate* people is known with any assurance. The circumstances with respect to Hellas are most favorable, since the enthusiasm for classical antiquity has led to a careful examination of the soil itself. The relatively numerous interments cover a relatively small area and consequently regional differences in population can be indicated with more specificity than when one must reconstruct a racial history out of deposits as scattered as Ur and Assur as is the case with Mesopotamia.

According to the comparative studies of Angel (1944), all the European racial types are represented, although in differing proportions, in all the periods of Hellenic history. The Mediterranean type predominates in all periods, but especially in the Neolithic and the Mycenean Periods. Those crania diagnosed as Nordic-Iranian achieve their highest frequency in the Middle Helladic Period, then proceed in general, with some chance variation, to diminish.

The fact becomes evident, at least in outline, that the Greek population of classical antiquity was composed of various strata. This fact would have been apparent from historical reports, philological, and cultural accounts even if we did not possess direct anthropological evidence. Two gifted populations were united. Indo-European tribes from the north thrust themselves into the southern portion of the Balkan peninsula to impose themselves upon the indigenous Mediterranean population and subsequently to amalgamate with them.

In the realm of the gods and that of myths, in the structure of society and the very life of the family, in the utilization of the soil, in the art style and last but not least in the speech of the Hellenes of the Classical Period, much of the cultural heritage of the Mediterranean makes itself evident. Therefore, the relationship with the immigrants could not have been only antagonistic, but must have also involved assimilation through peaceful intercourse (Krahe, 1939; Schachermeyr, 1939; Schwidetzky, 1954). One compares this with the description of the Greeks of classical times rendered by a historian of culture uninfluenced by biological considerations to which we have above alluded: its characteristic trait is that "the Greek essence harbored contradictions."

A similar longitudinal study, illustrating its racial history, was attempted for Egypt based on cranial series (Falkenburger, 1949). Such series and historical reports confirmed migrations, with the frequency of brachycephalic crania in the early dynastic period being identified with the impress and absorption of alien peoples. But this event occurred considerably after the time in which one would seek the genuinely creative impulse of the classic period of Egyptian antiquity.

For the great culture producing peoples of the Near East, the Sumerians and Babylonians, the Assyrians and the Persians, it is in general impossible to outline an adequate racial history based on substantial anthropological materials. Much the same is the case with the "Roman" people and the great cultural peoples of America, the components of which change in each temporal period.

In many cases, however, it is possible to make certain indirect conclusions concerning racial mixture based upon historic accounts concerning migrations. When something is known concerning the origins and ethnic character of the immigrants, one can attempt to evaluate the degree of genetic difference of the components involved in the mixture. It is evident from such accounts that, in fact, a mixture of peoples is to be found at the commencement of the history of every great culture-creating people. This process ultimately results in an ethnic synthesis—the result of incursion, mixture, and assimilation.

There are often groups, who in number and cultural significance approximate each other and are represented as essential elements in the new ethnic synthesis. The Egyptians of antiquity in the Dynastic Period were composed of three elements, one of Lower Egyptian peasants, the other of Upper Egyptian pastoralists, and one composed of Syrian-Palestinian immigrating population groups: "The fortunate union and mixture of these three components fostered the astonishing bloom of culture in the First Dynasty, 3000 years before Christ" (Scharff and Moortgat, 1950).

The Sumerians were patently racially heterogeneous by the time of their migration into the land of the Tigris and Euphrates, the result, probably of an ongoing mixture. In the land of their greatest historical achievements they assimilated an indigenous Caspian population. Still clearer, and historically better certified, is the mixed origin of the Babylonians. Sumerians and Akkadian Semites composed the principal constituent ethnic elements. The greatest period of Assyrian cultural history commenced with a population similar to that of Babylonia to which was added an infusion of Indo-European Mitanni.

A great culture in Mexico of antiquity developed as the Teotihuacan population was fundamentally altered by the Nahua influx from the north.

The ancient Italic population developed in much the same manner as the Hellenes—out of the superimposition of an Indo-European element (which left the imprint of its speech upon the subsequent culture) upon an already highly evolved non-Indo-European population of predominantly Mediterranean race.

There are also a significant number of examples to be drawn from the early history of contemporary civilized peoples. One need but remember the history of the Chinese people, which had its nucleus in the Hoangho Valley, whose power of assimilation gradually drew the mountain and forest peoples of what is today the southern provinces into their culture. Or one might refer to the history of the peoples of early Europe with its diverse incursions and mixtures of Celtic, Germanic, and Slavic tribes out of which the greatest and most significant peoples of our times have arisen.

Population Structure and Cultural Growth

ETHNIC GROUP mixtures can, in fact, parallel the ascent of a people, but that such mixtures stand in a causal relationship to such ascent is in no way unequivocal. The genetic explanation is not, in any case, the only one possible. The possible biological effect of racial mixture need not be such that it is conceived of as the cause of the ascent of peoples. In the first instance, two other causes are conceivable: (1) a purely socio-cultural cause conceived as environmental rather than genetic; and (2) a demographic cause.

We can discuss the socio-cultural cause briefly since it lies farthest from human biology. Culture develops through accumulation (Kroeber, 1948). Where two populations with diverse cultures come into contact, a spiritual enrichment can result which is entirely independent of the effect of genetic mixture. There are certainly enough examples of the simple borrowing of foreign cultures and cultural elements, which increase cultural potential without altering the population structure significantly.

Should one seek to establish hybrid vigor, as such, it would be necessary to furnish more compelling evidence than the fact that diverse population components have entered into the new ethnic unity. It would be necessary to indicate identifiable essential features which, though operating in a broader context, remain constant even in mixture. It is obvious that human biology, at least with respect to historic peoples, cannot provide such evidence. But even for historians and culture historians such evidence is difficult to provide and becomes possible only with a broad knowledge and a deep insight into their subject matter.

In this human biology might be able to assist here and there, in so far as it can indicate in which direction one can expect constants—that is to say genetically anchored essential traits. It could if it knew more about this matter itself. Unfortunately we find ourselves hindered by our limited knowledge concerning the hereditary determinants of individual and racial psychology—knowledge essential in the historical interpretation of anthropological facts.

With respect to the demographic effects of population mixture we stand on firmer ground. There exists a relationship between population density and the level of culture. In this respect one speaks of the law of the cultural pyramid (Rüstow, 1948). The extent of the base represented by the sustaining population stands in a determinate relationship to the height of the pyramid which indicates the level of cultural attainments. Civilizations rest upon specialized divison of labor which is possible only in a suitably large population at least part of which is relieved of the burden of producing for simple subsistence.

Cultural ascent has as a prerequisite the broadening of the population base. Any essential inroad into the demographic strength of a people would negatively affect the fulness of their cultural achievement. As a matter of fact the number of an ethnic community will be smaller the more extensive the space required for subsistence. Tribes which subsist on the level of a simple gathering and foraging economy, necessitating one square mile per individual to subsist, number approximately one hundred individuals. Those subsisting in a hunting or agrarian economy number approximately a thousand. A membership of ten or a hundred thousand becomes possible when the plow permits an increment in population.

The fully developed cultural peoples of antiquity, in the period of their broadest expansion, numbered approximately a million (Braidwood and Reed, 1959; Ratzel, 1912; Schwidetzky, 1952). In any event the "law of the cultural pyramid" is only a rule of thumb guide, if only because it is hardly possible to discover a measure for cultural levels which is at one and the same time strict and sensitive. The genuinely creative epochs of the peoples productive of great culture do not correspond with their periods of maximum demographic strength.

It is astonishing what level of decisive achievements in culture was attained with a limited population. The population of Sumeria numbered approximately a half million (independent estimates tendered by Schwidetzky, 1954; and Braidwood and Reed, 1959; compare Schneider, 1920; Wagner, 1902). The ancient Empire of the Mayans was estimated, through a consideration of the available sustenance, to have supported a population of three hundred thousand (Termer, 1951). With a more generous estimate, it was conceived to have sustained no more than that of Sumeria (Schwidetzky, 1953).

Egypt of antiquity achieved, under the last of the Pharaohs, a population of seven million. In the most creative period of the Old Kingdom the population was estimated at not more than a million (Beloch, 1886; Cleland, 1936; Dart, 1939). This was probably also the population of the Assyrian kingdom (estimate by Schwidetzky, 1954; Hunger, 1911; Manitius, 1909).

In the Golden Age of Hellas, after its significant population expansion, the population of Greece was around three million. Of these less than one and a half million were to be found in the Peloponnesus and central Greece, the nucleus of Greek life and culture. All of Italy had at the time of Augustus six million inhabitants, after an appreciable increment following the period of the Republic (Beloch, 1886). Nonetheless these are all populations larger than those found among "primitives" and all evidence a diversified division of labor and achievement.

All the foregoing instances of the mixture of populations in the earliest period of great cultural peoples signify also an increment in population. No great people has grown out of its own procreative power. The assimilation of alien ethnic groups has always played a role. The increase in the population base through ethnic assimilation apparently is an important prerequisite for an advanced culture. And it is conceivable that racial mixture is only a necessary consequence of this enlargement of the ethnic community without itself being the cause of its historic ascent.

The situation is here much the same as it is in all historical occurrences, enormously complicated. Therefore, it cannot be reduced to a simple biological formula with any assurance. A racial factor may be involved in this process. But one cannot thereby conclude that the alteration in the race structure of a people through the mixture of populations or other events can be causally related to cultural ascent.

Race Mixture and the Decline of Civilization

LET US TURN to the question whether there are negative effects ascribable to race mixture and what role these might play in the life history of peoples. In general the older individual studies on the theme of race mixture and disease are, in our own time, considered with a very critical eye.

In this context one is reminded of the researches of W. Abel (1933) concerning the disharmony among mulattoes or that of Lundborg (1931) concerning the incidence of tuberculosis among Lapp-Swedish hybrids. Such studies may rest on individual findings based on limited research materials and their interpretation

Race and the Biological History of Peoples

is in no sense unequivocal. That the greater the genetic distance between breeding groups the more serious the developmental difficulty of their progeny is indisputable. But that the racial intermixture among men transcends the critical threshold indicated by Stockard's studies of mixed mating among dogs is very doubtful.

Today, in general, one is disposed toward the conception that all human races can mix without difficulty. On the other hand, since the discovery of serological "incompatibility" the question whether unfavorable consequences can attend race mixture cannot be rejected without consideration. In any event we stand but on the threshold of the treatment of problems which probably will have significance for questions in history. If there is, in the psychological sphere, something corresponding to biochemical "incompatibility," it is completely unknown. And although one would tend to deny it, our experience with the genetics of blood groups should make us cautious with respect to such prejudices.

Race mixture in significant quantity can be established with some certainty through morphological and craniological considerations. This can be done not only for periods marking the beginnings of an ethnic community destined to become a culture-creating people, but also for late periods in the life of such peoples. Similarly, and at times in the bright light of history, this is supported by documentary accounts. The most carefully researched are the circumstances surrounding ancient Italy, with special consideration given to Rome. This has always served as the classic illustration of the deleterious effects of race mixing.

After the Punic Wars, a prodigious number of slaves accompanied precious metals taken out of the conquered territories and brought to Italy. They were employed in increasing numbers in agriculture upon the great estates and also in the commercial labor in urban factories. The majority of the forced migrants from the conquered lands lived, throughout the period of the Republic, largely in barracks and left few, if any, progeny.

But even during that time an increase in the citizenry was accomplished through the manumission of household slaves who originated, in the majority, from Greece and the Near East (Bang,

1910, 1912; Barrow, 1924; Duff, 1928; Strack, 1914). While Roman merchants, entrepreneurs and bureaucrats streamed into the conquered lands of the eastern Mediterranean and North Africa, Greek, Syrian, Thracian, and Illyrian merchants and businessmen emigrated to Rome (Mateescu, 1929; Pârvan, 1909; Solari, 1916, 1921; Vulpe, 1925).

Following the time of Caesar, the number of non-Italians increased in growing measure among the Roman senatorial and equestrian classes which until that time had been essentially Italian. This increase derived originally out of the Romanized provinces and then out of the Near Eastern lands which became part of the Empire but which were not Romanized. At the same time the manumitted slaves were admitted into the aristocracy of the provincial cities, the Decorian class, so that an unbroken progression of social mobility led from the class of slaves to the class of senators. In the Imperial Period this "alienation" can be certified with statistical precision. The number of the manumitted slaves identified through grave inscriptions amounted to, in different Italian regions and villages, from 15 to 48 percent. In Rome only 10 percent were of pure Italian ancestry (Frank, 1916).

Under Vespasian (69–79 A.D.), the first Near Easterners and North Africans appeared in the Senate. In the second century the native Italians constituted a small minority. The situation with the equestrian order was much the same. In the first century it was composed equally of Italians and non-Italians, while in the time of Trajan (98–117) to Septimus Severus (193–211) the Italians numbered but 40 percent, and in the third century they numbered less than 25 percent (Dessau, 1911; Gelzer, 1912; Kuebler, 1907; Lully, 1918; O'Brien Moore, 1935; Sherwin-White, 1939; Stech, 1912; Stein, 1927; Strasburger, 1936; Walson, 1929).

Similar infusion of aliens is evidenced during the final period in the vital life of other cultural peoples of antiquity. In Hellas the serious losses which resulted from the civil wars forced, in increasing numbers, the introduction of aliens to serve in the military forces and then to be accorded the rank of full citizen. In the fourth century B.C., Greece had more inhabitants than in the fifth, but only the aliens and slaves had increased in number (Beloch, 1886). In Athens, concerning which we are best informed, the number of *metics* had doubled while the slaves, who derived from a variety of origins, multiplied significantly (Diller, 1937; Sargent, 1924). "Every year one prepares mass interment," Isocrates lamented (436–338 B.C.), "without noticing that the graves are filled with citizens, while the phratries and the ranks of citizens are filled with those who do not belong in the State."

Northern Egypt in antiquity stood under the pressure of expansive and mobile peoples. In the revolutionary period at the end of the Old Kingdom, the "Prophet" Ipuwer complained (Ermann, 1919, 1923) of the accession of aliens: "The entire Delta is no longer insulated. . . . Aliens have all become Egyptians." In the Middle Kingdom the northern borders were successfully defended against military assault but the peaceful penetration of foreign peoples continued. Thus on the grave of Chnumhoteps II a Caananite prince is portrayed who, with his ethnic compatriots, seeks admission to Egypt. Even the Bible recounts such migrations.

Under Amenemhet III (1840–1792 B.C.) the drainage of the Fayum restored an extensive strip of land to settlement. This settlement included non-Egyptians. The stream of aliens was increased when during the New Kingdom Egypt became a military state and not only secured its own borders but conquered neighboring territories. Men were numbered among the riches which flowed into Egypt out of the conquered regions. Earlier, but few slaves were to be found in Egypt. With the conquests, Negro slaves out of Nubia and Asiatic prisoners of war were to meet the needs of Egypt as servants and the necessary labor force.

Even the army, which increasingly lost manpower in the necessary military defense of the outer regions, supplemented its forces with aliens who then succeeded to leading positions in the army and the government (Heichelheim, 1925; Schubart, 1927). "As this enormous number of aliens began to mix with the indigenous population the marked influx of alien blood began to make itself apparent in a modified visage" (Breasted, 1936). After the twenty-second Dynasty, political leadership passed into the hands of aliens. Libyans and Ethiopians mounted the throne of the Pharaohs.

And a final example: the history of the population of Mesopotamia, exposed on all sides, reveals not only a chain of military invasions but also a series of migrations. In the decrees of the government of the Third Dynasty of Ur (around 1250 B.C.) Churritic names appear regularly, representing at first a slow and subsequently a more rapid penetration from northern Assyria into the area of the great river systems. Individuals with Kassitic names appear more and more frequently as harvesters and peasants (Moortgat, 1950). Waves of Aramaics followed in ever new migrations: "wherever a vacancy existed, they thrust themselves in." In Babylonia the most numerous of the Aramaic tribes gave, finally, the land its name, Chaldea.

The Immigration Factor in Social Systems

IN ALL THESE cases the increasing "alienation" of the population proceeded parallel with the economic or cultural "decline," providing at least no chronological difficulty in suggesting a causal relationship between the two. But is racial mixture here, that is the biological fact, the real cause?

The events can be interpreted in an entirely different manner, that is as a consequence of sociological and socio-psychological factors. The security and the viability of a social system depends on an optimal mobility, that is an optimal relationship between accessibility and distance with respect to immigrants (Sorokin, 1933). The immigration can become so abundant that it cannot be culturally or linguistically assimilated. A weakening, and a final dissolution, of social systems and their cultural expressions must be the consequence. Reconstruction of social ties and forms of expression cannot follow the original tempo.

Obviously this was the case with respect to the Aramaic immigration into Babylonia. The migrants maintained their nomadic tribal organization. The irrigation system to which Sumer-Babylonia owed its fertility was not cultivated and gradually disintegrated. Fields and gardens were then reduced to wastelands or swamps.

Such difficulties in assimilation are something entirely different from the alteration of the genetic structure of a population through mixture. How far hereditary psychological barriers to assimilation existed among the immigrants, that is to say, how much a role the change in the genetic constitution of the population played, can hardly be indicated in historic cases. We are, with respect to recent cases, disposed to deny any such difficulty, because we observe an effortless assimilation of European civilization accomplished everywhere.

There exists, however, behind such difficulties in assimilation a biological consideration which clearly manifests itself but which is not one involving racial genetics but rather demography. This can be traced with special clarity in the Roman example and can be concluded with some conviction, or at least advanced with some evidence, for other historical cases. The conquest of the Empire loosed a stream of raw material and capital toward Italy. An intensification of the economy, a transformation from a landed economy to urban commerce and industry was the consequence. Subsequently, there was an increased demand for labor.

But the same political events, the conquest of the Empire, hindered meeting this demand out of the indigenous population. Emigration proceeded out of Italy toward the provinces. This migration was selective, that is, it was obvious that many capable, active, and aggressive individuals went into the provinces. "Throughout the civil war Gaul, Spain and Africa received waves of Roman migrants. . . ." (Rostovtzeff, 1932), and "the provincial Romans were the most creative and active possessed by the Empire, while the Romans of the City became ever more parasites and drones" (von Wartburg, 1939).

The intensification of the economy corresponded to a rise in the standard of living. This the Greek and Roman society of antiquity had in common with the modern West (although this is not true of all great cultural peoples). The increasing well-being and increased pretensions corresponded to a reduction in the number of children, which apparently was the consequence more of celibacy than the lack of fruitfulness in marriage (Zimmermann, 1947). As in the present, so in the past, the upper class was the pace setter of "family planning." Against this tendency the marriage law (lex Papia Poppea), the tax measures of Augustus of essentially demographic intent, and the biting satires of Juvenal were directed (Bouché-Leclercq, 1895; Jörs, 1893; Stella-Maranca, 1939).

The same series of demographic processes—extensive emigration, especially of the active elements, as well as the decline of the natural rate of growth in the population—stands behind the immigration of aliens. The Greek colonization of the western Mediterranean since the eighth century was fed by a rapidly increasing population.

In Hellenistic times, however, "a Greek colonization began which left the old colonial period far behind. In Egypt, Memphis became a half-Greek city. Along the Syrian coast Greeks lived in all the centers of commerce. Every prince commanded Greek mercenaries, officers, engineers and artisans in every realm of activity; each tiny court possessed a Greek 'cell'" (Kahrstedt, 1948). "The best parts of the population were given up to foreign lands" (Kornemann, 1941), where real wages were higher and there was greater opportunity for social advancement than in the competing minor states of the homeland. The center of Greek intellectual life located itself in Egyptian Alexandria.

But the natural rate of growth of the Greek population diminished, at least since the third century B.C. Thus, Polybius in the second century B.C. already conceived, in his famous indictment, the dearth of children as the real cause of the political misfortunes of Hellas: "In my time Greece in its entirety suffers from a lack of children and in general from a decline in population . . . although we are neither plagued by long wars nor contagious disease. Men have given themselves over to indolence, cupidity and a lust for pleasure. They do not wish to marry, or when they do, they are not disposed to bring up more than one or two children. . . ." (Landry, 1936; Moissidès, 1932; Myres, 1915).

With respect to population genetics those reports are of interest which indicate a selective process. The migration to the provinces comprised the active, gifted elements of the population, who could have, earlier, mastered the cultural and social assimilation of large numbers of immigrants. We have no proof that the immigrants, themselves, represented a "substandard" population group, reducing the qualitative level of the total population, at least with respect to Rome and Hellas, the best known examples. The rapid social ascent of the many freedmen, the increasing

Race and the Biological History of Peoples

penetration, even into the ruling political class, of aliens is evidence against such a thesis.

A change in the genetic structure of the population, that is, a "racial change," might very well have played a role in the cultural decline of the great cultural peoples of antiquity. But in so far as one is concerned with a reduction in quality one can trace this back to the selective process which was the consequence of emigration rather than the effect of racial mixture through immigration.

In summary it can, therefore, be said that racial mixture has accompanied the ascent as well as the decline of great cultural peoples. A simple causal relationship between the two occurrences cannot, with assurance, be forthcoming. Race mixture at the commencement of the history of a great culture-creating people gives rise to a demographic effect—an increase in the size of the population—which is more obvious than any genetic effect.

Even the "invigorating effect of the barbarian invasions" is more a demographic than a genetic effect: the return to naive, "barbaric" methods of population reproduction. A genetic effect of the mixture of population is probably not to be discounted. It is conceivable that population mixture increases the extent of variations in talent and thus affords special gifts for the diverse achievement of a culture-creating folk. Certainly it cannot be denied, given the extent of contemporary knowledge, that a stimulus for cultural evolution obtains in the accumulation of cultural elements delivered by different population components.

Race mixture in the late period of a great cultural people, the genetic effect of such mixture, cannot be decisive. Difficulties in the assimilation of immigrants and thereby an undermining of the social structure can explain the same features of decline. At least in the cases of Greece and Rome the qualitative impoverishment of the population—a negative change in the genetic structure—contributed to the decline. The emigration of the active and capable elements to the peripheral areas rather than racial mixture through immigration is conceived, from the point of view of population genetics, as the real causal factor.

Thus human biology conceives the biological background of

history as more complex and with a more critical demeanor than do the anthropological theories of history. It sees this background more clearly and is thereby justified in reiterating that history is not only a cultural process, but one in which population genetics and demographic factors play a significant part.

Literature

Abel, W., Zähne und Kiefer in ihren Wechselbeziehungen bei Buschmännern, Hottentotten, Negern, und deren Bastarden. *Zeits. Morph. Anthrop.*, 31: 314–361, 1933.
Angel, J. L., A racial analysis of the ancient Greeks. *Amer. J. Phys. Anthrop.*, N.S. 2: 329–376, 1944.

Bang, M., Die Herkunft der römischen Sklaven. *Mitt. Archäol. Inst. Rom. Abt.*, 25: 223–251, 1910; 27: 189–221, 1912.
Barrow, R. H., *Slavery in the Roman Empire.* New York, 1928.
Beloch, J., *Die Bevölkerung der griechisch-römischen Welt.* Leipzig, 1886.
Bengtson, H., Die Bedeutung der Eingeborenenbevölkerung in den hellenistischen Oststaaten. *Welt als Gesch.*, 11: 135–142, 1951.
Le Bon, G., *Psychologische Grundgesetze in der Völkerentwicklung.* Leipzig, 1922. (Paris, 1898.)
Bouché-Leclercq, A., Les lois démographiques d'Auguste. *Rev. Histor.*, 62: 241–292, 1895.
Braidwood, R. J. and C. A. Reed, The achievement and early consequences of food production: a consideration of the archeological and natural historical evidence. *Symp. Quant. Biol.*, 22: 19–31, 1957.
Breasted, J., *Geschichte Ägyptens.* Wien, 1936.

Castle, W. E., Race mixture and physical disharmonies. *Science*, 71: 603–606, 1930.
Cleland, W., *The Population Problem in Egypt.* Lancaster, 1936.
Comte, A., Cours de philosophie positive (6 volumes). Paris, 1830–1842.
Coon, C. S., *The Races of Europe.* New York, 1939.

Dart, R. A., Population fluctuation over 7000 years in Egypt. *Trans. Royal Society S. Africa*, 27: 95–145, 1939.
Dessau, H., Die Herkunft der Offiziere und Beamten des römischen Kaiserreichs während der ersten zwei Jahrhunderte seines Bestehens. *Hermes*, 45: 1–26, 1911.
Diller, A., Race mixture among the Greeks before Alexander. *Illinois studies in language and literature*, 20: 65–75, 1937.
Duff, A. M., *Freedman in the Early Roman Empire.* Oxford, 1928.
Dunn, L. C. and T. Dobzhansky, *Heredity, Race and Society.* New York, 1946.

Eickstedt, E. von, *Rassenkunde und Rassengeschichte der Menschheit.* Stuttgart, 1934.
Ermann, A., *Die Literatur der Ägypter.* Leipzig, 1923.
———, Die Mahnworte eines ägyptischen Propheten. *Sitz.-Ber. Preuss. Akad. Wiss., 42:* 804–815, 1919.

Falkenburger, F., Das Rassenproblem in Ägypten. *Homo, 1:* 56–64, 1949.
Frank, T., Race mixture in the Roman Empire. *Amer. Hist. Rev., 21:* 689–708, 1916.

Garn, S. M., *Human Races.* Springfield, 1961.
Gelzer, M., *Die Nobilität der römischen Republik.* Leipzig–Berlin, 1912.
de Gobineau, Graf A., Versuch über die Ungleichheit der Menschenrassen. German translation by L. Schemann (4 volumes). Stuttgart, 1891. (Essai sur l'inégalité des races humaines. 1853–55.)

Heichelheim, F., Die auswärtige Bevölkerung im Ptolemäerreich. *Klio, 18.* N.F.H. 5, Leipzig, 1925.
Herder, J. G., *Ideen zur Philosophie der Geschichte der Menschheit.* (4 volumes). Riga–Leipzig, 1784–1791.
———, *Fragmente über die neuere deutsche Literatur.* Leipzig, 1766–1767.
Hunger, J., *Heerwesen und Kriegführung der Assyrer.* Leipzig, 1911.

Jörs, P., *Die Ehegesetze des Augustus.* Marburg, 1893.

Kahrstedt, U., Die Bevölkerung des Altertums. *HWB Staatswiss., 2:* 655–670, 1924.
———, *Geschichte des griechisch-römischen Altertums.* München, 1948.
Klemm, G., *Allgemeine Kulturgeschichte der Menschheit* (10 volumes). Leipzig, 1843–52.
Kornemann, E., *Römische Geschichte* (2 volumes). Stuttgart, 1941.
Krahe, H., Die Vorgeschichte des Griechentums nach dem Zeugnis der Sprache. *Die Antike, 15:* 175–194, 1939.
Kretschmer, E., *Geniale Menschen.* Berlin, 1931.
Kroeber, A. L., *Anthropology.* New York, 1948.
Kübler, F., Equites Romani. In *Real-Encykl. klass. Altertumswiss.* Vol. 6, 272–312, 1907.

Landry, A., Quelques apercus concernant la dépopulation dans l'antiquité grécoromaine. *Revue historique, 177:* 1–33, 1936.
Lully, G., *De Senatorum Romanorum patria.* Roma, 1918.
Lundborg, H., Die Rassenmischung beim Menschen. *Bibliogr. Genetica, 7:* 1931.

Manitius, W., *Das stehende Heer der Assyrerkönige und seine Organisation.* Marburg, 1910.
Mateescu, G. G., I Traci nelle epigrafi de Roma. *Ephemeris Dacoromana, 1:* 57–290, 1923.

Meiners, C., Von den Varietäten und Abarten der Neger. *Götting. Hist. Magazin*, 6: 625–645, 1790.
Moissides, M., Le malthusianisme dans l'antiquité Grecque. *Janus, 36:* 169–179, 1932.
Moortgat, A., Geschichte Vorderasiens bis zum Hellenismus. In Scharff, A. and A. Moortgat, *Ägypten und Vorderasien im Altertum,* 193–535. München, 1950.
Myres, J. L., The cause of rise and fall in the population of the ancient world. *Eugenics Review, 7:* 15–45, 1915.

Nietzsche, F., *Jenseits von Gut und Böse. Nietzsches Werke,* Vol. 7. Leipzig, 1919.
Nilsson, M., The race problem of the Roman Empire. *Hereditas, 2:* 370–390, 1921.

O'Brien-Moore, D., Senatus. In *Real-Encyckl. klass. Altertumswiss.,* Suppl. 6, 660–812, 1935.

Pârvan, V., *Die Nationalität der Kaufleute im römischen Kaiserreich.* Breslau, 1909.

Ratzel, F., *Anthropogeographie: Die geographische Verbreitung des Menschen* (Volume 2). Stuttgart, 1912.
Rostovtzeff, M., *Gesellschaft und Wirtschaft im Römischen Kaiserreich* (2 volumes). Leipzig, 1932.
Rüstow, A., Entstehungs- und Lebensbedingungen der Hochkulturen. *Festgabe für Alfred Weber,* 399–433, 1948.

Sargent, Rachel Louisa, The size of the slave population at Athens during the fifth and fourth centuries before Christ. *Univ. of Illinois Studies in Social Sciences,* 12: 35–45, 1924.
Schachermeyr, F., Zur Rasse und Kultur im minoischen Kreta. *Wörter und Sachen,* 2: 97–157, 1931.
———, Zur Indogermanisierung Griechenlands. *Klio,* 32: 235–288, 1939.
Scharff, A. and A. Moortgat, *Ägypten und Vorderasien im Altertum.* München, 1950.
Schemann, L., *Die Rassenfragen im Schrifttum der Neuzeit.* München, 1931.
Schneider, A., *Die sumerische Tempelstadt.* Essen, 1920.
Schneider, H., *Philosophie der Geschichte* (2 volumes). Breslau, 1923.
———, *Die Kulturleistungen der Menschheit* (2 volumes). Leipzig, 1927–32.
Schubart, W., *Die Griechen in Ägypten.* Leipzig, 1927.
Schweitzer, B., Book review by M. Pohlenz vof "Der hellenische Mensch," Göttingen, 1947. *Dtsch. Lit. Zeits., 70:* 51–55, 1949.
Schwidetzky, I., Der Städtentypus: Stand und Aufgaben der Kausalanalyse. *Zeits. Rassenkunde,* 14: 190–208, 1944.
———, *Grundzüge der Völkerbiologie.* Stuttgart, 1950.
———, Bevölkerungsbiologie der frühgeschichtlichen Zeit. In *Historia Mundi,* Vol. 1, 217–222. München, 1952.

Schwidetzky, I., Betrug die Bevölkerung des Alten Reiches der Maya 300,000 oder 13 Millionen? *Homo, 4:* 102–107, 1953.
———, *Das Problem des Völkertodes: Eine Studie zur historischen Bevölkerungsbiologie.* Stuttgart, 1954.
——— (Editor), *Die neue Rassenkunde.* Stuttgart, 1962.
Sherwin-White, A. N., *The Roman Citizenship.* Oxford, 1939.
Solari, A., I Siri nell'Emilia antica. *Revista Indo-Greco-Italica, 5:* 35–37, 1921.
Sorokin, P. A., Life-span, age-composition, and mortality of social organizations. *Mensch en Maatschappij, 9:* 69–85, 1933.
Stech, B., Senatores Romani qui fuerint inde a Vespasiano usque ad Traiani exitum. *Klio, 10:* 121–142, Leipzig, 1912.
Stein, A., *Der römische Ritterstand: Ein Beitrag zur Sozial- und Personengeschichte des römischen Reiches.* München, 1927.
Stella Maranca, F., Le leggi demografiche di Augusto. Istituto di Studi Romani. Rome, 1939.
Stern, C., *Principles of Human Genetics.* San Francisco, 1955.
Strack, M. L., Die Freigelassenen in ihrer Bedeutung für die Gesellschaft der Alten. *Hist. Zeits., 112:* 1–28, 1914.
Strasburger, H., Nobiles. *Real-Encykl. klass. Altertumswiss.* Vol. 17, 785–791, 1936.

Termer, F., The density of population in the Southern and Northern Maya Empires as an archeological and geographical problem. *Sel. Pap. 29th. Internat. Congr. Americanists, 1:* 101–107. Chicago, 1951.

Vulpe, R., Gli Illiri dell'Italia Imperiale Romana. *Ephemeris Dacoromana, 3:* 129–258, 1925.

Walson, C. S., Oriental senators in the service of Rome. *J. Roman studies, 19:* 38–63, 1929.
Wagner, H., Die Überschätzung der Anbaufläche Babyloniens. *Nachr. Ges. Wiss. Göttingen Phil.-hist. Kl.,* 225–298, 1902.
Wartburg, W. von, *Die Entstehung der romanischen Völker.* Halle, 1939.

Zimmermann, C. C., *Family and Civilization.* New York–London, 1947.

PART 11
BIOLOGY

BIOGRAPHICAL NOTE

LUIGI GEDDA, *M.D., is Professor of Medical Genetics at the University of Rome and Director of the Gregor Mendel Institute of Medical Genetics and Twin Studies in Rome.*

Professor Gedda is one of the world's foremost authorities on twin studies, which are an essential method in the science of human genetics for determining the relative influence of heredity and environment. The Gregor Mendel Institute was founded by Dr. Gedda in 1953 to further such studies. Under his direction, many important studies have been conducted at the institute which have added considerably to the knowledge of the genetics of human anatomy and physiology, psychiatric disorders and medical abnormalities.

Professor Gedda is also founder and editor of the internationally-known journal, Acta Geneticae Medicae et Gemellologiae, *which publishes reports of research in the fields of medical genetics and twin studies from scientists throughout the world. He is the author of the nearly 1,400-page volume,* Studio dei Gemelli (1951), *which is the most comprehensive summary of twin studies and twin research yet written. An abridged English translation of this work was published in 1961 under the title* Twins in History and Science.

Dr. Gedda is active in Italian civic affairs. He was president of the Italian Youth of Catholic Action from 1926 to 1949 and later president of Italian Catholic Action, an adult group. He founded in 1948 the Civic Committee and edits the review Tabor.

A STUDY OF RACIAL AND SUBRACIAL CROSSING

Luigi Gedda

T HE STUDY OF race has, in the past, often been considered for extra-scientific reasons from two extreme perspectives: (a) the importance and import of "race" is exaggerated to the end that races, conceived of as different, may be graded and value judgments made according to their comparative positions on this "scale"; (b) the bio-psychological problem is either ignored or is pronounced solved. It is quite clear that both attitudes have been, in the main, political catalyzers. The first buttresses some form of negative discrimination; the second is frequently the recourse of would-be social engineers who, working for a more "harmonious" society, would reduce frictions by "action research."

Should science have deferred to such vested interests in other disciplines its achievements would have been minimal, its advance choked with misconstructions, misrepresentations, and calculated fraud. The alternative virtues of an uncommitted science, particularly in relation to the question of "race," presenting as it does, so many unsolved theoretical and practical scientific problems, are manifest. This is especially so now when greater attention is being given to accommodating different races to a common society. One of the most urgent problems is the reduction of ignorance with respect to the rising number of racial and subracial crossings whose human products will increasingly present their unique problems to society.

It is well known that all human crossings represent hybridizations for there are no pure lines in our species. Until comparatively recently, however, these hybridizations took place mainly within a number of more or less large demographic areas or "isolates." Their hereditary population traits had been selected, through the centuries, by the endogenous forces obeying the laws of specific inheritance, by the ecological forces, particularly those of climate and diet, and by the psychological forces innate in man, influencing in particular his choice in marriage. The operation of such forces on inbred populations over a period of thousands of years has resulted in higher frequencies of certain genes and gene-combinations in these populations. Furthermore, these gene-combinations are also more balanced and harmonic.

Because of these gene-frequency differences *between* population isolates, the most common of hybridizations, that of crossing *within* an isolate, is quite different from hybridization between individuals belonging to different isolates, subraces, or races.

Eugen Fischer's classic work on the Rehebother Bastaards in South-West Africa is an example of the enormously increased hereditary variability found in populations derived from a not yet stabilized interracial crossing. With regard to the various breeding frontiers, the most frequently crossed is undoubtedly that between population isolates. However, as the sociological pressures maintaining the subracial and racial frontiers diminish, movements across them as well shall become more prevalent.

Genetics, in its rapid development from the naturalistic to the human field and, in the latter, into medical and clinical applications, has brought into its compass genetic studies of entire populations—and from population genetics to the genetic study of racial problems the way is short. This has most recently been shown by the works of East and Jones, Hogben, Gates, Rife, Mayr, Simpson, Trevor, Glass, Boyd, Fraser Roberts, and others.

Hybridization has, since very early times, been due to a variety of factors. It may be worthwhile, therefore, to discuss the schema which I have used in my work on *War Mulattoes*.

In the very early past, as well as today, areas may be found in which interracial hybridization is endemic, due to different races occupying contiguous areas. The contacts which result give rise to various phenomena ranging from trade to hybridization. Such "border hybridization" occurs, for instance, in northern Africa, the principal contact area for Europeans and Negroes, and in India, with mixing between Indids, Mongoloids, and Veddoids, among others.

The colonialism of the last five hundred years has also contributed greatly to interracial hybridization. Inasmuch as the White man has been the principal agent of "colonial hybridization," the phenomenon has been that of "back-crossing" or of crosses between the White race and a colored autochthonous race. One example of this would be the so-called "Eurafricans" of Somaliland.[1]

A third mechanism of interracial crossing, that of "slave hybridization," has been of acknowledged importance in many countries. This has been especially important in the genesis of the American Negro population.

Type A hybridization (*border*), Type B (*colonialistic*), and Type C (*slave*) may coexist and give rise to phenomena of anthropological and genetical convergence. To give some idea of the quantitative relationships of these phenomena, I refer to Table 1, which compares the distribution of races in Central and South American countries. We assume that these figures date from 1957 and are only approximate. Nonetheless, what we are interested in are the mutual relationships of the ethnological components of these populations. We consider mestizos to be the product of the White x Amerindian crossing and mulattoes the product of White x Negro crossing. Thus, a mestizo is the product of colonial hybridization while a mulatto is one of slave hybridization.

The Crossing of Subraces

THE EVER increasing number of crossings between individuals of the same race but of different subraces may well work an

---

[1] As Somaliland was, before it reached independence, first a colony and then a protectorate under Italy, the term "Eurafrican" applies to the children of European (Italian) fathers x Somali mother unions. The traits of the parent races are blended without gross unbalance in these subjects. Somali mothers are very fond of these children who are often thought to represent, at least from the White man's viewpoint, an aesthetic improvement. It is also a fact that such children can be easily reabsorbed by the mother's "Cabila" (tribe).

TABLE 1
RACIAL DISTRIBUTION IN SOUTH AND CENTRAL AMERICA*
(1957)

Country	Percent Racial Distribution						Total Population in Thousands
	European White	American Indian	Mestizo	Negro and Mulatto	East Indian	Other†	
Mexico	15%	29%	55%	1%	—%	—%	31,426
Guatemala	5	60	35	1			3,349
Honduras	2	10	86	2			1,711
El Salvador	11	11	78	—			2,268
Nicaragua	17	5	69	9			1,302
Costa Rica	80	1	17	2			1,014
Panama	11	10	65	13			934
Colombia	20	7	68	5			13,227
Venezuela	20	7	65	8			6,130
Ecuador	15	60	22	3			3,777
Peru	15	46	38	—		1	9,923
Bolivia	15	53	32	—			3,235
Chile	30	5	65	—			7,005
Brazil	61	1	26	11		1	61,268
Paraguay	1	3	97	—			1,638
Uruguay	90	—	3	—			2,801
Argentina	97	—	3	—			19,678
Bermuda	40	—	—	60			43
Bahamas	15	—	—	85			111
Cuba	73	—	14	12		1	6,410
Haiti	—	—	—	100			3,390
Santo Domingo	15	—	—	85			2,613
Puerto Rico	75	—	—	25			2,350
Jamaica	23	—	—	77			1,687
Lesser Antilles	1–23	1	—	77–99			1,541
Trinidad	29	—	—	45	26		894
Belize	1	21	—	79	—		96
British Guiana	3	4	—	46	46	1	598
Dutch Guiana	2	3	—	47	48		340
French Guiana	5	4	—	91	—		35

* Based on *The Living Races of Man* (1965), by Carleton S. Coon.
† Mostly Chinese and Japanese.

appreciable change in the biology of man, and it therefore warrants careful study.

Our principal concern is with such crossings as occur in countries where the populations lived in separate isolates prior to this century and are now "exploding." In the older European populations, repeated additions over the centuries have overlapped to create mosaic populations which are genetically quite varied and yet sufficiently stable. Within these populations, such as that of Italy, we find, at only moderate distances from each other, samples of extremely different subraces. Here, for example, cimotrichous brachycephalic Alpine types are found but one thousand kilometers from the lissotrichous dolichocephalic southern Mediterranean types.[2]

In Italy the incidence of "domestic migration" has been increasing since the country reached political unity about ninety years ago. After the Second World War, the rate of this increase has risen sharply. This appears to be linked primarily to the demands of northern factories which have caused entire southern families to move to the Po Valley or to Liguria.

As shown in Table 2, the number of residents in certain regions

TABLE 2

POPULATION CHANGES IN NORTH ITALY (1951–1961)				
Regions	Resident Population		Change in Population	
	Nov. 4, 1951	Oct. 15, 1961	Absolute	Percent
Piedmont	3,518,177	3,889,962	+ 371,785	+10.6%
Aosta Valley	94,140	99,754	+ 5,614	+ 6.0
Liguria	1,566,961	1,717,630	+ 150,669	+ 9.6
Lombardy	6,566,154	7,390,492	+ 824,338	+12.6
Total	11,745,432	13,097,838	+1,352,406	+12.6%

of northern Italy has increased by 1,352,406 (from 11,745,432 to 13,097,838) within the decade from 1951–61. This is partially due to the increased number of births (428,172) and partially to the migratory movement (924,234). The latter has therefore contributed 68.34 percent of the total increase in population in these regions. The increases recorded for Piedmont and Liguria are wholly due to this migration, while in Lombardy the contribution of migration is only 61 percent.

Causes other than the attractions of industry contribute to the migration. Characteristic, for instance, is the Piedmont farmer's tendency to marry women coming from the regions around Sa-

---

[2] Subracial hybridization in Italy is more recent and significant than in other countries where this phenomenon has been occurring for some centuries (in America, for example). Ever since European populations have sent groups of Italian, Irish, French, Spanish, Polish, and other emigrants to America, mutual hybridization of the European White subraces has been taking place. While this is certainly a most important causal factor in the anthropological traits of the modern American, it is much too advanced to be studied in its formation.

lerno, Lucania and Calabria, since northern women, having become accustomed to urbanism often refuse to live and work in the country. In a country such as Italy, rich in demographic isolates which have consolidated over many centuries and which have inhabited very different ecological niches, such subracial crossing is of considerable importance.

To explore the various aspects of subracial hybridization caused by urbanism and by domestic migration, there is useful data in two papers issued by the Gregor Mendel Institute. One is by Gedda and Spaini (1962) on variations in skin and hair color in Roman school boys, and the other by Gedda and Brenci (1962) on increases of stature in the Italian population.

Let us analyze this data from the vantage point of possible subracial hybridization. Table 3 shows the gradations of skin color in eight hundred and forty-eight Roman school boys, both of whose parents came from the same region. Not each of the nineteen regions is listed in the table since some of them were represented by too small a number of subjects. However, the size of each of the samples and their mean values, based on three observations of skin and hair color, are indicated. The data were analyzed using the chi-square method.

In glancing through the table we notice the great variability in skin and hair color, which is related to the fact that both parents come from the same region. A larger percentage of the children of Sicilian parents, for instance, are dark-skinned and dark-haired while a large percentage of the children of Umbrian parents are light-skinned and blond-haired.

The results of subracial interregional crossings are a concrete example of the effects of panmixia, due to the explosion of isolates, on the transformation of traits which have been undergoing selection for a long time. In Fig. 1 we have singled out data from Table 3 which relate geographic location (Umbria, Calabria, and Sicily) with different hair color in Roman school boys whose parents were both born in the same region of Italy.

The study, undertaken by Gedda and Brenci on the effects of subracial hybridization in Italy, was concerned with the increase in average height in the Italian population. The figures in Table 4 represent successive measurements of: (a) twenty-year old mili-

TABLE 3

Parents Region of Origin	Number of Examined Individuals n	Hair Color										Skin Color							
		Black		Dark Brown		Fair		Red		χ^2	P	1°		2°		3°		χ^2	P
		ni[1]	pi[2]	ni	pi	ni	pi	ni	pi			ni	pi	ni	pi	ni	pi		
Abruzzi	91	16	12	60	60	14	18	1	1	2,221	ns[3]	40	39	45	45	6	7	0,167	ns
Calabria	48	7	6	32	32	9	9	0	1	0,167	ns	12	20	31	24	5	4	5,491	~0,05
Campania	58	9	8	39	38	9	11	1	1	0,514	ns	29	24	24	29	5	5	1,903	ns
Lazio	471	53	65	324	310	89	90	5	6	2,948	ns	202	198	233	236	36	37	0,145	ns
Marche	37	5	5	22	25	9	7	1	0	0,931	ns	16	16	18	18	3	3	0,000	ns
Puglia	55	4	8	43	36	8	10	0	1	3,761	ns	17	23	34	28	4	4	2,371	ns
Sicilia	49	15	7	27	32	7	9	0	1	10,367	0,01	18	21	23	24	8	4	4,469	~0,05
Umbria	39	4	5	20	26	15	8	0	0	7,709	0,05	24	17	14	19	1	3	5,530	~0,05
Subjects coming from the same region[4]	*848*	*113*	*119*	*567*	*559*	*160*	*162*	*8*	*11*	*1,033*	*ns*	*358*	*357*	*422*	*423*	*68*	*68*	*0,004*	*ns*
Control subjects coming from different regions	*636*	*90*	*87*	*411*	*419*	*124*	*122*	*11*	*8*	*0,287*	*ns*	*267*	*267*	*319*	*318*	*50*	*51*	*0,024*	*ns*
Sample Totals	*1484*	*203*	*203*	*978*	*978*	*284*	*284*	*19*	*19*	—	—	*625*	*625*	*741*	*741*	*118*	*118*	—	—

[1] Observed Frequencies.
[2] Expected Frequencies.
[3] Not Significant.
[4] The Experimental Frequencies of this line are obtained by adding the Frequencies of the eight previous lines.

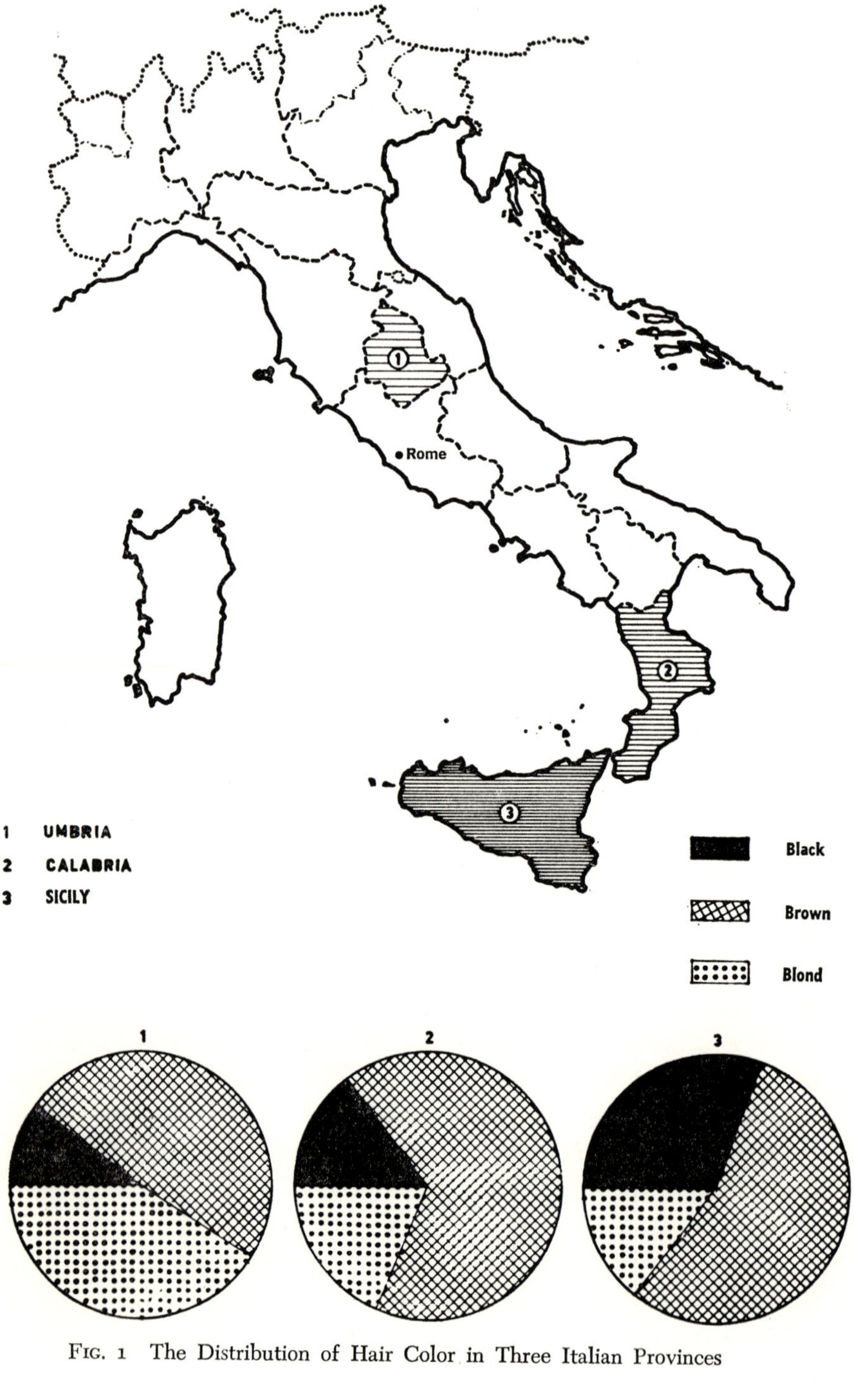

1	UMBRIA	
2	CALABRIA	
3	SICILY	

■ Black

▨ Brown

⋮ Blond

FIG. 1 The Distribution of Hair Color in Three Italian Provinces

A Study of Racial and Subracial Crossing

tary recruits taken over the sixty-year period from 1871 to 1931; and (b) the mean values for stature in the entire Italian population taken at ten-year intervals (excepting the years 1891 and 1921 for which no figures are available at Italy's Central Statistical Institute).

The increases in stature are compared with the corresponding values for the mean consanguinity index for Italy (ratio of first-cousin marriages to total marriages in Italy x 1000); and with an economic index (mean annual consumption per capita in thou-

TABLE 4

Years	Consanguinity (K)		Stature (ST)		Consumption per capita (CM)		Covariability	
	X_i	X_i^2	Y_i	Y_i^2	Z_i	Z_i^2	$X_i \cdot Y_i$	$Y_i \cdot Z_i$
1871	7.4	54.76	163.2	26634.24	1.8	3.24	1207.68	293.76
1881	6.0	36.00	163.7	26797.69	1.8	3.24	982.20	294.66
1901	4.9	24.01	165.0	27225.00	1.9	3.61	808.50	313.50
1911	4.2	17.64	166.0	27556.00	2.2	4.84	697.20	365.20
1931	4.4	19.36	167.5	28056.25	2.7	7.29	737.00	452.25
Σ	26.9	151.77	825.4	136269.18	10.4	22.22	4432.58	1719.37
D		7.05		12.15		0.59	8.07	2.54

$$r_{xy} = -0.8724 \qquad r_{yz} = +0.9478$$

sands of Lire, the value of the Lire being taken as that for 1938).

The correlation of the two indices is expressed by the index of Bravais. The correlation between stature and consanguinity is $r = -0.8724$, while that between stature and consumption per capita is $r = +0.9478$. It should be obvious that the consanguinity variable is assumed to reflect the influence of genetic factors, while the consumption per capita variable is assumed to reflect the influence of environmental factors.

Figure 2 reflects the changes over the years. While the downward sloping line of consanguinity crosses the upward line of stature, the latter is parallel to the line of consumption per capita. This indicates that reduced endogamy (reflected by the downtrend of consanguineous marriages) is a causal factor in the gradual increase of the mean stature. It is not the only causal factor, as indicated by its positive correlation with consumption. But it does

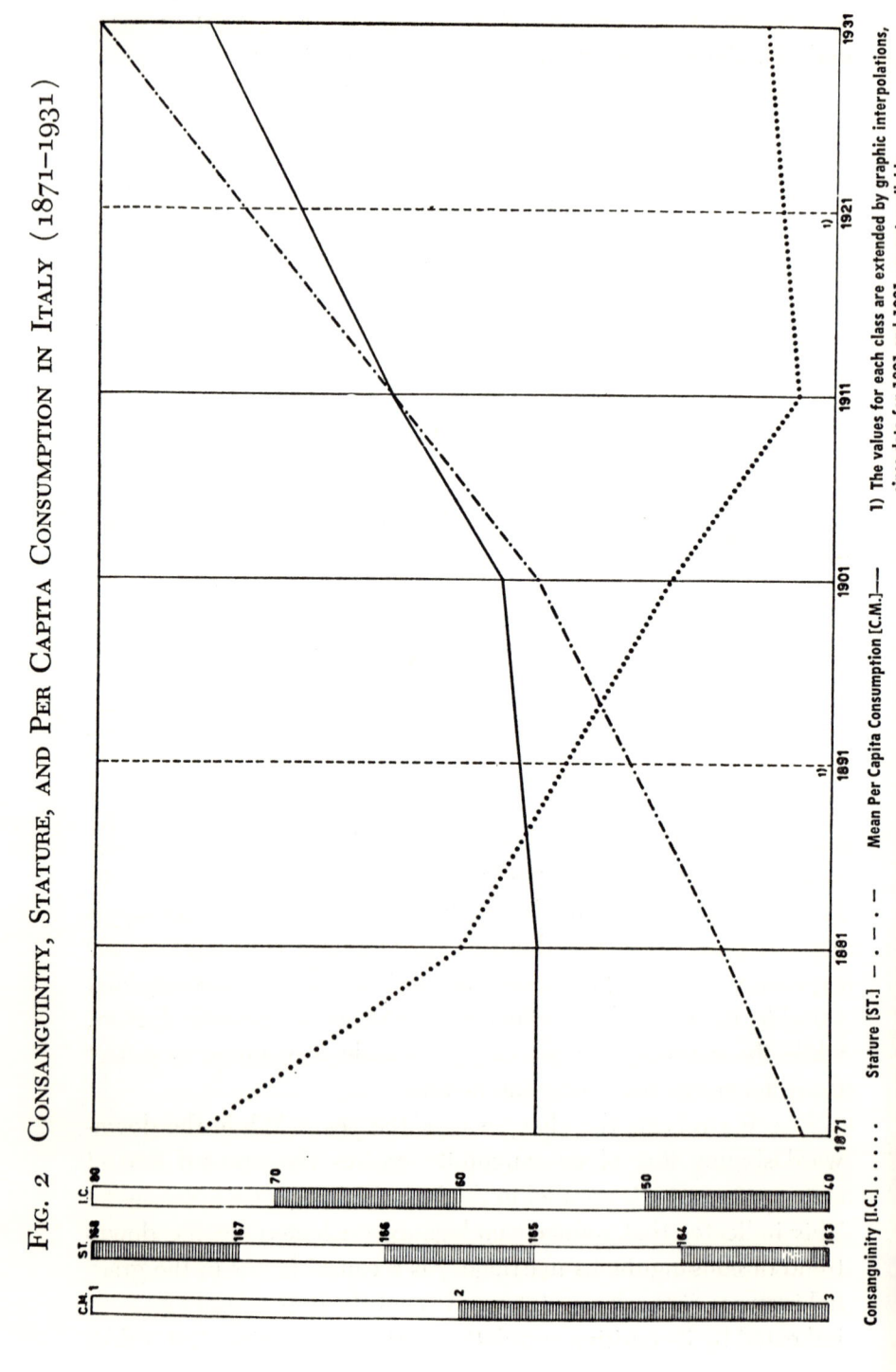

Fig. 2 Consanguinity, Stature, and Per Capita Consumption in Italy (1871–1931)

certainly have an influence which could be explained in various ways, one being through heterosis.

Beckman (1962) also studied the relationship between the stature of recruits and the parents' place of origin. He found that in Northern Sweden the stature of recruits whose parents were born in the same parish was significantly lower than that of those whose parents were born in different parishes. The phenomenon was reversed in Central Sweden and not significant in Southern Sweden. This may be due to the complexity of causal factors evidenced by our own research.

White and Colored Miscegenation

OVER THE PAST twenty years it has been possible to study the products of interracial crossing in the case of war mulattoes. These studies concern mixed-blood children left by Negro soldiers of occupation forces in areas with a White population, or by White soldiers of occupation forces in areas with a colored population.

Apart from some problems, these war mulattoes are valuable research material. The most important of the problems is that the father is nearly always unknown. This precludes a definite diagnosis of race which can then only be attempted through study of the case history or through a retroactive differential analysis with all of its inherent problems. Another problem is that of the legal and moral situation which emphasizes these individuals' abnormal condition in a largely homogeneous population which often rejects them.

Nonetheless there are several advantages in selecting this group for study. In the first place, under such an occupation the probability is higher of crossing taking place between such relatively pure and selected, mutually more differentiated racial stocks, than would be the case with individuals apt to cross under more conventional circumstances. We may assume that in the case of war hybridization we will find a higher number of traits for which parents and children correspond to the P and F_1 populations of the Mendelian pattern. Thus this type of hybridization affords exceptional conditions for the study of interracial crossing.

Another advantage derives from the fact that all of the war mulattoes were born within the same period or, at least, within a difference of only a very few years. Thus many ecological variables are common and the material is more homogeneous.

While mulattoes of the First World War (Moroccan father x European mother and Annamite father x European mother) have been studied by Wolfgang Abel (1937), those of the Second World War (White father x Japanese mother and Negro father x Japanese mother) have been studied in Japan by R. Ruggles Gates (1958).

The study of war mulattoes in Europe (on subjects born in Germany to White mothers and colored fathers) was undertaken by R. Sieg (1955). Since the fathers were unknown, it was impossible to exactly ascertain the paternal race. The material he studied included forty-eight males and fifty-two females, between three and seven years of age, born after the end of 1945. The fathers presumably belonged to the U.S. occupation forces.

Sieg's methodology included: general examinations for past and present diseases; dental examination including occlusion types; anthropometric measurements, skin color, hair color, and facial shape. He found a definite leptosomic tendency in the mulattoes, especially in the females. The leptosomic traits of the Negro fathers may be responsible, or they may be a phenomenon of heterosis. Sieg maintained that his study revealed no negative biological consequences attending interracial crossing.

A second series of studies was carried out by Gedda, Serio, and Mercuri (1960) on forty-four similar mulattoes between eight and twelve years of age, who were born in Italy of European mothers and colored fathers. The fathers of these mulattoes belonged to different colored races since the soldiers came from different armies (Negroes of the U.S. Army, Indians of the British Army, Negroes of the French Army, among others). Therefore the authors decided to identify the probable paternal race through the case histories and through an examination of the mulattoes' anthropological traits. Using that as a basis for separate analysis of the various crossing types, three groups were then obtained: NB

(Negro father x European mother), IB (Indian father x European mother), and a Mixed Group.[3]

I intend to demonstrate the significantly different characteristics of the mulatto by selectively sorting their data and comparing it statistically with corresponding data from the Italian population. This is an obvious element of comparison since all of the mothers in both groups were Italian. For comparative purposes, we have excluded mulattoes under ten years of age (as they form too small a sample) and all of the females. The material remaining includes twenty-three males divided into two classes: ten years of age (ten cases) and eleven years of age (thirteen cases). From data originally obtained we have thereby selected twenty-three items representing anthropometric traits or their derived indices. For each trait we calculated the arithmetic mean and variance.

The characteristics of the mulattoes were compared with the corresponding characteristics of a group of boys of the same age who were attending a boarding school in Rome. These boys are a representative sample of the Italian population. The same computations were made for this control group. The two series were then compared, using Student's t-statistic.

Table 5, which lists the results of this study, is divided into three sections for the convenience of the reader. A lists those traits that revealed significant differences in favor of the mulatto group; B lists those traits that revealed significant differences in favor of the European group. Traits for which there was no significant difference are listed in section C.

As compared with European boys of the same age, the mulatto is significantly plus-variant for the following traits: stature, sitting height, span, foot length, face height, facial index (Table 5, Section A). The gain in stature integrates the gain in sitting height and complements the gain in span. These measurements remind us of the widespread and well-grounded belief that in mulattoes the longitudinal development of the children exceeds that of the parental races. Yet we must observe, of course, that the plus-variance for mulattoes is proved only in relation to the maternal race. The mulattoes' plus-variance for face height and facial index

---

[3] The original data, without this further elaboration, were published *in extenso*, individual by individual, in order to allow others to analyze it further.

must be considered together with their minus-variance in several traits of cranial structure.

As a cautionary note, however, we should point out that the sample consists of individuals in an auxologic phase. We might well be faced, therefore, with an earlier rather than with a final development in the considered traits.

TABLE 5

MULATTOES   EUROPEANS

	Age	N.	μ	σ	Age	N.	μ	σ	t	p
Section A										
Stature	10–11	23	144.9	± 6.3	10–11	45	139.8	±8.5	2.537	0.05
Sitting height	10–11	23	75.1	± 3.2	10–11	45	71.8	±4.6	3.027	0.01
Span	10–11	23	146.9	± 6.3	10–11	45	139.8	±4.6	3.550	0.001
Foot length	10–11	23	24.2	± 1.9	10–11	45	22.8	±1.4	3.415	0.01
Face height	10–11	23	11.0	± 0.8	10–11	45	10.0	±0.7	5.263	0.001
Facial index	10–11	23	106.2	±10.7	10–11	45	99.0	±5.7	3.564	0.001
Section B										
Head height	10–11	23	12.5	± 1.0	10–11	45	13.7	±0.5	7.059	0.001
Head length	10–11	23	16.8	± 1.1	10–11	45	18.2	±0.6	6.364	0.001
Head breadth	10–11	23	11.9	± 0.8	10–11	45	14.4	±0.6	13.889	0.001
Nose height	10–11	23	3.9	± 0.4	10–11	45	4.2	±0.4	3.000	0.01
Cephalic index	10–11	23	71.1	± 6.2	10–11	45	79.1	±4.2	6.153	0.001
Section C										
Weight	10–11	23	36.1	± 6.7	10–11	45	36.0	±5.7	0.064	n s
Chest circumference	10–11	23	68.6	± 4.3	10–11	45	67.8	±3.9	0.769	n s
Hand length	10–11	23	15.6	± 0.8	10–11	45	15.6	±0.8	0.000	n s
Head circumference	10–11	23	52.8	± 1.5	10–11	45	52.9	±1.4	0.270	n s
Bizygomatic breadth	10–11	23	10.3	± 0.7	10–11	45	10.1	±0.6	1.948	n s
Ear height	10–11	23	6.3	± 0.6	10–11	45	6.1	±0.5	1.538	n s
Ear breadth	10–11	23	3.5	± 0.5	10–11	45	3.5	±0.4	0.000	n s
Nose breadth	10–11	23	2.6	± 0.6	10–11	45	2.7	±0.2	1.000	n s
Sitting height	10–11	23	52.0	± 2.0	10–11	45	51.5	±3.4	1.200	n s
Head height	10–11	23	74.8	± 8.5	10–11	45	75.2	±2.6	0.280	n s
Ear index	10–11	23	56.3	± 8.4	10–11	45	57.7	±4.9	9.654	n s
Nose index	10–11	23	67.0	±17.3	10–11	45	66.7	±8.7	0.094	n s

Table 5, Section *B* lists the traits for which a significant plus-variance was found for Europeans. These traits include cranial indices such as: head height, sagittal diameter, transverse diameter, and cephalic index. Length of nose also appears to be greater in the European group. But since this trait depends primarily on the shape of the nose, i.e., on the soft parts, it does not necessarily contradict the findings of Section *A* concerning facial height and facial index.

In the *Negro x White* crossings it appears that while the Negro imprint prevails in the facial bones, the cranial bones bear the stamp of the European mother.

In Section C of Table 5 are listed the twelve traits for which no significant differences between mulatto and European were found. As for weight, it is obvious that it is a product of environmental rather than of racial factors. For the remaining traits it is quite possible that a larger sample would reveal significant differences. However, the time factor in auxologic development may create situations that are not comparable.

The present analysis would seem to reaffirm the conclusions of the earlier Gedda, Serio, and Mercuri monograph that evidence of heterosis is not forthcoming with respect to this hybrid population since it is not possible to establish that the measurements characterizing mulatto offspring either coincide with or exceed those of the parental races.

An Increase in Hybridization

THERE IS A prevailing trend toward increased hybridization between subraces of the same race and between different races. This phenomenon has always been present. But its incidence is increasing today as a result of the increased physical and cultural contacts between peoples and because of the tendency of comtemporary civilization toward the elimination of the spiritual and cultural barriers still effective in restraining hybridization.

With the elimination of these obstacles the study of hybridization becomes of increased significance for two principal reasons. First, the phenomenon itself is of great scientific interest. Genetics will profit greatly by the study of these crossings, and they should be initiated before the phenomenon enters the phase of panmixia and precise analysis becomes difficult. Second, these studies may be particularly valuable in the analysis of genetic trait determination. The hereditary dynamics of racial and subracial phenotypes are generally difficult to study because all the members of the isolate share the same complex of traits and the mode of inheritance of these traits is not revealed through normal crossing.

The hybridization of races and subraces affords natural experimental data particularly in view of the fact that experimental crossing in man is hardly feasible. Such experimental inquiries can well reveal the hereditary dynamics of the transmission of diseases that pathology identifies as characteristics of given races or subraces.[4]

A further reason for specially considering the phenomena is that the total result of hybridization may well be a mankind quite changed in its physical as well as pathological and mental aspects. The emphasis on panmixia tends, in fact, to result in a certain amount of counter-selection and of genetic disharmonies.

Aside from the genetic factors of modification, there are environmental ones, such as diet, sanitation, working conditions and recreational facilities, all of which permit a wider and more exhaustive manifestation of normal genotypes. We should also consider the possibility of an increase in mutagenic radioactivity, with the resulting acceleration in mutation rates. Such biological changes may be further increased by somatic or germinal mutations induced by a new synthetic substance used in treatment or in work.

Consideration should also be given to the higher life expectancy which, as it increases the number of individuals of advanced age, will contribute to the altered collective physiognomy of future mankind. Such diverse but interesting phenomena are apt to change the anthropological and biological attributes of the human species.

Racial and ecologic differentiation has in the past had a vast influence on the psychical life of a population, directing the selection of the mental and vocational traits that were fundamental in the development of civilization. The psychological aspect of the phenomenon of panmixia is thus worth investigating while it is still in the preliminary, verifiable phase.

In the service of these inquiries the study of race should be conducted in an objective and calm manner in order that human and medical genetics may make a real and worthy contribution to man.

---

[4] See a paper by Saldanha (1962) as an example of the anthropological and medical malformations consequent upon immigration and a century of diverse crossings in a Brazilian rural community.

Literature

Abel, W., Über Europäer-Marokkaner und Europäer-Annamiter Kreuzungen. *Zeitschrift für Morphologie und Anthropologie*, 36: 311–329, 1937.

Beckman, L., The relation between stature and parental birth-place. *Acta Geneticae Medicae et Gemellologiae*, 11: 39–42, 1962.

Gates, R. Ruggles, Studies in race crossing: VIII. Japanese war children. *Zeitschrift für Morphologie und Anthropologie*, 49: 129–147, 1958.

Gedda, L. and G. Brenci, Nuova valutazione dei fattori causali ereditari e non ereditari nell'aumento della statura media degli Italiani. *Proceedings of the Second International Conference of Human Genetics*. Rome, 1962.

Gedda, L. and G. E. del Monte, Osservasioni sull'incrocio razziale in Somalia. *Proceedings of the Second International Conference of Human Genetics*. Rome, 1962.

Gedda, L. and G. Lena, Effeti della coesistenza de sottorazzo negridi nel Burundi. *Proceedings of the Second International Conference of Human Genetics*. Rome, 1962.

Gedda, L., A. Serio, and A. Mercuri, Il meticciato di guerra e altri casi. *Analecta Genetica*, No. 9, Edizioni Istituto Gregorio Mendel, 1960.

Gedda, L. and P. Spaini, Ricerche sulla composizione subrazziale della popolazione romana. *Proceedings of the Second International Conference of Human Genetics*, Rome, 1962.

O'Callaghan, S., *The Slave Trade*. London, 1961.

Saldanha, P. H., The genetic effects of immigration in a rural community of Sao Paulo, Brazil. *Acta Geneticae Medicae et Gemellologiae*, 11: 158–224, 1962.

Sieg, R., Mischlingskinder in Westdeutschland: eine anthropologische Studie an farbigen Kindern. *Beitrage zur Anthropologie*, No. 4, 9–79, 1955.

BIOGRAPHICAL NOTE

DAVID C. RIFE, M.A., Ph.D., *is a former Professor of Genetics at Ohio State University and now engaged in lecturing and writing on the subject.*

Professor Rife began his career as an instructor in science and agriculture at a Mission School in the Sudan, Africa. While at Ohio State University he served as chairman of its Institute of Genetics and also as consultant at the university's Geneticist Experimental Station.

He was Fulbright Lecturer at the University of Cairo, Egypt, and Fulbright Resident Scholar at Uganda, East Africa. He also served as livestock adviser for the International Co-operative Administration in Thailand, and as Deputy Science Attache of the United States Embassy in New Delhi, India.

Dr. Rife is a member of the American Association for the Advancement of Science, the Genetics Society of America, the Genetics Society of Egypt, and a former secretary of the American Society of Human Genetics.

He is the author of numerous articles and several books, including Heredity and Human Nature *(1959) and* Hybrids *(1965).*

RACE AND HEREDITY

David C. Rife

MEMBERS OF our species, *Homo sapiens,* are normally characterized by twenty-three pairs of chromosomes (Makino and Sasaki, 1961). These consist of twenty-two pairs of autosomes which are identical in males and females, and the X and Y chromosomes. The X chromosomes occur in pairs in females, while men possess an X and a Y.

The number of gene loci is constant within each chromosome. Thus, the total number of genes possessed by man is constant, with the exception of the difference in number between males and females, the latter having the higher number. The X chromosome is longer than the Y, and doubtless carries more genes. The total number of genes possessed by man is not known, but a recent estimate places the lower limit at approximately six thousand (Froto-Perroa, 1961).

All varieties of man are interfertile, and hybrids between the most diverse types produce fertile offspring. This interfertility, plus the uniformity in chromosome number, confirms the taxonomic classification of man into a single species, *Homo sapiens*. In general, the chromosome number is constant within a species, but differs from one species to another. Dissimilarity in number and kind of chromosomes is the primary reason for the sterility which frequently occurs in interspecific hybrids.

Species differ from one another with respect to both number and kind of chromosomes, whereas members of the same species have homologous chromosomes. This same principle may be stated in a different way, namely, species differ from one another in regard to both the total number of genes and kinds of genes, whereas members of the same species possess the same total number of genes, differing only in kinds.

The fact that all varieties of man belong to the same species greatly simplifies the problem of classification. We need not concern ourselves with cytological studies, when we are dealing with the classification of normal varieties of mankind. It is a problem of population genetics.

Populations and Genetic Variations

GENETIC VARIATIONS result from differences in the kind of genes at probably no more than 10 percent of all the gene loci. All members of the species are characterized by identical genes at the great majority of loci.

Gene differences are the result of mutations at various loci. The modern concept of the gene is that it is a portion of a chain of molecule of deoxyribonucleic acid, commonly referred to as DNA, running the length of the chromosome. A gene mutation is an alteration in the chemical structure of a sub-unit in the chain molecule, which is the gene locus. Genes are comparatively stable, the estimated rate of mutation in man ranging from one in ten thousand gametes to one in a million.

Mutations are not produced by what we think of as ordinary environmental influences such as climate, disease, food, experience, or training. They do not arise in response to a need. They can be produced by such artificial means as radiation by x-ray, gamma, beta, and neutron bombardment, and chemical mutagens. Although the precise mechanism of natural mutation is still unsolved, cosmic radiation is likely an important factor.

Artificially induced mutations occur at random. The majority of them are deleterious, and many are lethal. It is a matter of chance as to which genes will mutate, and the type of mutation. Experimental work on the production of synthetic mutations in plants now under way in many laboratories has resulted in some advantageous mutations, which enhance the yield and quality of crops. But each advantageous mutation has been produced at the ex-

Race and Heredity

pense of thousands of plants which had to be discarded. It has in no sense replaced conventional plant breeding. Directed mutations cannot be produced in man, and there is no foreseeable prospect for so doing.

Mutations provide the reservoir of variability for organic evolution. Chromosomes occur in pairs within the individual. When a mutation occurs within a particular cell in an individual, it follows that he carries one mutant gene, and one nonmutant gene at the locus. Gametes carry only one chromosome of each pair. If the mutation occurred in the germinal tissue, half of the gametes will carry the mutant gene, and half of them will carry its nonmutant homologue. Most mutations are recessive, and their effects are not apparent unless the individual received the mutant gene from each parent. Thus the effects of new mutations are usually not in evidence until a few generations after they occur.

Sometimes, for reasons to be discussed later, a mutant gene may completely supplant another within a population, that is to say, the population becomes pure or *homozygous* for the mutant gene. When this condition is attained, the gene is said to be *fixed* within the population. The gene from which it mutated, known as its *allele*, may be fixed in other populations. In such an event the populations differ completely from each other with respect to the genes in question.

Many hereditary variations result solely from one gene differences. The blood groups and hemoglobin variations are inherited in this simple fashion. In such cases trait and gene fixation correspond exactly. The expression of many traits, however, is determined by two or more pairs of genes. These include hair form, dermatoglyphics, pigmentation, and anthropometric variations. Here some of the genes may be fixed and others non-fixed for a particular trait. In this event, the trait is incompletely fixed. The variation in expression is limited.

Skin pigmentation and hair form are perhaps the best illustrations of traits which occur in this manner in some unmixed populations. Nilotic Negroes are characterized by blackish-brown skin and kinky hair, whereas Chinese populations are characterized by yellowish skin and straight hair. Straight hair and Mongoloid or Caucasoid skin color do not occur among unmixed Nilotic

Negroes. Conversely, kinky hair and blackish-brown skin do not occur among Chinese. The differences between Negroids and Mongoloids with respect to hair form and skin pigmentation are complete and fixed. Hair form is not fixed in Europeans, however, ranging from straight to very curly. Epicanthus, or inner fold of the eyelid, appears to be fixed among Mongoloids.

The foregoing examples are concerned with obvious differences in external appearance. Pigmentation of skin and hair form are the best known classical criteria for race. These are the most conspicuous of the relatively few fixed differences between human populations.

Many genes, especially those resulting from comparatively recent mutations, occur in only a portion of some populations, and are completely absent in others. These may be termed partially fixed genetic variations.

The Occurrence of Kuru Among a New Guinea Tribe

A SERIOUS neuropathological condition known as kuru occurs in the tribe of Fore, in the Eastern Highlands of New Guinea (Dobzhansky, 1960). There are approximately thirty thousand people in the tribe, inhabiting an area of approximately eight hundred and eighty-four square miles. Almost half of the women and one-tenth of the men die from this disease. As a consequence there are 2.5 males per female within the tribe.

Kuru appears to be simply inherited, being dominant in women and recessive in men. In other words, affected men have received a kuru gene from each parent, whereas women have the disease, even if they inherited it from only one parent. Heterozygous women may live long enough to bear one or two children. Kuru is not known to occur outside of the Fore tribe, although intermixture with other tribes may result in its dissemination. Quarantine measures are under consideration.

All four of the ABO blood groups are present in the majority of populations throughout the world, but there are a few exceptions. Pure Peruvian Indians are all of blood group O. Some tribes of Australian aborigines lack blood groups B and AB, indicating the complete absence of antigen B.

Sickle-cell anemia is another simply inherited variation which occurs in some populations, and is completely absent from others. It results from the homozygous condition of the cell sickling gene, and is thus recessive. Heterozygotes have been demonstrated to possess resistance to malaria, and the gene occurs most frequently in malarial areas (Allison, 1954). It occurs almost exclusively among Negroes, or people who have some Negro ancestry.

There are a few exceptions, however. Some of the hill tribes in western India have from 15 to 25 percent cell sicklers, although they show no other evidence of Negro ancestry. Cell sickling is completely absent from several other hill tribes. A few instances have been reported among Caucasoids in the Mediterranean area. Thus the gene responsible for cell sickling is restricted to Negroes, and to a few non-Negro populations.

Blond hair and blue eyes are completely missing in unmixed Mongoloid and Negroid populations. Although light pigmentation of hair and eyes is confined to people of European and mixed European descent, no European population is composed entirely of blue-eyed blonds. Even in Scandinavia a good proportion of the population is characterized by dark hair and eyes.

The forest pygmies in the Congo are always of short stature, in men ranging from four feet and three inches to five feet and three inches, the average being four feet and nine inches. Apparently the potentialities for tall stature are lacking in these pygmies, although they are present in many other populations characterized by relatively short average stature. The Japanese, for example, are noted for relatively short stature, yet an occasional one is tall. The genetic variation in stature, as well as in hair and eye color is quantitative and many genes are concerned. Short stature is incompletely fixed among pygmy tribes.

The Proportion of Specific Genes Cause Population Differences

QUANTITATIVE difference includes by far the majority of genetic differences between populations. These differences are in amount rather than in kind, quantity rather than quality. All of the genes responsible for such variations are present in each of the populations under consideration. These populations differ from one another in the proportions of these genes. The proportion of gametes which carry a particular gene is known as the frequency of the gene. If a gene is fixed, its frequency is 1.0.

The range of variability with respect to the frequency of a particular gene depends upon the size of the population. For example, individuals fall into three genotypes with respect to gene A, AA, Aa, and aa. Stated in terms of gene frequency, they are 1.0, 0.5 and 0.0. Gene frequencies in two individuals will fall into the following five categories: 1.00, 0.75, 0.50, 0.25, and 0.00. Populations of three fall into seven categories, those of four into nine, the general rule being $1 + 2n$, where n represents the size of the population.

Quantitative differences between populations are determined by non-fixed genes, that is to say, the frequencies of those genes under consideration are greater than 0.0, and less than 1.0. In other words, both alleles of the series are present in each population. This is an important distinction from situations where inter-population differences result from fixed and partially fixed genetic variations.

This difference is important in another respect. There is no way known to alter the frequencies of or to substitute for fixed genes, except through crossing with another population. There is no possibility of the Chinese altering their hair form to kinky through selection, or of African Negroes altering kinky hair to straight. It may be done by hair treatment for an individual, but this in no way affects his germ plasm. The expression of the genes is simply masked.

The situation is radically different for quantitative variations. It is possible to alter gene frequencies at will through selection. For example, there are marked differences between Chinese, Whites in the U.S.A., and Peruvian Indians in the percentages of the ABO blood groups, as follows:

Ethnic Group	Blood Type			
	O	A	B	AB
U.S.A. (Whites)	45%	42%	10%	3%
Chinese	42	25	25	8
Peruvian Indians	100	0	0	0

If, for some reason, it should be found that the distribution within Chinese is much more desirable than that within American Whites, it should be possible, through selective mating to eventually alter the distribution to that of Chinese, or vice versa. In other words, the genetic composition of populations in this category is subject to change through selection. Populations which differ markedly from each other may become quite similar through selection, or their differences may be increased. The limitation of selection for a particular gene is reached when it becomes fixed within a population.

The situation is quite different for populations in which the genes are fixed. Here selection is ineffective. Even though it should be deemed desirable for pure Peruvian Indians to have an ABO blood group distribution similar to that of Chinese, there would be no way of bringing it about. The same situation prevails with respect to traits characterized by continuous ranges of variation.

Let us return to a previous illustration. Congo pygmies and Japanese have relatively short stature. It would be impossible to raise the average stature of the pygmies up to that of the Swedes through generations of selection alone, but it might be done in the Japanese. Nutrition and other circumstances may partially mask the expression of genes for stature. Even if one were to assume these nonhereditary circumstances were equivalent, the foregoing statements concerning the effects of selection would doubtless hold true. The genetic potentialities for increasing in stature are surely present among Japanese, whereas they are very limited within the forest pygmies (or other pygmies, for that matter).

Unlike the blood groups and other simply inherited variations, many genes are doubtless involved in the inheritance of variations in stature, and the expression of the genetic potentiality may also be modified by nutrition and other factors (Jans, 1959). Many of man's outstanding variations, such as pigmentation, skeletal dimensions, dermatoglyphics, and physiological functioning exhibit continuous ranges of variation. Their final expression is the result of the interaction of multiple genes with environmental complexes. Nevertheless, heredity sets the limits of these variations.

In some populations these limits are more restricted than in others, as a result of gene fixation and incomplete trait fixation.

Definition of Races of Man

LET US NOW attempt to define race, keeping in mind the principles which have just been outlined. One dictionary defines a race as "the descendants of a common ancestor; a family, tribe, people or nation believed or presumed to belong to the same stock, a lineage." In a broad sense all mankind fits into the above category. But the term race is generally used to refer to major divisions within a species. *Homo sapiens* constitutes a single species, and the races of man are species subdivisions. In many respects they are analagous to breeds of domestic animals, which are also subdivisions of species.

The races of mankind are subdivisions of *Homo sapiens*, differing from each other with respect to a few fixed genes, and in the frequencies of many non-fixed genes.

A race is "pure" for fixed genes only. Human population differences in this respect are very few in number, far less than for the non-fixed genes. The situation is somewhat similar to that in breeds of livestock. Coat color, type of horns or their absence, type of combs, etc., are frequently used as breed trademarks. They are conspicuous and simply inherited, although they are of little or no real economic importance. The important differences between breeds, such as in production of meat, milk and eggs are largely the result of differences in gene frequencies. The possibilities for change in these traits are still there. Selection can still be effective.

Skin color and hair form are the best known marker traits for the races of mankind. African Negroes are characterized by blackish-brown skin and kinky hair, Asiatic Mongoloids by yellow skin and straight hair, and European whites by light skin. Both Africans and Asians are "purer" than Europeans, as genes for not only skin color, but hair and eye color, and hair form are fixed within unmixed representatives of these populations. Hair form and pigmentation of hair and eyes are far from fixed in Europeans.

Strictly speaking, of course, the popular classification of Europeans as "Whites," Africans as "Blacks," and Asians as "Yellows," is somewhat inaccurate. The majority of North Africans, the peoples of Asia Minor and Asiatic Indians are predominantly Caucasian, although there has been considerable mixture. For example, Asiatic Indians are characterized by Caucasoid features and varying shades of brown skin color. They are of mixed origin and they are not known to differ from other populations with regard to any fixed genes.

But the broad classification of people with respect to ethnogeographical origin does serve a useful purpose. The only place where one could find unmixed Negroes is in Africa. Unmixed Mongoloids are most likely to be found in Asia, and unmixed Caucasoids in Europe or in America, the latter being descended from European immigrants. Today it is becoming increasingly difficult to run across unmixed racial groups in any part of the world.

Even though we restrict our definition of a major or primary race to include only those populations which are characterized by a few fixed genes which are absent or non-fixed in other populations, the distinctions between races are frequently blurred by mixture, and divisions within the major racial groups. For instance, the Congo pygmies are a subdivision of the Negro race, their most outstanding difference being their short stature. They differ from other Negroes in that some genes for short stature are fixed within pygmies, but not in other Negroes.

The Negrito pygmies of the Philippines average less than five feet in stature, but are quite different from Congo pygmies in several other important respects. Negritos are characterized by relatively high frequencies of whorls on the fingertips and a low incidence of blood groups A and B (Weninger, 1957). Congo pygmies have unusually low frequencies of whorls on the fingertips and relatively high frequencies of blood groups A and B. Aside from stature, Congo and Negrito pygmies do not manifest striking resemblances. Congo pygmies comprise a subdivision of the Negro race, whereas Philippine pygmies show greater resemblances to primitive peoples in Australia and the Malay Archipelago.

The situation is quite different with respect to the South African Bushmen, a stone age race of whom only a few thousand still survive in the Kalahari desert. These people are also characterized by very short stature, quite similar to that of the Congo pygmies. But they differ from all other races of contemporary men with respect to a combination of traits, which are fixed within the population.

Perhaps the most remarkable of these is steatopygia, the protuding buttocks which are especially noticeable in the women. Another unique trait is the peculiar hair form known as "peppercorns," the hair occurring in isolated spirals. They are characterized by yellow skin, the inner epicanthus, flat nose, everted lips, and attached ear lobes. Although possessing some of the same characteristics as Mongoloids and Negroids they differ from each of them in several respects. They are a distinct race, not because of short stature alone, but because of a unique constellation of characteristics within the population.

Genetic Factors in Population Relationship

THE DEGREE of relationship between populations depends upon the number of fixed genes they have in common, and upon the degrees of similarities in frequencies of non-fixed genes. Thus in estimating the degree of genetic relationship between populations, it is essential to use several independent criteria. Similarity in one or two criteria may be pure chance and lead to quite erroneous conclusions, if based on these alone. Our present-day knowledge of the simple inheritance of the various blood groups, hemoglobins and many biochemical differences, and the growing appreciation of dermatoglyphics as a genetic tool in evaluating quantitative inheritance have greatly supplemented the older anthropometric criteria, such as anthropometric variations, pigmentation and hair form (Boyd, 1950).

With the exception of the major races, genetic differences between populations fall almost entirely in the categories of non-fixed and partially fixed genes. All known blood group differences belong in these categories. Although Peruvian Indians are

Race and Heredity

all of group O, there is no population in which Group O is completely lacking. No population is homozygous for cell sickling. Two Stone Age races, the South African Bushmen and Australian aborigines show the most extreme variations between populations in the incidence of patterns on fingertips. South African Bushmen have less than 20 percent whorls, while Australian aborigines have 70 percent (Cummins and Stetzler, 1951). Conversely, South African Bushmen have more arches than whorls, whereas Australian aborigines have less than 1 percent. Yet neither type of pattern is fixed in either population. It is of interest to note that the most extreme differences in this respect occur in two of the oldest contemporary populations, separated from each other longer, perhaps, than any others.

The degree of genetic difference between populations is very definitely correlated with cultural differences and geographic isolation from one another. The quantitative differences between populations show a tremendous range of variation, from those between major racial groups to those between minor ethnic groups.

The following factors are operative in the evolution of genetic differences between human populations: mutation, selection, isolation, and hybridization.

Mutation: The basis for genetic variation goes back to gene mutation. From the standpoint of the human life span, mutations rarely occur and the evolution of population variations is largely a matter of recombination of genes already present in the parent population.

Selection: The role of natural selection in bringing about genetic changes is more familiar and obvious to most people than those of the other factors to be discussed later. The high correlation between form and function was obvious to naturalists and keen observers long before the time of Mendel. Pre-Mendelians tended to ascribe these correlations to environment, assuming that acquired characteristics are inherited. Lamarck and his followers made what seemed at the time to be a most logical interpretation of their observations.

Today we know that cause and effect are in the reverse order of what Lamarck assumed. Mutations provided the genetic variability upon which environment acts as a selective agency. It does not cause the mutation, but instead serves to screen out genetic variations which are disadvantageous in particular environments.

Examples of the effectiveness of natural selection are abundant. One of the most remarkable is that of the geographical distribution of the gene responsible for cell sickling. Persons homozygous for cell sickling develop sickle-cell anemia, which is usually fatal. Heterozygotes do not develop the disease, but have been shown to have unusual resistance to malaria. The incidence of the gene is highest among peoples living in malarial areas. Natural selection for resistance to malaria is clearly indicated.

A similar situation exists with respect to Cooley's anemia, another simply inherited condition, in which heterozygotes appear to possess resistance to malaria. This disease occurs most frequently in the Po River valley in Italy, a region noted for its high incidence of malaria (Stern, 1960).

South American Indians have unusual lung capacity, an asset in the high Andes where the atmosphere is thin. The accumulations of fat on the buttocks of South African Bushmen apparently serve as a food reservoir during long intervals, during which no food is available. The flat, fat face and narrowed eye slit of Mongoloid peoples, above all in Eskimos and northern Siberians, serves to protect the eyes and nasal passages against the arctic cold, according to Howells (1959) and Coon, Garn, and Birdsell (1950). The occurrence of these same Mongoloid features among people in warmer climates is attributed to migration.

There is a pronounced correlation between latitude and pigmentation, beginning in Scandinavia and extending through southern Europe and northern Africa to the equator. This has frequently been cited as an adaptation of man to climate. Dark pigment affords protection against the burning rays of the sun. Skin cancer is reported to be a relatively frequent occurrence among albino African Negroes. The correlation between pigmentation and latitude does not hold true throughout the entire world, however, notably in the Western hemisphere.

There are also many examples of where there are no obvious correlations between form and function. There is no evidence, for example, of any functional importance for hair form, whether it

Race and Heredity

be kinky, curly, wavy, or straight. Obviously, mutations and natural selection are not the sole factors involved in the evolution of population differences.

Isolation: Migration of small populations has doubtless been an important element in bringing about inter-population differences. Suppose that the allelic genes A and a occur in equal frequencies in a large population. This means that half of the gametes carry A and half carry a. Members of the population occur in the following genotypic frequency: 1 AA, 2 Aa, 1 aa. If A is dominant to a, three-fourths of the inhabitants will show the dominant phenotype and one-fourth will show the recessive. Assuming that genes A and a are of no importance from the standpoint of selection, these proportions will remain constant from one generation to another. The population is in *genetic equilibrium.*

Let us further suppose that a man and a woman migrate from this population to an uninhabited island. What is the probability that the gene frequency will be the same as in the population from which they emigrated? The individual is double in his heredity. Therefore, it follows that two people will possess a total of four genes for each chromosome locus. The probability that the two immigrants will possess 2 A and 2 a is three in eight. There is also one chance in eight that either A or a will be fixed.

In other words the odds are against the gene frequencies remaining the same in the migrants as in the parent population. There is a possibility that one or the other allele may be fixed in the emigrants. The probabilities of differences in gene frequency among emigrants as compared to the parent population is directly related to the size of the emigrating population. The larger the number of emigrants, the less the probability of fixation of either allele. Conversely, the larger the emigrating population, the smaller will be the probability of gene frequencies being exactly the same as the parent population.

Many of the world's populations have doubtless stemmed from a small nucleus of emigrants. The American Indians are descendants of small bands of emigrants from Asia, who crossed what is now the Bering Strait. Similarly, indigenous peoples in islands of the south Pacific must have arisen from small migrations.

Genetic equilibrium cannot be maintained over a period of

several generations within small populations. Gene frequencies will fluctuate on a purely chance basis, and some genes may become fixed.

Let us go back to our illustration of the migrant couple. Assume that both are heterozygous, of genotype Aa. Suppose they have two children, a boy and a girl. The odds will be five to three against the gene frequencies remaining unaltered in their children, and three to one against both of them being heterozygous like their parents. This fluctuation in gene frequency, usually referred to as "genetic drift," will continue from one generation to another until gene fixation occurs. Genetic equilibrium can be maintained only in relatively large populations.

Hybridization: Hybridization has been an important factor in racial evolution. In recent centuries, due to better transportation facilities, it has become increasingly important in racial evolution, whereas the effectiveness of geographical isolation has decreased correspondingly. The most outstanding effect of hybridization is to increase genetic heterogeneity. Many gene fixations are broken, and gene frequencies are greatly altered. Hawaiians, American Negroes, Cape Colored of South Africa, the northern Sudanese, and Burmese are examples of populations of mixed origin.

Interaction of Heredity and Environment Produces Culture

HUMAN populations differ from one another in both heredity and culture. Cultural differences contribute much, although indirectly, to the evolution of genetic differences between populations. Culture itself is a product of the interaction of heredity and environment. This interplay is an essential element in bringing about human differences.

Culture is usually considered to be the non-biological inheritance of social customs from one generation to another. Under this heading may be included language, religion, traditional ways of doing things, educational systems, accumulations of literature and art, and all of the products of man's accumulated experience and ingenuity which are handed down through the centuries. These form very important portions of our environments, from birth onward.

The language or languages one speaks depends upon what he hears when he is beginning to talk. Any normal child will learn to speak any language or languages with ease, if he is exposed to them at an early age. Most of us profess the religion of our parents. The acquisition of various cultural attributes is a matter of environment, because it depends upon what impressions are conveyed to our minds through the sensory nervous system. Indeed, our ways of thinking and our attitudes depend to a very great extent upon cultural background.

But how can we account for the origins of culture, and the vastly different patterns of culture which are evident from one population to another? The ability to evolve cultures appears to be unique to man, and it is the chief distinction between man and other animals (Dobzhansky and Ashley-Montagu, 1947). The physical basis for the ability to evolve cultures is located in the cerebral cortex, a portion of the brain which is largely undeveloped in other animals. Like other organic evolutionary developments, it is biological and resulted from mutations.

Undoubtedly a whole series of mutations, rather than just one, have been responsible for the change. It is inconceivable that just one mutation could have brought such a drastic development. This is not the way evolution works. Mutations occurring at different times and in different places provided the physical background for the evolution of various cultures. There can be no doubt that not only individuals, but populations as well, differ from each other in their capacity to evolve various kinds of culture. It is inconceivable that all human populations are identical in this respect, and neither logic nor scientific observations give support to such a contention.

The way in which a particular culture evolves depends not only upon the cerebral cortex and external environmental influences, but also to some extent upon the entire biological make-up of the interbreeding population or "isolates," as biologists are wont to call them. There are innate differences in minimal nutritive requirements, sensitivity to pain, speed of perception, fear of high places, allergic reactions, sensitivity to heat and cold, manual dexterities, and physical drive. These and countless other differences could very well influence the directions in which various cultures evolve. Each of these variations in turn evolved from an intricate interaction of heredity and environment. One is forced to the conclusion, therefore, that people from different populations would not turn out to be the same, if all were reared in a common cultural background.

There is little or no evidence that people of today surpass in innate intelligence those who lived in the days of Socrates. We have made tremendous strides since then in education, economic growth and prosperity, scientific achievement, and world prestige. But this has been in a large measure due to our cultural heritage, rather than to increases in IQ. There is no reason to believe that introduction of modern techniques, gadgets, and educational methods into under-developed countries or among impoverished groups will in any way alter *innate* intellectual capacities.

The Influence of Cultural Barriers

CULTURAL differences can be just as effective as geographic isolation in restricting the size of human interbreeding populations. Language, religion, nationality, social-economic status, education, intelligence and race all serve as barriers to random choice of marriage partners. Religion has been among the most important of these.

The Hebrew religion is the cultural factor which has distinguished Jews throughout the world for over three thousand years. During this time they have been scattered over wide portions of the earth, although their original home was in Palestine. Today the new nation of Israel is made up of Jews, many of whom have migrated from North Africa, Yemen, Spain, Germany, Russia and even more remote areas. This reunion is occurring after centuries of separation.

Careful studies of the genetic make-up of modern Israelites shed interesting light on how religious differences may be correlated with genetic differences. Jewish immigrants from different regions manifest some significant differences in the ABO blood group frequencies (Mourant, 1954). Dermatoglyphics present a somewhat different picture. The fingerprints of Jewish immigrants from all over the world are remarkably similar. Fingerprint configurations are highly heritable. They are determined months before birth, and are non-affected by post-natal environment. These findings strongly suggest that Jews have not intermarried with Gentiles nearly as much as has been generally supposed. It must be added that the fingerprints of Jews differ significantly from those of non-Jews in the host countries (Sachs and Bat-Miriam, 1957). American Jews are characterized by highly significant differences from Protestants and Catholics in fingerprints and ABO blood groups. In general, American Jews closely resemble Syrians and Lebanese in serological, dermatoglyphic, and anthropometric characters.

Fingerprint configurations are perhaps the most outstanding example of polygenic non-pathological hereditary variations in man. As such they may be less subject to the effects of genetic drift than such simply inherited variations as the blood groups. Where two or more pairs of genes operate on a single trait, fluctuation in the frequency of one pair may be counterbalanced by opposite fluctuations in other pairs.

It is impossible to accurately assess the relative roles of selection and genetic drift in bringing about inter-population differences. Traits which may appear to be of no selective importance whatsoever can be conditioned by genes which also affect other traits of survival importance. Until recent years it was generally believed that the ABO blood groups were of no importance from the standpoint of survival. It has been shown that people of groups A and AB are more prone to cancer of the stomach than those of groups O and B, and that people of group O are more likely to be afflicted with peptic ulcer than those of the other groups (McConnell, 1956).

The bulk of evidence strongly indicates that the ancestors of the American Indians were East Asians. Blood group B is rare among all tribes of American Indians, but occurs in a fourth to a third of East Asians. The frequency of blood group B gradually increases from western Europe to eastern Asia. It is conceivable that genetic drift may not be solely responsible for these differences. Perhaps antigen B has positive survival importance in Asia, and is of negative survival importance in other regions. Then, too, it is possible that mutations to antigen B may occur more frequently in Asia than in other parts of the world. Whatever the relative roles of selection and drift may be in accounting for these differences, we know that they exist. Furthermore, inter-population differences in genetic make-up and culture are so closely interwoven that they cannot be disentangled.

In so far as a trait may be conditioned by heredity, we may expect both populations and individuals to differ from one another. Evidence that heredity is entirely or partially responsible for individual variations in a trait may be taken as convincing evidence that populations differ from each other in like manner. This principle applies to behavioral variations as surely as to serological and anthropometric variations. Culture may mask or accentuate the expression of hereditary differences, but it cannot alter the genotype.

The bulk of psychological data strongly indicates many significant inter-population differences with respect to speed of perception, conformity, general intelligence, emotional reactions and numerous other aspects of behavior (Porteus, 1961 and Terman, 1947). Culture background doubtless plays a role in bringing about the differences, and in so far as this affects test scores, the tests lack complete validity for population comparisons. Even if these scores are repudiated for inter-population comparisons, but are accepted as valid evidence for individual comparisons within populations, we must accept the verdict of the latter.

If they give no evidence for innate individual differences, then we have no grounds for assuming that the inter-population differences may be in part due to heredity. Conversely, if the tests give real evidence of innate individual differences, sheer logic compels us to infer that inter-population differences are present, even if they have not been tested. This need not imply that all populations differ from all others in all genetic traits. But the conclusion seems inescapable that many real inter-population variations do exist. The burden of proof rests upon those who contend that there are no innate differences between populations in genetic potentials for various aspects of behavior.

Let us assume that completely valid tests should be devised measuring speed of reaction. Suppose that these tests reveal that population X rates higher, on the average, than population Y. However, a few people in Y rate as high as any of those in X. One might safely conclude from this that all of the genes necessary for the highest rating are present in both populations. None of the genes responsible for variation in expression of the trait appear to be absent in either population. The inter-population differences are quantitative, and population Y has the potentiality for raising its average score to that of X in future generations, through selection. Suppose there is a third population Z, which rates lower on the average than either X or Y. Furthermore, none of the people in it score as high as several of the best in population X. We can logically infer that Z may not possess the genetic potential for great improvement in average speed of perception, even though selection may be practiced over a period of many generations.

The Result of Racial Amalgamation

WHAT ARE THE biological effects of extensive racial intermixture? Will it eventually bring about a uniform blend, in accord with the conventional concept of the melting pot? The answer is no. While it does tend to eliminate and blur the differences between ethnic groups, individual differences are increased by a corresponding amount. The total variability is the same as it was before, but it is now distributed in a different manner.

Thus when Negroes and Whites intermarry all of their children are intermediate and mulatto. But the next generation will produce many shades of pigmentation, varying between those of the Negro and the White ancestors. There will be several shades of skin color in the mixed populations, rather than just two. The mixed population is thus more variable, but the intermediate gradations serve to render extreme differences less obvious. Unless rigorous selection is carried out extensively for preferred shades, segregation of different shades will be a continuous process from generation to generation. Complete uniformity will never be attained.

The situation may be visualized as follows. Think of the genes as marbles, those for dark skin color as brown, and those for light skin color as white. A dark race may be compared to a bag containing brown, a light race as containing white marbles. Mixing of races may then be compared to taking a bag of brown marbles and one of white marbles, and dumping them into a single bowl. When shaken thoroughly and viewed from a distance, the shade will be intermediate between the brown and white. This represents the first generation hybrid.

The comparison of the next generation may be represented by bags containing four marbles each, drawn at random from the bowl. As the marbles are drawn at random it is quite obvious that varying combinations of brown and white will occur within the bags. Most of them will have both colors, but occasionally one will have only brown, or only white. These bags may be thought of as the second generation within the mixed population. Like the bags of marbles, several shades of pigment will appear, ranging from one extreme to the other.

The following generation would be formed in the same manner. That is to say, all of the marbles are again poured into the big bowl, and again placed into bags at random, four in each. In each successive generation the process is repeated.

It is quite apparent that the distributions of marbles within bags will be constant from one generation to another. The total variability remains constant. Hybridization has simply altered the distribution, but not the amount of variability. The population is in genetic equilibrium.

Although the total genetic variability remains constant, individual differences have increased at the expense of group differences. The parent populations were composed of only two kinds of populations and individuals, either all brown or all white. The hybrid population will consist of individuals of five shades of pigment, ranging from brown to white (following the assumption that only four genes are concerned). The sharp contrast between the parent populations is reduced among individuals in the hybrids.

The same principle holds for all other hereditary variations, and for the most part they will occur independently of each other.

Race and Heredity

Thus hair form, skeletal dimensions, hand prints, facial features, tooth conformation, and numerous other traits will exhibit a tremendous range of variation within the mixed population, and for the most part independently of each other. Furthermore, this individual variability will remain from one generation to another.

The story is different concerning cultural variations. Uniformity may be expected rather quickly. As a matter of fact, populations of mixed origin provide good source material for evaluations of the roles of heredity and environment. In so far as a trait is hereditary, individual variability will not diminish from one generation to another. But when the trait is environmental, uniformity may be quickly attained within mixed populations, especially when living in the same city or geographical area.

Individual genetic variability is increasing today for still another reason. Modern advances in medicine and other fields of science have greatly reduced the effectiveness of natural selection in eliminating those with constitutional deficiencies and susceptibilities to various diseases. Great advances have also been made in our understanding of nutritional requirements and deficiencies. Natural selection against nutritional deficiencies is becoming less and less effective, even in the far corners of the world.

Meanwhile, there is every reason to believe that natural mutations are occurring at the same rate as they have for thousands of years. The germ plasm is unaffected by medication and food of the individual, except that the possibilities for the transference of deleterious genes to oncoming generations is greatly enhanced.

The total store of genetic variability is thus increasing at an ever accelerated rate in modern man. This trend, plus racial intermixture is bringing about a continuous increase in the degrees of genetic difference between individuals throughout the entire world.

Hybrid Vigor and Miscegenation

THERE REMAINS yet another aspect of the biological effects of miscegenation which is frequently misunderstood. The popular belief is that wide crosses, whether in man or other living organisms, always result in offspring more vigorous than either parent. This is commonly known as hybrid vigor, although professional biologists and agriculturists frequently use the term "heterosis."

Almost everyone today knows the story of hybrid corn and how it has stepped up production. Hybrids in many plants and animals have proved their worth to farmers and horticulturists. The question naturally arises as to the possibilities of improving mankind through extensive racial intermixture.

Before answering this question, it may be worthwhile to consider just what is meant by "hybrid vigor." The mule, resulting from mating a jackass with a mare, is usually cited as the classical example of a hybrid that combines the toughness and endurance of the donkey with the strength of the horse. It possesses some of the most desirable qualities and lacks some of the undesirable qualities of each of its parents.

But the mule is actually a poor example of hybrid vigor, in the sense in which the term is used by plant and animal breeders. It is usually sterile with "no pride in ancestry or hope of posterity." This holds true for most inter-specific crosses in animals. The number of chromosomes usually varies from one species to another. This interferes with normal pairing of chromosomes at the time of germ cell formation, which in turn results in sterility.

Practical plant and animal breeders, as a rule, are concerned with hybridization within species, where they can be reasonably certain of obtaining fertile offspring from the hybrids. All mankind belongs to the same species, *Homo sapiens,* and hybrids between the most distantly related varieties show no reduction in fertility. Thus we need not concern ourselves here with hybrid sterility.

The primary task of the breeder is to select good genes and cull undesirable ones through hybridization and selection. His task is analagous to that of a traffic officer who directs the flow of germ plasm from one generation to another. He seeks to combine desirable lines of germ plasm and to eliminate the undesirable. Essentially, he directs the regrouping of genes.

Hybrid vigor is usually defined by animal and plant breeders as an increase over the vigor possessed by either parent. Vigor expresses itself in a variety of ways—in yield, production, lusty growth, general health and balance. In man it may also include intelligence and ability.

Strictly speaking, a hybrid is the offspring of parents who differ from each other in one or more genes. In that sense, all men are hybrids. Even in plants and animals the only "pure" strains are those which have been highly inbred. In the usual sense "hybrid" means the offspring of different breeds, strains, or varieties. In men, it is usually interpreted as referring to people of mixed racial origin.

Although the causes of hybrid vigor are not yet fully understood, the complementary action of genes brought in from different strains has been shown to be of considerable importance. The classical example of this was analyzed by Keeble and Pellow (1910) in England. They crossed two varieties of peas, each of intermediate height. The hybrid offspring were taller than either parent. One of the parent varieties was characterized by many joints spaced relatively close on the stems, whereas the other variety had few joints spaced widely apart. The hybrids had received a dominant gene from each parent, one resulting in many joints, the other in widely spaced joints. These hybrid peas did not breed true in future generations, but as might be predicted, segregated into tall, intermediate, and short plants.

Hybrid corn is the most famous of all hybrids within species (Crabb, 1947). The farmer must purchase new seed each year, as second generation hybrid offspring are characterized by marked declines in yield and uniformity. The use of hybrid seed corn alone has increased the acre yield from 25 to 50 percent.

Highly inbred lines are the parent stock for commercial hybrid seed corn. These lines are the result of six to eight successive generations of self-fertilization, and this intensive inbreeding brings to light undesirable recessive traits which are culled out. But the general vigor of these inbred lines declines. This is especially noticeable during the first half of the process, the lines gradually leveling off and attaining remarkable uniformity after five or six generations.

The inbreeding process has made it possible to sift out many undesirable genes. But the corn breeder is not as efficient at this as is nature. In other words, along with elimination of many obviously undesirable characteristics, man unconsciously selects out genes responsible for vigor and yield.

Although thousands of inbred lines have been produced, relatively small percentages of them are selected and retained for the production of commercial hybrid seed corn. Some combinations greatly outyield others. Furthermore, the best hybrid in one region may do poorly elsewhere. The successful production of hybrid seed corn is thus preceded by careful and rigid selection over a period of years.

Many commercial hybrid seed firms now produce hybrid chickens. The parents of these hybrids are the result of three to four successive generations of brother-sister matings. The degree of inbreeding is much less intensive than for the inbred lines in corn. Brother-sister matings are only half as intensive inbreeding as self-fertilization, and it is carried on for only half as many generations. There is good reason for this, as longer periods of inbreeding in chickens—and other animals for that matter—result in losses of fertility, and great difficulties are encountered in maintaining the lines. Furthermore, much more capital is invested per chicken than per corn plant. Here, again, careful selection is practiced for breeding stock.

Other methods are also employed in the production of hybrid livestock. The Santa Gertrudes is the only breed of cattle which originated in the United States. Over half a century ago Brahman cattle were crossed with Shorthorns at the King Ranch at the southern tip of Texas (Rhoad, 1949). These hybrids provided the foundation stock from which the Santa Gertrudes breed developed. This breed combines the heat tolerance and parasitic resistance of Brahmans with the quick maturity and good beef qualities of Shorthorns.

Careful selection of Brahman and Shorthorn foundation stock—plus constant selection for over fifty years after the initial crosses—were put into the building of the breed. Constant culling of poor stock and the extensive use of outstanding animals for breeding purposes were necessary to attain the goal. The Santa Gertrudes not only possess highly desirable beef qualities and excellent suitabilities for hot climates, but also comprise a breed characterized by a uniform red color and reduction of the Brah-

Race and Heredity

man hump. They are definitely superior to either the Brahman or the Shorthorn for beef purposes in the southwest.

Various other techniques are employed by breeders in the production and utilization of hybrid vigor in domestic animals and cultivated plants. But, in all instances where it is successful, careful selection is an essential element. Hybridization between different breeds or varieties, unaccompanied by selection, is no assurance of attaining hybrid vigor in the offspring. Dogs provide a good example of this. Mongrels are frequently inferior to their purebred ancestors, as no selection has been practised for outstanding vigor. The success stories of hybrid corn, Santa Gertrudes cattle, and other outstanding hybrids overemphasize the hybridization aspect and underemphasize the importance of careful selection.

What about hybrid vigor in man? Now that racial intermarriage is more common than ever before, should this result in an increase in vigor? The answer to the latter question is *no*. Man is already a highly heterogeneous animal, and no "pure" races exist today. The inbred strains of corn are relatively "pure" genetically, the plants in each manifesting amazing uniformity, even to the most casual observer. But the inbred lines which go into particular crosses frequently differ remarkably from each other.

Shorthorn and Brahman cattle are not closely related, although they are interfertile. Some zoologists classify them as belonging to different species. Accordingly, Shorthorn along with other European breeds are classified as *Bos taurus*, whereas Brahman and other Indian cattle are classified as *Bos indicus*. Others classify them as different subspecies. Regardless of zoological classification, the differences between them surpass those between the most distantly related ethnic groups.

Human beings are so heterogeneous that no hybrid vigor should be expected except in rare and isolated cases. Wide crosses are made on a more or less haphazard basis, with little or no thought being directed towards improvement of mankind. Selection is not practiced either before or after hybridization.

The offspring of hybrids are usually characterized by marked declines in vigor and uniformity. Farmers avoid this by buying hybrid seed corn each year. The founders of the Santa Gertrudes avoided it by many years of rigid selection among the Shorthorn-Brahman hybrids, and subsequently were able to produce a relatively uniform breed. Consequently, hybridization in man is not analogous to that practiced by plant and animal breeders.

In general, the degree of hybrid vigor attainable is negatively correlated with the degree of relationship between the parents. Many social scientists insist that the term "race" should not be used in speaking of varieties of mankind, on account of the absence of "pure races." Hence, they, of all people, should not expect hybrid vigor to be an attribute of human populations of mixed origins.

Talented Ethnic Groups Who Have Abstained From Interracial Marriages

THUS, WE SHOULD not expect miscegenation to be accompanied by marked increases in vigor. Furthermore, it has *not* been observed. On the contrary, some of the most talented populations in the world have abstained from extensive inter-marriage with those of other ethnic groups. Prominent among them are the Jews, the Copts, the Icelanders and the Parsis. Selection rather than hybridization seems to have been an important element in accounting for their outstanding abilities.

Approximately 10 percent of the population of Egypt are Coptic Christians. These have contributed much to the leadership of Egypt, especially in commercial and intellectual activities. Egypt was overrun and conquered by the Arabs in the seventh century A.D. The Mohammedan religion and the Arabic language and culture were introduced at that time. The Copts were there centuries before this and represent the most undiluted remnant of the descendants of the ancient Egyptians. The Muslims consist of mixtures of Arabs, Egyptians and Sudanese.

The people of Iceland are world renowned for their literacy and their outstanding achievements in intellectual output (Huntington, 1945). They are predominantly of Scandinavian descent, their ancestors having migrated there during the eighth and ninth centuries. Iceland is a bleak and cold island, and at times has been subject to volcanic eruptions which have wrought great damage.

There are approximately eighty thousand Parsis in India today, about half of whom live in Bombay. They are descended from the Zoroastrians, or ancient Fire-Worshippers of Persia, who migrated to Bombay in 766 A.D. Their ancestors were subjected to severe hardships and even persecution at times. Yet they are generally recognized as among the most competent people in India. They are well-known for their achievements in commerce and science.

None of the foregoing populations can be classed as hybrids, so their achievements cannot be attributed to hybrid vigor. Each of them, with the exception of the Icelanders, has been subjected to persecution at times. Selection, rather than hybrid vigor, appears to have been at least partially responsible for their outstanding qualities.

In spite of the lack of positive evidence for hybrid vigor in contemporary ethnic groups of mixed origins, there is no reason to believe that hybridization *per se* brings about deterioration in mankind. It does bring about greater individual variability in biological makeup, and at the same time reduces group differences.

From a strictly biological point of view, there would seem to be no advantages to be gained from miscegenation, which would not likewise accrue from different racial groups living side by side, but not interbreeding. The same range of genetic variability would still be there.

Literature

Allison, C. A., Protection afforded by sickle-cell trait against subtertian malarial infection. *Brit. Med. J.*, 6: 290–294, 1954.

Boyd, W. C., *Genetics and the Races of Man*. Boston, 1950.

Coon, C. S., S. M. Garn, and J. S. Birdsell, Races: a study of race formation in man. Springfield, 1950.
Crabb, A. R. *The Hybrid-Corn Makers*. New Brunswick, 1947.
Cummins, H. and F. M. Stetzler, Dermatoglyphics in Australian Aborigines. *Amer. J. Physical Anthropology*, 9: 455–560, 1951.

Dobzhansky, T., Eugenics in New Guinea. *Science, 132:* 75–77, 1960.
Dobzhansky, T., and M. F. Ashley-Montagu, Natural selection and the mental capacities of mankind. *Science, 106:* 587–590, 1947.

Froto-Perroa, O., Number of gene loci and total mutation rate in man. *Amer. Nat., 115:* 217–222, 1961.

Howells, W., *Mankind in the Making.* New York, 1959.
Huntington, E., *Mainsprings of Civilization.* New York, 1945.

Jans, C., La croissance ponderale du nourisson pygmee (Bambuti-Ituri). *Ann. Soc. Belge. Med. Trop., 39:* 851–863, 1959.

Keeble, F. and C. Pellew, The mode of inheritance of and time of flowering in peas (*Pisum sativum*). *Journ. Gen., 1:* 47–50, 1910.

Makino, S. and M. Sasaki, A study of somatic chromosomes in a Japanese population. *Amer. J. Human Genetics, 13:* 47–63, 1961.
McConnell, R. B., Selection and the ABO blood group locus. *Ann. N.Y. Acad. Sci., 65:* 1–32, 1956.
Mourant, A. E., *The Distribution of the Human Blood Groups.* Oxford, 1954.

Porteus, S. D., Ethnic group differences. *The Mankind Quart., 1:* 187–200, 1961.

Rhoad, O. A., The Santa Gertrudes breed. *J. Hered., 40:* 114–126, 1949.
Rife, D. C., Populations of hybrid origin as source material for the detection of linkage. *Amer. J. Human Genetics, 6:* 26–33, 1954a.
———, Dermatoglyphics as ethnic criteria. *Amer. J. Human Genetics, 6:* 319–327, 1954b.
———, The myth of the melting pot: genetic variability and racial intermixture. *Amer. J. Human Genetics, 1:* 248–251, 1954c.
———, *Heredity and Human Nature.* New York, 1959.

Sachs, L. and M. Bat-Miriam, The genetics of Jewish Populations: 1. Fingerprint patterns in Jewish populations in Israel. *Amer. J. Human Genetics, 9:* 117–127, 1957.
Stern, C., *Principles of Human Genetics.* San Francisco, 1960.

Terman, L. M., *The Gifted Child Grows Up.* Stanford, 1947.

Weninger, M., Der Beitrag des Haustleistens systems zur Pygmäenproblem. *Zeits. Morph. Anthrop., 45:* 207–234, 1957.

BIOGRAPHICAL NOTE

CLARENCE P. OLIVER, *M.A., Ph.D., is Professor and Chairman of the Department of Zoology of the University of Texas. He has held this position for over twenty years, and was formerly at the University of Minnesota where he was director of the Dight Institute for Human Heredity.*

Professor Oliver is a former president of both the Genetics Society of America and the American Society of Human Genetics. He is also a member of the American Eugenics Society, the Federation of American Societies for Experimental Biology, the American Association for Cancer Research, and the International Association for Dental Research.

Dr. Oliver has conducted extensive research in the fields of human genetics, the genetics of human cancer, the gene action in Drosophila alleles, *and the mutation process and radiation effects of* Drosophila. *He has served as co-editor of* Genetics *and is the author of many articles dealing with genetics and human biology. He is co-author of the book a* Guide to the Study of the Anatomy of the Shark, Necturus and the Cat (1947).

THE RACES OF MAN
AND HUMAN GENETICS

C. P. Oliver

A MORE ADEQUATE understanding of the formation of subspecies and of species can be reached if studies based upon plants as well as animals are considered. One subdivision can supply answers which are more difficult to unravel from studies of other groups. Differentiation into races may not seem to be so complicated a process but agreements and understandings among workers are at least as difficult to attain. It might seem preferable, therefore, in any discussion of races to include more organisms than *Drosophila* and man, which are the examples used principally in this presentation. The limit placed on organisms to be used, though, is made as a matter of expediency and not due to lack of appreciation for the many studies which have been made with other organisms.

The Problem of Race and Species Definitions

SYSTEMATISTS do not agree on a definition for species. An acceptable definition for race is no easier to formulate than is a definition for species. Race is not just a thing. It is a situation in a biological process (Howells, 1959), involving conditions which under adequate circumstances can lead to separation of biologically related individuals into species. Subdivisions classified as races have not become sexually isolated and, therefore, will not be mistakenly identified genetically as different species. Races are populations that differ genetically and may be distinguishable phenotypically (Patterson and Stone, 1952).

Biologically, populations having different gene pools are considered separate races. Each has its characteristic sets of alleles and the differences may be great. Nevertheless, two races could and would cross freely if they occupied the same area and if other circumstances related to their habits did not prevent it. Races, therefore, are geographically separated from each other or they are kept apart by an ecological barrier. Otherwise, there would be an exchange of genes between them and observable differences would become only individual variations among members of a race.

One might question whether information collected from racial studies of zoological specimens can be applied to mankind. Biologically, man is an animal. It must be kept in mind, though, that many populations of men do not face a struggle with nature in the same sense that other animals do. The evolution of culture in the history of mankind has counteracted to some extent selection by nature. But selection in human populations nevertheless has occurred and continues to occur.

During early civilizations, the major races of mankind were isolated geographically from each other even though isolation probably was in most instances never absolute. Gradually over many generations each of the races would be expected to have developed its own gene pool which included alleles unique to that race. Certainly not all members of the race would have carried the unique alleles. Other races, though, living in separate areas would have been free of the alleles because of lack of mutation or due to loss by selection. With increase in world population and the development of methods of transportation, members of one race migrated to areas occupied by other races. Where numbers of members of two races were brought together, social patterns, religion, and other cultural practices often limited the free exchange of genes and prevented complete fusion of the two gene pools.

Diversity Within a Population Unit

TO SOME individuals the term race indicates a population unit which includes members who are always identifiable as such. This opinion of course is not correct. Two races might be so strikingly different phenotypically that any individual could be properly classified according to his race, provided that no mixing or hybridization had taken place. This would be true for the giant and standard races of *Drosophila montana*. On the other hand, two races may differ only to a minor extent, particularly in their observable characters.

In a genetic sense, a pure or homozygous race will not be found (Dobzhansky, 1955). Genic or chromosomal differences exist in the genetic pool of any population unit. Due to these differences, individuals among whom matings occur produce progeny which can be expected to show individual variations. With the production of gametes, recombinations of chromosomes as well as crossing over between homologous chromosomes result in new combinations of genes. Any individual that is not homozygous, the fate for all when the total genotype is considered, will thus produce a number of different kinds of gametes. Sexual reproduction brings together a variety of gametes from the mates. Not all progeny can be expected to have the same or identical combinations of genetic material.

Even if the unexpected were to occur and a population unit were to originate from two identical, homozygous individuals, the genetic purity would not exist for long. Experimental geneticists have encountered this difficulty in many investigations. In a study of any series of alleles, for example in *Drosophila melanogaster*, it is essential to eliminate all latent modifying genes in the chromosomes, including the one which carries the gene under study. This can be done by the use of proper breeding methods. But the homogeneity does not last.

Within time, the homozygosity, except for the alleles and possibly closely associated regions of the chromosome, begins to break down. Mutations occur spontaneously. Any one gene may have a low mutation rate, possibly as low as one in a hundred thousand cells. If all genes are considered, though, the overall rate becomes very high. If ten thousand genes represent the total haploid condition, the mutation rate becomes one per ten gametes, assuming that all genes mutate with equal frequency.

With each passing generation, additional mutations occur. Different cultures or strains will gradually become different genetically. They may have identical or similar mutations but it is not necessarily true that all mutations will be identical. In fact that seems to be unlikely. Consequently within a number of generations the strains lose their homogeneity. The mutant genes may not result in morphologic traits. They can nevertheless have a modifying effect upon the genes under study.

In any natural population, mutations have occurred again and again. The mutations in association with selection result in polymorphism within the unit. This may involve chromosomal rearrangements or gene differences with the latter resulting in differences in phenotypes, otherwise they may not be recognizable. The phenotypes or rearrangements are not necessarily distributed evenly over the population. Often, there are pockets of high and pockets of low frequencies for the mutants.

Polymorphism also occurs in any population of mankind. This variation has been reported especially with blood types. Since the discovery by Landsteiner of the four main ABO blood groups in man, anthropologists and geneticists have determined the blood group frequencies in many of the areas of the earth. Each population, with few exceptions, carries the three major alleles in its gene pool. Relative frequencies of the alleles differ in the various areas occupied by one population unit of large size. The basis for retention of polymorphism for the ABO groups is not well understood, but selection may be a factor. Evidence is being collected which shows that blood group genotypes cannot be considered to have a neutral selective value.

Diversity Among Population Units

AFTER TWO natural populations become separated geographically or ecologically so that breeding between them does not occur, the alleles and chromosomal rearrangements in the two genetic pools will begin to differ in pattern, in their relative proportions and combinations. With the passing of sufficient time, the two populations may be expected to differ genetically and the differences will be considered racial. Yet within each group some of the combinations from the original genetic pool will be retained. To some extent, therefore, members of the two populations will overlap genetically.

The degree of difference between two races will depend upon a number of factors. Migration of one or more members from one race to the area or niche occupied by another will cause a mingling of gene pools. Mutations occur regularly. Adaptation to fit each race or unit of the race to its unique environment will effect changes in the gene pools. Alleles or chromosomal patterns lost through adaptation will not always be the same for the two races.

Geographic races have been found to differ in relative frequencies of types of chromosomal arrangements. The differences are to some extent quantitative but qualitative differences also occur. A striking example of polymorphism within a race and among races of one species has been reported for *Drosophila montana* (Moorhead, 1954; Stone, Guest, and Wilson, 1960). Three races have been found in three widely separated geographical areas. One population, the standard *montana,* was found in the Rocky Mountain area of the United States. A second population, giant *montana,* was discovered in the Pacific Northwest area. More recently another population has been reported from Canada and Alaska.

The three main populations are alike phenotypically with the exception that giant *montana* is larger than either of the other two. Interbreeding occurs easily and the hybrids are viable and fertile. Hybrids between giant *montana* and standard *montana* are intermediate in size, suggesting to Moorhead that size difference is a result of more than one gene.

Karotypes of the three races are identical but they differ in inversion patterns. Giant *montana* has fourteen inversions that are not found in standard *montana* (Moorhead, 1954). Alaskan-Canadian *montana* has seven inversions unlike those found in the other two forms (Stone, Guest, and Wilson, 1960).

Among twenty-three strains of giant *montana* and among

strains of the other races, polymorphism with respect to chromosomal pattern was reported. Many inversions were heterozygous and therefore not fixed. The three main groups, or races, are widely separated geographically. Chromosomal patterns representing the genetic pools differ among races. Yet they share some common inversions and are morphologically very similar.

Human races have their characteristic frequencies of genes. This is shown by the reports on distribution of blood type antigens and hemoglobin types. Regardless of the fact that many of the genes responsible for ABO, Rh and MN blood types occur in some members of all races, certain alleles may be absent or very uncommon in one racial group in comparison to others. Some of the American Indians lack the gene for antigen A. The Basque population has a high frequency of Rh-negative, higher than the frequencies found in other groups in that same race and in other races. Siamese and a few other populations apparently lack that recessive gene. All members of the population, however, carry some of the alleles responsible for Rh-positive. In most instances, though, races of people differ quantitatively. All races carry the genes responsible for the MN major blood groups. Most populations have very similar frequencies of groups M, MN, and N, but a few exceptions occur. The Eskimo has a relatively high frequency of the allele for M. Australian natives have a high frequency of N.

Study of Genic Constitution

RACES ARE groups of organisms belonging to a species which have not differentiated to the point that they are classified as separate species. Racial classification in a zoological sense is based primarily upon physical characteristics (Shapiro, in Linton, 1945). This concept applies as well to man, particularly for those investigators who group and classify human populations according to physical and anthropological measurements.

All men are recognized genetically as members of a single species. Racial groups do exist. Mixing of gene pools occurs where association between races takes place and this has prevented the development of sexual isolating factors which would be necessary for differentiation into species. If a population unit occupies a large geographic area, the introduced genes will not be evenly distributed. Pockets of a unit can remain free of the introduced genes because of isolation. For scientific reasons, geneticists should study the comparative genetics of the various groups, to determine the degrees of similarity and of difference, and to study the causes and effects of the variations.

Patterson and Stone (1952), in a discussion of genetic diversity among species, referred to an ideal approach which includes determining the number of gene loci in various species and the number of gene differences between species. They recognized the difficulty and one might say the impracticability of the problem because of the lack of knowledge about the many variables that would be involved.

Unquestionably the study of total gene differences among races in zoological organisms including man would be very involved. No two men are exactly alike. Monozygous twins have the same genotypes, provided no mutations altered a gene after twinning took place. Yet these twins can be expected to differ to some extent because of an environmental effect. Genic differences among members of a group will be found. Within one race, groups separated by conditions of life will have genic differences.

In the past, obvious and easily measured phenotypes were used in population genetics. Men differ in many other genetically determined traits which are discoverable only by laboratory tests. New methods of study and new discoveries continue to make available characters which can be studied. Just recently a new blood antigen caused by a sex-linked gene has been reported (Mann et al., 1962). It occurs at least in the Caucasian and Negro races. With the great increase in number of antigens and serum proteins, geneticists have reached the point where it becomes necessary to decide on how many traits can be studied if one wants to use a large number of members per race.

Mourant (in Harrison, 1961) stated that in Europe a genetical analysis of the populations is being achieved. He referred to Beckman's report on populations in Sweden in which a number of blood types vary in concordance with one another. The data were obtainable through medico-legal paternity testing. In many countries such data will not be so readily available. Yet, the changing patterns of life and rapid transportation now available make it imperative that racial differences be determined, as completely as possible, before the opportunity is lost.

Admittedly the study of the distribution of many genes, the ideal method, will be a tedious task. Geneticists, though, owe it to mankind to undertake the studies. The birth of genetics in itself is an example of the value to be gained in detailed studies, close observations, and accurate recording of particulate data. Estimating the number of genes certainly will be inaccurate until we have better knowledge about what constitutes a gene. Investigators can, though, do adequate work with what is available. A mere count of the genes will not give the information that is needed unless a study is also made of the effects of these genes on individuals living under various conditions (Penrose, in Roberts and Harrison, 1959).

Origin of Genetic Diversity

RACIAL DIFFERENCES can be detected only if more than one phenotype is known. Phenotypes based on genic cause can differ only if allelic forms exist. Alleles arise as a result of mutations. Mutations, then, are one source of diversity among population units. An understanding of the origin and preservation of mutant genes becomes important if comparative genetical studies are to be made.

Recurrent mutations deserve particular attention. Any mutant gene has a good chance to be lost due to selection or chance. If the mutation occurs a number of times, the allele has a better chance to survive. Then one is faced with the problem of determining whether recurrent mutations are truly identical mutations. If they are not, presumed similarity may be so only superficially. Penrose (in Roberts and Harrison, 1959) has called attention to the possible inaccuracy in the assumption that mutations which seem to be repeated necessarily occur at the same locus.

During the formative years of genetics, a gene was thought to be associated with a single, specific locus of a chromosome. Mutants which had similar phenotypes, as phenotypes are described, were considered to involve the same, single locus if the mutants met accepted tests for allelism. This strict opinion is no longer acceptable.

A series of mutants involving the lozenge (lz) locus on the X-chromosome of *Drosophila melanogaster* have been discovered. The several mutants function in a similar manner in that they affect the roughness of the surface and the pigmentation of the eye. These are the most easily detected differences in comparison with normal characters, but each mutant also causes the alteration of a number of other structures of the body (Oliver, 1947). With one exception, though, each of the mutants which were studied could be easily distinguished by its phenotype from the other alleles in the classical sense in that females heterozygous for two of the mutants were not normal, or non-mutant. Yet in a series of tests using females heterozygous for spectacle (lz^s), and glossy (lz^g), crossing over occurred between the two alleles (Oliver, 1940). Homozygous spectacle and glossy have very distinct differences in eye color and structure, and heterozygous spectacle/glossy females can be distinguished from either homozygote although they are somewhat similar to glossy.

The heterozygous females were mated to glossy males. Only mutant types of progeny were expected, but two per 1000 of them had normal eyes, and examination established that they were normal for all other characters affected by the mutants. The reversions to normal were always associated with crossing over as shown by marker genes located on each side of the lz locus. It was presumed that crossing over occurred between the two alleles. Later, Green and Green (1949) made studies of several lozenge alleles and proved that three separate loci in the lozenge gene were involved. In other words, the gene involves an area or a region of the chromosome, not a single locus in the classical sense.

Clusters of genes having similar functions and reacting phenotypically as though each cluster represents multiple alleles of a single gene have been reported in several organisms. For animals, three examples will be mentioned. Lewis (1942, 1945, 1951, 1955) and Green (1955) have discussed the data for a number of cases in *Drosophila*. Dunn (1956) has reported the evidence on a series of genes, *t* alleles, in mice which affect the tail and other traits. Dunn states that evidence is lacking that any of the alleles of independent origin are identical. In man, the Rhesus series of genes affecting the Rh (CDE) antigens are considered by some investigators to be located close together in an area of a chromosome.

Mutations make possible new forms of genes which give material for differentiation of members of species into races. Mutations, however, cannot be looked upon as the only source for change. The suggestion has been made that the mutation rate in mankind is much too slow to be the important factor in formation of racial differences, particularly when one considers the short period of time involved (Krogman, in Linton, 1945).

Although the mutation rate alone most likely is not adequate to account for all differences, it is hardly advisable to consider the total mutation rate to be slow. Any one gene will mutate spontaneously only once in several thousand cells. If all genes of an organism are considered, however, the total rate is high.

Duplications of chromosomes or of parts of chromosomes increase the number of available genes which might be important as a source for changes. In animals, this phenomenon cannot be depended upon to give much lasting variability. Duplications resulting in an abnormal genetic balance tend to reduce viability of the organism. A small duplication, though, may persist and give no evidence of damage to the animal.

Mutant genes in the genome of an animal are a basis for interaction with various other genes. The interaction may produce different phenotypes and alter viability. Dobzhansky and his associates have made studies of genetic variability through recombination (Dobzhansky, Levene, Spassky, and Spassky, 1959; Spiess and Allen, 1961). Spiess and Allen working with *Drosophila melanogaster* as laboratory populations found a wide spread of viability, including a high percentage of lethals, due to recombination of chromosomes. Dobzhansky (in Roberts and Harrison, 1959) has made the suggestion that genetic variability depends on recombination to a greater extent than on recurrent mutations, at least in organisms with genetic structures similar to those in *Drosophila*.

Similar Phenotypes With Different Genes

SIMILAR PHENOTYPES sometimes involve different genes or genotypes. They may occur as mimics as a result of mutations at different loci (Patterson and Stone, 1952). In *Drosophila virilis*, mutant vermillion on the X-chromosome and also mutant cardinal on the fourth chromosome lack brown pigment in the eyes, each gene controlling the production of kynurenine which is necessary for pigment development. *Drosophila melanogaster* has one mutant gene on the X-chromosome which causes almost complete absence of any pigment, resulting in white eyes. The same phenotype will appear in flies that are homozygous for two autosomal genes, scarlet and brown.

Two members of a cluster of genes, those called multiple alleles in the past, can produce identical phenotypes. More complete study, though, can show that the genic actions are not completely identical. In the lozenge series, spectacle (lz^s) and spectacle-Bishop (lz^{sB}) are indistinguishable in that each affects all of the several characters related to the lozenge effects, and to exactly the same extent (Cummings, 1946; Oliver and Cummings, 1947). Eyes are glassy smooth, lacking facets, with an appearance of light brown pigment except for a rim of red color. Heterozygous lz^s/lz^{sB} females are identical to either homozygote, even in cellular structure of the eyes as shown by histological sections (Clayton, 1954). Nevertheless, lz^s and lz^{sB} differ in their interactions with lozenge (lz). In females lz/lz^s, the eyes are almost normal in phenotype (Oliver and Green, 1944) whereas lz/lz^{sB} females have a phenotype intermediate between homozygous lz and homozygous lz^{sB}.

Some of the "identical" hemoglobin mutants in man are not the same even though first descriptions so classified them. Ingram (1961) referred to three hemoglobin-D variants. They have the same motility, and by this electrophoretic behavior alone the several D hemoglobins would be considered identical. Peptide analyses have shown that they are quite distinct. They do not have the same molecular identity. One hemoglobin-D involves a chemical change in the alpha chain. Two others are associated with the beta chain but involve alterations at different positions. Another hemoglobin-D, reported by Bowman and Ingram (1961), may be identical to one of the known beta types.

Different amino acid substitutions have also been established for G hemoglobins. Honolulu-G and Philadelphia-G involve substitutions at non-identical positions in the alpha chain. San Jose-G involves the beta chain (Sutton, 1961). Bowman, Moreland, and Schneider (1962) have recently reported another G-hemoglobin, Galveston-G, which involves the beta chain but at a position different from the one associated with San Jose-G.

Presumably S hemoglobins as so far identified in the United States and in Africa have molecular identity. Hemoglobin-S has been reported occurring in several other areas of the world. This could mean that the variant has risen by mutation more than once. More information about the molecular structure of the hemoglobin found in the various areas may show that these similar phenotypes are not always identical.

Ingram (1961) and Allison (in Harrison, 1961) have called attention to possible dangers if anthropologists use rare, abnormal hemoglobins as racial markers. Any case of similar phenotype involving separate mutations must stand the test for being identical. Observers usually choose the most striking character to identify a mutant. Similarity can therefore be misleading.

Natural Selection and Adaptation

EVERY INDIVIDUAL faces selective forces which act to alter his genetic constitution and to mold him. Any structure is somehow a result of adaptation or response to selection, although the force will be effective in such manner as to develop the organism into a harmonious unit. Selection is made on genotypes rather than on the individual characters, and brings about the most favorable combination of the genotype for the existing circumstances (Howells, 1959; Penrose, in Roberts and Harrison, 1959).

Patterson and Stone (1952) discuss in some detail the numerous experiments carried on by Dobzhansky and co-workers, showing the relationship between genetic differences and natural selection. The remarkable story is worthy of reading for anyone who is interested in genetic variability. Gene rearrangements as evidenced by chromosomal alterations respond to niches in nature and to changes in surrounding circumstances. In some localities, rearrangement had different properties than in other localities. Frequency of an arrangement was related to the altitude of the locality and to other conditions. Gene arrangements from different populations were found to have different selective values.

Genes vary in their response to environment. This can be seen especially with genes which are autonomous with respect to the other genes in the genome. Some genotypes bring about their related phenotype under all known external conditions while the others may produce different phenotypes if external conditions vary.

Genes which control the development of a trait may have their actions altered in response to a particular environmental agent. The vestigial gene (vg) in *Drosophila melanogaster* causes the absence, or almost complete absence, of wings. Ordinarily it is recessive to the gene for normal, or non-vestigial, wing. Homozygous vg can be made to exert an influence on wing development so as to result in the production of wings which approach normal if temperature control is exerted at the proper time in larval development (Narnly, 1936). The dominant homozygote produces normal wings regardless of temperature.

It is possible, though, to bring about an effect of vg in a heterozygote by use of modifying genes. Green (1946) and Green and Oliver (1940) used minute genes to prolong the instar periods of development and found that under those circumstances heterozygous vestigial brought about scalloping and notching of the wings, in some cases to an extreme degree. If by small duplications an extra vg was added to the genotype, prolongation caused even more extreme reduction in the wings where only one vg^+, or normal, gene was present. In this sense, therefore, the gene vg

cannot be said to be autonomous from the other genes in the genotype.

Development, then, is a result of interaction between the genotype and the environment. We know too little about this phase of genetics, that associated with development. Even less is known about developmental genetics as applied to man.

Natural selection acts on the basis of the reproductive fitness of an individual. An organism with the best genotypic complex, one which permits him to survive longer and to be more fertile, will be the parent of a greater number of progeny of the next generation. His genes will enrich the gene pool in contrast to his competitor who has a less favorable genotype. This is not saying, of course, that the genes retained in greater numbers are necessarily those one might choose as being ideal. Net fertility is the measure of fitness, i.e., not total number of progeny, but the number which reach the mean age which the parents reproduced (Clarke, in Roberts and Harrison, 1959).

Penrose (in Roberts and Harrison, 1959) suggests that mate selection as well as relative fitness and genotype frequencies may alter natural selection. Inbreeding and assortive matings in man tend to increase the proportion of homozygotes. Whether this modification in relative genotypic frequencies brings about more or fewer of the advantageous combinations, the effect will be to increase the speed of selection.

Pleiotropism and Genetic Unbalance

GENES ACT BY the control of biochemical processes. They produce or influence an enzyme which is effective in metabolism. We do not know definitely whether a gene controls only one or more than one biochemical process. It is a question as to how many tissues the gene helps to control. Some genes show a pleiotropic effect and cause more than one part of the body to be modified. But pleiotropism is currently recognized by the end product of development. Possibly one process is controlled to effect these body variants.

In man recent investigations have shown that some multi-system defects are apparently due to genetic unbalance, where a whole or a part of a chromosome is duplicated. Not every case of multiple defects in man can be considered, however, as related to chromosomal abnormalities. Hereditary syndromes are known for which the interpretation of a single gene-pair involvement can be made. One example is the Laurence-Moon-Bardet-Biedl syndrome involving skeletal defects, obesity, hypogenitalism, and mental deficiency.

Other organisms are known to have genes which have pleiotropic effects. In *Drosophila*, at least, it is possible to establish the fact that a gene has manifold effects. The gene vg affects not only the wings, but also the balancers. Absence of pigment in the eyes is the most striking effect of gene w, but some of the mutants of the locus also affect the internal reproductive structures of the female.

The lozenge series is a most striking example of manifold effects of a gene because so many characters are altered by the sex-linked, recessive gene. Each allele affects the eyes, claws and pulvilli, and internal genitalia of females, as well as other traits (Oliver, 1947). Presumably one developmental process is involved and this is a failure or cessation of cellular differentiation. Lack of development of the female genital ducts can be traced to a point in differentiation where growth stops (Anderson, 1945).

Pleiotropic effects of the gene lozenge have been shown to be related to a single locus (or cluster). Isogenic strains were used, as has been reported. Salivary gland chromosomes are normal in quantity and quality. An unreported case of a lozenge-like mutant in *Drosophila virilis* also showed externally the multiple effects found with the lozenge gene in *Drosophila melanogaster*.

Potential selective pressure against the lozenge gene can be detected in at least two of the multiple effects of the gene, viability and fertility. The observations indicate that a single mutant gene can be a factor in selection, although one should not reason that selection in every set of circumstances is on a single gene rather than on the genotype as a complex. Mutant spectacle (lz^s) has a low life expectancy, at least under ordinary laboratory conditions. This effect of the gene seems to be secondary. The claws on the feet are small and weak and the pulvilli are almost completely absent.

Under regular culture conditions, the flies have difficulty pulling themselves from the pupal case. Even if they emerge, they often get caught in the food and die because with the abnormal pulvilli they cannot climb on glass. Under altered circumstances where very dry food conditions are used, spectacle males and females survive (show emergence) in great numbers and live for several days.

Another secondary effect of the lozenge gene in *Drosophila* shows how one gene may sometimes be a factor in reduction of fertility. Females homozygous for any one of the alleles were considered sterile until more detailed studies were made of them. Fertility is greatly reduced and, as has been stated, the females lack parts of the genital ducts. Sperm are stored in the tubular receptacle of the female but very quickly those sperm lose motility (Anderson, 1945). The effects seem to be related to the abnormal ducts. Females continue to produce eggs in great numbers but eggs are fertilized only for a few hours after insemination. New sperm, if added, will again give viable zygotes but only for a brief period of time (Oliver and Anderson, 1945).

The Effects of Interaction

GENES IN THEIR control of variation in an organism differ in their degrees of effect. Some genes exert a strong, individual influence on development of a trait, whether it is a variant within a race or is a racial difference. These genes may, of course, be responsive to selective agents. Even though the genotype as a whole may be the combination which responds to an environmental agent, one gene can make the difference between whether the organism benefits or suffers harm from a particular environment.

This relationship is shown between certain genes for blood types and the response of an organism to disease. Aird and Bentall (1953) reported evidence that blood groups in man are closely related to the tendency for cancer of the stomach to occur.

Antigen A existed in the patients more often than would be expected on the basis of relative blood group frequencies in the population. Subsequently a number of investigators in different countries have reported on the relationship between ABO blood groups and diseases. Some of the results have been summarized by Roberts (1959). In most of the reports, the frequency of group A in gastric cancer patients was higher than in control cases, and the frequency of group O was lower. Duodenal ulceration showed an opposite relationship, with the frequency of group O being higher than group A in patients.

Buckwalter and Tweed (1962) have investigated the Rh and MN blood types among individuals having several diseases. They reported a significantly higher frequency of duodenal and gastric ulcer patients having the R^1R^2 genotype than would be expected by chance. There was strong evidence also of a relationship between the Rhesus blood groups and gastric cancer. Apparently the only strong association between the MN genotypes and disease is the occurrence of homozygous N in rheumatic fever cases.

Experimental geneticists have for a long time recognized that gene control alone does not govern the characters or traits of an organism. They attempt to control the environment in any genetic tests made in the laboratory by subjecting the experimental and control cultures to the same conditions except one that might be under study. Investigations with so-called pure lines made soon after the rediscovery of Mendelism called attention to environmental effects on organisms as well as showed that heredity must be given consideration.

Within a given line, variability among progeny occurred even though the line was genetically as homogenous as selection could make it. These differences were to a considerable extent the effect of environment. A second line was as variable as the other but the average measurements of the two lines were distinctly different. The between line differences can be considered due to heredity. One genotype can cause an organism to develop farther along a given direction than can a second genotype under the same environmental conditions.

In some instances the effect on one gene by other genes in the genotype is not easy to detect except under specific circumstances. The modifiers may be suppressor genes which increase the effect of the major gene. Examples of such action are numerous in experimental organisms.

Man also has an interesting gene interaction involving the ABO and the Rh blood systems. Incompatibility for the ABO system seems to offer some protection against erythroblastosis due to Rh incompatibility. An O, Rh-negative woman having an A, Rh-positive child is less likely to be sensitized to the Rh antigen than is true where no ABO incompatibility exists (Levine, 1958).

Gene interaction can be effective in preventing the loss or rapid loss of one gene by, in a sense, protecting it from the environment. Contrariwise, a gene in its customary combination with the other genes in the pool can lose its beneficial effects if other alleles are brought into the pool. It is true that little evidence is available to support that opinion. It is just as true that very few investigations on the matter have been made except possibly on the easily observed, overall phenotype.

An important consideration about genic differences between two races is the nature of the genes involved. A trait, or character, will sometimes develop because of a single or a pair of mutant genes. Actually, multiple genes function together to cause any general trait as it is described. If the trait is a variant one, and more than one mutant gene is involved the character is likely to be a blend, in a sense, of the several individual gene actions. On the other hand, if the trait is not considered mutant for the population unit, the fact that several genes are functioning to produce the general trait will be recognized only if mutants occur.

Interacting genes do not necessarily have the same degree of effect on the trait. If the interacting genes individually have small effects, the action of any one gene will at best be difficult to measure. Quantitative characters do exist. Two population units sometimes differ in quantitative characters and since such traits do not segregate and are not too suitable for genetical analysis, the study of them in racial differences is far from a simple task.

Systematists consider another order of gene action in bringing about changes of evolutionary significance. These are polygenes, those genes with small individual effects but acting similarly in the production of the trait. Unquestionably polygenes are important enough to be given consideration in genetical studies. They have an important place in genic balance and in adaptation. It is hardly accurate to conclude that differences between human races are dependent on polygenic combinations. Genes having more measurable and striking effects on the morphology of an individual cannot be ignored.

Man and Evolutionary Processes

MAN IS SOMETIMES given special consideration in discussions of evolutionary processes. The statement is made that man now is free of natural selection. Penrose (in Roberts and Harrison, 1959) expressed an opinion that the belief that natural selection in man has been abolished by civilization, or culture, is based on superficial reasoning. The evolution of culture has placed man in a position to exert some control over his environment and to adapt his altered genotype to the culture in which he lives. He can reduce or increase the selective value of a genotype.

The human organism is plastic and is responsive to environmental conditioning. Unfortunately some individuals take an extreme point of view and go on the assumption that culture is the only circumstance to be considered. In effect man has the potentiality to develop within a range rather than be limited to a single expression of a genotype (Shapiro, in Linton, 1945). Yet there is a limit to this flexibility.

In so far as genes are effective in governing an individual's response to an environment, members of any race should differ in their reaction to their common culture. Population units, or races, have different gene pools. They should under the same circumstances be expected to respond differently to an environment, or a common culture. The differences may show as different rates of fertility, or viability, or in other ways.

In studies of population genetics, investigators have determined the distribution of particular characters, and therefore, genotypes. The reports have sometimes included data about environmental conditions which presumably are associated with the characters. Some traits are world-wide in their distributions. All races have the traits but the allelic frequencies may differ for the gene pools. The ABO blood types are typical of this kind of distribution. In a similar manner, serum proteins, hemoglobins, intellectual capacity, and other general groups of traits occur among all racial groups. In some cases, though, variant types are not so widely distributed.

Variant hemoglobins may occur only in some racial groups or in relatively small areas of a region occupied by one race. Hemoglobin-S occurs with high frequency in some areas of central Africa. It also is found, with a lesser frequency, in regions around the Mediterranean Sea and in certain groups in Arabia and India. Other areas of the world seem to be free of S hemoglobin except where migration has introduced it.

Geneticists are interested in the causes of the scattered distribution of the gene Hb^s and in the different frequencies with which it occurs in the various regions of the world. An environmental agent, malaria, is thought to be an effective selector in favor of the heterozygote in comparison to either of the homozygotes. Resistance of the heterozygote to malignant malaria is stronger than in those individuals homozygous for non-sickle, A hemoglobin. The resistance also compensates for the loss of the Hb^s gene in homozygous sickle hemoglobin individuals (Allison, in Harrison, 1961). Livingstone (1958) has given an explanation for the frequency differences in sickle hemoglobin in areas of Africa. It is related to the progress of agriculture in equatorial forest regions which resulted in conditions favorable to the mosquito.

The spread or appearance of S hemoglobin in other areas of the world cannot be explained very easily. Allison (in Harrison, 1961) questions the use of the distribution of S hemoglobin as an indication of waves of migration, or the use of relative frequencies to estimate the contribution of one population to another group. Gene Hb^s would be expected to remain in an area only because malaria was present, that being the powerful selective force operating on genotype $Hb^s Hb^A$.

Some migrants into new regions have retained a high frequency of the gene. The Black Carib (Firschein, 1961) were native Africans who were taken into the Caribbean area. They were shipwrecked and for a time lived on an island until they eventually reached the mainland. Now there are pockets of descendants who live culturally separated from the other inhabitants of the area. Each pocket has its own individual frequency of Hb^s, but many show a very high frequency. Malaria can be a factor in the retention of the gene.

If migration cannot account for the widely distributed pockets of sickle hemoglobin over the world, other interpretations must be made. Mutations might account for the different centers. Malaria as a selective agent in the regions would be surmised and probably correctly so, provided the mutant genes were identical or responded alike to the environmental agent. As was discussed in an earlier part, though, recurrent mutants which seem to be identical may prove not to be the same if detailed studies are made of them.

Genetic drift as a means to account for Hb^s frequency differences cannot be ignored. It will result in variations in frequency in a finite population due to sampling errors. In a small population, drift can result in change in gene frequency over a period of time. The known relationship between $Hb^s Hb^A$ and malaria causes one to question whether genetic drift can be used to explain frequency differences. It is also true that current knowledge of the relationship between ABO blood groups and diseases raises a question about the advisability of depending upon genetic drift to explain frequency differences of those blood groups.

More Knowledge of Genes and Human Races Needed

RACIAL GENOTYPIC differences in organisms with a genetic system similar to *Drosophila* are readily recognizable. This is particularly true for chromosomal variants. Morphological characters may distinguish one race from the other as is true for giant *montana* and standard *montana*. Phenotypes are given as marker characters in recognition of many species. Human races differ phenotypically, also, although members within one race show wide diversity. Traits requiring closer examination for recognition are now being discovered and will result in more complete data for population studies.

Polygenes, as they are understood, will in total effect influence the balance involved in species and in race differentiation. The opinion that multiple genes each having a small individual effect on a trait are of primary importance can inhibit to a considerable extent the study of population genetics if it is followed too strictly. With current methods available, the effects of a gene in the polygene series are difficult to study although methods being developed should be helpful in the future.

Genetics has not developed from the study of phenotypes as a whole, nor in attempts to limit the study to traits caused by multiple factors. Genetical investigations begin with a variant type. Analysis of the mutant leads to an understanding about the action of the responsible gene, the relationship of the gene to different genotypic combinations, and the effect of environmental agents on the action of the gene. By this method, a phenotype is broken up into discernible parts for more detailed examination.

Little is known about races in field animals. Even less is known about races in mankind. Arguments are plentiful but not too convincing. Agreements are certainly not an ordinary event. The study of race in modern man has been an undesired performance for many geneticists who are well-trained for the work. As a consequence, observations have been inadequate for scientific purposes and a well-developed body of real biological knowledge about human races is absent or at least meager (Howells, 1959). Studies of human races are also complicated by emotion and distrust. With man being the animal that he is, maybe we should not expect anything else. With man being intelligent and wanting to know the truth, we are justified in expecting something else.

Geneticists should want to know the facts about the genetical patterns in human racial groups. Some similarities obviously exist because all men are members of the same species. They carry identical genes although many of the genes are allelic in form and not the same in all populations. Where similarities are present, that information should be made known and the studies continued from that basis. Also, differences between races can be expected to occur. Races which since the origin of man have occupied different regions will have differences (Howells, 1959). Biological laws are responsible for them.

Where differences exist, this should be made known so that more study can be carried on. Some data are on hand but more information is needed if a scientific understanding of racial differences is to be had. In order to have sufficient information, more variants caused by single gene differences (or multiple gene involvement if that can be measured) must be studied to determine the distribution, selective value and response of the altered genotype to various environments. For many years, traits available for the studies were rather scarce.

New methods for study of genes and gene action have opened up new avenues of approach to the problem. The progress in biochemical genetics can be expected to increase our knowledge even more than one could have anticipated just a few years ago. This method can become helpful in the studies of normal traits which have a wide range of expression, such as human intelligence. It can eventually lead to methods for understanding adaptation to environmental agents and possibly response to selective pressures. If it proves to be desirable, an environment most suitable to a given genotype can be selected.

There is still the question as to who will make the necessary detailed and time consuming studies. Now with the newer procedures, a young individual can devote himself to the study of human genetics. He can get results and recognition without the delay that human geneticists have faced in the past. The work will be most fruitful if it comes from the efforts of those who are interested in the problem for scientific reasons and who can conduct the research dispassionately. There are those among geneticists and those in other fields who can meet the challenge if they will.

Literature

Aird, I., and H. H. Bentall, Relationship between cancer of the stomach and the ABO blood groups. *British Medical Journal*, 1: 799–807, 1953.

Anderson, R. C., A study of the factors affecting fertility of lozenge females of *Drosophila melanogaster. Genetics*, 30: 280–296, 1945.

Bowman, B. H., and V. M. Ingram, Abnormal human haemoglobins. VII: The comparison of normal human haemoglobin and haemoglobin D. *Biochimica et Biophysica Acta.*, 53: 569–573, 1961.

———, J. H. Moreland, and R. G. Schneider, A new haemoglobin variant, haemoglobin G. *Nature, 193:* 1298–1300, 1962.

Buckwalter, J. A., and G. V. Tweed, The Rhesus and MN blood groups and disease. *Journal American Medical Association, 179:* 479–485, 1962.

Clayton, F. E., Phenotypic abnormalities of the eye of lozenge compounds in *Drosophila melanogaster*. *University of Texas Publication 5422:* 189–209, 1954.

Cummings, K., *A study of a series of multiple alleles at the lozenge locus in Drosophila melanogaster*. Minneapolis, 1946.

Dobzhansky, T., *Evolution, Genetics, and Man*. New York, 1955.

———, H. Levene, B. Spassky, and N. Spassky, Release of genetic variability through recombination: III *Drosophila prosaltans*. *Genetics, 44:* 75–92, 1959.

Firschein, I. L., Population dynamics of the sickle-cell trait in the Black Caribs of British Honduras, Central America. *American Journal Human Genetics, 13:* 233–254, 1961.

Green, M. M., A study in gene action using different dosages and alleles of vestigial in *Drosophila melanogaster*. *Genetics, 31:* 1–20, 1946.

———, Pseudoallelism and the gene concept. *American Naturalist, 89:* 65–71, 1955.

———, and K. C. Green, Crossing over between alleles at the lozenge locus in *Drosophila melanogaster*. *Proceedings National Academy of Sciences, 35:* 586–591, 1949.

———, and C. P. Oliver, The action of certain mutants upon the penetrance of heterozygous vestigial wing in *Drosophila melanogaster*. *Genetics, 25:* 584–592, 1940.

Harnly, M. H., The temperature-effective periods and the growth curves for length and area of the vestigial wings of *Drosophila melanogaster*. *Genetics, 21:* 84–103, 1936.

Harrison, G. A. (Editor), *Genetical Variation in Human Populations*. Oxford, 1961.

Howells, W., *Mankind in the Making*. New York, 1959.

Ingram, V. M., *Hemoglobin and Its Abnormalities*. Springfield, 1961.

Levine, P., The influence of the ABO system on Rh hemolytic disease. *Human Biology, 30:* 14–28, 1958.

Lewis, E. B., The star and asteroid loci in *Drosophila melanogaster*. *Genetics, 27:* 134–154, 1942.

Lewis, E. B., The relation of repeats to position effect in Drosophila melanogaster. Genetics, 39: 137–166, 1945.
———, Pseudoallelism and gene evolution. Cold Spring Harbor Symposia on Quantitative Biology, 16: 159–174, 1951.
———, Some aspects of position pseudoallelism. American Naturalist, 89: 73–89, 1955.
Linton, Ralph (Editor), The Science of Man in the World Crisis. New York, 1945.
Livingstone, F. B., Anthropological implications of sickle cell distribution in West Africa. American Anthropologist, 60: 533–562, 1958.

Mann, J. D., A. Cahan, A. G. Gelb, N. Fisher, J. Hamper, P. Tippett, R. Sanger, and R. R. Race, A sex-linked blood group. Lancet, 1(7219): 8–10, 1962.
Moorhead, P. S., Chromosome variation in giant forms of Drosophila montana. University of Texas Publication 5422: 106–129, 1954.

Oliver, C. P., A reversion to wild-type associated with crossing-over in Drosophila melanogaster. Proceedings Nat. Acad. Sci., 26: 452–454, 1940.
———, Interrelationship between eye color and facet arrangement in lozenge alleles of Drosophila melanogaster. University of Texas Publication 4720: 167–184, 1947.
———, and R. C. Anderson, The effect of rematings on the fecundity of an infertile mutant female. American Naturalist, 79: 89–94, 1945.
———, and K. C. Cummings, Dominance and interaction effects of four isogenic lozenge alleles in Drosophila melanogaster. Anatomical Record, 99: 629, 1947.
———, and M. M. Green, Heterosis in compounds of lozenge alleles in Drosophila melanogaster. Genetics, 29: 331–347, 1944.

Patterson, J. T., and W. S. Stone, Evolution in the Genus Drosophila. New York, 1952.

Roberts, D. F., and J. A. Fraser, Some associations between blood groups and disease. British Medical Bulletin, 15: 129–133, 1959.
———, and G. A. Harrison (Editors), Natural Selection in Human Populations. Oxford, 1959.

Spiess, E. B., and A. C. Allen, Release of genetic variability through recombinations: VII. Second and third chromosomes of Drosophila melanogaster. Genetics, 46: 1531–1553, 1961.
Stone, W. S., W. C. Guest, and F. D. Wilson, The evolutionary implications of the cytological polymorphism and phylogeny of the virilis group of Drosophila. Proceedings Nat. Acad. Sci., 46: 350–361, 1960.
Sutton, H. E., Genes, Enzymes, and Inherited Diseases. New York, 1961.

BIOGRAPHICAL NOTE

ROBERT E. KUTTNER, M.A., Ph.D., *is Research Associate in Biochemistry in the Department of Obstetrics and Gynecology at the University of Chicago. He joined the faculty in 1965.*

Before he assumed his present position Dr. Kuttner was at Creighton University for five years, where he was also a Research Associate in Biochemistry. Before that he was engaged in brain chemistry and brain physiology research at the Institute of Living, Hartford, Conn. He has also served as a research assistant at the University of Connecticut and as a member of the research staff at the Brookhaven National Laboratory, Long Island, N.Y.

Dr. Kuttner is a contributing editor of the Mankind Quarterly, *an international journal dealing with the various sciences related to the races of man, and is the author of articles and reviews in the fields of physiological chemistry, neurochemistry, biology, psychology and anthropology, which have been published in various scientific journals.*

He is a member of the American Association for the Advancement of Science, the British Eugenics Society, the International Institute of Sociology, the Nebraska Academy of Science, the New York Academy of Science, and the American Eugenics Society.

BIOCHEMICAL ANTHROPOLOGY

Robert E. Kuttner

THE LINK BETWEEN physical anthropology and biochemistry at first glance may appear remote. It can be readily established, however, that many of the classical sorting criteria of anthropology are based on manifestations of chemical activity. Skin color helps distinguish the primary races and it is evident that the quantity of pigment is a chemical parameter. Stature is also regarded as an anthropological index. Yet it is well known that human height is partly determined by endocrine functions which once again involve measurable amounts of body chemicals. With these examples in mind, the claim that biochemistry may be promising as a tool to aid in the classification of populations is seen to deserve serious consideration.

The application of biochemical methods to anthropology can greatly stimulate progress in this field. Race taxonomies in the past depended almost exclusively on the descriptive anatomy of skin and bone. Pigmentation, osteometric constants, and eye, nose, and hair form provided the principal items in every scheme of classification. Somewhat inadvertently anthropologists made skin and bone the sole measures of man. But despite all the permutations and combinations of these two elements, over 75 percent of the body mass was left out of the calculations. With fossil remains, this was unavoidable; with living races, it was inexcusable. The body contains many thousands of substances, some of which most certainly vary in quantity or type with ethnic identity. In this light it is regrettable to note how rarely until recent years tissue or blood studies were employed in anthropological research.

Before the domain of biochemical anthropology is marked out, recognition must be given to some contrary views of the eminent biochemist, Professor Roger J. Williams. In a lecture published under the title "Chemical Anthropology—An Open Door" (Williams, 1958), he strongly emphasized the chemical individuality of every human, and repeatedly called attention to the tremendous variability of biological and biochemical constants even when so called "normal" ranges are considered. Recognition of the diversity, or as better described, the individuality of life is blurred by the existing tendency to reduce wide ranges of data to statistical averages (Williams, 1956, 1960a, 1960b).

The protest against this practice is fully justified, especially when the fact of distortion is forgotten in the casual use or citation of an artificial constant. But it is true that nature always suffers a distortion when abstractions are created. To complain against idealized abstractions is to complain against the method of science. A perfect gas no more exists than an average man. Yet the former concept is indispensable to physical chemists, and the latter is of considerable service to social scientists. Real phenomena are invariably blurred by abstractions but as compensation we often obtain more precise mathematical or logical models to guide our thinking. To renounce mathematical summaries in sciences such as psychology and biology is to retreat into chaos. Statistics may disguise fine differences but they can also reduce the anarchy of raw data to manageable proportions.

The ensuing sections survey some of the known biochemical "constants" characterizing humanity. The immediate hope, of course, is to discover finer sub-constants that can be added to the taxonomic tools of anthropology. This approach, the use of chemical taxonomic criteria, has been applied with moderate success to the field of biology as a whole. The techniques employed in comparative biochemistry may be illustrated by examples drawn from one pioneering volume devoted to this topic (Florkin, 1959).

Biochemical Methods and Techniques

CHEMICAL ANATOMISTS have found that vertebrates can be distinguished from invertebrates by determining the monovalent-divalent ion ratio in body fluids. The ratio is two or more times higher for vertebrates. Furthermore, the energy reservoir for vertebrate metabolism resides in a compound called phosphocreatine, while for the more primitive phyla a different chemical called phosphoarginine is usually found. Thus, both quantitative and qualitative chemical criteria are available to aid zoologists. The above is a simple problem with which taxonomists need no assistance. With certain transitional life-forms, however, chemical data have been of value in tracing evolutionary connections.

It is well recognized that human chemistry is influenced by many factors—diet, season, climate, age, sex, disease, stress, and exercise—to list only the obvious ones. These factors make data interpretation difficult but it is encouraging to note that physical anthropology has survived similar limitations. Sorting criteria for anthropologists include items like stature and pigmentation, qualities known to be influenced by diet and climate. This has not invalidated these criteria but merely refined their application. Similarly, biochemistry must find a way to separate the stable genetic elements from the superimposed environmental influences before its data can serve the purposes of classification.

Counter-balancing the variability mentioned above is a remarkable homeostasis which characterizes all living things. This homeostasis keeps within narrow ranges many important chemical constituents of the body. Blood salinity and acidity, for examples, scarcely show any variation, though with these factors even small changes can be significant to health. Between the ephemeral statistics of individual differences and the rigidity of homeostasis lies the territory of biochemical anthropology.

Biochemical "constants," when processed down to the irreducible minimum variation, are destined to be more erratic than conventional anthropological data in that they may reflect transient metabolic states. Classical anthropologists have the happy assurance that after their specimens attain full growth their metrical indices remain unchanged. This naturally cannot apply to biochemical anthropology since it is not dead bone but metabolizing tissue which is being studied and classified. The difficulties are greater but the results promise to be infinitely more rewarding.

Biochemical anthropology is interwoven with clinical chemistry and every small advance may contribute profoundly to the diagnosis of disease. Physical anthropology, for much of its history, was allied only with anatomy, and it was more a passive recipient than an active contributor to medical knowledge.

Biochemical taxonomy deals with dynamic systems and it is apparent that standardized techniques are even more crucial than for its anatomical sister science. Before population and racial norms can be established, agreement has to be reached on laboratory methods that provide the most precise measurements. Uniform training, reagents, instruments, and techniques will do much to reduce the range of deviation in data reported from different laboratories. The need for improved standardization is made evident by a check on one hundred and seventy hospital laboratories in Canada. Over 40 percent of the tests carried out on "unknowns" were outside of the allowable limits for error (Tonks, 1963).

Nutritional Substances

IN A PRELIMINARY survey it is wise to omit biochemical substances that are chiefly derived from the diet. Interpretation of analyses of such substances would be very difficult from a taxonomic viewpoint. Vitamins and minerals enter into this category and for the purpose of this review must be left undiscussed. The same considerations probably apply also to the fluoride content of teeth though there is much interesting work on this subject.

In Boston, an area with low fluoride levels in the water supply, the enamel and dentin contained the expected low levels in teeth, 54 and 86 parts-per-million respectively. Comparisons with samples from five cities in India gave averages two to five times higher for enamel and three to eight times higher for dentin. Eskimos approximated Hindu values. Soldiers in Pakistan and Iran also had elevated dental fluoride. Since recruits were drawn from all parts of these countries and the likelihood of high fluoride concentrations in diet and drink in all these separate regions seems remote, a possibility exists that the deposition of fluoride may not be exclusively dependent on intake, as has been suggested (Shaw, et al., 1959), but may be modified by individually or racially determined rates of mineralization.

Anatomists are familiar with the effects of racial variation in mineralization of bone. According to a study on vertebrae, ribs, sacra, and limb bones, Negro skeletal material was appreciably denser than White samples except for ribs and tibiae (Trotter, et al., 1960). The fact of denser bones may account for the much lower incidence of hip fractures in the Negro female (Gyepes, et al., 1962). The role of nutrition in this case is uncertain. Negro school girls have been reported to consume more dietary calcium and phosphorus, the bone-forming elements, than adolescent White females (Wharton, 1963). A superior mineral diet can obviously contribute to bone strength.

On the other hand, individuals of Asiatic race have lighter, less compact skeletons than Caucasians (Garn, et al., 1964). Poor diet does not appear to be the factor behind this observation since diminished compact bone is present in both Asiatic-born Chinese and Japanese individuals and in American-born Asians, the latter group enjoying the nutritional abundance that characterizes a successful socio-economic class. In addition, children of mixed Chinese-Caucasian ancestry have intermediate values for compact bone. Race thus appears to clearly influence the body utilization of nutritional elements.

The type of body fat is considered to be a function of diet. Analyses of autopsy and surgical material from many parts of the world have been carried out and the findings related to diet intake. Jamaicans tend to have body fat rich in lauric and myristic acids due to ingesting coconuts with high concentrations of these substances (Hegsted, et al., 1962). Japanese fat contains long chain, twenty-carbon fatty acids due to the appreciable consumption of fish oils.

Cholesterol

CHOLESTEROL is a complex, solid alcohol which is generally classified as a fatty substance. It is the parent compound for many hormones in the body. Great importance is attached to cholesterol because when excess amounts are deposited on arterial walls, a degenerative condition called atherosclerosis results which is intimately related to high-mortality cardiovascular diseases. Cholesterol is of dual origin, partly synthesized by tissues and partly obtained from the diet.

It is known from family and twin studies that cholesterol levels in the blood are determined by both genetic and environmental factors (Schaefer, et al., 1958; Adlersberg, et al., 1959). Monozygotic twins living together show little scatter in their serum cholesterol values (Meyer, 1962). Even when monozygotic twins live apart and are exposed to presumably different diets and environments, the variance between pairs is no greater or is less than the variance for dizygotic twins living together.

So far it has not been possible to sort out completely genetic, dietary, and other environmental influences (stress, exercise, etc.) on cholesterol blood concentrations though such factors along with age and sex are known to be extremely important.

Plasma cholesterol values for Europeans and White Americans may range from 50 to 100 percent higher than for non-Caucasians inhabiting backward areas. It is almost always found that differences between ethnic groups reflect socio-economic status. Upper class Nigerians, for example, have cholesterol levels comparable to Europeans (Edozien, 1958a). Increased prosperity usually implies a richer meat diet with a resulting elevation in body cholesterol. This may be seen in the decreasing difference between French and Moslem Algerians over the course of a generation as colonial progress improved the Moslem diet (Juillan, et al., 1960). Well nourished Asians living in Hawaii have cholesterol levels identical to Caucasians (Adamson, 1960).

Opposed to the large mass of data linking diet and cholesterol, there are reports of relatively low cholesterol values in Navajo

Indians despite a fat intake not much less than the American average (Gilbert, 1955; Page, et al., 1956). The implication of these reports was that the Navajo had genetic protection against diet-elevated cholesterol and its presumed correlate, coronary artery disease. The Navajo shows a number of other statistically significant differences in his serum lipids from normal Whites that may in part be accounted for by either a high incidence of tuberculosis or a relatively meager caloric diet (Kositchek, et al., 1961). A later study on other American Indians also gave cholesterol analyses lower than for Whites. However, a genetic or ethnic factor seems eliminated by the observation that full-blooded and mixed-ancestry Indians had similar cholesterol levels (Abraham and Miller, 1959).

The Eskimos represent another interesting ethnic group. These people consume unusually high amounts of meat (Heinbecker, 1928; Thomas, 1927). Yet evidence indicates that their cholesterol level is the same or lower than that of White North Americans (Alexander, 1949; Corcoran, et al., 1937; Sinclair, et al., 1949). This may perhaps be due to a special biochemical adaption.

Serum Proteins

SERUM PROTEINS offer promise as taxonomic aids. They are completely of endogenous origin, synthesized from the raw material of the diet. As such, they reflect the chemical activity of the body more directly than many other blood components. Various techniques of separation (chromatography, electrophoresis, salt fractionation) have been developed and have revealed quantitative and qualitative differences.

The main protein fractions are albumin, α_1-globulin, α_2-globulin, β-globulin, and γ-globulin. They are identified most readily by differential migration in an electrical field, albumin moving fastest and γ-globulin slowest. Certain refined modifications permit a further separation into additional protein subtypes.

Albumin, the main protein component, has occasionally been reported to vary in quantity according to racial group. The evidence is still incomplete but it appears probable that albumin levels reflect the adequacy of dietary protein intake (Bronte-Stewart, et al., 1961).

Twin studies carried out on Swedish, Danish, and Dutch pairs indicate that monozygotes usually resemble each other more closely in concentrations of various serum protein fractions than dizygotes (Leonhardt, 1962).

α2-Globulins are a diverse family of proteins that include the haptoglobins. This latter class of proteins are able to bind hemoglobin, the oxygen carrying substance of red cells. The clinical meaning of this fact is obscure but it has been noted that in some hemolytic anemias the serum haptoglobin content falls sharply. The function of these proteins may be to remove from circulation any hemoglobin released from fragmented red cells.

Two haptoglobin types have been distinguished, called Hp-1 and Hp-2. The heterozygous state (Hp 1-2) and an "ahaptoglobinemic" condition marked by the absence of the protein have also been identified. About 50 percent of native Africans from Nigeria, Liberia, and the Ivory Coast are homozygous for haptoglobin 1. Less than 10 percent show type 2 (Allison, et al., 1958; Sutton, et al., 1956; Neel, et al., 1961). Summarized statistics on Caucasians reveal that under 20 percent are homozygous type 1 and 30 percent or more are homozygous type 2 (Budtz-Olsen, 1958).

Racially mixed American Negroes are intermediate between Whites and Africans (Giblett, 1959). Australian aborigines are 20 percent or lower in type 2 individuals but different geographic populations may resemble high type 1 Negroes or low type 1 Caucasians (Budtz-Olsen, 1958). New Guinea Melanesians follow the African Negro pattern (Curtain, 1959). Central American Indians are about 35 percent homozygous type 1 and 15 percent homozygous type 2 (Sutton, et al., 1960).

Several reviews have given geographic clines for the haptoglobin-1 gene (Boyd, 1963; Parker and Bearn, 1961; Giblett, 1962). India and Ceylon report the lowest frequencies, ranging from 15 to 17 percent (Giblett, 1962). A small group of Indians living in Malaya had a frequency of only 9 percent (Steinberg, et al., 1961a). Radiating outward from the sub-continent to Pakistan,

Iran, Thailand, and Malaya, frequencies of 22–24 percent were encountered.

Chinese and Japanese on the Asian mainland, in Taiwan, or in America, had a frequency between 26 to 34 percent for the Hp-1 allele (Giblett, 1962, 1963; Parker and Bearn, 1961). Values for Polynesians were 45–60 percent; in New Guinea 64 percent, falling to 37 to 63 percent in Australian aborigines with a low of 17 percent found in the Western Desert. The gene frequency is 38 percent for a Filipino sample, intermediate between Oceanic and Asian values (Blackwell, et al., 1964).

As the Bering Straits are crossed, the frequency increases over Asian means to 33 percent for Alaskan Eskimo, 44 percent for Alaskan Indian, 45 to 60 percent for North American Indians, with Central American and Venezuelan frequencies of 53–59 percent, going to a high of 73–75 percent for Indians in Peru and Chile. A North-South gradient for the Hp-1 gene is evident in the Western Hemisphere.

Moving into Europe, values of 42 to 46 percent are found in many sample Caucasian populations from Poland to England, from Norway to Italy. In Africa, below the Sudan, frequencies range upward from 53 percent for the Zulu, 60 percent for the Congo, and 60–80 percent in Liberia and Nigeria. This also suggests a gradient reaching a peak in the wet, tropical fever areas. The Congo pygmy has a frequency of 40 percent, the South African Bushman below 30 percent.

No theory has explained the world distribution of haptoglobin gene types. What selective forces produced the existing pattern of gene gradients are unknown. Both Hp-1 and Hp-2 protein bind hemoglobin equally well so that a meaningful functional difference cannot be assigned to the action of either gene.

Primates other than man have haptoglobin-1 type serum proteins (Arends, 1960). In some primate sera, faint bands corresponding to haptoglobin-2 have been observed to occur along with the main Hp-1 protein band on electrophoretic separations. Nevertheless, this does not suggest primate Hp 1-2 heterozygosity since in the human heterozygote the bands for Hp-1 and Hp-2 are of the same intensity (Makela, 1960; Parker and Bearn, 1961).

Haptoglobin-1 appears to be the original primate gene which mutated to the Hp-2 form recently in human evolution. From the anthropological perspective the problem is extremely complex. Human populations possess both gene types but the frequencies vary for different ethnic and racial groups. By haptoglobin sorting, some populations may be classified but not individuals.

The β-globulins include a class of proteins called transferrins that have iron-binding properties. These proteins transport iron to the marrow and other storage sites and likewise carry out the reverse process. The various transferrins are distinguished by their mobilities in an electrical field. Transferrin C is the commonest protein of this class and is found in most populations with frequencies of over 90 percent. Faster migrating transferrins are called B. Those that move slower than C are called D.

A tabulation of published data indicates that Caucasians are about 99 percent homozygous CC, the heterozygous BC electrophoretic pattern accounting for the remaining 1 percent of the serum samples (Lai, 1961). Liberian Negroes are 92.5 percent CC and 6.9 percent CD, the frequency of the transferrin-C gene (Tf-C) being 96 percent (Neel, et al., 1961). In other African and American Negro populations the CD heterozygote occurs with a frequency of 3 to 10 percent and sometimes more (Lai, 1961; Parker and Bearn, 1961). The African Bushman is 87.6 percent CC, 11.5 percent CD and 0.9 percent DD; the Hottentot is 94.1 percent CC and 5.9 percent CD; the Zulu is 97.3 percent CC and 2.7 percent CD (Lai, 1961). Since the Hottentot is usually considered to be a hybrid race composed of Southern Bantu and Bushman elements, it is interesting to find that the Hottentot CD frequency is intermediate between Zulu and Bush values.

Australian Aborigines have been reported to be 55 to 78 percent CC and 41 to 22 percent CD, with 4 percent DD (Lai, 1961; Giblett, 1962). This calculates to Tf-C gene frequency estimates of 75 to 89 percent. Papuans from New Guinea are quite similar to Australians being 81–84 percent homozygous CC, around 16 percent heterozygous CD, and 3–8 percent homozygous DD. Alaskan and Canadian Eskimos are 100 percent CC (Giblett, 1962; Parker and Bearn, 1961). Chinese Americans, Formosans, and Chinese in Malaya show the CD heterozygote condition 6 percent, 4.3 per-

Biochemical Anthropology

cent, and 6.8 percent respectively, and Thailanders 7.2 percent (Parker and Bearn, 1961; Giblett, 1962; Lai, 1961). Central American Indians are 98–99 percent CC, and about 1 percent BC and 1 percent CD (Sutton, et al., 1960; Lai, 1961). In this last case, there is some possibility of admixture with Whites and Negroes. The Navajo Indian is 7.4 percent BC and the Venezuelan Yupa Indian (a Carib tribe) is 42 percent CD and 16 percent DD (Giblett, 1962; Arends and Gallango, 1964).

Biochemistry Findings and Racial Variations

THIS ARRAY of data does not permit ready anthropological interpretation. It seems that among the major races, the Caucasian varies least from the 99 percent CC homozygous condition, the Negro and Asian Mongol races being recorded as CD heterozygous with a frequency of 5–10 percent. A high frequency of variation from the CC homozygous state is common in the minor races and in marginal populations (Indians, Bushmen, Australasians). This may be due to the factor of genetic drift in small populations or to the necessity for extensive inbreeding in near-extinct populations.

It is also clear that since the minor races and marginal populations occupy less favorable habitats, different selective forces may operate on these groups with the end result that different transferrin types may be conserved for some still unguessed biochemical advantage. So far as is known, the different transferrin molecules are equally efficient in transporting iron (Giblett, 1962). Thus, some other function must be sought in the search for selective advantage.

Refined methodology has shown that the B and D transferrin proteins can be further subdivided on the basis of small differences in electrophoretic mobility. Thus, though Negro and Chinese may both be 5–10 percent CD heterozygous, the D transferrins in the blood are not the same. The Chinese transferrin, called Dchi, moves slightly faster than the Negro transferrin, called D_1 (Parker, et al., 1961). The Venezuelan Yupa Indian D protein is considered identical to the Chinese (Arends, 1964).

The Navajo B protein is also known to differ from the Caucasian B (Parker, et al., 1961), the former called B_0–1, the latter, B_2. Information is lacking on B and D forms of transferrin in other races and populations. The different rates of migration in electrical fields for these various transferrins are due to mutations that change a single amino acid in the protein molecules which in turn may change the electrical charge by a single ion.

It may be remarked that the transferrin picture among the lower primates is even more complex and obscure than among the human races, so no taxonomic help can be expected from this quarter.

The γ-globulin proteins are responsible for immunological protection against disease. High levels are believed to reflect exposure to disease. And since exposure is a function of life span, aged animals and humans tend to show elevated concentrations (Bronte-Stewart, et al., 1961; Larson, 1959; Suarez, et al., 1957). Negroes in as widely separated regions as Brazil (Medeiros Neto and Hoxter, 1960), the Netherland Antilles (Luyken, et al., 1959), and Nigeria (Edozien, 1958a, b), have greater γ-globulin serum contents than Whites. Inferior nutrition and medical care may be responsible for this difference. Before poor health exerts its influence, young Negro (Luyken, 1959) and Navajo children (Straus, et al., 1959) show γ-globulin concentration markedly below adult values. This "racial" difference can perhaps be explained by endemic tropical fevers and parasitic infestation, and a more complete history of sub-clinical diseases. Whites occupying the same habitat as Negroes also have raised γ-globulin levels (Luyken, et al., 1959).

The role of diet is also implicated. Liver damage caused by prolonged protein malnutrition is held by some to account for the Negro protein pattern. This explanation has not been accepted for the Nigerian sample (Edozien, 1958a, b), however, since natives with normal hepatic function still show low albumin and high γ-globulin. A genetic racial factor is thus not completely eliminated. The trend toward lower albumin values has appeared in other reports (Medeiros Neto, 1960; Luykens, 1959), but has not reached statistical significance upon analysis.

It is rather interesting to note that a report from a Negro

university questions the possible ethnic basis for γ-globulin differences (Johnson and Wong, 1961). Healthy Negro athletes were not found to have elevated γ-globulin levels. The sample was based on only seven Negro students. A more complete study of sixty-two healthy Caucasians and sixty-two healthy American Negroes once again confirmed serum protein differences with a probability of only one in one thousand that the variations found were due to chance (Pollak, et al., 1961). Serum albumin was low and γ-globulin was found to be high. The most recent studies on Brazilian and African Negroes confirm the earlier findings of high γ-globulin and low albumin (Trabulsi, et al., 1963; Passarello, 1964).

Perhaps the best current study was conducted on the Bantu, Cape Colored, and Europeans of the Cape Peninsula (Bronte-Stewart, et al., 1961). The Bantu had higher γ-globulin at all ranges of protein intake and at all ages. The Cape Colored, a hybrid group, were intermediate between the parent stocks. Since the Cape Colored subjects were also intermediate on the socioeconomic scale, which reflects itself in nutritional adequacy and quality of medical care, neither genetic nor environmental factors could be eliminated as determinants of serum protein for this group. The authors cite other reports indicating that protein levels in newborn Whites and Negroes are similar up until the first year of life. Additional work on the very young is crucial for settling the issue of genetic versus environmental influences.

In view of the repeated association between high γ-globulin and low albumin, it is of interest to find that the therapeutic infusion of large amounts of γ-globulin into patients results in a fall in serum albumin levels (Coon, et al., 1961). This experimental fact obviously has bearing on the above noted association.

Another biochemical test that can distinguish populations is the analysis for urinary β-aminoisobutyric acid. This compound is a product of nucleic acid metabolism. Both high and low excretors have been reported, with high excretion being attributed to homozygosity for a single recessive gene. A number of studies indicate that Chinese and Japanese excrete more of this compound than Caucasians (Sutton and Clark, 1955; DeGrouchy and Sutton, 1957). A summary of current data reveals 10 percent of American Whites to be high excretors compared to 23 percent of Alaskan Eskimos, over 50 percent of Alaskan and Athabascan Indians, and over 80 percent of Micronesian islanders (Blumberg and Gartler, 1959). Ethnic groups of Asiatic origin thus appear to be the focus for this gene.

Serum Electrolytes and Pepsinogen

DIFFERENCES IN serum electrolytes have been detected but whether they are of genetic or environmental origin is not yet established. Potassium is slightly elevated in natives of South India (Henrotte, et al., 1960a). Europeans resident in India also have elevated potassium which suggests a climatic influence. A sorting of Madras Indians into a dark-skinned, platyrrhine class ("Dravidians"), and a lighter colored, leptorrhine group ("Aryans"), led to the finding that the "Aryans" resembled Europeans in having low serum potassium (Henrotte, 1960b). Lowered adrenal gland activity is believed to cause hyperpotassemia. The inhabitants of Madagascar have high potassium levels (Ruf, 1960). Indonesians, on the other hand, show potassium values similar to Europeans, but lower sodium values (Maruna and Tie, 1958).

No genetic analysis has been done on humans but careful work on sheep has led to the identification of high and low potassium breeds (Kidwell, et al., 1959; Mounib, and Evans, 1960). It must be stated that explanations of electrolyte differences as due to adrenal responses to heat acclimitization have not progressed beyond short-term experiments on man (Streeten, et al., 1960).

The inactive precursor of the digestive enzyme of the stomach is called pepsinogen. About 1 percent of the gastric secretion of pepsinogen enters the blood. Acidifying samples of blood activate the enzyme and measurement of this activity gives an estimate of the proteolytic function of the stomach. Hypersecretors of pepsin are prone to develop duodenal ulcers.

Ethnic differences in blood pepsinogen have been reported according to a survey of one thousand young army conscripts (Croog, 1957). Men of Irish origin had significantly more enzyme activity than soldiers of German, Italian, and Jewish extraction. Negro recruits had intermediate values. In another study on older, hospitalized Negroes and Caucasians, no racial variations were observed (Sievers, 1959). It was noted, however, that individuals with type O blood averaged higher values on the pepsin test than patients with A or B type blood.

Further investigation revealed that American Indians of Sioux linguistic stock had elevated pepsinogen with an average 30 percent greater than Caucasians (Kuttner, 1964). A small migrant Mexican population composed chiefly of mestizos was also found to have high pepsinogen activity (Kuttner, et al., 1965). Since Indians possess mainly type O blood, part of this elevated enzyme activity may be due to this genetic trait rather than to the racial factor.

Salivary Amylase and Uric Acid

AMYLASE IS the salivary and pancreatic enzyme that digests starch. Bantu Negroes have high amylase activity while Kalahari Bushmen exhibit low activity (Squires, 1953). Europeans have intermediate values. Diet is believed to influence enzyme levels. The above findings are explained by the high starch (cereal) diet of the Bantu and the carnivorous diet of the Bushmen. No racial difference in amylase was found in urbanized Sioux Indians and Caucasian medical students (Searles and Kuttner, 1965).

Uric acid is a nitrogenous substance formed in the body from the breakdown of nucleic acids. The nucleic acids themselves are either synthesized by the cells or ingested with the diet. Excess uric acid is associated with gouty arthritis. In this condition meat intake is usually curtailed since this food category is rich in nucleic acids.

It has been observed that Filipino males average 20 percent higher serum uric acid levels than Caucasian males of the same age and subsisting on a roughly equivalent diet (Decker, et al., 1962). The method used for analysis showed 5 milligrams of uric acid per 100 milliliters of serum in the Caucasian series. Using a different methodology, other workers were not able to demonstrate hyperuricemia in Filipinos. However, in this older study no Caucasian comparison bloods were tested simultaneously with the Filipino samples (Guevara and Cabuenos, 1961).

Another Pacific population, the Maori of New Zealand, tend to have high blood uric acid, 59 percent of a male population falling into the abnormal range (Prior, et al., 1964). Five males out of one hundred and ten had a history of classical gout, for an incidence rate ten-fold greater than for New Zealanders of European origin. Earlier surveys suggested a gout rate of 8 to 10 percent (Lennane, et al., 1960). A predisposition to develop gout can be inherited.

A sex-linked genetic mutation manifesting itself by an enzyme deficiency in red cells has been noted to vary in incidence according to racial origin. Glucose-6-phosphate dehydrogenase activity is reduced 90 percent in afflicted individuals. When this condition occurs, the red cells are unusually prone to undergo hemolysis on exposure to certain sensitizing chemicals. The disease was observed in World War II among American troops in the Pacific areas after antimalarial therapy with synthetic drugs. Over 10 percent of Negroes, compared to less than 1 percent of Europeans, show the characteristic hemolytic reaction after dosing with challenging drugs (Marks and Gross, 1959).

The disorder has also been found fairly common in Oriental Jews, Greeks, Sardinians, and other groups bordering around the Mediterranean Sea. The Mediterranean variant can be distinguished from the disease as it occurs among other Caucasians (Kirkman, et al., 1964). In Whites, the trait may be genetically distinct since leucocytes as well as red cells are depleted of the enzyme (Marks, et al., 1959). About 2.5 percent of Chinese and 5 percent of Indians examined in Singapore had low enzyme activity (Vella, 1959). A later screening of Chinese patients in Hong Kong gave an incidence of 5.5 percent (Chan, et al., 1964).

The disease resembles the severe Caucasian rather than the mild Negro form in that in some instances no enzyme could be demonstrated in the erythrocyte samples. In Puerto Rico, a racially mixed area, 3.6 percent of an unselected population numbering over one thousand subjects showed the deficiency (Saurez, et al., 1961). The significance of this wide-spread mutation is obscure. In a recent review, it was pointed out that the geographic distribution of drug-induced hemolytic anemia coincided with malarial regions, and that the deficiency may confer a relative immunity to populations carrying the trait (Allison, 1961).

Hemoglobins

HEMOGLOBIN (Hb) is the iron-porphyrin-protein complex in red cells that has the function of transporting oxygen. The protein portion consists of two pairs of polypeptide chains for a total of four. A mutation affecting a single gene can alter by a single amino acid the composition of one of these chains to give a hemoglobin molecule with radically changed properties.

The frequency of aberrant hemoglobin types varies with racial groups. In sickle cell anemia, the substitution of a valine for a glutamic acid residue in one pair of peptide chains converts normal hemoglobin-A into hemoglobin-S. More than 10 percent of equatorial African Negroes are heterozygous for Hb-S, with frequencies of 40 percent for some groups. When the sickling gene is homozygous the victim rarely lives to maturity. In the heterozygote, between 30 to 40 percent of the hemoglobin is of the abnormal type but the subject is generally symptom-free. Selection for the sickling trait occurred in Africa and other fever regions since the heterozygote has superior resistance to the malarial parasite (Allison, 1961). It is rarely found south of the Zambesi River, the line that divides Equatorial Africa from the temperate zone.

Many other abnormal hemoglobins are known but only a few attain an appreciable incidence. Of the common ones, hemoglobin C is found in West Africa. Negroes living east of the Niger River only infrequently show Hb-C on testing (Lehmann and Mwokolo, 1959). In north Ghana, in contrast, over 20 percent of some tribes carry the Hb-C gene. The homozygous condition for hemoglobin C results in a mild hemolytic anemia that lacks the fatal consequences of homozygosity for Hb-S.

Hemoglobin E is another common variant. It also differs by a single amino acid from normal Hb-A (Hunt and Ingram, 1959). Unlike S and C, Hb-E is concentrated in Southeast Asia, one in twenty Malayans, one in two hundred Indians and Nepalese, and one in three hundred Chinese showing the trait (Vella, 1958). It is not known against what specific diseases protection is afforded by Hb-C and Hb-E.

Racially unmixed Europeans very rarely display the above hemoglobin anomolies. Hemoglobin S does occur in Greece and among aboriginal tribes in India. It appears that hemoglobins S, C, and E are molecular adaptations to tropical fevers and would not be expected to be common in colder climates. Certain European populations in malarial zones along the Mediterranean coast have accumulated genes that may confer some still undetermined selective advantage without, however, developing any deviant hemoglobins. Rather, a mutation has arisen which preserves into adult life a hemoglobin characteristic of fetal or intrauterine life (hemoglobin F). This condition, called thalassemia or Mediterranean anemia, occurs on occasion with other abnormal hemoglobins to give a very complex pathological, genetic, and chemical picture (Vella, 1959).

Of special importance is the data on thalassemia in Liberia. A recent survey shows no exceptional incidence of fetal hemoglobin in Liberians who are unprotected by Hb-S from malaria (Neel, et al., 1961). This casts some doubt on early suggestions that the thalassemia phenotype has a selective advantage in fever zones. Evidence from Greece also fails to show a close association between the incidence of thalassemia and malaria endemicity (Stamatoyannopoulos and Fessas, 1964).

Miscellaneous Factors

THE ETHNIC distribution of a number of other biochemical factors have been studied and some of these are sufficiently interesting to warrant mention.

The drug, isoniazid, used in treating tuberculosis, is metabolically inactivated in the body at different rates. The frequency of slow, intermediate, and rapid inactivators varies with race. A greater percentage of fast inactivators is found in northern populations. Among the Ainu, 50 percent are rapid inactivators, in contrast to 20 percent among the Thai (Sunahara, 1961). References to other groups are cited in the report.

An inherited factor which inhibits rheumatoid arthritic serum from agglutinating certain specially treated red cells has been found in the γ-globulin protein fraction of blood. Almost 100 percent of Asiatics, Pygmies, Eskimos and Negroes have the inhibitor while 40 to 60 percent of White population samples show the trait (Grubb, 1959; Steinberg, et al., 1961). This factor is called Gm(a). Similar factors have been identified, including Gm(x) and another Gm-like gene, which show great variation among races (Steinberg, et al., 1960, 1961).

It is obvious from this brief sampling of the subject matter of biochemical anthropology that the scope of the field is too broad to permit convenient summarization. The selection of papers was arbitrary and many important references could not be cited. In some cases, the data are merely suggestive and final interpretations are not possible. The next few years will bring the necessary new work to allow a valid assessment of the significance and utility of biochemical approaches to anthropology.

Ethnic differences of two kinds were listed—sharply qualitative, involving genetic polymorphism, as with hemoglobins, haptoglobins, and transferrins, and quantitative differences, relating to average concentration of serum substances in racial groups (cholesterol, γ-globulin). Since the former are more clearly genetic, they are of the most immediate promise as differentiating taxonomic criteria. These factors are not by themselves absolute determinants of race. The different haptoglobins, for instance, are found in individuals from every race. It is therefore not possible to sort individuals by chemical tests. Populations, however, can be identified by noting the frequency of the different biochemical factors.

The parallel between biochemical anthropology and sero-anthropology is evident. By studying the blood types of large numbers of donors, sero-anthropologists have observed a number of pertinent correlations. Approximately 30 percent of people of Mongol stock have type B blood. Asia is thus the locus of the highest concentration. Type O blood predominates in American Indians, and Rh negative blood reaches its highest incidence among the Basques of the Pyrenees. Yet type O and type B bloods are found throughout the world, and Rh negativity is also widely distributed.

Sero-anthropologists have reconciled themselves to this individual variation by dealing only with group frequencies in setting up anthropological systems. In a similar manner, biochemical anthropologists must deal with populations and not with individuals. The preliminary data in this speciality already indicate that biochemical criteria will cut across the lines of classical races. This is not unanticipated as the traditional races themselves show overlapping of many anatomical features (head indices, eye color, etc.).

An Aid to the Study of Races

BIOCHEMICAL anthropology is certain to contribute information on mutation rates, on the migration of genes, and on selective forces in the environment. When sufficient data are available, gene gradients can be plotted, and the spread of mutations from any one center can be determined. Type B blood, for example, is believed to have entered Europe during the many historical invasions from Asia. The geographical distribution of biochemical factors may reveal similar gene gradients and provide evidence of population movements.

Some of the newly discovered factors may have become stabilized in ethnic groups by virtue of a protective action against some environmental hazard. This is the function of hemoglobin S in malarial regions. A more thorough knowledge of the selective forces in a particular habitat may ultimately be correlated with biochemical novelties in the indigenous populations. Such studies may reveal, to cite one possibility, why diabetes is virtually absent in Eskimos (Scott and Griffith, 1957).

Many biochemical traits may have resulted from adaptive changes in populations. Human ecology is still an unexplored area despite several excellent analytical studies on the influences of heat, cold, altitude, and nutrition (Newman, 1960, 1961). By defining new traits, biochemical anthropology contributes to the solution of many problems concerning human plasticity and the evolution of races. The adaptive potential of man may be illustrated by reference to a group of Venezuelan Indians living in a region of iodine deficiency, who have highly active thyroid glands, but who show no signs of palpable goiter (Roche, 1959). Such instances of biochemical variation can be greatly multiplied.

A few correlations may be noted even from the very incomplete data available for survey. High serum uric acid has been found for two widely separated oceanic populations, the Maori and the Filipino. Whether common geographic, dietary, or racial factors are responsible remains to be ascertained. Negative correlations also exist, such as the virtual absence of hemoglobinopathies among American Indians despite the tropical habitat some of them occupy. This finding, like many others, remains to be probed by future investigations.

It has not been the intention of this review to do more than sketch in the horizons. The task of introducing a dynamic new science is not difficult but to summarize it defeats the best efforts of any reviewer. It may be sufficient to say that in terms of new discoveries to come, biochemical anthropology promises to be an extremely stimulating contributor to our knowledge of human biology.

Literature

Abraham, S. and Miller, D. C., Serum cholesterol levels in American Indians. *Public Health Reports, 74,* 392, 1959.

Adamson, L. F., Serum cholesterol concentrations in various ethnic groups in Hawaii. *J. Nutrition, 71,* 27, 1960.

Adlersberg, D. and Schaefer, L. E., The interplay of heredity and environment in the regulation of circulating lipids and in atherogenesis. *Amer. J. Med., 26,* 1, 1959.

Alexander, F., A medical survey of the Aleutian Islands. *New England J. Med., 240,* 1035, 1949.

Allison, A. C., Genetic factors in resistance to malaria. *Ann. N.Y. Acad. Sci., 91,* 710, 1961.

———, Blumberg, B. S., and Rees, A. P., Haptoglobin types in British, Spanish Basque, and Nigerian African populations. *Nature, 181,* 824, 1958.

Arends, T. and de Rodriguez, M. L. G., Haptoglobin in monkeys. *Nature, 185,* 325, 1960.

———, and Gallango, M. L., Transferrins in Venezuelan Indians: High frequency of a slow-moving variant. *Science, 143,* 367, 1964.

Blackwell, R. Q., Chen, H. H., Chen, H. C., and Uylangco, C. V., Haptoglobin distribution in a Filipino population. *Nature*, 202, 814, 1964.

Blumberg, B. S., and Gartler, S. M., High prevalence of high-level β-aminoisobutyric acid excretors in Micronesians. *Nature*, 184, 1990, 1959.

Boyd, W. C., Genetics and the Human Race. *Science*, 140, 1057, 1963.

Bronte-Stewart, B., Antonis, A., Rose-Innes, C., and Moodie, A. D., An interracial study on the serum protein pattern of adult men in Southern Africa. *Amer. J. Clin. Nutr.*, 9, 596, 1961.

Budtz-Olsen, O. E., Haptoglobins and hemoglobins in Australian Aborigines, with a simple method for the estimation of haptoglobins. *Med. J. Austral.*, 689, 1958.

Chan, J. K., Todd, D., and Wong, C. C., Erythrocyte glucose-6-phosphate dehydrogenase deficiency in Chinese. *British Med. J.*, 2, 102, 1964.

Coon, W. W., Iob, V., Wolfman, E. F., Hodgson, P. E., and McMath, M., Experiences with large infusions of gamma globulin. *Amer. J. Surg.*, 102, 548, 1961.

Corcoran, A. C., and Rabinowitz, I. M., A study of the blood lipids and blood proteins in Canadian Eastern Arctic Eskimos. *Biochem. J.*, 31, 343, 1937.

Croog, S. H., Relation of plasma pepsinogen level to ethnic origins. *U.S. Armed Forces Med. J.*, 8, 795, 1957.

Curtain, C. C., Starch-gel electrophoresis of Melanesian sera. *Austral. J. Sci.*, 21, 195, 1959.

Decker, J. L., Lane, J. J., and Reynolds, W. E., Hyperuricemia in a male Filipino population. *Arthritis and Rheumat.*, 5, 144, 1962.

DeGrouchy, J. and Sutton, H. E., A genetic study of β-aminoisobutyric acid excretion. *Amer. J. Human Genetics*, 9, 76, 1957.

Edozien, J. C., Biochemical "normals" in Nigerians. *West African Med. J.*, 7, 121, 1958a.

———, Chemical evaluation of hepatic function in Nigerians. *J. Clin. Pathol.*, 11, 437, 1958b.

Florkin, M., *Biochemical Evolution*. Academic Press, N.Y., 1949.

Garn, S. M., Pao, E. M., and Rihl, M. E., Compact bone in Chinese and Japanese. *Science*, 143, 1439, 1964.

Giblett, E. R., Haptoglobin types in American Negroes. *Nature*, 183, 192, 1959.

———, Haptoglobins and transferrins in Pacific populations. *Eugenics Quart.*, 9, 45, 1962.

———, and Brooks, L. E., Haptoglobin sub-types in three racial groups. *Nature*, 197, 576, 1963.

Gilbert, J., Absence of coronary thrombosis in Navajo Indians. *California Med.*, 82, 114, 1955.

Grubb, R., Hereditary gamma globulin groups in man. *Biochemistry of Human Genetics*. Little, Brown and Co., Boston, 1959.

Guevara, R., and Cabuenos, V. G., Normal values for blood chemical constituents among Filipinos. *Philippine J. Sci.*, 90, 479, 1961.

Gyepes, M., Mellins, H. Z., and Katz, I., The low incidence of fracture of the hip in the Negro. *J. Amer. Med. Assoc.*, 181, 1073, 1962.

Hegsted, D. M., Jack, C. W., and Stare, F. J., The composition of human adipose tissue from several parts of the world. *Amer. J. Clin. Nutr.*, 10, 11, 1962.
Heinbecker, P., Studies on the metabolism of Eskimos. *J. Biol. Chem.*, 80, 461, 1928.
Henrotte, J. G., Ranganathan, G., and Krishnamurthi, G., Normal values of plasma potassium, sodium, cholesterol, and proteins and of blood glucose in South Indian People, in reference to Western standards. *Experientia*, 16, 350, 1960a.
———, Relation entre certaines caractéristiques anatomiques et physiologiques des Indiens de Madras. *J. Physiologie*, 52, 117, 1960b.
Hunt, J. A., and Ingram, V. M., Abnormal human hemoglobins: Human hemoglobin E: the chemical effect of gene mutation. *Nature*, 184, 870, 1959.

Johnson, T. F., and Wong, H. Y. C., Comparison of paper electrophoretic serum protein values for young healthy American Negro and white men. *Amer. J. Med. Sci.*, 241, 116, 1961.
Juillan, M., and Bats-Maillet, Y., La cholesterolemie des populations de l'Algerie. *Arch. Instit. Pasteur (Algeria)*, 38, 151, 1960.

Kidwell, J. F., Bohman, V. R., Wade, M. A., Haverland, L. H., and Hunter, J. E. Evidence of genetic control of blood potassium concentration in sheep. *J. Heredity*, 50, 275, 1959.
Kirkman, H. N., Schettini, F., and Pickard, B. M., Mediterranean variant of glucose-6-phosphate dehydrogenase. *J. Lab. Clin. Med.*, 63, 726, 1964.
Kositchek, R. J., Wurm, M. A., and Straus, R., Biochemical studies in full-blooded Navajo Indians: II-Lipids and lipoproteins. *Circulation*, 23, 219, 1961.
Kuttner, R. E., Serum pepsinogen in urbanized Sioux Indians. *J. Natl. Med. Assoc.*, 56, 471, 1964.
———, and Mailander, J. C., Serum pepsinogen in migrant Mexicans and stressed Caucasians. *J. Natl. Med. Assoc.*, 57, 109, 1965.

Lai, L. Y. C., Serum transferrins in Malays, Chinese, and Indians in Malaya. *Austral. J. Sci.*, 23, 228, 1961.
Larson, B. L., and Touchberry, R. W., Blood serum level as a function of age. *J. Animal Sci.*, 18, 983, 1959.
Lehmann, H., and Mwokolo, C., The river Niger as a barrier in the spread eastward of hemoglobin C: a survey of hemoglobin C in the Ibo. *Nature*, 183, 1587, 1959.
Lennane, G. A. Q., Rose, B. S., and Isdale, I. C., Gout in the Maori. *Ann. Rheumatic Diseases*, 19, 120, 1960.
Leonhardt, T., The quantitative variation of serum proteins: electrophoretic studies of twin materials. *Acta genet. (Basel)*, 12, 251, 1962.
Luyken, R., Luyken-Koning, F. W. M., and Van Dam-Bakker, A. W. I., Nutritional survey on the Windward Islands (Netherlands Antilles). *Trop. Geograph. Med.*, 11, 49, 1959.

Makela, O., Renkonen, O. V., and Salonen, E., Electrophoretic patterns of haptoglobins in apes. *Nature*, 185, 852, 1960.
Marks, P. A. and Gross, R. T., Drug-induced hemolytic anemias and congenital galactosemia. *Bull. N.Y. Acad. Med.*, 35, 433, 1959.

Marks, P. A., Banks, J., and Gross, R. T., Glucose-6-phosphate dehydrogenase thermostability in leucocytes of Negroes and Caucasians with erythrocyte deficiency of this enzyme. *Biochem. Biophys. Res. Comm.*, 1, 199, 1959.

Maruna, R. F. L., and Tie, O. E., Physiologisch and pathologisch chemische untersuchungen in Indonesien. *Clin. Chim. Acta*, 3, 1958.

Medeiros Neto, G. A., and Hoxter, G., Estudo electroforético das proteinas séricas em indivíduos normais das racas branca e preta. *Rev. Hosp. Clin. (Brazil)*, 15, 103, 1960.

Meyer, K., Serum cholesterol and heredity: a twin study. *Acta Medica Scand.*, 172, 401, 1962.

Mounib, M. S., and Evans, J. V., The potassium and sodium contents of sheep tissues in relation to the potassium content of erythrocytes and the age of the animal. *Biochem. J.*, 75, 77, 1960.

Neel, J. V., Robinson, A. R., Zuelzer, W. W., Livingstone, F. B., and Sutton, H. E., The frequency of elevations in the A_2 and the fetal hemoglobin fractions in the natives of Liberia and adjacent regions, with data on haptoglobin and transferrin types. *Amer. J. Human Genet.*, 13, 262, 1961.

Newman, M. T., Adaptations in the physique of American aborigines to nutritional factors. *Human Biol.*, 32, 288, 1960.

———, Biological adaptation of man to his environment: heat, cold, altitude, and nutrition. *Ann. N.Y. Acad. Sci.*, 91, 617, 1961.

Page, I. H., Lewis, L. A., and Gilbert, J., Plasma lipids and proteins and their relationship to coronary disease among Navajo Indians. *Circulation*, 13, 675, 1956.

Parker, W. C., and Bearn, A. G., Haptoglobin and transferrin variation in humans and primates: two new transferrins in Chinese and Japanese populations. *Ann. Human Genet. (London)*, 25, 227, 1961.

Passarello, P., Electrophoretic analysis of the serum proteins of 173 N'Zakara Negroes (Central African Republic). *Ric. Sci., Rend. Sez. B.*, 4, 155, 1964. (*Chemical Abstracts*, Aug. 31, 1964).

Pollak, V. E., Mandema, E., Doig, A. B., Moore, M., and Kar, R. M., Observations on electrophoresis of serum proteins from healthy North American Caucasians and Negro subjects and from patients with systemic lupus erythematosus. *J. Lab. Clin. Med.*, 58, 353, 1961.

Prior, I. A. M., Rose, B. S., and Davidson, F., Metabolic maladies in New Zealand Maoris. *British Med. J.*, 1, 1065, 1964.

Roche, M., Elevated thyroidal I^{131} uptake in the absence of goiter in isolated Venezuelan Indians. *J. Clin. Endocrinol. and Metabolism*, 19, 1440, 1959.

Ruf, J., Les principales constantes biochimiques du serum de differents groupes ethniques Malgaches et Comoriens en rapport avec leur ecologie (kaliemie et natremie). *Arch. Instit. Pasteur (Madagascar)*, 27, 212, 1957.

Schaefer, L. E., Adlersberg, D., and Steinberg. A. G., Heredity, environment, and serum cholesterol. *Circulation*, 17, 537, 1958.

Scott, E. M., and Griffith, I. V., Diabetes mellitus in Eskimos. *Metabolism*, 6, 320, 1957.

Searles, R. P. and Kuttner, R. E., Salivary and serum amylase in American Indians. *Proc. Nebraska Acad. Sci., Lincoln, 75th Annual Meeting;* p. 11, 1965.

Shaw, J. H., Resnick, J. B., and Sweeney, E. A., Fluoride content of human teeth from the Orient and the Canadian Arctic. *J. Dental Res.*, 38, 129, 1959.

Sievers, M. L., Hereditary aspects of gastric secretory function: race and ABO blood groups in relationship to acid and pepsin production. *Amer. J. Med.*, 27, 246, 1959.

Sinclair, R. G., Brown, G. M., and Cronk, L. B., Serum lipides of Eskimos: effect of a high fat diet (pemmican) and of fasting. *Federation Proc.*, 8, 251, 1949.

Squires, B. J., Human salivary amylase secretion in relation to diet. *J. Physiology*, 119, 153, 1953.

Stamatoyannopoulos, G. and Fessas, P., Thalassemia, glucose-6-phosphate dehydrogenase deficiency, sickling, and malarial endemicity in Greece: a study of five areas. *British Med. J.*, 1, 875, 1964.

Steinberg, A. G., Giles, B. B., and Stauffer, R., A Gm-like factor present in Negroes and rare or absent in whites: its relation to Gm^a and Gm^x. *Amer. J. Hum. Genetics*, 12, 44, 1960.

———, Stauffer, R., Blumberg, B. S., and Fudenberg, H., Gm phenotypes and genotypes in U.S. whites and Negroes; in American Indians and Eskimos; in Africans; and in Micronesians. *Amer. J. Hum. Genetics*, 13, 205, 1961.

———, Lai, L. Y. C., Vos, G. H., Singh, R. B., and Lim, T. W., Genetic and population studies of the blood types and serum factors among Indians and Chinese from Malaya. *Amer. J. Hum. Genetics*, 13, 355, 1961a.

Straus, R., Gilbert, J., and Wurm, M., Biochemical studies in full-blooded Navajo Indians. *Circulation*, 19, 420, 1959.

Streeten, D. H. P., Conn, J. W., Louis, L. H., Fajans, S. S., Seltzer, H. S., Johnson, R. D., Gittler, R. D., and Dube, A. H., Secondary aldosteronism: metabolic and adrenocortical responses of normal men to high environmental temperatures. *Metabolism*, 9, 1071, 1960.

Suarez, Sr., R. M., Olavarrieta, S., Buso, R., Suarez, Jr., R. M., and Sabater, J., Studies on blood proteins in healthy Puerto Rican adults and in various animal species. *Bol. Asoc. Med. Puerto Rico*, 49, 115, 1957.

Suarez, R. M., Olavarrieta, S., Buso, R., Meyer, L. M., Suarez, Jr., R. M., Glucose-6-phosphate dehydrogenase deficiency among certain Puerto Rican groups. *Bol. Asoc. Med. Puerto Rico*, 53, 41, 1961.

Sunahara, S., Urano, M., and Ogawa, M., Genetical and geographical studies on isoniazid inactivation. *Science*, 134, 1530, 1961.

Sutton, H. E., and Clark, P. J., A biochemical study of Chinese and Caucasoids. *Amer. J. Phys. Anthrop.*, 13, 53, 1955.

———, Neel, J. V., Binson, G., and Zuelzer, W. W., Serum protein differences between Africans and Caucasians. *Nature*, 178, 1287, 1956.

———, Matson, G. A., Robinson, A. R., and Koucky, R. W., Distribution of haptoglobin, transferrin, and hemoglobin types among Indians of Southern Mexico and Guatemala. *Amer. J. Hum. Genetics*, 12, 338, 1960.

Thomas, W. A., Health of a carnivorous race: a study of the Eskimo. *J. Amer. Med. Assoc.*, 88, 1559, 1927.

Tonks, D. B., A study of the accuracy and precision of clinical chemistry determinations in 170 Canadian laboratories. *Clin. Chem.*, 9, 217, 1963.

Trabulsi, L. R., daSilva, L. C., Martinez, J. O., Pontes, J. F., Electrophoretic studies on the serum proteins of healthy adult Brazilians of different racial groups. *Rev. Inst. Med. Trop. Sao Paulo, 5,* 190, 1963. (*Chem. Abstracts,* June 22, 1964).

Trotter, M., Broman, G. E., and Peterson, R. R., Densities of bones of white and Negro skeletons. *J. Bone and Joint Surgery, 42A,* 50, 1960.

Vella, F., The incidence of abnormal hemoglobin variants in Singapore and Malaya. *Indian J. Child Health,* 804, 1958.

———, The erythrocyte. *Gaz. Univ. Malaya Med. Soc., 7–8,* 19, 1959.

Wharton, M. A., Nutritive intake of adolescents: a study in Southern Illinois. *J. Amer. Dietetic Assoc., 42,* 306, 1963.

Williams, R. J., *Biochemical Individuality,* John Wiley and Sons, N.Y., 1956.

———, Chemical anthropology—an open door. *Amer. Scientist, 46,* 1, 1958.

———, Why human genetics? *J. Heredity, 51,* 91, 1960a.

———, Etiological research in the light of the facts of individuality. *Texas Rep. Biol. Med., 18,* 168, 1960b.

PART III
SOCIOLOGY

BIOGRAPHICAL NOTE

C. D. DARLINGTON, M.A., D.Sc., F.R.S., is Sherardian Professor of Botany at Oxford University. He is a former president of the British Genetical Society and a Fellow of the Royal Society of London and a recipient of its Royal Medal. Professor Darlington is also a Fellow of Wye College and Magdalen College, Oxford, and a foreign member of the Academy of the Lincei in Rome and of the Royal Danish Academy.

Professor Darlington is internationally known for his contributions to the sciences of cytology, genetics and evolutionary theory. His work has been published in French, German, Italian, Spanish and Japanese as well as English. Among the more well-known of his books is The Facts of Life *(1953), which deals with the history of genetics in relation to man and includes an account of the Lysenko controversy. A revised and enlarged edition of this work was published in 1964 under the title* Genetics and Man.

Dr. Darlington is the author of a number of books, including The Conflict of Science and Society *(1948),* The Elements of Genetics *(1949),* The Evolution of Genetic Systems *(2nd. Edition, 1958),* Darwin's Place in History *(1959),* Chromosome Botany and the Origins of Cultivated Plants *(2nd Edition, 1962), to name only a few.*

HUMAN SOCIETY AND GENETICS

C. D. Darlington

F OR A HUNDRED YEARS genetics and history have been within speaking distance of one another (Galton, 1869; Fisher, 1930; Darlington, 1943). But only during the last twenty years have advances on both sides brought them into direct contact. The contact is on a widening front. In dealing with human populations, historically or geographically, socially or medically, in examining the fossil remains of man and his works and their physical dating, in considering the effects of changes in climate, vegetation or coastline, in elucidating the origins of domestication in plants and animals and in following its consequences, in relating phonetic and linguistic evolution to the movements of populations, in all these directions we are no longer able to keep asunder historical and genetical interpretations of what has happened.

Recent summaries (Grant, 1951; Coon, 1954; Zirkle, 1959; Clark, 1961) have put many new views in perspective. So also have the great recent advances in the genetics of human behavior and disease (Fuller and Thompson, 1960; Vogel, 1961). We need to formulate new and explicit hypotheses putting the genetic and historical evidence in relation to one another. We have to expose and examine the assumptions that have been made in the past, often unconscious assumptions made on either side about the processes examined by the other side. I am here going to give a sketch—a preliminary sketch—of what seems to be wanted for these purposes.

Early Man

THE STUDY OF early remains in South Africa has revealed a sequence of events in the evolution of man which was quite unexpected before their first discovery by Raymond Dart in 1925. It is now clear that the erect two-footed habit, necessary for the life of man in open country favored a tool-using development of the hands. Furthermore, the handling of tools favored the making of tools; and this in turn favored a shift from a vegetarian to an omnivorous diet (Robinson, 1962). The later sequence, the development of a more complex intelligence, the larger brain, the longer infancy, and the connected family with its almost continuous sexual activity (shared only with the gibbon) had, of course, long been assumed.

In these sequences we have connections which are genetically intelligible. They suggest that at each stage man's own invention had depended upon changes in nervous and mental, muscular and skeletal organization. Further, these changes had been favored in their origin and in their maintenance by processes of natural selection. But, above all, these changes had themselves led to an exaggeration of the advantage which had given rise to them.

The principle of self-exaggeration leading to continued change in one direction has long been known in the evolution of the foot of the horse. But such orthogenesis for the man's head is of greater consequence than for the horse's hoof. With man each invention was due to hereditary ability. Each invention gave a greater advantage to more ability of a similar kind. It sharpened the selection against those who could not exploit it.

Casting our minds forward we may note that this principle works today on a larger scale than ever before. Every advance in science increases the selective disadvantage of a lack of scientific capacity. It is not however one kind of ability, but rather hundreds of different kinds of ability, which are concerned. The environment has diversified the means of expression for ability, and vice versa. Thus culture has been given the appearance of creating man although man undoubtedly created culture—man always came first.

Directed evolution has a second important consequence. Man expanded, as Coon has shown (Coon, 1962), perhaps half a million years ago to occupy parts of Europe, Asia, and Africa. Here his races diverged. They became adapted to regional differences of climate, disease, and mode of life. They diverged notably in skin color, in skull shape, and in the apparatus of their developing speech. These divergent changes affected temperament and physique. Accompanying them no doubt were directed changes which led to general increases in intelligence and hence to a parallel evolution of the European, Mongolian, and Negro peoples that are living today.

A second great expansion came with modern man some forty thousand years ago. His skill in making tools then began to show itself in the variety of tools he could make for hunting, fishing, woodwork, boatbuilding, basket work, and so on. These opened up greater supplies of food and permitted exploration and colonization which extended man's range. The main expansion, in Coon's view, came from southwest and east Asia. These new skills demanded, favored, and enhanced the twin gifts of teaching and teachability. They favored the further elaboration of vocal organs and of their nervous control, and they led to increasing regional diversity in speech (Brosnahan, 1961).

Inbreeding and Outbreeding

SPEECH COMBINED with the spread of man over wide regions of the earth was bound to facilitate two important changes in human breeding. On the one hand, differences in speech always create barriers to interbreeding. They are bound to emphasize and particularize the tribal limits to mating. Today they have largely superceded the differences in smell, and in susceptibility to smell, such as still help to preserve the genetic integrity of the African pygmy (Coon, 1962). On the other hand, speech was bound to assist the recognition and also the definition of kinship. A crisis in the evolution of human breeding systems was then bound to arise. We have the evidence of its results.

Consider the development of human breeding. Originally man was in the same position of not recognizing his kindred as all other animals. Now he recognized them and had a name for them. He was bound to be either attracted to what we call incest or repelled from it. If he was attracted he was bound to create homogeneous groups incapable of varying. Such groups often arise in animal and plant evolution. But being invariable they are incapable of adaptation and they never survive for long. They are dead ends (Darlington, 1958a). The human races which expanded were therefore bound to be those which by their genetic character, their instinct, were repelled from incest.

Survey of surviving human tribes and peoples shows that this instinct against inbreeding has been inherited by all of them. Being socially advantageous and instinctively correct it has become a part of universal human morality (Darlington, 1961). It has created and maintained tribes which, even when homogeneous in appearance, are genetically capable of releasing variation. This they regularly do when the size of the group expands or contracts. Such adaptations to the future needs of changing conditions is one which exists throughout sexually reproducing organisms.

At the same time the rules for breeding, whose variations in detail are of little genetic importance, give a coherence to all primitive communities. They give them also an interest in kinship and descent which extends irrationally to the most advanced peoples today where it still supports the institutions of aristocracy and monarchy.

The coherence of primitive communities is due to their uniformity. They show no regular genetic differences beyond the difference of sex and the polymorphisms which they widely share with animal species. The differences in the work that individuals do derive only from differences in sex and age. In consequence inborn differences between classes are unknown and leadership is feeble or non-existent. The primitive people which have maintained their prehuman tribal character have done so by obeying the rules of outbreeding developed during the paleolithic period. These are superimposed on rules of inbreeding, mating within the tribe, which go back to the beginnings of sexual reproduction (Darlington, 1960).

It was no doubt at this revolutionary moment that man, with infinite variations, reversed his mating posture and set in motion those processes of sexual selection first noticed by Darwin (1871), processes which, as Haldane (1924) has suggested, transformed the Venus of Brassempouy into the Venus of Milo.

The Last Paleolithic Expansion

THE LAST general expansion of man, which I prefer to call paleolithic rather than mesolithic, began perhaps in southwest Asia about forty thousand years ago. It swept man outwards into South Africa, over the dry Bering Strait into America, and last of all into Australia (Coon, 1962). The movement continued until 1400 A.D. when the Eskimos colonized Greenland. The genetic adaptation to varied climates and diseases which accompanied this movement was successful in proportion to the variability of available populations.

Thus it is evidently because the American colonizers had been filtered through an arctic zone within the last fifteen thousand years that they have never had the pigment mutations of the Negro, Negrito, and other black races of the Old World. America never had black people until they were brought over as slaves from Africa in 1520 A.D. Indeed native people on the Gulf of Venezuela still have to paint their faces black to avoid sunburn. This difference further indicates that the valuable mutations from brown to black are very rare in man.

A second aspect of local adaptation was the appearance of races adapted to resist malarial infection through the production of indigestible hemoglobins. These races carry genes which are fatal in the pure state but in the hybrid state prevent the propagation of the malaria parasite without incapacitating the human being. Gene mutations having such effects seem to have arisen in some variety, probably during the last paleolithic expansion. Since they were about as rare as the pigment mutations, different mutations have reached equilibrium in different geographical regions and races (Allison, 1961).

It is not only from malaria and other diseases that such mutations protect human beings. They protect them from disturbance by other less well adapted human races. They have thus helped to maintain, together with their sharp geographical boundaries, a conservatism or backwardness (as we like to put it) in many tropical populations (Livingstone, 1958; Motulsky, 1961).

Another evolutionary property revealed by the paleolithic expansion concerns the B blood group. This blood group is determined by the least frequent of the three balanced alleles or elements of the multiple ABO gene system. It has been lost in the gorilla. But in common with the chimpanzee most human populations still possess it. The B group however has been lost in the most rapidly moving of the expanding peoples, those which have spread furthest, into South America, south Australia, and east Polynesia (Mourant, 1959). Possibly this loss has been assisted by the concurrent loss of diseases such as smallpox and bubonic plague which the B group may help to resist (Vogel, 1961). In any case, we see that the genetic and medical sources of evidence, themselves independent, are independently attested by the archaeological dating of the paleolithic expansion.

The Origin of Agriculture

THE LATTER END of this period of paleolithic movement from 10,000 to 5,000 B.C. was a time of rapid climatic change. The last ice age, after sixty thousand years of relative stability, gave place to the warm or interglacial period we now enjoy (Zeuner, 1959; Godwin, 1960). The sea has generally risen about four hundred feet, and locally where the ice lay, the land has risen up to one hundred feet. America and Asia, Australia and New Guinea, Britain and Europe became separated by ocean. The Alps have become passable, the Mediterranean impassable. Thus, breaking the great centrifugal movements of the paleolithic expansion there must have been great cross movements of men following the retreat of the ice. There must also have been sudden stoppages.

Human Society and Genetics

Such situations of movement and crisis favor evolutionary change. In man, as in other organisms, a rapid alternation of mixing and isolation, of outbreeding and inbreeding, destabilizes genetic populations. At the same time it is bound to accentuate selective processes and lead to the greatest racial diversity. Further, these movements and hence their effects were evidently concentrated in certain regions, at certain migratory crossroads. The most obvious of these are in southwest Asia and in Central America. It is not surprising therefore that in these regions in the eighth millennium B.C. in the Old World, and, quite independently three millennia later in the New World, men using their wits should have discovered new modes of life. They learnt, in fact, how to propagate the grain they had formerly only collected and stored for eating.

The excavations at Jericho at the western end and at various places on the northern and eastern side have shown that the site was the Fertile Crescent. Wheat and barley were the living agents to which we must attach the foundation of agriculture (Braidwood, 1960; Helbaek, 1959). It was no sudden discovery. It was rather an evolutionary process, the last quiescent period of human history.

Over a period of at least a hundred human generations (and this must always be the unit of our evolutionary measurement), groups of men slowly expanded and developed their settlements. As their agricultural production increased they came to depend less and less on hunting and collecting. They began to make pottery and they learnt also to keep grazing animals for meat, milk and wool (Reed, 1959; Kenyon, 1957). Slowly their settlements grew larger and they began to fortify them against their neighbors. War as well as trade added to the causes of mixture and instability.

These discoveries enable us to put a new face on what Gordon Childe called the Neolithic Revolution (Childe, 1942). Previously every invention of man had had, I would say, an autocatalytic effect. It had encouraged the multiplication of those who were genetically capable of using it. And these in turn were most likely to be kindred of those who made the invention. Man had therefore for many ages been unconsciously changing the conditions of his own evolution. He had been unconsciously selecting himself.

Now he began unconsciously selecting something else, his chosen food plants. Instead of shattering their ears, and spreading their hulled grain with barbed awns, instead of cross-breeding and maintaining great variability with flowering and germinating spread raggedly over the season, they began to adopt a habit hitherto unknown, that of the cultivated crop plants. The crops of grain shot into ear on one day, the flowers opened all at once and often they began to be self-fertilizing instead of cross-fertilizing. The ear itself became tough, the grain thrashed out, and the seed ripened and germinated quickly and together (Engelbrecht, 1961; Vavilov, 1926).

These changes arose from the unintended selection inherent in regular sowing, regular tillage and regular harvesting. Hereditary mutations leading to these new characteristics, and also to increased yields of grain, favored the propagation of each crop in turn as it came under man's care. And when the cultivator migrated into a new country he began to harvest the seeds of the weeds along with his crop. He had soon, without knowing it, created a new crop, rye instead of wheat, or one millet instead of another. Conscious and unconscious selection have thus worked together in the improvement, the acclimatization, and the substitution of crops, processes which have continued over most of the world down to the present day (Darlington, 1963).

The Neolithic Expansion

THESE PROCESSES led to the slow growth in numbers of the first tribes of cultivators. Supplied with regular and increasing sources of food, they began to spread east and west, and more slowly north and south, of their original territory. As they did so the conditions of the last paleolithic expansion inevitably repeated themselves: colonization, adaptation, and diversification. In addition several quite novel situations arose.

The new crop plants were dependent on man for their propagation. They were therefore unconsciously selected to prosper under these new conditions. They became domesticated races. But the reactions of crop and cultivator were reciprocal. The new cultivators were now dependent on their crops for their own propagation. They were therefore also being unconsciously selected to prosper under these new conditions. They too became domesticated races. They became fitted for their new life, unfitted for their old life, and no longer free but tied to their land and their crops; or, as they might have said, to the Earth Goddess who rewarded their devotions.

The change in the character of selection arising from the dependence of men on crops and crops on men is fundamental to the understanding of human history. Prior to cultivation the man and the future crop plant were separately selected in relation to the rest of nature. After cultivation each became overpoweringly important to the other and the interdependence gradually came to exclude most of the rest of nature. The combination became what it still remains for those most deeply involved: MAN-AND-CROP, a new symbiotic unit in evolution.

In this way after a hundred generations, with varying hybridization but with unvarying selection, races of cultivators arose. They had been slowly selected for success. And success had depended, as those who are accustomed to cultivation know, on industry and patience, forethought and skill. The new cultivators had learnt to handle the seed, the plant and the soil. The novel abilities which distinguished them from other kinds of men are inherited by the successful grain-growers of most of the Old World today. They continue everywhere to demonstrate a love of home, a feeling for the earth and the crops, and a sense of property, which were unknown to any who had gone before them.

An instructive control to this great neolithic experiment, for so we have to regard it, was run in the New World. There the cultivation of maize, beans, and potatoes led to the growth of similar races of cultivators (Clark, 1961; Darlington, 1963). But where, in both Old and New Worlds, the easier cultivation of the roots of lower protein content, of yams and manioc, was taken up, it always propagated peoples of a less industrious character (Burkill, 1951).

The contrast between domestication of animals in the Old World, and its effective absence in the New, shows us several other aspects of the neolithic experiment. In the Old World animal husbandry followed agriculture after one or two millennia, just as Abel followed Cain in the book of Genesis. First the sheep and the goat, later the ox and the pig, later still the ass (from the Sudan), and last of all the horse (from central Asia) and the camel, were taken into protection by cultivators who could offer them the security of accommodation. As with the crops, these animals were unconsciously selected for their usefulness to their keepers, and vice versa.

The farmers were now in a position to expand their activities and to diversify their means of livelihood. Coming to the edge of the drier steppe they were able to drop their cultivation and return partly or wholly to a wandering life. Hybridization and selection in these new conditions produced new races of nomads who in the fourth millennium B.C. began to extend far beyond the limits of cultivation. These new kinds of herdsmen were more alert and enterprising than the soilbound cultivators. Just as the grain growers were more alert than the root growers, so the horse and cattlemen were more enterprizing than the swineherds and they were no doubt partly responsible for the more rapid expansion of the neolithic peoples in the Old World than in the New.

The rate of spread of the herdsmen over the Old World is not easy to record. But the spread of the new cultivators has been tentatively mapped and dated. Their entrance into Egypt in the fifth millennium, and into India and Europe in the fourth millennium, is well authenticated. The first steps in China in the third millennium still need to be more fully known. The character of the expansion in Europe has been sketched very clearly by Gordon Childe (1958). The advancing tribes were at first homogeneous, socially undifferentiated, indeed paleolithic except in the density of the populations and the stability of their settlements. This expansion continued until the cultivable world was largely occupied, that is, until the Maori arrived in New Zealand and the Bantu in South Africa in the last millennium.

Wherever they went these new people created a stable market for the paleolithic peoples, the forest and steppe peoples, who everywhere surrounded them. Trade led to cooperation as it does between purely paleolithic tribes today. Sporadically, but inevitably, it also led to hybridization and genetic recombination necessary both for acclimitization to new latitudes and the production of new communities. There was an efflorescence of new trades, like flint knapping, salt panning, boat building, sea trading, and a multiplication of new peoples prospering in certain localities and busily or even furiously searching for fresh sources of supply and fresh chances of demand.

Inventions, Tribes and Castes

THE NEW activities and customs arising in the new hybrid populations included specific inventions and discoveries. Some of these, like basketwork and pottery, were probably feminine inventions. They were copied, like the improvements of agriculture, and they spread through whole tribes. Others, beginning in the third millennium B.C. with the discoveries of what could be done with metal ores, were probably masculine inventions. They spread by a method that was new and with results that were unparalleled in human or any other evolution.

For the processes discovered were kept secret. They were enveloped in magic, and they were propagated by their discoverers from father to son. What had happened? We may say that the instinct for inbreeding or assortative mating which underlay tribal separation had received a sudden additional social and economic incentive. It was an incentive which has continued down to the present day. The result was that the inventive metal-working families multiplied proportionately to their success. They migrated wherever they could find markets for their work, that is, wherever the cultivators and the stockbreeders had preceded them and even beyond. The descendents of these people are still found as metal-working castes, over large parts of Arabia (Doughty, 1921), India and Africa. In Europe we know a branch of them as the Romany-speaking Gypsies.

This process or origin of new breeds, castes or races from inside old groups is a special case of what the experimental breeder knows as *disruptive selection* (Mather, 1955). The invention cuts off those who know it from interbreeding with those who do not.

The inventors who know it are selected for skill in exploiting it. The rest who do not know it are unselected. The community is disrupted genetically and divided occupationally.

Usually the inventors prospered and spread, and culture is said to have prospered and spread. Sometimes they died out and culture is said to have degenerated (Raglan, 1962). When they prospered, the new castes of metal-workers provided, first of all, the tools, the hoe, the spade, and later the metal-shared plough, which were the means of increasing the density and distribution of the whole cultivating population. Secondly, they provided weapons whose use led to the next decisive steps in the evolution of society.

Paleolithic peoples, at least the men, had fought with one another, killed one another, and even kept their captives to be ceremonially eaten. But now with more effective weapons and more diverse employments, entirely novel opportunities arose. Captives could be kept alive. They could be used to cultivate the soil, to mine the ore, to row the ships, and generally to support and enrich their captors. They could be castrated and treated as expendable. Or they could be bred to form a new caste, or two new castes, pure and hybrid.

Serfdom of indigenous populations and slavery of imported populations became the bases of civilized society. In an immense variety of genetic situations (several of them described in Deuteronomy, XX and XXI), they have remained so until our own age (Mendelsohn, 1949). The patient peasants who had made the Neolithic Revolution found themselves in the Bronze Age at the bottom of society. There they have continued ever since.

How did this come about? Warrior groups arising by disruptive selection imposed their rule on peasant societies and were able to demand service in return for protection. They created feudal types of society. Such societies arose independently in ancient Egypt, and in medieval Europe, in China and Japan, and in many parts of Africa at many periods. They have been said to depend on the relationship whereby a man, a vassal, offers to serve his lord in exchange for protection. The man at the bottom of the system, bearing its ultimate burdens, was always the cultivator (Bloch, 1949). This contract nominally kept the system going.

What however called it into existence, and made it work and

endure, was not a respect for force, for custom, or for an idea in law, but always a deeper principle. It was the inborn character of the cultivator, the character which made him prefer the security of cultivation to the hazards of freedom. It made him prefer his own land to anything else in the world. This inborn character is what was created by the long millennia of neolithic selection.

The metal workers were too scarce, too skillful, and above all too uncommitted to lose their status. They have wandered everywhere freely over the earth forming their castes but contributing also to other castes. Craftsmen and technicians everywhere are descended from the smiths of the Bronze and Iron Age. And through hybridization with the scribes and other inventors they have no doubt contributed to the origin of the most skilled profession of all—the priesthood.

Summing up: the origins of stratified societies with classes following different occupations, and exercising different skills, which they transmit by teaching and by heredity, is always to be traced to one genetic principle, that of a combination of different races, breeds or stocks. And the separation of their classes is always maintained by the genetic principle of assortative or discriminatory mating, a continuation of tribal endogamy from the paleolithic time. But the combinations arose in various ways, either by inventive disruption, by friendly cooperation or by fierce conflict (Darlington, 1958b). They are maintained in various ways, by various expressions of power, various modes of protection, balanced one with another. On the one hand, there was the strength of military castes armed with bronze and iron to conquer and to enslave by force. On the other hand, there was the peaceful guidance of priestly castes equipped only with their intellectual gifts and magical and ceremonial devices. Neither has ever been able to maintain itself for long alone, and the political compromises and the genetic relations of the two have filled a large part of recorded history.

The City and the Nation

AT THE BEGINNING of the Bronze Age there were no doubt already available on the rich alluvial lands of the Euphrates, Nile and Indus valleys, peoples with diverse skills, temperaments and instincts, peoples dependent on one another in the way needed for the creation of cities. Genetic diversity (and not, as Flinders Petrie once suggested, hybrid vigor) was and always has been the key to the prosperity of cities. But beyond diversity and interdependence other quite new faculties were wanted. The first was an ability to live in dense populations, a question of genetic adaptation to crowding and disease. A second was the ability to live together with very unlike people, a question of instinct and temperament. A third was the ability to breed under these unprecedented conditions. These properties are not to be taken for granted. They were not characteristic of paleolithic man nor indeed, we have reason to believe, of any of his ancestors.

One of the needs created by the new settlements was thus tolerance of mixture. Paleolithic hunters, fishers and gatherers are still in the habit of meeting and exchanging their goods. Early neolithic villages often bear witness to a similar arrangement. Two settlements are pitched next to one another evidently to facilitate a permanent exchange. The two groups of people meet but they do not freely mingle.

Animal experiments on the control of population show that this habit of keeping apart is as deeply ingrained in rats as in men. If two colonies of rats are mixed their fertility at once declines (Coon, 1961). It is not surprising that men and women, who are at least as sensitive as rats, keep apart and still keep apart, so far as the placing or construction of their dwellings allows, in the groups which work and commerce draw together. But the genetic causes as well as consequences of this keeping apart and drawing together are vastly important for the evolution of human society.

It was necessary by selective breeding to break down the reactions and instincts of primitive man in some of these respects. The Egyptians, for example, did not overcome the obstacles to city life for sixteen hundred years, i.e., until after the invasion and, as I would say, hybridization of the Hyksos people (Mumford, 1961). People in cities have now for one hundred and fifty generations lived under a continual pressure of selection which has favored those who can survive and breed under these conditions. A partial and locally variable success has been achieved and the proportion of mankind capable of living and breeding in cities has, for better or for worse, slowly increased. Now there are even people who prefer it.

The ability to live in close proximity with other kinds of people than one's own, however, is a gift which has never been acquired in any society except under the selective elimination of slavery. The inability to meet in a full sense this requirement of living together is indeed the reason why social classes keep apart. People following the same trade live together, first in their own villages, secondly in their own quarters or streets of a town. They keep together and breed together. They keep apart and breed apart from others. Exceptionally or sporadically, illegitimately or polygamously, but in all cases selectively, they cross-breed between groups.

How often cross-breeding occurs depends on the degree and obviousness of the difference between the groups. What matters of course is the subjective difference, for color of skin means much to some people, little to others. This is not a rational matter. It is largely a genetic and instinctive matter. Whether it is communal or individual depends on the religious guidance which may be given by a priestly caste. The Priests and Brahmins have thus molded the evolution of Jewish and Hindu society. The Priests of Delphi were less concerned with this problem. The governing classes of ancient cities however never forgot their breeding policy. It was only because the patricians of Athens and of Rome were willing to relax their rules that their republics could in the end become empires (Fustel de Coulanges, 1864). Sparta and Venice by their glory and decay demonstrate experimentally the consequences of the opposite course of increasing exclusiveness.

The consequence of limited breeding, selectively limited, between social classes is to remove slowly the former racial distinction between them. Through a diffusion of genes, society becomes homogeneous in the socially irrelevant differentials. These include not only blood group frequencies but even sometimes body size, which, in Archaic Egypt, for example, ceased after a few generations, to distinguish the foreign dynastic caste from the indigenous servile race (Emery, 1961).

The different ecological niches in the structure of society

created by racial differences continue to be filled adaptively when the superficial differences between classes have been submerged. But they are filled by a selection of genes in new combinations following interbreeding from the different racial sources.

Thus a young nation with physically contrasted classes becomes an old nation which is physically and temperamentally much more homogenous. This is what Livy means when he refers to the Roman people in Book II as developing in the course of many generations a sense of community. The same kind of change had taken place in the Greek City States. It took place in England in the twelve generations following the Norman Conquest. Indeed the same process overtook all the nations of Europe as they crystallized in their modern and separate shapes during the Middle Ages. In these instances the spread of a common language established a breeding community and helped to confirm the feeling of belonging together which arises from even the most limited genetic exchange.

The Linguistic Expansions

THE FIRST achievements of the neolithic expansion were the establishment of the three valley civilizations by the combination with paleolithic peoples as illustrated in the epic of Gilgamesh. But the farming populations spread in all directions and wherever they went they encountered sparse hunting and collecting tribes, all of them nomadic. Wherever they went also, apart from the three valleys, they encountered a harder life. The Danube valley was rich but colder and wetter. Nubia, North Africa, Arabia, and Central Asia were dryer and poorer. In all these places cultivators survived and increased by hybridizing with native populations.

The evidence consists in the mixed character of the skulls recovered (Coon, 1958) and in the mixed, diversified, and altogether new customs arising (Atkinson, 1956). Hybridization, hitherto rare and localized at crossroads, was now and henceforth connected with all human movement. Inevitably it produced by genetic recombination new races fitted for new habits of life and marked by new languages, or families of languages.

The first two of these new peoples, the Hamites and the Semites, arose too early for their sources to be located except that they were probably on the borders of the Fertile Crescent itself. The third of the new peoples came from further away, from the Danube region, and we know them as the Aryans. We know them by their separate linguistic inheritance, their common stock of words (Thieme, 1958). Some of them like the words for grain crops seem to have been their own. Others, like the words for copper, for the socketed axe, and for domestic cattle, they owed to the Sumerians (Piggott, 1952). It seems that men from Sumer, perhaps over many generations, had traveled among the mixed and developing peoples. These men had carried with them their arts, the things they made, and the words for them. They had helped to create new societies with a diversity of talents and skills which set them on their way to expansion.

In the third millennium these Aryans moved into Italy, Switzerland, Germany, Britain, Scandinavia and the Ukraine. To the archaeologist they may appear as secondary and tertiary neolithic people. The first were unstratified agricultural tribes, the second primitive agricultural nations with bronzesmiths, priests and traders. These people where they moved north into almost uninhabited Lithuania, preserved unchanged their earliest ancestral form of speech. But where they met and subjected large paleolithic populations their language changed more. They gave rise to Celtic in the west, Hittite, Greek and Latin in the south, Persian and Sanskrit in the east.

Meanwhile, from Egypt and Arabia similar vast movements began which took the other new peoples, the Hamites and Semites, with their crops, their stock, and their languages, across North Africa to the Maghreb, up the Nile into Nubia, across the desert into the happy land, *Arabia felix*, the Yemen, and on into the highlands of Ethiopia (Seligman, 1957; Moscati, 1959).

We know how these linguistic expansions took place since they were repeated in historic times. Place names show that the Celts covered Europe in their time from Galicia to Galatia, from the Don to the Dee (Taylor, 1864). The Goths and the Slavs followed the pattern of the Celts a millennium later. So also on a smaller scale, and in their own way, did the Vikings (Brøndsted, 1960).

And in the historic period the great Muslim expansions likewise caused an enormous spread of Arabic language, culture, and race (Levy, 1957). A little earlier had come the Indonesian and Bantu expansions (Wrigley, 1962).

All these great movements, the early ones in the bronze age, the later ones in the iron age, arose from small groups, originally even single families, prospering by unusual gifts and becoming governing classes, multiplying polygamously and imposing their language on subject peoples.

The Indonesians subdued not people but the sea. They owed their success to their possession of yams and bananas (Simmonds, 1962) and to their skill in navigation which carried them over the Pacific, the Indian and even perhaps the Atlantic Ocean (Hornell, 1946). But all the others owed their success to their ability by force, by diplomacy, and by priestcraft to organize and govern the peoples they overcame. Their habits meant that they were usually selected equally for their sexual fertility and for their warlike and technical skill. Breeding as much as fighting was a genetic condition of their sustained success.

Yet another condition of success of the new peoples was their ability to maintain themselves by new methods and under more difficult conditions. One of their principal means was by exploiting animals, especially the horse in the Russian steppes and later the camel in the Arabian and African deserts. By means of these animals they were able to abandon settled life and to traverse immense distances with speed multiplied in secular terms a hundred or a thousand fold. The Scythians and their horse-riding predecessors provided the link between the Danube and the nascent Chinese civilization in the second and first millennium B.C. It was probably millets (first *Setaria* then *Panicum*) as grain for horses as well as for men that enabled them to take their flocks across Asia. And in doing so this carried the practice of agriculture and stockbreeding from south Russia to the valley of the Yellow River (Darlington, 1963; Watson, 1960).

Not only breeding and fighting, but also riding was therefore a genetic condition of success. In the end, for the Semites as well as for the Aryans, the horse was as much the conqueror as the man. And it became the symbol, as it had been the instrument, of their mastery of society. It is not surprizing that where the horse came to its limit in Abyssinia civilization also, for a thousand years, came to a standstill (Seligman, 1957). Disease held back the advance of new races of men and new species of animals alike.

The nomadic herdsmen and horsemen, even those who had lost all use and all talent for agriculture, as we saw were derived by hybridization and selection from the earliest settled cultivators. The evolution was formerly thought to have been the other way round but the reasons for the mistake are now clear. The nomadic life was simpler. In its movement it looked more like hunting life. And it covered an immense area of the world in advance of any cultivation. By the speed of its expansion it had run away from the evidence of its sedentary beginnings.

The New Peoples

THE SPREADING Hamites, Semites and Aryans, although beginning as a minority of rulers, by dominating or assimilating the paleolithic peoples destroyed over a vast area the languages they spoke. Thus the numbers of languages in Europe, Asia and Africa, from the Atlantic to the Indian Ocean, continually diminished during the Bronze and Iron Ages. In the new stratified societies arising, the new governing class languages became the means of unity for larger populations and territories. Conversely the great diversity of local aboriginal languages still surviving in America is related to the absence of the great conquering expansions which flooded over the paleolithic Old World.

The paleolithic populations who adopted the new languages had their own racial character in regard to their vocal organs and mental structure. They naturally therefore changed the character of their new speech (Ballard and Bond, 1960). For this reason in etymology and grammar, the languages of Europe, now Aryan, became split, as we saw, into Latin and Celtic, Teutonic and Slavic.

Phonetically also they diverged, but this divergence demonstrably cuts across the linguistic divisions. The TH phoneme, critical in this respect, corresponds with blood group frequency contours of paleolithic and neolithic origin. It cuts right across the linguistic divisions between Latin and Celtic, and even between Aryan and Basque, which are effectively of post-neolithic and governing class origin. The linguist has naturally been baffled by these complicated circumstances and has used non-genetic terms such as "substrate" to explain the result (Darlington, 1947).

The reciprocal aspect of mixture and hybridization between neolithic and paleolithic people is seen not only, as we noticed, linguistically but also archaeologically. Neolithic arts were introduced to the hunting peoples on the arctic and tropical fringes of cultivation. Some of the introductions were merely by trade. But when they were genuinely incorporated in the activities of the people, as happened with pottery in Japan and in Africa, they were probably the result of hybridization and they are appropriately classified by archaeologists as *sub-neolithic* (Clark, 1961).

The Hamitic, Semitic and Aryan expansions were, like earlier ones, centrifugal and in all directions. One side of them may therefore be seen as a continuation of the general outward neolithic movement. The other side however lay in the reverse and inward direction. The expanding peoples turned back towards the neolithic center, towards the region of greatest resources and also of greatest resistance.

The Semites from Arabia conquered and assimilated Sumer. The Nubians from the south briefly subdued Egypt. And when they were thrown out by the Assyrians they took with them to Meroe the men who founded the iron-working castes of Africa (Arkell, 1955). From the north, on the other hand, the Aryans, coming as Hittites, Greeks and Persians, carved enduring kingdoms out of the whole northern edge of the ancient east. These struggles resulted in new elaborations of government and more complex social stratification which were successively generated by the Persian, the Macedonian and the Roman empires.

This inward movement brought a new opposition into view which has often been noticed. Between the first cultivators who established agriculture on the Indus, the Euphrates and the Nile, in Lydia, Crete and Etruria, on the one hand, and the new Bronze Age races on the other, there was a contrast in the relations of the sexes. Among the first cultivators women were important. They took a large part in the work and worship of the community. The mother goddess and her priestesses later dominated their societies. Amongst them the myth of the Amazons came into flower and queens often ruled the country (Seltman, 1954).

The Aryans and Semites however were at first, and in their governing classes continued to be, dominated by the male. Whether the contrast between the new people and the old perhaps had its roots in a contrast between collectors and hunters of the paleolithic we do not know. Since however it commonly distinguishes animal species it is undoubtedly an adaptive and genetic contrast and one which can arise by natural selection.

This contrast between races still exists. We see it represented by the difference between matrilinear and patrilinear forms of inheritance and habitation in Africa. And, in India, the neolithic southern populations are matrilinear and even matriarchal while the northern Aryan populations are dominated by the male (Hutton, 1946). When, therefore, in the ancient east the incoming races became differentiated as governing classes it was the male predominance and the male gods of the Hittites, the Persians, the Greeks, the Romans, the Jews and the Arabs which displaced the female predominance of their predecessors. The religious ideas of the lower orders, as Fustel de Coulanges has explained, were little regarded in the Iron Age city. It was only much later, in medieval Europe, that the cult of the mother goddess emerged from the depths once more, perhaps through the influence of a peasant and celibate priesthood (Childe, 1958; Fleure, 1951).

Population Control

LET US NOW ASK what the great increases in mere density of human populations in the Neolithic and Bronze Ages meant for human behavior. How did the expanding societies accommodate themselves to their unprecedented situation?

In all animal species the capacity for reproduction allows the population to increase quickly when the supply of food increases. Under ordinary conditions when the food supply is stable or diminishing and the population is at or above its optimum density, the species restricts its numbers. This it does by reducing or postponing egg production, by killing off some of the young, and in general by individual actions under instinctive or physiological control (Coon, 1961; Wynne-Edwards, 1962). These mechanisms are assisted by a variety of social devices which foreshadow human morality and also human social behavior. For they depend on communication by sight and sound and on ceremonial gatherings where sexual markings and display are used for identification by the same sex as much as for admiration by the opposite sex.

The result of all this activity is that conflict as well as famine is avoided. The assertion of rights in territory for tribes and for families not only regulates reproduction; it also preserves the sources of food, that is the habitat. The regulating apparatus is continually in action without any threat of starvation. It represents a genetically, instinctively and physiologically controlled property of the breeding system and one evolved by processes of natural selection. If we apply Darwin's terms, it also represents the basic animal morality. For all animals live by destruction of plants or of other animals. And this is a restraint of destruction which serves the double purpose of providing the right habitat for the parents while protecting it for their posterity.

The building in of genetic controls to the breeding mechanism is an example of the close mutual adaptation of all the materials and processes of heredity, variation and reproduction, extended in time and in space, which is characteristic of the evolution of genetic systems (Darlington, 1958). The mutations and recombinations of genes in the cell and the instincts of individuals in mating are all related to the adaptation of one system in evolution. And in this system the regulation of territory, of social behavior, and of sexual fertility are all necessary parts.

What happens in man? The situation was made clear by Carr-Saunders (1922) in man some time before it was understood in animals. Under paleolithic conditions the principles of restriction found in animals still applied. An instinctive feeling for territory is still indeed characteristic of civilized peoples. But amongst all paleolithic peoples control of propagation has been universally practiced. Before sexual life begins initiation is required. Afterwards infanticide is the best known method of limitation. It is

Human Society and Genetics

always selective, usually against the female, when it has the further effect of promoting homosexuality or polyandry. Abortion is perhaps equally important. Human sacrifice, whether of widows or captives, was also formerly a widespread means of population control.

The agricultural revolution led to a change, indeed a reversal, in the selective situation which had operated throughout time. Settled farming made it possible to provide for increases, not rapid but still unprecedented increases, of the farming population. Most of the world was open to their colonization. Two great evolutionary changes were therefore favored during the long quiescent period of the neolithic and we know that they occurred. First, as Darwin (1871) suggested, there was an increase in the natural fertility. Secondly, there was a shedding of the instinctive paleolithic restrictions on multiplication and on unlimited exploitation of the habitat. Slowly the brakes were taken off and the great population explosion began.

The shedding of the instinctive restrictions on multiplication was no doubt itself due to decay of the selective pressures supporting them. Later, however, the change in attitude found religious expression and guidance. Great religions, we must not forget, have always been propagated by breeding. Their lasting success has been proportional to the care and discernment with which they organized the survival and sexual reproduction of the faithful.

The founders of Hinduism and Judaism were explicit on these questions in both general covenants and particular laws. The founders of Christianity at first hesitated, but not for long, and their successors (in competition and in contrast with the rival exponents of Mithraism) learnt to direct their rules and rituals towards increasing the population, that is the Christian population.

And finally Islam may be said, in these respects, to have learnt its lesson from the successes and mistakes of its predecessors. Its miraculous expansion several times repeated, was the result of a well-balanced policy. First, then, was the forbidding of abortion, infanticide, homosexuality, and internecine war. Secondly there was the replacing of these means of limitation by the grand devices of multiplication: foreign conquest, slavery and polygyny. And thirdly, there was the introducing of medically sound rules for cleanliness.

The biological successes of past millennia are not of course a guarantee of future prosperity. The standards of sexual behavior established by Christianity which have fostered a cult of sin, and the untempered subordination of women established by Islam, have left both religions with a control of the breeding system which compares unfavorably with the parental Judaism.

All advanced societies were thus first stratified, and then selected for enhanced multiplication. This led to enhanced competition and even conflict. Their equipment for conflict continually improved during five millennia. These societies have therefore always expanded to limits fixed by pestilence, famine and war. Up to the time of Malthus, advanced societies had been increasing unchecked either by instinctive or rational limitations. We were first clearly told this by Malthus and we know it from our own observations.

We must note therefore an historic misunderstanding. The idea of natural selection was taken from Malthus by Darwin and applied to all plants and animals. He based it not upon wild life, nor even upon paleolithic or pagan life, but upon advanced man enlightened by the great religions. The idea of nature "red in the tooth and claw" came not from nature but from the most recent struggles out of which civilization had been emerging (Darlington, 1959).

Destruction of Habitat and Migration

NOT ONLY limitation of the population but also preservation of the habitat was no doubt partly under instinctive control before the development of agriculture. But with agriculture far-sighted instincts suited to customary situations were replaced by short-sighted reasons and short-term solutions. And the results, earlier as well as later, were frequently disastrous.

The earliest cultivators took pains to preserve the soil and the water on which they depended for their crops. Probably before the fifth millennium the corniche ploughing, giving those terraces which were to girdle the earth, had begun to stretch round the hillsides of the Fertile Crescent. But as these structures grew they became more vulnerable. Every war led to their destruction. One people after another lost the soil on which it lived. Moreover, irrigation had its own dangers. Sumeria was the first to suffer from these, salted and silted out of existence (Adams and Jacobson, 1958).

With the domestication of animals, overgrazing destroyed the vegetation of much of Syria and Palestine, its effect passing later to Greece, Italy and North Africa. Finally, as the population grew, land became scarce. The felling of trees for timber and fuel was no longer made good. Forests were felled or burnt for arable space (Joshua XVII:15). And ships had to be built. The Phoenicians felled their cedars to sell them to Egypt as well as to build their own fleets. The Minoans ruled the Mediterranean by cutting down their forests to build ships.

As each society in turn destroyed its habitat, it lost its population. But the loss was always selective. It was the governing and technical classes which moved on to where the living was better. As the olive took the place of the cypress on the white mountains of Crete, modest farmers gathered their harvests. But the princes had departed.

The princes sailed to new lands taking with them, fortunately the vine, the olive and the alphabet, less fortunately the sheep and the goat. The movement has continued ever since. The Lydians, and some Cretans too, no doubt, established themselves in Etruria, the Phoenicians in Carthage, the Greeks in the Crimea, in Sicily and in Provence. Wherever they went they felled timber and grazed flocks and herds. And into North Africa, four thousand years after the goat, they brought the camel to complete its work. The climate fluctuated but it did not change for the worse in its physical foundations. It had changed earlier. The vegetation, however, which could have been a buffer against the effects of this change, was now devastated. The humus of these lands, accumulated over a whole age, was often washed away in a few centuries (Lowdermilk, 1944; Thomas, 1956).

The order in which civilization advanced was also the succession of its decay, the decay of the soil, and of the society. After Sumeria, Crete through its small size suffered early. North Africa through its low rainfall suffered next. Hannibal's invasion of Gaul was already a recognition of the diminished resources of the southern side of the Mediterranean. The fall of Carthage in a sense foreshadowed the decline of Rome.

The one people who failed to ruin their foundations were the Egyptians. In relative importance, Egypt has, to be sure, diminished over its five millennia of continuous cultivation. Its citizens suffered a fearful encounter with the Arab invaders. For six centuries they endured the celibate Mamelukes. Their governing classes have risen and fallen. But the soil has never been spoilt, and the irrigation system has never needed to be seriously altered. Not, at least, until it had to accommodate cotton as a perennial crop in the nineteenth century (Hutchinson, 1962). The cultivators and the cultivation have therefore survived—almost unchanged.

Thus the impact of Semites from the south and Aryans from the north, herdsmen and horsemen, on the ancient east produced successively the first great multiracial syntheses of civilization. But each collapsed when it exhausted its habitat. The governors and the administrators, the priests and the craftsmen, then moved on. They moved away from the center, northwards and westwards, from Assyria to Persia, from Greece to Rome.

The Carrying of Civilization

IN THE EARLIEST civilizations we do not exactly know where the founders came from. We merely guess that the first dynastic race of Egypt came from Syria or from Libya in 3200 B.C. But already with the Hittites we know they had assimilated Assyrian traders and craftsmen before they became famous (Ozgüç, 1962). The Minoans were probably priests from Syria, nobles from Anatolia, seamen from the Cyclades and Phoenicia, and craftsmen from Egypt (Huxley, 1961). The founders of archaic Athens were partly Mycenaean, partly Ionian, partly local, and partly northerners. But new societies were always supplied with the artisans, usually with the priests, and sometimes with the governors, from older societies. The places, the names and the speech changed, but the people were in part, an indispensable part, the same.

There is thus a genetic continuity between the castes and classes who carry the culture from the old to the new. These castes and classes mix slightly, slowly and always selectively, with the governors above and the slaves and serfs beneath. We can see the effects of differences in these mixtures and rates of mixture, in the different Greek city states. For the mountain barriers between them made *epigamia*, or crossbreeding, difficult and soon law reinforced custom. In consequence, when migration ceased, the Greek societies increasingly diverged in racial character and social structure. Indeed they diverged to the point at which their chief aim was to destroy one another.

These barriers between Greek and Greek as well as between Greek and barbarian were nearly broken down by the Persians. They were in the end broken down by Alexander when he introduced the Persian system of racial cooperation, the system of Cyrus and Darius, to the western world. It was a system which Alexander had capped with a Greek governing class. Or rather a hybrid governing class for one glorious day he married them all to Persian wives. The Greeks who thought they had invented this system blessed it with the name of *homonoia* (Tarn, 1933).

Geographical and genetic conditions in their interaction determine not only static but also dynamic or revolutionary differences between societies. The good communications of Italy after six generations of effort allowed the Roman Republic to expand and to absorb technical and governing classes from the Etruscan empire in the north, artists and scholars from the Greek colonies in the south, clerks, poets and writers from both. But it succeeded in doing so only because after a long struggle the patricians had admitted the plebeians, that is the immigrant population of Rome, to a limited partnership and selective interbreeding.

A political system was established which was also a breeding system. It ensured the selective diffusion of the ancient civilized genetic materials into the Roman governing class who could have become civilized in no other way. This system expanded under the empire when the selective emancipation of intelligent slaves, mostly Greek-speaking, from the markets of Delos and Chios, fed the Roman administration with the people it needed for undertaking the government of the world.

We see the working of these principles of selective movement as much in the decline as in the rise of the Roman Empire. The dispersal of the administratively talented men to the provinces and their concentration in the new eastern capital both depended on the impoverishment of Italy and the consequent redistribution of the sources of food and raw materials. This led to the decay of communications and the reestablishment of regional breeding populations, first for the peasantry, now fixed to the soil, and then for the higher classes.

The tetrarchy of Diocletian acknowledged the advancing disintegration. The barbarian invasions arose through the development of agriculture, the work of the iron axe and the iron plough in central Europe between 200 B.C. and 400 A.D., which fed and bred large new populations of Teutons and Slavs, the materials of the third Aryan expansion.

The invasions themselves broke down the barriers between the parts of Europe once again. They also opened the way for a new kind of movement. Owing to the administrative power and missionary momentum of the Roman Church, merchants, technicians, and a new race of clerks, began to carry civilization at last into the northern countries. All these processes were genetic and depended on the movement of people from the spoilt into the unspoilt country. But they were reinforced by intellectual and religious incentives.

The succession of empires is thus, in my view, due to the selective movement of people, the many different kinds of people, whose cooperation is necessary to make an empire, and whose separate breeding is necessary to sustain a diversified culture.

The principle, *ubi bene, ibi patria*, which the sedentary European has often applied to the eastern immigrant can be applied to any intelligent group in any unstable stratified society. Without it civilization would have died where it began. For ideas do not fly on wings. They march on foot. Cultures do not multiply in a vacuum. They arise from the work of men, who have to be fed by cultivation of the soil. It is these men who multiply and they do so by processes of sexual reproduction following the instinctive laws of inbreeding, outbreeding, and assortative mating established in the earlier evolution of our species.

Religion, Race and Culture

THE GREAT collective problem of the Bronze Age was the reconciling of class separation with national unity. The differences between Sumeria, Egypt, and India, in the intelligence and temperament of their priestly and other castes, as well as in their geographical conditions led to quite different approaches and successes in dealing with it. The military, priestly, and kingly contributions to national coherence were different.

In India dense populations, sharply differentiated in color were able to preserve a stable balance by making a religion of cooperation between groups which should keep a respectful distance apart and should never interbreed without penalty. It was a system invented by the priestly caste and it gave them a highly favored position. Today it remains a system which has preserved Hindu society for three thousand years with less change than has ever been known elsewhere. And it is still capable of assimilating and preserving unlimited racial diversity (Hutton, 1946).

Egypt shows us an almost equal conservatism for an almost equal period. But it was the geographical isolation of the country, the richness of its soil and the unexplained numerical stability of its people that preserved it. Sumeria by contrast passed down its inheritance of people and ideas not only to the outer Aryans but also, through successive empires, to the multi-racial societies of Assyria and Persia where worship or near-worship of the Great King united the whole community.

The contrast between these large communities and the small community of the Jews which they attempted to absorb or liquidate is instructive. For, as time went on, cooperation between races and respect for the King or for Caesar meant less and less to the Jews. They existed by virtue of their respect for their own God. It was the laws of this God and his prophets, the long historical and literary record of their relations with him, that mattered to the Jews and made them what they were. Those who did not respect their laws, their history, and their covenant, disappeared. They were the ten lost tribes and a great many more. Others who did respect these things were absorbed by the Jews to share their way of life (Orlinsky, 1960; Fishberg, 1911).

So the Jews as a race have evolved under changing conditions, first as an independent nation, and later as a migrating caste fitted into multi-racial societies. Several times in different places they even indulged themselves with success in a missionary effort to convert the Gentiles and absorb the converts into their lower orders. Through all these changes Judaism remains, even more than Brahminism, a system of ideas selectively propagated by genetic processes which it has itself prescribed in the ritual of circumcision. Only by this means has the system preserved itself through the appalling vicissitudes of three thousand years.

Look now at the fruits of these contrasted religious and genetic habits. The Assyrian and Persian empires soon disappeared. The principles they used and the administrative and technical classes they employed were passed on to the Hellenistic and Roman empires and indeed to the Roman Church and to modern Europe. Yet the languages they spoke, the laws they invoked, the gods they worshipped, the names they gave themselves, were continually changing. Their history, oscillating between misery and glory, was continually interrupted by the breakdown of society. The genetic continuity was concealed by the confusion of crossbreeding. And parts of the culture were in consequence repeatedly lost. It is the same kind of loss for the same genetic reason as has happened again and again with primitive peoples (Raglan, 1939).

Not so with the Jews. The disasters inflicted on them by the Babylonians, the Greeks and the Romans, by the exile and the Diaspora, in fact freed them from the peasant basis on which every other nation has rested. In spite of catastrophe, indeed on account of catastrophe, the strict and formal continuity of race has been preserved in the learned classes, first in the priesthood, later after A.D. 70, in the rabbinate.

This preservation was due, of course, to the intellectual character of these classes, their ethical, literary and historic sense, and their obstinate belief in the superiority of their opinion to those of all others. So it was that the Jews were able to preserve almost all the sublime literature they had created while the Persians and the Greeks lost a large part of theirs. So it was also, paradoxically, that in due course Judaism was able to inspire both Christianity and Islam with ideas which went even beyond *homonoia* in promoting the unity of mankind.

We may be grateful therefore for highly divergent systems of belief and breeding. Not least may we be grateful for the contrast in attitude of policy between Christianity and Islam. For the intolerance which Christianity derived from Judaism enabled it, having won Rome, to occupy the virgin soil of northern Europe and keep it for five hundred years without division. But Islam faced with the most ancient societies in the heart of its territory was forced to adopt a principle of religious toleration. The Caliph was content to make the Christians and the Jews pay for the cost of being governed by Muslims while keeping their own beliefs (Levy, 1957). It is for this reason that the ancient east today, chiefly under Muslim rule, contains within itself so many of the diverse racial minorities of its own past, each genetically preserved by its religion, and each preserving its differentiated crafts, skills and traditions.

The religious intolerance of Christians might have destroyed their civilization if their beliefs had been uniform. But the racial differentiation of Europe progressing by local inbreeding during the Middle Ages inevitably led to rebellion against control from one center whether political or religious. And when minorities within the boundaries of the old Roman Empire had to seek refuge in northern countries the effect was always beneficial.

Spain, to be sure, lost much with her Jews. France lost less with her Huguenots, for she could afford to lose them. But to England, Holland, and Prussia they both made a priceless contribution (Wilson, 1959). They had those high technical capacities which seem to be genetically correlated, whether amongst Calvinists, Mozabites or Jews, with stern religious convictions (Alport,

1954). They continued the centrifugal movement of specialized talent which had played the crucial part in the development of all advanced societies.

Mental Traits and Evolution

THIS BRIEF sketch is enough to show the kinds of evidence, and the kinds of argument that can, I believe, be legitimately used, when we seek to establish the relations, often so intricate, between genetics and history. All previous evolution had depended on selection among varying individuals whose differences were revealed by the mode of breeding.

In man the evolution of his mental character has, without his knowing it, controlled, diversified and continually disturbed the processes of both selection and breeding. Every invention he has made, whether technical or intellectual, has thus affected a change in his own character by its success. A vortex of hybridization at a critical moment in the Old and in the New World gave him his start, the chance of his most momentous series of inventions, the processes and creations of agriculture. It set him off on a new course of which he was quite unaware. For when he began to select his crops, they also began to select him.

Another entirely new course was taken when certain men made the discovery that they could cooperate with their enemies instead of killing them. They then invented stratified societies, a painful discovery which succeeded because, as Sorokin (1927) has shown, it proved to be indispensable for maintaining a diversified culture. Moreover these stratified societies have never arisen except by the related processes of disruptive selection and race combination. They have therefore created the basis of recurrent hybridization which has released variation in all later societies.

The continual new modes of maintaining class structure developed or adopted by governing classes, military or priestly, have in turn continually varied the modes of evolution of societies. Their purposes have been usually practical and often shortsighted. They have been usually unfortunate and often disastrous. But out of their immense diversity new successful elaborations, new inventions, have been selected.

The processes by which human societies evolve are thus in principle the same as those working at a prehuman stage of evolution. But the modes of working, the intellectual and social considerations which govern human breeding and selection are, for better or for worse, characteristically human, interwoven and multifarious. In no respect, however, are they to be regarded as outside the scope of genetic enquiry.

Literature

Adams, R. M. and Jacobson, T., Salt and silt in ancient Mesopotamian agriculture. *Science, 128:* 1251–1258, 1958.
Allison, A. C., Abnormal haemoglobins. *Genetical Variation in Human Populations.* Oxford: Pergamon, 1961.
Alport, E. A., The Mzab. *J. Royal Anthrop. Inst., 84:* 34–44, 1954.
Arkell, A. J., *History of the Sudan.* Manchester: Manchester Univ. Press, 1955.
Atkinson, R. J. C., *Stonehenge.* London, 1956.

Ballard, C. F. and Bond, E. K., Variation of jaw-form and oro-facial behaviour. *Speech Path. Ther., 3:* 55–63, 1960.
Berthollet, A., *History of Hebrew Civilisation.* London: Harrap, 1926.
Bloch, M., *La Société féodale.* Paris, 1949.
Braidwood, R. J. et al., Prehistoric investigations in Iraqi Kurdistan. *Studies in Ancient Oriental Civilizations, 31:* 1960.
Brøndsted, J., *The Vikings.* London: Penguin, 1960.
Brosnahan, L. F., *The Sounds of Language.* Cambridge: Heffer, 1961.
Burkill, I. H., The greater yam in the service of man. *Adv. Sci., 7:* 443–448, 1951.

Carr-Saunders, A. M., *The Population Problem: A Study in Human Evolution.* Oxford: Oxford University Press, 1922.
Childe, V. G., *What Happened in History.* London: Penguin, 1942.
———, *The Pre-History of European Society.* London: Penguin, 1958.
Clark, G., *World Prehistory.* Cambridge: Camb. Univ. Press, 1961.
Coon, C. S., *History of Man.* London: Cape, 1954.
———, et al., Crowding, stress, and natural selection. *Proc. Nat. Acad. Sciences, 47:* 427–464, 1961.
———, *The Origin of Races.* New York: Knopf, 1962.

Darlington, C. D., Race, class & mating in the evolution of man. *Nature, 152:* 1943.
———, The genetic component of language. *Heredity, 1:* 269–286. 1947.
———, *The Facts of Life.* London: Unwin, 1953.
———, *Evolution of Genetic Systems.* Edinburgh: Oliver & Boyd, 1958a.
———, The control of evolution in man. *Eugenics Rev., 50:* 169–178, 1958b.

Darlington, C. D., *Darwin's Place in History*, Oxford: Oxford Univ. Press, 1959.
———, Cousin marriage and the evolution of the breeding system in man. *Heredity*, 14: 297–332, 1960.
———, Instincts and morals, *Rationalist Annual*, 31: 23–24, 1961.
———, *Chromosome Botany and the Origins of Cultivated Plants* (2nd edit.) London: Unwin, 1963.
Darwin, Charles, *The Descent of Man and Selection in Relation to Sex*. London, 1871.
Doughty, C. M., *Travels in Arabia Deserta*. London: Cape, 1921.

Emery, W. B., *Archaic Egypt*. London: Penguin, 1961.
Engelbrecht, T., Über die Entstehung einiger feldmässig angebauter Kulturpflanzen. *Geog. Zeits.*, 22: 328–334, 1916.

Fishberg, M., *The Jews*. London: W. Scott, 1911.
Fisher, R. A., *The Genetical Theory of Natural Selection*. Oxford: Oxford Univ. Press, 1930.
Fleure, H. J., *Natural History of Man in Britain*. London: Collins, 1951.
Fuller, J. L. and Thompson, W. R., *Behavior Genetics*. New York: Wiley, 1960.
Fustel de Coulanges, N. D., *La Cité antique*. Paris, 1864.

Galton, F., *Hereditary Genius*. London: Collins, 1962 (1st edit. 1869).
Godwin, H., Radiocarbon dating and quaternary history in Britain, *Proceedings of the Royal Society* (B), 153: 287–320, 1960.
Grant, M., *Ancient History*. London: Methuen, 1951.

Haldane, J. B. S., *Daedalus or Science and the Future*. London: K. Paul, 1924.
Helbaek, H., Domestication of food plants in the Old World. *Science*, 130: 365–372, 1959.
Hornell, J., *Water Transport: Origins and Early Evolution*. Cambridge: Cambridge Univ. Press, 1946.
Hutchinson, J. B., History and relationships of the world's cottons. *Endeavour*, 21: 5–15, 1962.
Hutton, J. H., *Caste in India*. Cambridge: Cambridge Univ. Press, 1946.
Huxley, G. L., *Crete and the Luwians*. Oxford: Oxford Univ. Press, 1961.

Kenyon, K., *Digging up Jericho*. London: Benn, 1957.

Levy, R., *Social Structure of Islam*. Cambridge: Cambridge Univ. Press, 1957.
Livingstone, F. B., Anthropological implications of sickle cell gene distribution in West Africa. *Amer. Anthrop.*, 60: 533–562, 1958.
Lowdermilk, W. C., *Palestine, Land of Promise*, London, 1944.
Mather, K., Polymorphism as an outcome of disruptive selection. *Evolution*, 9: 52–61, 1955.

Mendelsohn, I., *Slavery in the Ancient Near East*. New York: Oxford Univ. Press, 1949.

Moscati, S., *The Semites in Ancient History.* Cardiff, 1959.
Motulsky, A. G., Metabolic polymorphisms and the role of infectious diseases in human evolution. *Processes of Human Evolution,* 28–62. Detroit: Wayne Univ. Press, 1961.
Mourant, A. E., Blood groups and anthropology. *Brit. Med. Bull.,* 15: 140–142, 1959.
Mumford, L., *The City in History.* London: Secker, 1961.

Orlinsky, H. M., *Ancient Israel.* Ithaca: Cornell Univ. Press, 1960.
Ozgüc, T., An Assyrian trading post. *Sci. Amer.,* 208: 96–106, 1962.

Piggott, S., *Prehistoric India.* London: Penguin, 1952.
Raglan, Lord, *How Came Civilisation.* London: Methuen, 1939.
———, Prehistoric men—what can we know of them? *Rationalist Annual,* 32: 31–41, 1962.
Reed, C. A., Animal domestication in the prehistoric Near East. *Science,* 130: 1629–1639, 1959.
Robinson, J. T., Origin & adaptive radiation of the Australopithecines. *Evolution and Hominisation.* Stuttgart: Fischer, 1962.

Seligman, C. G., *Races of Africa.* Oxford: Oxford Univ. Press, 1957.
Seltman, C., *Women in Antiquity.* London: Thames, 1954.
Simmonds, N. W., *The Evolution of the Bananas.* London: Longmans, 1962.
Sorokin, P., *Social Mobility.* New York: Harper, 1927.

Tarn, W. W., Alexander the Great and the unity of mankind. *Raleigh Lecture* (*Brit. Acad.*). London, 1933.
Taylor, I., *Words and Places.* London: Macmillan, 1864.
Thieme, P., The Indo-European language. *Sci. Amer.,* 199: 63–74, 1958.
Thomas, T. L. (Editor), *Man's Role in Changing the Face of the Earth.* Chicago: Chicago Univ. Press, 1956.

Vavilov, N. I., Studies on the origin of cultivated plants. *Bull. App. Botany,* 16: 139–248, 1926.
Vogel, F., *Handbuch der allgemeinen Humangenetik.* Berlin: Springer, 1961.

Watson, W., *Archaeology in China.* London: Parrish, 1960.
Wilson, F. M., *They Came as Strangers.* London: Hamilton, 1959.
Wrigley, C., Linguistic clues to African history. *J. Afr. Hist.,* 3: 269–272, 1962.
Wynne-Edwards, V. C., *Animal Dispersion in Relation to Social Behaviour.* Edinburgh: Oliver & Boyd, 1962.

Zeuner, F. E., *The Pleistocene Period: Its Climate, Chronology, and Faunal Successions.* London: Hutchinson, 1959.
Zirkle, C., *Evolution, Marxism, and the Social Scene.* Philadelphia: Univ. of Pennsylvania Press, 1959.

BIOGRAPHICAL NOTE

CORRADO GINI, *D. Jur., D. Econ., D.Sc., one of Italy's leading sociologists, was Professor Emeritus of the University of Rome at the time of his death in 1965. He was the founder and director of the Institute of Statistics at the Universities of Rome and Padua, and president of the Italian Committee for the Study of Population Problems.*

Dr. Gini conducted anthropometric and demographic studies in Palestine, Mexico, Poland and Lithuania. He was president of the International Institute of Sociology and was the organizer and president of the National Congresses of Eugenics and Genetics in Milan (1924), Rome (1929), Bologna (1938) and Milan (1949), and of the XVI International Congress of Sociology in Rome (1950).

Professor Gini was the recipient of a number of distinguished awards for his work in sociology and was honorary president of the Latin-American Sociological Association. He was an honorary member of scientific societies in Argentina, Belgium, Hungary, Switzerland, Czechoslovakia, Mexico, India and Italy.

Dr. Gini was the editor of Revue Internationale de Sociologie, Genus *and* Metron. *He is the author of over seventy volumes, seven hundred articles and four hundred reviews. Among his more notable works are* Patologia economica *(1957),* Economica lavorista—Problemi del Lavoro *(1956) and* Le Medie *(1957).*

RACE AND SOCIOLOGY*

Corrado Gini

Racism in all its forms affirms that there are differences which qualify a specific race, or certain races, as superior to all others. The tendency to render such judgments seems endemic to human nature because its traces are to be found in the earliest history of mankind. Indeed, there is evidence to indicate that this tendency was more pronounced at one time than it is today.

For example, in the most ancient of the Near Eastern civilizations, each people had its own national diety (Marduk in Babylonia, Assur in Nineveh, Ammon in Egypt, Jehovah among the Jews) to whom preeminence was ascribed. From this preeminence of the national diety, naturally followed the superiority of the people under its protection. The Greeks and Romans considered all other peoples as inferior, whom they identified as barbarians.

Even in our own time many primitive populations identify the individuals who belong to their own race with the word for man,[1]

---

* This article is based upon the lectures in sociology delivered by Professor Gini at the University of Rome, commencing in 1926 and especially developed in the academic years from 1948 to 1955. The lectures have been published as a textbook for students in several editions. The last one, adopted also in other universities, is entitled *Corso di Sociologia* (Rome: Edizioni "Ricerche," 1957). A new edition is now in preparation.

The bibliographical notes are editorial and concern partly other more detailed works by Professor Gini, which support and amplify the views presented in his exposition, and partly works of others, often posterior to Gini's original work, which develop the same line of thought.

[1] "Each tribe in distinguishing itself from its neighbors arrogates to itself the appellation 'men,' designating others 'non-men.' Each community conceives of

or people. This is the case with respect to the Eskimos, the various Indian tribes in North America, the Fuegians, the Andaman Islanders, and the Bantu. It is also probably the case with respect to many other peoples. This indicates that to them alien peoples are not men. They are beasts, and do not constitute a people, but a herd.[2]

Every ethnic group, therefore, considers itself the sole representative of the human race, irrespective of the existence of other men. In other words, while we have a zoological conception of men, because we consider them members of the species *Homo sapiens*, our progenitors had, and contemporary primitives actually entertain, a political conception. For them only that individual who belongs to their own social group is properly a man.

It is to be noted that the developed zoological conception of man has become manifest under the progressive expansion of social groups. The political conception of man gave way to the more universal conception as a consequence of a number of influences: alliances which habituated men to consider, even if only temporarily, men of other social groups as their equals; demographic, economic, and cultural exchanges that attenuated the heterogeneity of the various political groups; and, finally, science which regularly focused attention upon the substantial affinities between the various human races.

It is also necessary to consider the influence of the three great world religions, Buddhism, Christianity and Islam, which extended to all men, who had embraced their faith, the concept of human brotherhood. However, during the modern period Catholic theologians debated whether the American Indians did or did

---

itself, with an a priori conviction of the most categorical sort, as somehow unique, superior, and favored of the gods." A. J. Gregor, "On the Nature of Prejudice," *Eugenics Review*, 52, number 4, January, 1961, p. 217; cf. H. Fairchild, *Race and Nationality*. New York, 1947, p. 4 f.; R. Park, *Race and Culture*. Glencoe, 1950, p. 87.

[2] This is not to say that beasts are ill-treated. Just the contrary. If they amuse us, if we like them, if, above all, they are useful, they are well treated. No man in the world, probably, has ever been the object of such prodigal care and attention as have been race horses and pure bred dogs. When, however, they no longer answer our needs, animals are sold or slaughtered. Their treatment can be excessively good, but it is always regulated by our pleasure or profit. Cf. C. Gini, *Le rilevazioni statistiche tra le popolazione primitive*. Rome, 1942, p. 271.

not possess a soul, that is to say, whether they should be considered men on a parity with Europeans.[3]

In any event this mental attitude, derived from an egocentric principle, which still persists among primitives, explains their seemingly contradictory behavior with respect to Whites. Primitives, considering only themselves men, treat others like animals. Their occasional benevolent behavior with respect to Whites is analogous to that which we evince toward a dog, cat or lamb. Our attitudes in this case are dictated by a mild disposition or self-interest, not humanity or a consciousness of common moral ties.[4] For this reason primitives may suddenly alter their attachments in accordance with their interests, killing those Whites who had imagined themselves in the primitives' good graces.

Race Consciousness in Civilized Societies

HISTORY demonstrates further that racial tendencies have manifested themselves recently among many civilized peoples. There are the examples of the anti-Semitic campaigns conducted in many European countries and, with particular feeling, in National Socialist Germany, of the struggle which still rages today in Palestine between the Arabs and Jews, of the manifestations of racial antipathy evidenced by White Americans with respect to their Negro co-nationals.

One of the most conspicuous examples of racism is that offered by the Japanese. They were, in fact, prohibited during the Tokugawa period (1542–1868) from leaving Japan, while strangers were prohibited from entering under threat of the gravest of sanctions. Another example is that offered by the history of Spain

---

[3] Christian theologians of all denominations have long concerned themselves with the problem of the fundamental equality and inequality of human races. It was a preoccupation as early as the time of Augustine (*City of God*, XVI, 8). In our own time the thesis that the "Nordic Peoples" are the elect of God occupies a central position in the creed of the British Israel Association.

[4] "The first phase of race and culture contacts is characterized by contacts that are not truly social, in the sense that persons with different racial and cultural backgrounds who are brought together are not members of the same moral order . . . they hardly regard each other as completely human." E. Frazier, *Race and Culture Contacts in the Modern World*. New York, 1957, p. 32.

where, having just achieved national unity, first the Moors, then the Jews and ultimately the fruits of mixed marriages with Catholics, were expelled. Finally, it should be remembered that a racial consciousness, at least in part, inspired the restrictive immigration legislation of the United States of America, Canada and other Commonwealth nations.[5]

One can maintain that racism is a special case of conformist tendencies, through which each population seeks to remove from its immediate association minorities which depart from itself in some fundamental fashion and which, therefore, are difficult to assimilate.[6] It is to be noted that sometimes racial strife concealed itself under different guises—religious and dynastic among others. It is very probable that the struggle between Christians and Mohammedans which culminated in the Crusades, that of the Catholics against the Huguenots of France, that of the Protestants against the Catholics in England, and that of the Catholics against the followers of Huss in Czechoslovakia, as well as the religious struggles in Central Europe, and so forth, were directed against individuals who distinguished themselves from the majority as much by virtue of their physical, intellectual or moral character as by their religious faith.

All these considerations provide support for the contention that racism, be it a mental attitude or a political orientation, having manifested itself in one guise or another in all times and in all places, arises out of an innate disposition in man.[7]

The Question of "Pure" Races

IF THIS disposition is understood to be directed toward the maintenance of a "pure race," it would seem that its efforts, from a

---

[5] Cf. C. Gini, *Aspetti demografici del conflitto*. Milan, "Collana dei corsi di cultura per i dirigenti di aziende industriali," 1942.

[6] Cf. C. Gini, *Nascita, evoluzione e morte delle nazioni*. Rome: Offices of the Review "Metron," 1930, p. 83; "Aree e centri culturali," *Genus*, VI–VIII, 1943–1949, p. 24; "Problemes demographiques en Europe," *Genus*, XI No. 1–4, 1955, pp. 46–48; "El problema de la asimilacion cultural," *Revista de la Facultad de Ciencias Economicas de la Universidad de Cuyo*, May–August, September–December, 1955.

[7] Cf. A. Keith, *The Place of Prejudice in Modern Civilization*. New York, 1931; A. J. Gregor, "The Biosocial Nature of Prejudice," *Genus*, XVIII No. 1–4, 1962.

scientific point of view, are spent in the pursuit of an unattainable goal. First and foremost it seems that primary pure races, or pure lines, that is, those which descend from homogeneous progenitors, do not actually exist. As a matter of fact, as far as we recede in time, there is always evidence of populations with variable anthropological traits.[8]

The empirical evidence indicates that even in the most remote epochs of prehistory, from which cranial series have been preserved, individuals belonging to the same population differ substantially among themselves with respect to cephalic index and other skeletal characteristics. Therefore, it has never been possible to retrace perfectly homogeneous populations.[9] Take the North Europeans, for example, their mythology and folklore tell us of brunet individuals, and we know that brunets with prominent, arched brow ridges existed in antiquity even in Scandinavia.

There is further reason to doubt the existence of pure races in the literal sense. The study of genetics indicates that it is probable that the origin of man is to be ascribed to the crossing of diverse biological forms. This hypothesis is based on the consideration that the chromosomes of the germ cells of man are forty-six in number and upon the fact that the greater part of human characteristics depend on multiple determinants or factors. Man, consequently, probably constitutes a polyploid form derived from repeated crossings.

This phenomenon is certainly verified with respect to certain vegetable species, for example with grain, and is probably true for the diverse canine races. Polyploid forms have a greater power of resistance and of adaptation and are consequently diffused over a larger area than the normal diploid species. Thus, if man is essentially a polyploid form,[10] one can hardly talk of pure races in the formal sense and probably not even of a pure species.

There is, however, another sense in which one speaks of a pure

---

[8] E. E. Hunt, "Anthropometry, Genetics and Racial History," *American Anthropologist*, 61, 1959; D. Gorjanovic-Kramberger, *Der diluviale Mensch von Krapina in Kroatien*. Wiesbaden: Kreidel, 1906.

[9] Cf. F. Weidenreich, *Apes, Giants and Men*. Chicago, 1946, p. 102 f.; G. Sergi, *Origine e diffusione della stirpe mediterranea*. Rome, 1895, p. 18 f.

[10] Cf. H. Weinert, *Biologische Grundlagen fuer Rassenkunde und Rassenhygiene*. Stuttgart: Enke, 1943.

race. It is specifically in the racist sense. In this instance one does not refer to primary pure races but to pure secondary races.[11] Within this concept when one talks of pure-blooded horses, one does not intend to imply descent, without crossing, from a single race. Rather, one knows that they are the product of a cross between Arabian and English steeds.

One speaks therefore of a pure secondary race when one speaks of individuals produced by this crossing, who by dint of isolation and endogamy, have produced individuals whose characteristics, when not identical, vary in accordance to chance. Thus pure bloods may not all display the same features, and among purebred Angora cats some have one yellow eye and a blue one. This is a variation which constitutes the greatest disparity. They are nonetheless creatures of pure race because the mixture of the modalities of the diverse characteristics is such that the distribution in all lines obtains the maximum homogeneity compatible with the genetic composition of the race itself.

In this sense one can also speak of pure races among men. These are found, above all, as ethnic groups or population isolates, such as those studied in the expeditions of the Italian Committee for the Study of Population Problems.[12]

Race, People and Nation

AT THIS POINT let us examine the relationships which obtain between the concepts race, people and nation, which are often confused. As we have seen, the concept race, strictly conceived, is primarily a zoological concept, which we can define as "a group of individuals whose phenotype displays a particular combination of normal characteristics, transmissible and variable within determinate limits." A people is, on the other hand, a sociological entity, the product of a historico-cultural process in which the unity of

---

[11] Cf. C. Gini, *Le basi scientifiche della politica della popolazione.* Rome: Offices of the Review "Metron," 1931, chap. XIII.

[12] Cf. C. Gini, *Saggi di demografia.* Rome: Italian Committee for the Study of Population Problems, 1934, p. 746; *Appunti sulle spedizioni scientifiche del Comitato Italiano per lo studio dei problemi della popolazione* Rome: Italian Committee for the Study of Population Problems, 1943.

language plays an essential role. A nation, which will be defined below, can be formed of diverse races and peoples who share a common cultural patrimony.

There are, in fact, nations which include several races, such as the United States, Brazil, Mexico, and the Union of Soviet Socialist Republics. Others include several languages, as is the case in Switzerland and Belgium. On the other hand there are races and languages diffused over an area divided into many nations. Thus the Spaniards form distinct political entities in the Iberian peninsula and South America and the Anglo-Saxons of England have expanded to populate the United States, Canada, Australia, New Zealand, and so forth. In many cases, therefore, the concepts race, people, and nation, strictly defined, do not in fact coincide. Nevertheless the apparent intention of racial policies in some states in the recent past was to make the nation form a racial unity.

A pure race, as we have indicated, is a biological concept which in the primary sense presupposes descent from the same stock. A nation can be, instead, defined as a complex of individuals united by a common consciousness of their spiritual unity, the product of a common historico-cultural patrimony, and a faith in a common destiny. This consciousness does not merely consist of the simple group sentiment which constitutes the base of all societies, even the most primitive, and which may persist even without the indicated exigencies of a spiritual and cultural order.

The solidarity which rests at the base of national consciousness is the consequence of a number of factors. For example, one of the most important of these is the unity of language, which, however, does not seem absolutely necessary. In Belgium and Switzerland, in fact, there coexist two and four ethnic groups, respectively, each of which uses its own language. Nonetheless national consciousness and the sentiment of social solidarity are in these two countries very strong. To the linguistic element one can add racial unity, but even this, as we have indicated, is not essential. In this measure one can say that theoretically race and nation constitute two different concepts.

It must, however, be observed that a nation, when it constitutes a political unity which has long endured, tends to acquire particular characteristics, first social and then racial. Political and social individuality inevitably brings with it a certain measure of isolation that has the effect of developing in the nation particular biological characteristics.[13] This phenomenon is verified especially when one considers populations that have long remained isolated.[14]

The Racial Composition of Various Nations

THE JAPANESE, for example, are a population whose racial composition is mixed, being derived from the crossing of very diverse races. The populations which originally lived in the Japanese isles, the Ainu—remnants of which still live in the islands of Hokkaido, Sakhalin and the Kuriles—were of Caucasoid derivation. Malay elements were added to those, which left their imprint on the type of habitation and the mode of dress. Later Mongoloid populations were added among whom the Yamato, who subjugated the others, left a lasting impression of their own characteristics. All these components are today almost completely fused to form a new relatively homogeneous race or population.

It can be maintained that the more prolonged the isolation the more the secondary race becomes pure.[15] In the case of Japan, isolation has been very much accentuated, and for more than three centuries isolation was absolute because of the prevailing dispositions of the Tokugawa epoch to which we have already alluded.

Another example of the convergence between race and nation is provided by Great Britain. The population of the British Isles is at present racially homogeneous, possessing singular characteristics. As a consequence of this it is easier to distinguish an English-

---

[13] C. Gini, *Nascita* . . . , p. 100, n. 31, cf. p. 77; "The Testing of Negro Intelligence," *Mankind Quarterly*, Vol. I, No. 2, October, 1960; cf. A. J. Gregor, "Sociology and the Anthropobiological Sciences," *Memoire de XIXe Congres International de Sociologie*. Mexico, D. F.: Comite Organisateur, 1960, II, p. 96 f.

[14] Cf. L. Dunn, *Heredity and Evolution in Human Populations*. Cambridge, 1959; C. del Real y Ramos, *Sociologia pre y protohistorica*. Madrid: Instituto de Estudios Politicos, 1961, p. 101 f.

[15] Cf. C. Gini, "Progresso o decadenza?" *Rivista di Politica Economica*, XLIX, May–September, 1959, p. 29.

man from an individual from the Continent than it is to distinguish between two individuals from the Continent who belong to different nations.

Nonetheless, contemporary Englishmen trace their descent from races very different among themselves.[16] The substratum is formed of a dolichocephalic, Mediterranean population which still persists today in Wales. There have been added, in successive waves, first pre-Aryan, brachycephalic populations, then, in several waves, the blond, dolichocephalic Indo-Europeans: Celts, Saxons, Danes, Normans, and so forth. From the fusion of these races, which has been more complete in England than in the other British regions, arose the Anglo-Saxons, who today possess well-defined characteristics. The fusion was probably greatly facilitated during those periods of conformism at which time, as we have indicated, under different pretexts, heterogeneous elements were eliminated.

While among the countries with which we have been concerned the fusion of diverse elements has already been accomplished, in others this is not yet the case. But the general process seems to be, and to have been, everywhere the same. The anthropological history of the French nation presents an analogous picture, derived as it has been from the superposition of peoples of Germanic derivation, from whom France received its name, upon the precedent population of Alpine, Mediterranean and Nordic origins. Germany similarly developed as a consequence of the combination of Nordic populations and Alpines with some traces of Mediterranean blood imported through the Roman conquest.[17] The same races, although in different proportions, enter into the constitution of the Italian population.

In antiquity the civilizations of Greece and of Etruria or Rome had, according to tradition supported by considerable evidence, a similar origin: the invasions of populations which superimposed themselves upon an indigenous people more or less diverse.[18]

[16] Cf. C. Gini, *Nascita* . . . , p. 73.
[17] Cf. the interesting discussion in E. von Eickstedt, *Die rassischen Grundlagen des deutschen Volkes*. Berlin: Schaffstein, 1934.
[18] Cf. G. Oberziner, *Origine della plebe romana*. Genoa, 1901; *Patriziato e plebe*. Milan, 1912; C. Gini, *Le basi* . . . , chap. XIII.

Group Sentiment and Race Formation

GROUP sentiment, determined by physical, social, cultural or administrative factors, coupled with the hostility of neighboring groups, promotes isolation, and through isolation and selection the complete fusion of the adiacritic race is gradually accomplished to produce a "new" or "purified" race.[19] This constitutes the biological consequence of group sentiment. With these considerations in mind a nation can be defined as a group of persons having a given individuality not only from a political and cultural, but, ultimately, also from a biological point of view.

Racial consciousness, a complex of sentiments fostering sociocultural and ultimately biological conformity, manifested in our own times is often seemingly the product of economic and political exigencies. For example, the restriction of immigration of Orientals, Latins, and Slavs into the United States was prompted, according to many, by the consideration that these immigrants, coming from populations suffering a standard of living inferior to that of the host nation, would work for minimum compensation, resulting in ruinous competition for American labor. This economic factor certainly contributed much to determine, but was not the exclusive cause of, the restriction of immigration. The researches of Franz Boas[20] led some to believe that by restricting immigration it would be possible to realize, in a short space of time, a desired racial unity.[21]

In the case of National Socialist racial legislation in Germany there was an attempt to eliminate heterogeneous socio-cultural as

---

[19] Cf. E. Colin, *Elements of Genetics*. New York: McGraw-Hill, 1956, p. 293 f.; N. Timofeeff-Ressowsky, "Sulla Questione dell'isolamento territoriale entro popolazioni specifiche," *Scientia Genetica*, I, 1939, pp. 76–85, "Genetica e evoluzione," *ibid.*, pp. 278–281.

[20] F. Boas, *Changes in Bodily Form of Descendents of Immigrants: First Report*. Washington: Government Printing Office, 1911.

[21] There can be little serious doubt that the racial writings of Madison Grant (*The Passing of the Great Race*. New York, 1930) and of Lothrop Stoddard (*Revolt Against Civilization*. New York, 1922; *Racial Realities in Europe*. New York, 1925) significantly influenced the formulation of this legislation (cf. H. Guenther, *Racial Elements of European History*. London, 1927).

well as anthropological elements. The Jews were particularly sin-
led out for having maintained their religious and ethnic independence. Racial consciousness manifested itself as a concerted
effort to achieve national homogeneity, a homogeneity which extended to spheres as varied as language, dress, cultural and artistic enterprise.[22]

In view of its varied manifestations it has been questioned
whether it is correct to refer to this tendency as racist. It has been
contended that, in essence, the term is inappropriate in so far as
this tendency seeks not only the biological purity of race but also
the conformity of sentiment. In fact, in the discussion which took
place in National Socialist Germany to determine the characteristics of the "German Man," it was decided that the most secure
was that of feeling oneself German.

When, therefore, one speaks of racism, that term should be
understood not in the strictly biological sense, but also with cultural and social connotation. The term "ethnism" has been suggested, as a consequence, which more scientifically corresponds to
the practical disposition of the tendency. But the term "ethnism"
finds scant response in common language and therefore one continues to speak of racism.

We have suggested that there are significant reasons for the
employment of the term racism. Group sentiment, and the disposition toward conformity which it occasions, leads to the voluntary
or forced elimination of heterogeneous elements in a population as well as fostering the biological fusion of those remaining.
Thus understood the term racism has a socio-cultural as well as a
biological significance.[23] Group identity[24] promotes conformity in
feelings and behavior, smoothing out existing differences, leading,
finally, to biological assimilation of existing components.

Some comment should here be made with respect to this general process toward uniformity. On the one hand there are practi-

[22] Cf. C. Gini, "Authority and the Individual During the Different States of the Evolution of Nations," in *Authority and the Individual*. Cambridge, 1937, p. 254.
[23] Cf. A. J. Gregor, "Corrado Gini and the Theory of Race Formation." *Sociology and Social Research*, January, 1961.
[24] Cf. A. Niceforo's discussion of this concept in "Schematico profilo di una sociologia generale in cinquanta paragrafi." *Rivista italiana de economia, demografia e statistica*, XI, Number 3–4, July–December, 1957.

cal limitations to the possibility of transcending a certain measure. On the other hand there would seem to be grave disabilities for society attending the achievement of absolute homogeneity.

The Influence of Geographic Factors

AT LEAST part of the anthropological differences which distinguish subgroups arise as a consequence of geographic factors and cannot, therefore, be abolished. Thus, within the Japanese and British populations there are notable local differences. In Italy there are, and there will always be, differences between northern and southern populations, between urban and rural populations, between those of the mountains and those of the plain, between those of the coast and those of the interior, and so forth.

Anthropological differences are not only ineradicable, but it would be inopportune to attempt their abolition. Modern society, because of the demands of our technological civilization, necessitates specialization and division of labor. The various activities demand diverse endowments. Therefore it is beneficial that the characteristics of the population remain varied and well distributed.

This circumstance is, in fact, one of the major factors in the success of the Italian people in many spheres of science and art. In Italy conjoined with the peoples of speculative tendencies of the South, we have the essentially practical peoples of the North. The Lombards possess the talents of industry and commerce, the Piedmontese a strong military spirit, the Tuscans, the Umbrians, and the Venetians an elevated artistic sense, and so forth. Therefore, the necessity of recognizing the utility, from many points of view,[25] of the tendency toward homogeneity should not lead to the exaggeration that it can and should be absolutely complete.

[25] "Homogeneity of physical characteristics, interests and feelings, which leads to reciprocal sympathy and conformity in behavior, or mutual tolerance, which smoothes out the existing differences, permits the spontaneous realization of social consensus. But this cannot be attained without the pressure of authority if the people are heterogeneous in respect to race or social position, with contrasting interests and divergent feelings, and moreover, uncompromising." C. Gini, "Authority and the Individual . . . ," *op. cit.*, p. 254.

Race and Sociology

Some reference should also be made to the concept of the nation as a race in formation. Intimations of this theory were early formulated by Sir Arthur Keith.[26] And it was articulated with some precision in my own, quite independently developed, presentation at a demographic conference in Chicago in 1929.[27]

Keith sought to discover the reasons why racist policies have had so frequent a manifestation in all times and all places. He attempted to discover whether race consciousness had a real utility and if so what it could be. One of the reasons which at first glance seems plausible is that among men, as among domestic animals, pure races are more highly prized because one values their hereditary patrimony and the merit of those individual characteristics to be transmitted to future generations. In hybrid races, on the other hand, undesirable recessive traits can reappear in successive generations. But this phenomenon of recessiveness, which was revealed by Mendel, could not have been recognized in the past. Therefore it seems impossible that racist policies could be determined at such a time in order to avoid the appearance of undesirable recessive traits.

Keith consequently attempted to uncover the basis of racist dispositions in biological utility. If these tendencies were not utilitarian throughout the evolution of humanity they would have become extinct. If they were maintained they evidently answer some specific exigency. According to Keith the diversity of races affords the variations upon which a selective environment can operate.

If the multiplicity of types served no evolutionary purpose, natural selection would favor the uniformity of all human races and one would observe a systematic tendency in this direction. Instead, even today, among the diverse races there continues the same heterogeneity which has always prevailed.

History demonstrates how, in the development of a race, there follows a period of expansion, one of stability, and one of decline. For example, the Caucasoid or White race is now in a state of

---

[26] A. Keith, *Nationality and Race from an Anthropologist's Point of View.* London: Oxford University, 1919. For a later, more sophisticated presentation, see A. Keith, *Evolution and Ethics*, New York, 1947; *A New Theory of Human Evolution*, New York, 1949.

[27] C. Gini. "The Cyclical Rise and Fall of Population." Chicago, 1929.

virtual stasis[28] after having traversed a period of broad expansion.[29] The ostensibly Caucasoid peoples who still retain considerable power of expansion, as in Russia and South America, are in reality more or less biologically mixed with other races. This cyclical pattern of expansion and contraction seems to decisively influence the propagation and substitution of races. In this respect Keith's explanation is not exhaustive.

Racism and Evolution

TO PROVIDE a significant account of how racism functions within the context of the broad evolutionary process, it is instructive to consider how animal breeders, the most consistent of racists, comport themselves with respect to pure bred races in their charge. They know that the returns on a pure race are not continuous. A pure race, once established, often degenerates and loses its fecundity and resistance. Therefore two races are crossed, even diverse races, and sometimes one obtains hybrid vigor or heterosis.[30]

Among the varieties thus obtained only the most vigorous are selected and their characteristics are fixed by having them reproduce in reproductive isolation, obtaining a new pure race. When even this commences to degenerate, one has recourse to new mixtures.[31]

Something similar obviously obtains for the human race where reproductive isolation is fostered by nationalism, by conformity,

---

[28] Cf. C. Gini, "Die Krise des Buergertums und die Bevoelkerungspolitik der totalitaeren Staaten." *Zeitschrift fuer die gesamte Staatswissenschaft,* 103, Number 2, 1943.

[29] Cf. C. Gini, *Corso di Sociologia.* Rome: Ricerche, 1957, chap. III; *Demographie et Sociologie.* Istanbul: Basimevi, 1952; "I problemi demografici nei secoli XIX e XX," *Questioni de storia contemporanea.* Milan: Marzorati, 1954.

[30] "It is necessary to note that the new races and nations, which one encounters in history, constitute only a minute part of the new types derived from crosses. They represent the rare successful attempts out of the enormous majority of attempts which proved abortive, either because the products of the crosses were not qualitatively favorable or were not sufficiently fecund . . ." C. Gini, *Nascita . . . ,* p. 81, cf. p. 79.

[31] Cf. E. East and D. Jones, *Inbreeding and Outbreeding.* London, 1917, pp. 31–35, 98, 114, 195, 201–209.

and by racist policies, while hybridization attends the constant expansive tendency made itself felt among political entities which were very small: clans, tribes, cities, and so forth. Subsequently, the transition was made from small political groups to larger aggregates, the minor units uniting among themselves giving way to a larger community animated by the aforementioned disposition toward homogenization. When a certain level of fusion was achieved, the moment for a vaster political expansion manifested itself which was followed by a new racial phase.[32]

Thus, gradually, from the condition of the tribe, if not of the primal family, a transition was effected to the village, the city, the state, and finally to a superstate phase, that of the United States of America and the Commonwealth of Britain. Today there is thought of a supernational complex vaster still. This constitutes the general tendency. There are periods, however, in which, because of the decline of civilization and of populations, contrary tendencies prevail, as occurred after the fall of the Roman Empire.

Obviously the anthropological factor is very important in the attempt to understand the nature, evolution and history of man as a social animal. In such an attempt the concept race figures in a critical way. We have concerned ourselves with this factor because it has been of prime importance in our own time.

[32] Cf. C. Gini, "L'evolution des groupements socieux." *XIV Congres International de Sociologie*, Bucharest, 1939.

BIOGRAPHICAL NOTE

A. JAMES GREGOR, M.A., Ph.D., *is Associate Professor of Social and Political Philosophy at the University of Kentucky. He is regional secretary of the Institut International de Sociologie and co-editor of* Revue Internationale Sociologie. *He is also division secretary of the Society for the Philosophical Study of Dialectical Materialism and a member of the American Philosophical Association, the American Sociological Association, the American Academy of Political and Social Science, the Southern Society for Philosophy and Psychology, the Kentucky Psychological Association, and the New York Academy of Sciences.*

Professor Gregor has conducted pyschological and sociological field studies in Central Australia among the Wailbri, Pintubi and Aranda aborigines and has done similar research among the Venda and Zulu Bantu in South Africa, and among the indigenous tribes of South West Africa. He is the author of numerous articles and several monographs. He is also the author of A Survey of Marxism: Problems in Philosophy and the Theory of History *(Random House, 1965).*

EVOLUTIONARY THEORY, RACE AND SOCIETY

A. James Gregor

Sociology, as the science of man in association, is an admittedly immature discipline.[1] As a consequence sociologists tend to be methodologically self-conscious. During the inter-war years this self-consciousness led to an avoidance of theory and theory construction and those disposed to entertain or pursue them were subject to polite odium. There was a general neglect of theory, a failure to make careful inventory of the intellectual patrimony bequeathed by the sociology of the nineteenth and early twentieth century. But those who neglected theory early found themselves condemned to painfully reformulate concepts and insights discerned with admirable clarity by their predecessors, for "facts" revealed themselves to be quite meaningless outside a theoretical context.

A theory, as theories tend to be understood in immature disciplines, is a determinate set of propositions which synthesizes observed regularities in a co-ordinated and coherent manner. One service of theory is its ability to relate phenomena from what appear to be, at first sight, disparate ranges of phenomena. In this sense theory provides a more parsimonious description of a wider range of natural phenomena than would be possible without it. In so doing, theory "explains" by revealing relationships between variables hitherto conceived as unrelated.

Explanations further provide the elements necessary for prediction: the law-like generalizations under which particular instances can be subsumed.[2] Theories, therefore, ideally equip the experimental scientist with predictive power and can serve as programmatic guides to the research enterprise. A theory is, minimally, a coherent statement of the results of research already accomplished and a program for future research.

In their impulse toward more comprehensive explanation, theories tend to become increasingly inclusive. This is particularly true in the case of sociology where, traditionally, there has been a tendency toward the gradual convergence of functional propositions generated by social psychology, social anthropology, ethnology and genetics. The theoretic gain realized by such convergence is expressed in terms of general orientations towards research findings, suggesting the types of variables and their possible interrelations which must be taken into account for adequate comprehension of the phenomenal field under scrutiny. As programmatic guides to research, on the other hand, the propositions of a theory must be couched in terms of clearly defined concepts, internally consistent, and capable of generating verification studies.

Sociology, at its present stage of development, finds it difficult to satisfy all these requirements. As a discipline it employs the language and the logic of ordinary discourse. Theoretical discussions remain, by and large, discursive rather than formal. Sociologists rarely attain the level of formal sophistication which characterizes the mature sciences. They have devised few formulae adequate to express the relationship between sociological variables. While there are admirable beginnings, these efforts are generally restricted to the codification of low range empirical generalizations.

Within this general context, the present essay is conceived as a contribution to general theory construction in sociology in the sense that it calls attention to a theory of intermediate range which suggests the types of variables, and their possible interrelationships, which must be taken into consideration to understand what is generally identified as "race prejudice." The theory itself was first outlined in the work of Ludwig Gumplowicz and its elements found expression in the work of notables such as Gaetano Mosca, William Graham Sumner, Arthur Keith and Corrado Gini.

That Gumplowicz's discursive theory has been long neglected is to be lamented. That it has been so neglected is the consequence of a number of influences, some legitimate and some not. Among the legitimate reasons for neglect is the general vagueness of the theory, its inability to generate testable propositions. The development of new research techniques and increasing analytic sophistication, however, tend to mitigate the strength of this objection. Among the illegitimate reasons for neglect is the indisposition on the part of contemporary social science practitioners to admit that the concept race has *any* explanatory or descriptive force.

The conviction seems to obtain that any recognition of the theoretical utility of racial concepts supports, in some unspecified sense, racial discrimination and racial violence. The fact that race concepts have been misapplied in the past[3] does not, of course, constitute a compelling argument for their present abandonment. It merely argues that one must insulate oneself against misapplication.

Ethnocentrism and Human Behavior

WHAT PASSES AS "race prejudice" is today generally recognized as but a single variety of a whole class of related ethnocentric responses[4] exemplified in normal human behavior.[5] The general agreement which obtains among specialists concerning the characterization of the sociopsychological syndrome identified as ethnocentrism,[6] its analogues among all social animals, and its putative universality among men,[7] afford strong presumptive evidence that we are dealing with behavior somehow rooted in the nature of man.[8]

All social animals apparently evince a disposition to identify with only select members of their own species. Within every species of social animal we find the existence and maintenance of independent, self-regarding groups which evince, irrespective of the variety of forms it takes, manifest preference for members of their own immediate community to the systematic exclusion of out-group members of the same species.[9] The assumption in citing such evidence is that human behavioral characteristics, particularly so universal a trait complex as ethnocentricity, have anlagen, analogies and homologies in non-human forms—and that the study of types which have the greatest degree of general morphological affinity to man may yield insights useful in understanding and interpretating problems of human behavior.[10]

While all analogical reasoning runs considerable hazard there is an increasing disposition, as a consequence of the painstaking work of behavior geneticists, to more seriously consider the animal anlagen and animal analogues of human social behavior in the effort to attain more comprehensive understanding. Thus Bettleheim and Janowitz have recently drawn an instructive parallel between the phenomenon of "territoriality" among social animals, the disposition of a group of social animals to defend a specific territorial confine against trespass by out-group members of the same species, and the human problems of residential segregation.[11]

That group exclusiveness, in-group preference, out-group avoidance and territorial segregation, characterize, in a variety of forms, the social behavior of not only man's closest primate relatives but apparently all non-primate vertebrate and invertebrate social animals as well, affords strong presumptive evidence against the theses that its basis lies in "convenience" and that such behavior patterns can be assumed or abandoned at will.[12] From time immemorial men have distinguished themselves on the basis of tribal, caste, class, national and/or racial differences, the explicit form of distinction determined largely by the historic, socioeconomic and political circumstances in which the particular human community finds itself.

These differences are never looked upon philosophically. They are one or the other or all together, made the ground for discrimination. At best, in highly sophisticated communities, differences are tolerated—but even then, under the least pressure, they become the focal point of group antagonism. Exclusiveness and preference collect around differences. These differences can reside in attitudes, religious or political opinions, speech, aesthetic or gustatory preferences, technical achievements or observable physical differences.[13] In varying context, in different areas of competition, one or the other or several in combination will be of primary importance.

Whatever the case, the generic social fact is that each association of men is animated by a "consciousness of kind," an identification of like members, a preferred association which characteristically conceives itself, with an apriori conviction of the most categorical and incorrigible sort, as somehow unique, superior and favored of nature.[14]

Development of Gumplowicz Theory

EFFORTS ON THE part of behavioral scientists to integrate these facts in a systematically related set of propositions have produced a variety of explanatory and descriptive accounts more widely used in social science than perhaps any other theoretical formulations.[15]

In general these formulations harken back to William Graham Sumner's account of "ethnocentrism" to be found in his classic *Folkways*. As a matter of fact the theoretical account of ethnocentrism is at least a generation older. Certainly as early as 1881 (a generation before the appearance of *Folkways*) Ludwig Gumplowicz provided a theoretical account of the psychosocial phenomena Sumner described, and similarly identified the constellation of behaviors under scrutiny as "ethnocentrism" (*Ethnocentrismus*).[16]

By 1883 the conception of mankind divided "at all times and in all places" into self-regarding communities each convinced of its own superiority and each animated by in-group amity and out-group diffidence had matured into the classic exposition of *Der Rassenkampf*.[17] Its influence radiated throughout Europe and the United States. Sumner's account was, in fact, an admirably summary account of Gumplowicz' theoretical contentions.[18] By 1896 the conception of ethnocentrism had become, in fact, commonplace among social theorists. Mosca, in his *Elementi di scienza politica*,[19] maintained:

"Mankind is divided into social groups each of which is set apart from other groups by beliefs, sentiments, habits and interests that are peculiar to it. The individuals who belong to one such group are held together by a consciousness of common brotherhood and held apart from other groups by passions and tendencies that are more or less antagonistic and mutually repellent."

Since that time the theme has been recurrent in the professional literature and received its last full statement and unqualified endorsement in Alfredo Niceforo's "Schematico profilo di una sociologia generale in cinquanta paragrafi," which was published in 1957.[20] Like Gumplowicz, Niceforo conceived aggregates of human beings, men in association, to be the irreducible elements of the science of sociology. Each such group is animated by a "sentiment of identity" and held together by a general "attraction of similars and repulsion of dissimilars." Each such community, furthermore, harbors a sense of superiority, what Niceforo called "group egocentricity," highly resistant to counterjudgment. Given these psychosocial dispositions the contacts between such self-regarding groups is characterized by diffidence, if not hostility.[21]

The general "theory" of ethnocentrism, recurrent in the literature, is certainly as old as Gumplowicz's *Rechtsstaat und Socialismus*. What is interesting to note is that for Gumplowicz ethnocentrism had biogenetic as well as psychosocial implications, an insight only recently rediscovered by contemporary social theorists. Gumplowicz made the former implications explicit by identifying his conception of what he had earlier called "ethnocentism" as "syngenism," each heterogeneous and irreducible social element of his theory a "consanguineous circle" that through protracted social isolation tends to become a biological race.[22] This is an aspect of Gumplowicz's theory only recently revived in the work of Arthur Keith and Corrado Gini.

Long before the advent of population genetics Gumplowicz advanced a populationist conception of race, identifying "races" as endogamous social isolates, communities of delimited territorial confines characterized by restricted gene-flow, breeding circles (*Blutgemeinschaften*) governed by mating rules which limit access to the common gene-pool. These mating rules were inculcated by what Gumplowicz identified as "social suggestion,"[23] a process which results in induced preferences—a disposition to identify with a preferred association. Thus, the general theory of ethnocentrism implied, in effect, propositions having biogenetic as well as psychosocial significance.

Gumplowicz conceived differences as both the cause and the result of social isolation and hereditary differences as marking off races.[24] Differences in language, religion, political organization, morals, aesthetic and gustatory preferences were enough to activate sentiments of repugnance on the part of each self-regarding community that restricted, as a consequence, inter-group gene-flow. Given sufficient time restricted gene-flow would tend to fix hereditary differences between allopatric (and in the cases of classes and castes, sympatric) groups.

The general theory of ethnocentrism advanced by Gumplowicz had, as a constituent, a special theory of raciogenesis. The special theory was either explicitly rejected by those who followed Gumplowicz (as in the case of Mosca) or simply neglected (as was the case with Sumner). Only recently have the merits of Gumplowicz's original insights become obvious. These insights urge themselves upon us as a consequence of special developments in dynamic anthropology and population genetics.

Physical Anthropology and Race

FOR SOME TIME it has been apparent that anthropology has entered a critical transitional phase in its development. The question is whether this phase marks a stage in the process of maturation of what had hitherto been an immature, essentially classificatory science (albeit with some pretentions of grandeur) or whether it marks the passing of a fundamentally useless discipline whose greatest service was to keep a considerable number of men harmlessly employed for an inordinate time.[25] As a matter of fact, physical anthropology, critically self conscious of itself as a consequence of professional[26] and popular[27] attacks leveled against it, gives all the evidence of maturing into a science of man prepared to benefit through a convergence of biological, psychological and sociological theory.

The first critical objection to the enterprise of the physical anthropologist has been that the *homme moyen* of Quetelet, the *tipo medio* of Morselli and Mantegazza, and the "phenotypic statistical abstraction" of which Kluckhohn speaks, have no counterpart in nature.[28] There is no race of man, in nature, displaying an absolute uniformity in any given constellation of metrical or non-metrical hereditary characteristics. What one does find is a natural distribution, variations (at least within major races) which may be plotted on a monomodal curve, through which one race, or sub-race, merges imperceptibly, as a "clinal population," into another.

The physical anthropologist originally selected a discrete number of subjects and, by dint of measurements and observations, abstracted a "polar" or "ideal" type; the inclusiveness or exclusiveness of the subsequent unit series determined by the number of variables he employed in abstracting this polar type. The number of races distinguished was a function of the number of variables considered. If but one variable was employed (i.e., pigmentation), two "pure" races might be conjured up with hybrid intermediates satisfying the empiric necessity of explaining the observed gradual transition from one minor race to the other.[29]

In an area such as Europe the physical anthropologist could "discover" one, two, or one hundred "races,"[30] the multiplicity being determined by the number of variables considered, the convenience afforded by some special classification and/or simple common sense. For heuristic purposes it may be convenient to recognize only a small number of "major" or "geographic" races while, for detailed consideration of the inhabitants of a limited area, sharper distinctions may be entertained.

The argument directed against this entire preoccupation is simply: if racial classification is, even in part, arbitrary and a matter of convenience, what has such classification to do with man, as we find him in the natural world, i.e., man as a denizen of social, religious, political, and economic associations? An answer, important because of its implications for our special considerations, here, has been forthcoming in the contemporary work of Coon, Darlington, Gates, and Gini, and has been, in recent years, gaining increased support.

Modern Conception of Race

THE CONTEMPORARY conception, in the sociological tradition of Gumplowicz, is simply that race is a dynamic, not a static, constant—that the natural variability which characterizes man affords the prime matter of evolution—that evolution proceeds through the agency of the natural associations in which men are to be found and that such associations are sustained by a disposition man shares with all social animals to associate with only select members of his own species.[31] Evolution proceeds by virtue of the resultant social isolation which fosters endogamous self-regarding breeding communities.

Man has systematically, throughout time, isolated himself in preferred associations. As a primitive those associations were "hordal" or tribal. The associations among contemporary men are more complex and diverse. If any of these associations are anything more than transient, systematic in-group preferences and out-group avoidance result in more or less systematic endogamy—mating systems more or less effective in concentrating genotypes in "pure" lines, retaining and fostering the genetic variations which are the raw material of microevolution.[32]

As a consequence, a multiplicity of inbred lines are sustained and promoted, the riches of genic diversity (otherwise lost in panmixia) preserved.[33] Variations, preserved and fostered through protracted social isolation (not to concern ourselves here with geographic isolation) produce the local or minor races (a population which differs from other populations in the relative frequency of determinate genes)[34] with which the physical anthropologist occupies himself.[35] The intraspecific competition and substitution of such local variations through natural selection completes the theoretical picture of the microevolutionary process.

Such a conception is predicated on the notion of a "natural disposition" on the part of individuals to associate only with preferred members of their own species. As we have seen, sociologists have long been aware of such a behavioral disposition, the natural corollary of which, in the face of contact with out-groups, is generally flight among animals[36] and avoidance and prejudice among men.

Local associations among men are sustained by a "sentiment of identity" generated through similarities in political allegiance, accoutrement, custom, language, origin, culture, or perceivable physical difference. The importance of physical similarity is that it is permanent and transmissible in accountable fashion, and consequently, is perhaps the most important single similarity upon which man's disposition to distinguish his group from others fixes itself. Man has regularly assigned individuals who display gross physical differences from his own group to an entirely different moral and aesthetic order.[37]

Enduring associations based upon socioperceptual differences become closed breeding circles,[38] populations in which components biologically assimilate to gradually produce, given sufficient time, pandiacritic or anthropologically distinct races. Local or "parish" races can be found at various stages of differentiation: an *adiacritic* phase where the biological process has only recently begun, where phenotypic variability may be prominent in relative abundance—a *mesodiacritic* phase, where more phenotypic uniformity is in evidence—and an ultimate *pandiacritic* phase, the end result of an evolutionary process.

Dynamics of Mate Selection

CONTEMPORARY population theory thus suggests an intimate connection between social or reproductive isolation and evolution, a connection rich in obvious sociological implications. The dynamics of mate selection, the factors involved in and determining the nature of breeding communities and breeding systems, are of critical importance in the attempt to understand the microevolution of any species.[39] Mating, among men, is limited not by immediate fertility but by specified rules of exogamy and endogamy, by the sanctions imposed upon breeding outside the "marriage circle." This "repugnance to outbreeding"[40] is the common property of all animals: ". . . naturalists and students of wild populations have shown clearly that local races of animals may exhibit marked mating preferences, usually favoring mates of their own race."[41] Among men this preference may manifest itself by establishing breeding communities of varying stability.

In contemporary society these preferences manifest themselves as national, class, religious, and racial preferences (and corresponding national, class, religious, and racial avoidance). That these preferences constitute the basis of "racial prejudice" is now generally recognized and the social isolation which is its natural consequence is recognized as theoretically essential to the understanding of the process of human microevolution.[42]

As we have suggested, these endogamous communities are more or less effective agencies in concentrating genotypes in pure lines.[43] Such groups tend to meet but not mingle. They constitute, for all intents and purposes, "race-cradles," isolates of varying stability which preserve and foster genetic differences. If "races" are understood to constitute populations which differ from other populations in the relative frequency of determinate genes, then breeding isolates even of recent vintage, maintaining specific genetic differences which they preserve by their manifest repugnance to outbreeding, constitute races. "Races," in the abstract or classificatory sense, are the end result of a long process of isolation and inbreeding in which a diagnostic constellation of anthropometric traits become "fixed."

The confusion which has attended discussions of "race prejudice" has largely been the consequence of the fact that in past and contemporary literature "race," while having an almost intolerably broad connotation, has rarely been found to have a precise denotation. This circumstance has invoked varying reactions among social scientists. Some have simply advocated abandonment of the term; some have employed it in so careless a fashion as to bring it into disrepute.

Gumplowicz and Gini (among others) on the other hand, have employed it with commendable consistency to designate a dynamic, or historic constant fully in accord with contemporary evolutionary theory. "Races" can be incipient, possessed at one stage, of little more than a "desire" to become a race in the anthropometric sense, that is, possessed of a systematic preference scale which proscribes outbreeding and maintains a climate fostering biologic isolation and, given time, genetic homeostasis, phenotypic uniformity. The latter consequence is a result of the former disposition. Geographic isolation, genetic drift, and selection, to further the analysis, conduces to the formation of "grand" or major races, i.e., "geographic races."

An adequate appraisal of the phenomena we identify as race prejudice can only be consequent upon a correct analysis of the concept "race," an appreciation of the factors involved in human microevolution, and an understanding of the psychosocial disposition of individuals to identify with only select numbers of their own species as the result of conditioning during a critical phase in primary socialization.

Consciousness of Kind

AT THE TURN of the century, when Franklin Giddings articulated the concept of in-group amity as "consciousness of kind,"[44] the tendency was to treat the behavior associated with this aspect of ethnocentrism as "instinctive," a term seemingly justified by the universality of the trait complex. There can be little serious doubt that the "sentiment of identity," what Niceforo calls the "invariable law" of "attraction of similars and repulsion of dissimilars,"[45] is somehow rooted in the nature of man, a nature which man shares in its most significant features with all social animals. But to call man's intra-group (or inter-group) responses "instinctive" does not convey much information. Some account of what is essentially attitude formation is required to complete the assessment of the biosocial nature of preferential association.

As has been suggested, a group is sustained by mutual attraction. The members of the group are attracted to each other and abstract from observed similarity notions of ideal beauty and appropriate dress, and find in their common customs and usages the self-evident rules for proper conduct. The disposition to identify with a group of select membership characterizes man as a social animal; the specific object choice for such identification will be determined by the circumstances in which he is nurtured.

In every complex society men react selectively to their fellows and preferential association is based upon observable differences.[46] Such preferences, in evolutionary time, made a group more cohesive, they provided a guide in avoiding potential predators. Individuals and groups possessed of such disposition would have a greater survival potential than those but weakly possessed of it. Possession of such an ethnocentric trait complex, i.e., the disposition to identify with members of a select community of individuals, would therefore favor the survival of groups so disposed[47] and as a consequence, such a disposition would tend to become universal,[48] "part of Nature's evolutionary machinery."[49]

In simple primitive societies, where the members of out-groups are generally of the same racial confraternity, enmities are elicited as a consequence of cultural differences, modes of speech, differences in accoutrement, custom, and personal adornment. Sociologists and social psychologists have long been aware of these facts. What has been lacking has been a genetic account of the development of attitudes that would sustain such universal behavior patterns—behavior patterns which characterize all social animals. In our own time materials provided by ethologists, sociologists, child psychologists, and social psychologists have begun to take on the outlines of a general theory of group behavior which affords a theoretical account of the formation of ethnocentric attitudes necessary for a comprehensive account of the process of human evolution.

The study of the psychological mechanisms which foster group isolation, establishing a breeding community of defined extent, has only begun. The establishment of preferences fixes certain norms of mate selection and marks the confines of a marriage circle. Such discriminatory preferences are apparently fixed at an early or primary socialization stage when children find themselves in an environment where they are regularly exposed, generally, only to members of their own physical type, class, and cultural background. These preferences have shown themselves to be but little subject to alteration after the period of primary socialization has been undergone.[50]

The importance, within the context of the evolution of man, of the fixing of these preference scales so significant in microevolution has been touched upon by various authors since the time of Darwin himself. Mating preferences insure genetic continuity to variations, thus permitting a wider range of material upon which selective agencies may act. The theoretical need for such a disposition to preferential mating has long been recognized: the variations afforded by such dispositionally motivated isolation provide for the substitution of types through natural and artificial selection.

"Developmental Identification"

THE PROCESS by virtue of which the individual identifies with a specific group has been described as "developmental identification."[51] This identification with a reference group probably has its roots, in part, in the basic nurturance relationship between the child and his family group, that is to say, since the infant is almost totally dependent upon those charged with his care he begins to associate primary-drive reduction with certain (visual and auditory) cues provided by those ministering to his needs. These cues take on a secondary reward value for the child.[52] The familiar face of a mother is comforting, an unfamiliar face is discomfiting.[53] These cues associated with the valued person or persons become self-rewarding.[54] This process can conveniently be termed primary socialization.[55]

Since in this primary reference group the perceptual cues of the valued persons (physical appearance, patterns of speech, etc.) are those which are, or will ultimately be, shared by the infant, the emotional basis of generalized self-acceptance is securely laid down. Much of this primary emotional charge is associated with physical appearance, since this is one of the principal perceptual cues to which the organism is conditioned. "This means . . . that [the] basic sociosensory perception of difference in physique plays a powerful role in the conscious, and probably still more powerful role in the unconscious, group identification."[56]

The development of a coherent self-system is a function of

group identity. Before the ego has been fully developed it appropriates a perceptual symbol that assists it in distinguishing itself from others.[57] Primary socialization takes place in an environment of high salience, in a situation where elementary perceptual cues attend the gratification of primary drives. Thus by the age of about two and a half to four the child "has a definite consciousness of kind, of his own kind."[58]

Only in the very recent past has the process of individual ego development become the subject of systematic consideration. A shift from preoccupation with the psychology of the unconscious and mechanisms of repression to the psychology of ego development has led to a more positive appraisal of what had been, almost universally, condemned as "prejudice." That the child, in the necessary process of ego development, organizes the data of his macrospheric social world under a bipolarity of types, valued and disvalued, good and bad, is now recognized as a major source of ego strength. The individual child in its synthesizing and developmental efforts, subsumes under a valued ego ideal those characteristics which he shares with those with whom he stands in nurturance relationship.

The existence of a powerful ideal implies as its contrast a negative prototype characterized by differences which distinguish it from the valued ideal. As a consequence attributes of high social visibility constitute prime identifying traits of both positive and negative prototypes. The white child, in the process of developing a viable self-image, identifies "white" physical traits as good, superior, beautiful and potent, a readiness to assign value predicates which we recognize as diagnostic of ethnocentric disposition. The ability of the child to identify himself with the valued prototype in terms of evident physical and cultural similarities enhances self-esteem and is the source of enormously valuable ego strength.[59]

This process of "primary socialization," the identification of the individual with his social group, with its obverse diffidence with respect to out-groups, has its obvious analogue among lower animal life forms. What has been called "secondary socialization," the process by which the child is encouraged to be like valued persons in the groups to which he is socialized is mediated by speech and organized education but requires as a necessary antecedent that the child possess a generalized need or secondary drive to increase the measure of similarity he shares with those individuals he values.

Those in the larger society after whom the child is expected to model himself normally share the more obvious sociosensory traits with those of the child's primary family group and the child has an initial bias to regard them as valued. The child manifests what Ichheiser calls a "possibly irresistibly strong" tendency to associate real value with observed similarity—he evinces an "attitudinal set."[60]

From whatever empirical evidence is available it seems that the child, as the obverse of a generalized favorable bias with respect to those with whom he normally shares some sociosensory traits, possesses a generalized and relatively undifferentiated unfavorable attitude toward a group characterized by differences of high visibility.[61] This constitutes a generalized attitude articulated during the earliest developmental stages of the individual's life so charged with emotion that it persists thereafter with singular tenacity.[62]

Similarity and Preference

THIS ATTITUDINAL bias reveals itself in a positive relationship between perceived similarity and preference.[63] Positive values are ascribed to the traits of the reference group,[64] while out-group traits, particularly those possessed of high visibility, are conceived of, at best, as curious, and in contact situations are deprecated.[65] For example, while all groups use ethnophaulisms (verbalized group disparagements) such disparagements most frequently refer to manifest physical differences, and then, second in rank order, to highly visible cultural differences.[66]

Nursery school children of about four years of age clearly give evidence of these dispositions, although awareness can be plotted on a continuum from low (involving something like 15 percent of the group) to high (involving some 32 percent of the group.)[67] Lasker remarks: "We see among children around five years of age recognition of racial differences in individuals with an emotional bias in favor of his own and adverse to some other race. No cases are reported in which children become aware of racial difference without a feeling about the matter."[68]

Studies conducted with children from three to seven provide evidence for such contentions.[69] Goodman's early report of studies with children ranging in age from about two and a half to four lends further corroboration. Disposed as he is, the child tends, subsequently, to be characterized by "biased" social perception, i.e., to be disposed to note and recall instances of negative out-group behavior, emphasizing differences and departures, and exaggerating the number of out-group members in his immediate environs.[70] The out-group, in effect, becomes a "conceptualized object" possessed of traits which need not necessarily have any direct qualitative or quantitative correspondence with the characteristics of the actual out-group.[71] A relatively well defined stereotype is articulated. These characteristics persist into maturity. Adult whites, for example, identify Negroes as "black" when they are in effect brown; white police officers will regularly overestimate the number of arrests they have made involving Negroes[72] and white witnesses will overestimate the number of Negroes at the scene of a crime.

Such a reaction pattern with respect to the out-group can be exaggerated by real or fancied threats of economic competition, status displacement, or general hostility.[73] Prejudice then passes from stereotype and emotional enmity to action.[74] Unfulfilled needs, economic competition, and personality disabilities can act as stimulants to the expression of prejudice and its virulence or lack of it, but they cannot be conceived of, in any exhaustive sense, as the *causes* of race prejudice.[75]

There was a time when it could be maintained that the importance of obvious physical differences between groups could be minimized in rendering an account of the dynamics of inter-group relations. Racial "amity" in Hawaii and Brazil were frequently cited as cases in point. Increasing sophistication and more systematic collection of empirical data indicate that wherever data is available racial avoidance can be documented in the relationship between groups of high social visibility in protracted contact.[76]

There is, of course, no uniform pattern of specifically interracial responses because the life situation of each group differs. Often mature individuals will be members of a number of different reference groups, each casting the individual in a different role, each group animated by a different value system,[77] designed to enhance its viability. An individual in one institutional situation may display admirable "tolerance" for out-group members and in another manifest explicit enmity,[78] but the responses can only be meaningfully understood against a background of generalized ethnocentrism and group dynamics.

In our own immediate society, as distinct from primitive communities, response patterns in interethnic and interracial relations will vary for a variety of reasons. As an illustration, it is often the case that in certain institutional situations individuals will learn the appropriate verbal etiquette of intergroup and interracial discourse, in those institutions an earmark of status, and in interview situations will register a relatively rapid diminution of "prejudice" as a consequence of having learned the requisite language,[79] while, as a matter of fact, Gittler[80] and Stember[81] indicate that the generalized negative response toward outgroups, developed very early in life, is extremely resistant to change. Overt behavior is often at complete variance with verbal behavior.

Horowitz's data indicates that negative attitudes toward Negroes in the United States are constant, irrespective of whether the white children have little personal contact (by attending segregated schools) or whether the subjects derived from North or South, from urban or rural environments.[82] Clark's findings similarly indicate a general consistency of negative response.[83]

Adult Response More Variable

ADULT RESPONSES in our society will show increased variability because the various roles in which the mature individual is cast in a complex community are more heavily laden with consequences bearing on his status, economic opportunities, bargaining position, institutionalized functions, and responsibilities. These can operate to mollify, alter or exaggerate negative response toward out-groups. Needless to say, the negative responses toward out-groups having high social visibility are most resistant to change.[84]

There are, on the other hand, singular circumstances in which group members are systematically taught, in order to enhance the survival potential of the group, not to display what would otherwise be a normal avoidance pattern even with respect to out-groups possessed of high visibility. Jews and Communists in the United States, for example, regularly give overt evidence of a low index of bias toward Negroes. Their peculiar situation, in which the Jew conceives of himself forever standing in the shadow of oppression, and the Communist in the shadow of repression, explain these anomalous response patterns. Their marginal position necessitates especially adapted responses.

Jews in the United States, for example, evince low bias attitudes toward Negroes, but are apparently as prejudiced against other ethnic groups as non-Jews.[85] Jewish children, it would seem, are specifically taught *not* to evidence bias against Negroes with whose fate the Jews tend to identify themselves.[86] Jews in Israel, on the other hand, show marked prejudice against "dark citizens."

Communists in the United States, in turn, while they record low bias against ethnic and racial groups, show pathological enmity toward the conceptualized "capitalists" in what Sprague has termed the "rivalry of intolerances."[87] Communists in the Soviet Union, in comparison, give ample evidence of ethnic and racial bias.[88]

Singularities in their life situation often tax groups to the extent that their manifest responses show engaging departures from otherwise universal behavior patterns. Individuals, and entire groups, may become xenocentric as a consequence of frustration, threat, personal rejection, and status deprivation.[89] But their behavior is comprehensible within the compass of a general theory of ethnocentric intergroup dynamics and is understood as a displacement of elemental response patterns.

Such a theory suggests that in primary socialization the emergent ego comes to associate certain highly visible perceptual traits with value, and certain perceptual "symbols" become associated with primary drive gratification. The individual ascribes value to those possessed of such traits. He is comfortable in their presence and anxious in their absence. The child shares those valued traits with primary family members. This constitutes the core of self-acceptance. Certainly by the time the child reaches the age of three or four he has conceptualized an "ideal group" characterized by a constellation of sociosensory traits (traits having high social visibility). He can distinguish between "his" group and other groups.

He enters secondary groups possessed of this bias. Generally such groups can become "his" group without psychic tension—they generally evidence the same major sociosensory traits as his primary group. Sociometric choice in the macrosphere is made on the basis of real or fancied similarity. The ongoing process of secondary socialization takes place without psychodynamic tension: the child proceeds to imitate the valued persons who share with him evident similarities. The persons of the secondary groups are infused with the value associated with those of the primary group with whom they share observable traits.

The ability of the individual to identify with the valued persons he is imitating, making himself like unto them, enhances his own self-esteem. The individual, the primary group, and the secondary groups share the common nucleus of visible similarity. The manifest tendency of such groups is to value their distinctive traits, be they physical or cultural, to make interpersonal selection on the basis of perceived similarity, and to enter into selective associations, associations of preference, the obverse of which is the latent or manifest avoidance of those groups which are, in lesser or greater degree, dissimilar.

The Basis of Racial Prejudice

THERE SEEMS to be little doubt that ethnocentrism is the primitive, generic tendency of group life, around which the attitude of specifically racial prejudices develops[90] in the course of the normal psychodynamic process of individual ego development in a society where groups characterized by distinctive racial livery come into sustained contact.[91]

We are now in a position to better understand some important aspects of the dynamics of intergroup relations. Much of contemporary theory in micro- and macroevolution turn on the evident disposition of groups to maintain breeding circles of limited compass. Contemporary anthropologists have postulated the necessity of such isolating mechanisms of a psychosocial order to provide a fully articulated account of the processes governing evolution. Sociologists have identified the trait complex involved as "ethnocentrism." What has been lacking has been a substantive account of the process of individual attitude formation compatible with observed collective response. In our own time theoretical accounts of the psychology of ego development have been moving in just such a direction. Should these accounts prove satisfactory they would fill out the theoretical sketch left us by Ludwig Gumplowicz.

The outline of a general theory of ethnocentrism left to the social sciences by Gumplowicz anticipated, to a surprising degree, developments in the related sciences of anthropology, genetics, sociology and psychology. "Ethnocentrism" has proved to be one of the most widely employed and suggestive of the concepts in the behavioral sciences. The dynamic concept of race, as it has been advanced by population geneticists, supplements and is itself implied as a collateral to ethnocentrism. What Gumplowicz identified as "social suggestion" (an identifying complex term adopted by Sumner after him) reveals itself in the contemporary guise of primary and secondary socialization, developmental identification, concepts becoming increasingly important in the psychology of individual ego development. Contemporary behavioral science has done much to vindicate the pioneer work of Gumplowicz. That he has been so long neglected is unfortunate.

For the general theory of ethnocentrism as it was advanced by Gumplowicz to achieve the stature of a bona fide theory in social science it is necessary that it prove capable of generating verification studies, of enumerating constituent variables and the putative relationship that obtains between them, of providing a scaling technique for the measure of ethnocentricity and its relationship to group formation and intergroup relations, of techniques measuring gene flow between adjacent population groups that give evidence of the ethnocentric syndrome as well as suggesting longitudinal and factor analytic studies of the development of attitudes.

Most of the empirical research that would serve to thus fill in the theoretical sketch left by Gumplowicz has only begun. A renewal of interest in the work of Gumplowicz should, however, provide programmatic suggestions that would be invaluable in research design. The satisfaction of at least such requirements would advance Gumplowicz's conceptions from the level of a plausible explanation sketch to the first level of general verification. Ludwig Gumplowicz has left us a broad and suggestive account—it is both a help and a challenge.

Notes

[1] Cf. R. K. Merton, *Social Theory and Social Structure* (Revised edition. New York, 1963), Introduction.

[2] Cf. C. G. Hempel, *Aspects of Scientific Explanation* (New York, 1965); G. C. Homans, "Contemporary Theory in Sociology," in *Handbook of Modern Sociology* (R. E. L. Faris, ed. Chicago, 1964), pp. 951–953.

[3] Cf. Gossett's account of Ward's application of Gumplowicz's conceptions in T. F. Gossett, *Race: The History of an Idea in America* (Dallas, 1963), pp. 165–167.

[4] R. Park, *Race and Culture* (New York, 1964), pp. 231 f.; P. I. Rose, *They and We: Racial and Ethnic Relations in the United States* (New York, 1964), pp. 73–77.

[5] G. W. Allport, *The Nature of Prejudice* (Garden City, 1958), Chaps. 2–4.

[6] Cf. D. T. Campbell, R. A. LeVine, "A Proposal for Cooperative Cross-Cultural Research on Ethnocentrism," *The Journal of Conflict Resolution*, 1961, 5, 83 n. 3.

[7] W. G. Sumner, *Folkways: A Study of the Sociological Importance of Usages, Manners, Customs, Mores and Morals* (New York, 1960), pp. 27 ff.

[8] ". . . it is probably unfortunately true—that prejudice is part of our nature. . . ." B. Bettelheim and M. Janowitz, *Social Change and Prejudice* (New York, 1964), p. 52.

[9] A. Keith, *A New Theory of Human Evolution* (New York, 1949), p. 39.

[10] C. R. Carpenter, "Societies of Monkeys and Apes," *Biological Symposia*, 1942, 8, 177, reproduced in *Primate Social Behavior* (C. H. Southwick, ed. New York, 1963), p. 24.

[11] Bettleheim, Janowitz, *op. cit.*, pp. 61–65.

[12] For a popular but nonetheless significant account of this thesis, vide R. Ardrey, *African Genesis* (New York, 1961).

[13] C. Gini, "El problema de la asimilacion cultural." *Revista de la Facultad de Ciencias Economicas de la Universidad Nacional de Cuyo*, May–August, September–December, 1955.

[14] Such a generalization must, of course, be insulated by a *cateris paribus* clause. Under normal conditions the in-group amity-out-group enmity dichotomy can be expected to maintain. In complex societies however, particularly where as a consequence of the functioning of this disposition and the superordination of a

Evolutionary Theory, Race and Society

class, race or ethnic in-group, status deprived groups obtain, individuals from those subordinate communities may manifest xenocentric orientations. This is a relatively common phenomenon in stratified society and is the special subject of reference group theory. This issue will be touched upon in the course of our exposition, but limitations of space preclude exhaustive treatment.

[15] For an excellent treatment of the range and variety of theoretical propositions in "ethnocentricity theory" vide D. T. Campbell and R. A. LeVine, *Propositions About Ethnocentrism from Social Science Theories* (Mimeographed, March, 1965).

[16] L. Gumplowicz, *Rechtsstaat und Socialismus* (Innsbruck, 1881), pp. 70–78.

[17] L. Gumplowicz, *Der Rassenkampf: sociologische Untersuchungen* (Innsbruck, 1883).

[18] By 1899 Gumplowicz' *Grundriss der Sociologie* was rendered into English by Frederick Moore as the *Outlines of Sociology* (Philadelphia, 1899). The first edition of *Die sociologische Staatsidee* appeared in 1893 and a second edition in 1902. A comparison of Sumner's account with that found in almost any of Gumplowicz' writings indicates their close affinities.

[19] G. Mosca, *Elementi di scienza politica* (Bari, 1953), I, 111.

[20] A. Niceforo, "Schematico profilo di una sociologia generale in cinquanta paragrafi," *Revista Italiana di Economia, Demografia e Statistica*, 1957, 11, 1–43.

[21] *Ibid.*, paras. II, XLII, X, XXXIX.

[22] Cf. Gumplowicz, *Outlines* . . . , p. 145.

[23] Gumplowicz, *Sociologische Staatsidee*, section vii.

[24] Gumplowicz, *Der Rassenkampf*, p. 193 f.

[25] ". . . the time is long overdue to recognize that the discipline designated physical anthropology, conceived in any terms other than its relevance to stock-taking in the tailoring and furnishing trades, is a blind alley in the landscape of biological science, like its parent phrenology, harmless as a hobby for the opulent aged, but with no rational claim to support from the public purse." L. Hogben, "Darwinism and Human Society: Society in Retrospect," *Darwinism and the Study of Man* (M. Banton, ed. London, 1961), p. 48.

[26] W. Boyd, *Genetics and the Races of Man* (Boston, 1950).

[27] F. Ortiz, *El Engaño de las Razas* (Havana, 1946); M. Ashley Montagu, *Man's Most Dangerous Myth* (New York, 1952).

[28] A. J. Gregor, "The Logic of Race Classification," *Genus*, 1958, 14, 1–4.

[29] Something like this is frequently found in naive race theories; cf. J. Sayers, *Can the White Race Survive?* (Washington, 1929); O. Hauser, *Der Blonde Mensch* (Danzig, 1930); K. Weinlaender, *Rassenkunde, Rassenpaedagogik, und Rassenpolitik* (Weissenburg, 1933).

[30] C. Coon, S. Garn, "On the Number of Races of Mankind," *American Anthropologist*, 1955, 57, 5; A. Keith, *A New Theory* . . . , Chap. 33.

[31] C. Waddington, "The Human Evolutionary System," *Darwinism and the Study of Society*, p. 67; C. Darlington, "The Control of Evolution in Man," *Eugenics Review*, 1958, 50, 172; A. J. Gregor, "Corrado Gini and the Theory of Race Formation," *Sociology and Social Research*, 1961, 45, 175–181.

[32] N. Timofeeff-Ressowsky, "Sulla questione dell'isolamento territoriale entro popolazioni specifiche," *Scientia Genetica*, 1939, 1, 78–85; A. Keith, *The Place of Prejudice in Modern Civilization* (New York, 1931) p. 9.

[33] R. A. Fisher, *The Theory of Inbreeding* (London, 1949) p. 120.

[34] L. Dunn, *Heredity and Evolution in Human Populations* (Cambridge, 1959) p. 90.

[35] C. Gini, *Le basi scientifiche della politica della popolazione* (Catania, 1931), Chap. 40, *Corso di Sociologia* (Rome, 1957) p. 152 f., *Nascita, evoluzione e morte delle nazioni* (Rome, 1930) pp. 77, 81, 86, 100 n. 31.

[36] D. Freedman, "The Flight Response and Critical Periods in Social Development," *Mémoire du XIXe Congrès International de Sociologie* (Mexico, D.F., 1960), II, 39–53.

[37] C. Gini, *Le Rilevazioni statistiche tra le popolazioni primitive* (Rome, 1942) p. 270 ff.

[38] L. Dunn, *Race and Biology* (Paris, 1951), p. 25.

[39] Darlington, *op. cit.*, p. 171.

[40] Darlington, *op. cit.*, p. 172.

[41] Waddington, *op. cit.*, p. 67.

[42] Cf. C. Coon, *The Origin of Races* (New York, 1962), pp. 103–106, *The Living Races of Man* (New York, 1965), pp. 30–33; R. Biasutti, *Razze e popoli della terra* (Turin, 1941), I, 300 f.; A. J. Gregor, "Sociology and the Anthropobiological Sciences," *Mémoire . . .* , II, 83–106.

[43] Hogben, *op. cit.*, p. 45.

[44] Cf. F. Giddings, "Sociology and the Abstract Sciences: the Origin of the Social Feelings," *Annals of the American Academy of Political and Social Science*, 1895, 5, 750.

[45] Niceforo, "Schematico profilo . . . ," para. X.

[46] Cf. G. A. Lundberg, "Some Neglected Aspects of the 'Minorities' Problem," *Modern Age* (Summer, 1958), p. 286.

[47] Cf. B. Berry, *Race Relations* (New York, 1951), p. 78 f.

[48] Cf. Campbell and LeVine, "A Proposal for Cooperative Cultural Research on Ethnocentrism," *op. cit.*, p. 85.

[49] A. Keith, *Nationality and Race from an Anthropologist's Point of View* (London, 1919), p. 32 f. Cf. also his *The Place of Prejudice in Modern Civilisation*.

[50] M. Jahoda, *Race Relations and Mental Health* (Paris, 1960), p. 38–40.

[51] Cf. O. H. Mowrer, *Learning Theory and Personality Dynamics* (New York, 1950).

[52] Cf. J. R. Davitz, "Social Perception and Sociometric Choice of Children," *Journal of Abnormal and Social Psychology*, 1955, 50, 175, and M. Ashley Montagu, "The Origin and Nature of Social Life and the Biological Basis of Cooperation," *Journal of Social Psychology*, 1949, 29, 275 f., 279.

[53] Cf. A. T. Jersild, "Emotional Development," in *Manual of Child Psychology* (L. Carmichael, ed. New York, 1954).

[54] J. P. Scott, "The Process of Socialization in Animal and Human Societies," *Mémoire . . .* , II, 242.

[55] *Ibid.*, pp. 237–244.

[56] G. Ichheiser, "Sociopsychological and Cultural Factors in Race Relations," *The American Journal of Sociology*, 1949, 54, 396. Cf. Allport, *op. cit.*, p. 286.

[57] "The following discussion is limited to children's emergent awareness of themselves, with reference to a specific social grouping. It deals with the beginnings of race consciousness conceived as a function of ego-development." R. Horowitz, "Racial Aspects of Self-Identification in Nursery School Children," *Journal of Psychology*, 1939, 7, 99.

[58] Goodman, *op. cit.* Cf. M. E. Goodman, "Evidence Concerning the Genesis of Interracial Attitudes," *American Anthropologist*, 1948, 48, 624–630.

[59] The literature devoted to this aspect of the general theory of ethnocentricity is abundant. Among the most significant treatments are E. H. Erikson's *Childhood and Society* (New York, 1963), and his "Identity and the Life Cycle," in *Psychological Issues* (G. S. Klein, ed. New York, 1959), particularly pp. 19–31. Cf. also Bettelheim and Janowitz, *op. cit.*, pp. 53–61, where a relatively positive appraisal of "prejudice" and its role in ego development is given. Unfortunately, the authors still identify the disposition to entertain a polarity of ideal types as in

some sense "defensive" rather than as a necessary constitutive process in ego development.

[60] Ichheiser, op. cit.

[61] R. Black and W. Dennis, "The Development of Stereotypes Concerning the Negro," *The Journal of Abnormal and Social Psychology*, 1943, 38, 525–531.

[62] "Another characteristic of primary socialization is that it takes place relatively rapidly and has very long lasting effects, both on infantile and adult life. It determines the close relatives of the animal and incidentally those for which it has a preference in mating. It also has a marked effect on social fighting. Mice raised as litter mates rarely fight each other as adults. Puppies reared in the same way form a dominance order without serious fighting which they maintain into adult life. Strangers, on the other hand, are usually attacked. We may wonder how these findings apply to human behavior," Scott, op. cit., p. 242. Gini, in an extensive report on children raised by various species of animals, reports that children undergoing primary socialization in animal groups never appear fully to identify with humans even after long inter-human contact. Cf. Gini, *Corso di Sociologia*, p. 242; J. B. Gittler, "Man and His Prejudices," *Scientific Monthly*, 1949, 69, 43–47

[63] Cf. F. E. Fiedler, "Assumed Similarity Measures as Predictors of Team Effectiveness," *Journal of Abnormal and Social Psychology*, 1954, 49, 381–388; W. G. Warrington and F. G. Blaisdell, "Unconscious Attitudes as Correlates of Sociometric Choice in a Social Group," *ibid.*, 1952, 47, 790–796, and Davitz, op. cit., pp. 173–176.

[64] Goodman, *Race Awareness* . . . , pp. 34–37. Cf. K. L. Llewellyn, "Education and the Family: Certain Unsolved Problems," in *The Family: Its Function and Destiny* (R. N. Anshen, ed. New York, 1949), pp. 277–298.

[65] Cf. C. I. Glicksberg, "Psychoanalysis and the Negro Problem," *Phylon*, 1956, 17, 43–44.

[66] E. P. Palmore, "Ethnophaulisms and Ethnocentrism," *The American Journal of Sociology*, 1962, 67, 442–445.

[67] Goodman, *Race Awareness* . . . , chap. 5.

[68] B. Lasker, *Race Attitudes in Children* (New York, 1929), p. 4.

[69] A. J. Gregor and D. A. McPherson, "Racial Attitudes among White and Negro Children in a Deep-South Standard Metropolitan Area," *Journal of Social Psychology*, 1966, 68, 95–106 and "Racial Preference and Ego-Identity among White and Bantu Children in the Republic of South Africa," *Genetic Psychology Monographs*, 1966, 73, 217–253.

[70] "It is proposed that the young white child acquires first of all, a generally unfavorable attitude toward the Negro, which makes him unwilling to attribute to the Negro any 'good' traits." R. Blake and W. Dennis, "The Development of Stereotypes Concerning the Negro," *Journal of Abnormal and Social Psychology*, 1943, 38, 530.

[71] H. Blumer, "The Nature of Race Prejudice," *Social Processes in Hawaii*, 1954, 18, 11.

[72] W. M. Kephart, "Negro Visibility," *American Sociological Review*, 1954, 19, 462–467.

[73] Cf. H. Blumer, "Race Prejudice as a Sense of Group Position," *Pacific Sociological Review*, 1958, 1, 3–7.

[74] Cf. B. Kramer, "Dimensions of Prejudice," *Journal of Psychology*, 1949, 27, 393 f.

[75] Cf. S. Mekeel, "Cultural Aids to Constructive Race Relations," *Mental Hygiene*, 1945, 29, 185.

[76] "The first phase of race and culture contacts is characterized by contacts that are not truly social, in the sense that persons with different racial and cultural

backgrounds who are brought together are not members of the same moral order . . . they hardly regard each other as completely human." E. Frazier, *Race and Culture Contacts in the Modern World* (New York, 1957). Cf. Gini, *Le rilevazioni* . . . , pp. 270 ff.; A. J. Gregor, "On the Nature of Prejudice," *Eugenics Review*, 1961, 3, 10–18. For articles devoted to specific areas vide A. Lind, "Post War Attitudes Regarding Race Relations in Hawaii," *Social Forces in Hawaii*, 1947, 11, 18–28; B. Gorman, "Speech, Prejudice and the School in Hawaii," *Ibid.*, p. 74; D. V. Springer, "Awareness of Racial Differences by Preschool Children in Hawaii," *Genetic Psychology Monographs*, 1950, 41, 215–270; R. Bastide and P. van den Berghe, "Stereotypes, Norms and Interracial Behavior in Sao Paulo, Brazil," *American Sociological Review*, 1957, 22, 689–694; R. Sereno, "Cryptomelanism: A Study of Color Relations and Personal Insecurity in Puerto Rico," *Psychiatry*, 1946, 19, 261–269; G. E. Simpson, "Political Cultism in West Kingston, Jamaica," *Social and Economic Studies*, 1955, 4, 133–149, and "The Ras Tafari Movement in Jamaica; A Study of Race and Class Conflict," *Social Forces*, 1955, 34, 167–171; E. Williams, "The Contemporary Pattern of Race Relations in the Caribbeans," *Phylon*, 1955, 16, 367–379; J. Comas, "Latin America," *International Social Science Journal*, 1961, 13, 271–299; C. Senior, "Race Relations and Labor Supply in Great Britain," *Social Problems*, 1957, 4, 302–312; R. D. Wilson, "Note on Negro-White Relations in Canada," *Social Forces*, 1949, 28, 77–78; R. Bastide, "African Students in France," *International Social Science Bulletin*, 1956, 8, 489–492.

[77] J. D. Lohman and D. C. Reitzes, "Note on Race Relations in Mass Society," *American Journal of Sociology*, 1952, 58, 240–246.

[78] Cf. W. B. Brookover and J. B. Holland, "An Inquiry into the Meaning of Minority Group Attitude Expressions," *American Sociological Review*, 1952, 17, 196–202.

[79] Cf. for example, G. M. Gilbert, "Stereotype Persistence and Change among College Students," *Journal of Abnormal and Social Psychology*, 1951, 46, 245–254; L. A. Kahn, "The Organization of Attitudes Toward the Negro as a Function of Education," *Psychological Monographs*, 1951, 65, 1–39; and M. Reimann, "How Children Become Prejudiced," *Commentary*, 1951, 11, 90.

[80] Gittler, *op. cit.*, pp. 45–47.

[81] C. H. Stember, *Education and Attitude Change: the Effect of Schooling on Prejudice Against Minority Groups* (New York, 1961).

[82] E. L. Horowitz, "The Development of Attitude Toward the Negro," *Archives of Psychology*, 1936, 194, 5–47.

[83] K. B. Clark and M. Clark, "Racial Identification and Preference in Negro Children," in *Readings in Social Psychology* (T. M. Newcomb and E. L. Hartley, eds., New York, 1952), pp. 551–560.

[84] Cf. D. H. Russell and I. Robertson, "Influencing Attitudes Toward Minority Groups in a Junior High School," *School Review*, 1947, 55, 205–213.

[85] E. L. Hartley and R. E. Hartley, *Fundamentals of Social Psychology* (New York, 1952), p. 709.

[86] "When we ask the question, 'What is the stake of the Jewish people in the fight for Negro rights?' it is easy enough to recite some of the ready answers . . . we must see how large the problems of the Negro people loom in the shaping of our destiny . . . It must concern us because the oppression of the Negro people, economically and politically, is a main prop for anti-Semitic forces in our land." S. Goldner, *The Jewish People and the Fight for Negro Rights* (Los Angeles: Committee for Negro-Jewish Relations, 1953), pp. 5 ff. Cf. F. W. Westie and M. L. Westie, "The Social Distance Pyramid: Relationships Between Caste and Class," *American Journal of Sociology*, 1957, 63, 195.

[87] T. W. Sprague, "The Rivalry of Intolerances in Race Relations," *Social Forces*, 1949, 28, 68–76.

[88] Cf. W. J. Kolarz, "Race Relations in the Soviet Union," in *Race Relations in World Perspective* (A. Lind, ed., Honolulu, 1955), pp. 187–216.

[89] D. P. Kent and R. G. Burnight, "Group Centrism in Complex Societies," *American Journal of Sociology*, 1951, 57, 256–259. Cf. A. J. Gregor and C. P. Armstrong, "Integrated Schools and Negro Character Development," *Psychiatry*, 1964, 27, 69–72.

[90] Cf. Blumer, "The Nature of Race Prejudice," *op. cit.*, p. 13.

[91] Cf. A. J. Gregor, "Ethnocentrism among the Australian Aborigines: Some Preliminary Notes," *Sociological Quarterly*, 1963, 4, 162–167.

BIOGRAPHICAL NOTE

GEORGE A. LUNDBERG, M.A., Ph.D., LL.D., is *Professor Emeritus of Sociology of the University of Washington and served as chairman of the Sociology Department for nearly twenty years. He is widely known for his many original applications of mathematical and statistical techniques to social science problems.*

The University of Minnesota in 1951 awarded Professor Lundberg its Distinguished Achievement Medal, *with the citation, "Pioneer in Applying Scientific Method to Sociology—Worthy of Special Commendation for Outstanding Achievement." The University of North Dakota honored him in 1958 with a LL.D. degree.*

Dr. Lundberg has served as President of the American Sociological Society, the Sociological Research Association, the Eastern Sociological Society, and the Pacific Sociological Society. He is a Fellow of the American Association for the Advancement of Science, and a member of the Institute of Mathematical Statistics, the American Statistical Association, the Population Association of America, the Psychometric Society, and the Economometric Society.

He was the editor of Sociometry *from 1941 to 1947, and is the author of more than eighty articles and monographs and six books. Among his more notable books are* Foundations of Sociology (1939), Can Science Save Us? (1947) *and* Sociology (1954).

SELECTIVE ASSOCIATION OF ETHNIC GROUPS

George A. Lundberg

THE EMPIRICAL research reported in this study constitutes a pilot project for the principal purpose of developing techniques for scientifically studying, on a larger scale and with improved technique, selective association among human individuals and groups. The research here presented of course makes no claim as to the applicability of our results to other groups in other cities, in other states and countries, in the absence of further tests.

However, the phenomenon under study, namely, selective association, is universal and amenable to objective study by the general methods here employed. We believe also that research of this type is greatly needed before intelligent action can be taken for the prohibition, prevention, or amelioration of the many maladjustments that are likely to follow in the wake of a drastic program of interference with customary practices of selective association.[1]

Although the study here reported was undertaken and completed before the current interest in school segregation developed, its relevance to that subject will be readily apparent. However, we are interested here not only in selective association of Negro-White high school students but also in the selective association among other "racial" as well as ethnic, socio-economic, and religious groups. We are interested not primarily in the concrete cases of selective association currently agitating the public but in the larger and more permanent phenomenon as it has existed and will probably continue to exist long after current examples have disappeared.

This larger aspect of the subject involves not only individuals and local groups but selective association as we find it in large segments of population including state, national, and international groupings. The enormous development of public opinion measurement in recent decades makes possible large-scale attitude studies among national and international groups which bear directly on selective association, and all that such association means in national and international tensions.[2] In short, our interests far transcend the subject of high school attitudes and selective association in Seattle. We are interested in methods of research into a universal phenomenon, namely, the selective attitudes and associations in which all people engage.

The research reported in the following pages, then, is designed primarily to discover and test methods of objective inquiry into a subject of recognized general importance. Incidentally, we are interested in the degree to which racial and/or ethnic groups of high school students in a modern northern city relatively free from the grosser forms of intergroup tensions are nevertheless disposed to respond selectively in various degrees to specified groups, including subgroups of their own classification.

Specifically, this study reports, the extent to which students in a large American high school choose associates for four different types of social relationships from their own ethnic group and from other ethnic groups; the relative popularity of the different ethnic groups as reflected in the choices of members of each group; and the association of certain factors (sex, school class, age, membership in organizations, and socio-economic status) with the number and kind of choices made.

The Subjects and Method of the Study

THIS PARTICULAR high school was selected for analysis because it draws its students not only from the crowded "skid-row" district, but also from some of the wealthiest and most "restricted" neighborhoods of the city. At the time of the study, the total enrollment was 1,544 students, 1,360 of whom filled in

Selective Association of Ethnic Groups

questionnaires. This represents 88 percent of the total enrollment who were present in school on May 27, 1948. The 12 percent not returning questionnaires represent the usual number of absentees on any given day, plus one of those present whose schedule was too defective to be included.

The ethnic background of the majority of the students was non-Jewish White (59.6 percent), while 15.9 percent were Jewish, 9.6 percent Japanese, 8.5 percent Negro, 4.8 percent Chinese, and 1.6 percent "other" (Filipino, Hawaiian, and Indian).[3] The non-Jewish Whites were nearly all descended from northwestern Europeans. The parents of 32.7 percent of the students were managers, owners, or professional workers.

The students ranged in age from thirteen to twenty years old, and except for a very small freshman class (4.6 percent), were equally distributed by school classes. The two sexes were equally represented. Nearly one-third of the students held part-time jobs and nearly two-thirds planned to attend college. About half the students belonged (or had belonged) to school organizations, and 21.5 percent held (or had held) school offices. One-fifth belonged to the scholastic honor society. Ten percent were Roman Catholic, 43 percent Protestant, 16 percent Jewish, and 3 percent "other" (mostly Buddhist), while 28 percent attended no church. The non-Jewish White majority did not differ markedly from the minorities, taken as a whole, in any of these respects except religion.[4]

The principal data were secured through a questionnaire which, in addition to the usual questions regarding the student's personal characteristics, school class, membership in organizations, socio-economic status, and plans after completing high school, called for the following information:

1. Name three students whom you would like to have represent your high school next week at a big national meeting of high school students.

2. If all the students were asked to help on a school picnic, which three students would you like to work with?

3. If you could have a *date* with *anyone in this school*, which three people would you choose?

4. Who are your three best friends in this high school (boys or girls)?[5]

The questionnaires were administered by the teachers, after an explanatory statement, during first period classes. No attempt was made to give the questionnaire to absentees. However, school officials gave us their file of advisor's cards which gave most of the data (other than answers to the choice questions) for the absent individuals.[6]

The first general objective was to answer the question: What is the relative degree of ethnocentrism of the different ethnic groups with respect to choosing leaders, work partners, dates, and best friends? To answer this question the number of choices which each ethnic group gave to itself and to each other group on each of the four questions were tabulated. The Criswell self-preference index[7] was then computed for each ethnic group on each of these questions. The word "ethnocentrism" in this paper is defined entirely in terms of the Criswell index.

A second general question which the study undertook to answer was the following: What characteristics are associated with choosing members of out-groups, and what characteristics are associated with ethnocentrism? Since the comparatively small number of members of the different minorities permitted a more intensive analysis of their characteristics,[8] only the data for non-Jewish Whites were subjected to machine tabulation. For each non-Jewish White an IBM card was punched giving his background characteristics, and for each question, whether he chose (a) no one, (b) only other non-Jewish Whites, or (c) one or more out-group persons. Then cross-tabulations were made for each question for each background characteristic according to whether the individual made an out-group choice or not. The hypothesis of no association was then tested for each table by the chi-square technique using the .05 critical level.

For the minority groups the technique used was similar enough to allow a comparison.[9] Each choice was classified according to whether it was given to the in-group or to the out-group (i.e., other groups taken as a whole). Then, as for the majority group, the hypothesis that there was no association between each characteristic and out-group choosing was tested by the chi-square technique, again using the .05 level of significance.

As will appear below, the data when analyzed yield answers to

Selective Association of Ethnic Groups

a very large number of specific questions in addition to the general questions discussed above. Examination of the principal questions of choice will show that the first three questions pose hypothetical situations, whereas the fourth question asks for information about an actually existing situation. Also, the relationships of leadership, work-partnership, dating, and friendship were selected on the hypothesis that each of their relationships arouse different degrees of in-group and out-group attitudes. That is, we were interested to discover whether and to what extent in-group attitudes vary according to the relationship specified and whether the order of variation is the same for all groups. For example, do all groups show highest ethnocentrism on dating and lowest on choice of leaders? What is the social distance (as measured by the Criswell index) of each group to every other group in each of the four relationships into which inquiry was made? Numerous other questions to which the data yield answers will be specified as they arise.

Frequency and Overlapping of Choices

THE STUDENTS answering the questionnaire chose 3,489 friends, 3,432 leaders, 3,199 work partners, and 2,352 dates.[10]

Some evidence of the degree to which each of the four questions did, in fact, tap different areas or degrees of sociability may be found in the extent to which students chose the same or different persons on each question. The frequency with which the same person was picked on each pair of questions was as follows:

1. Work Friendship 1010
2. Work-Leadership 632
3. Leadership-Friendship 374
4. Work-Dating 259
5. Leadership-Dating 232
6. Dating-Friendship........................ 143

By far the most popular combination was Work-Friendship, which is followed in frequency by Work-Leadership; it may be that students have two criteria in mind when choosing persons with whom to work, namely, someone they like—a friend, and someone who will get the work done. The latter may also be a principal quality desired in a leader, hence the high duplication of choices for work partners and leaders.

On the other hand, only comparatively infrequently do students appear to feel that the person desired for leadership must be also their friend, and even less frequently do they feel that they would care to date with the person they have chosen for leadership. Likewise, they apparently find that the sentimental aspect of dating is not compatible with the best work relationship. Least of all do they find the same person in the role of both friend and date.[11]

Out of the 10,139 total choices made, there were 8,120 cases in which the individual was chosen on only one question by the same chooser. This indicates that the questions used were rather effective in distinguishing different roles and the extent to which different persons are thought of as best fulfilling different roles. In 1,724 cases the same individual was chosen on two questions by the same person; in 280 cases the same individual was chosen on three questions by the same person; and in only 15 cases was the same individual chosen on all four questions by the same person. The most common three-question combination was leadership-work-friendship; 194 such cases occurred.

The Choices of the Different Ethnic Groups

THE GENERAL index of self-preference for each of the ethnic groups (as against all outsiders taken together) on each question is given in Table 1. Every ethnic group showed a preference for

TABLE 1
GENERAL CRISWELL INDEX OF SELF-PREFERENCE FOR EACH ETHNIC GROUP ON EACH QUESTION

Ethnic Group	Leadership	Work	Dating	Friendship
Non-Jewish White	8.5	8.5	14.7	6.3
Chinese	3.2	12.2	34.1	47.8
Japanese	2.7	6.2	12.2	53.2
Jewish	1.2	3.6	3.7	16.7
Negro	7.4	10.6	22.4	66.4

its own members in each of the four relationships covered by the questions (i.e., all the indices are more than 1.0).

We find the lowest ethnocentrism is shown by Jews in choosing leaders, and the greatest by Negroes in choosing friends. It may be that Jews, being relatively popular with the rest of the school, are friendly in return, while Negroes, who were very infrequently chosen as friends by the other groups, retaliated by making few out-group choices of friends. If so, however, the Negroes appear to have over-compensated in their retaliation because they were conspicuously *more* disposed to avoid choosing friends among other groups than these other groups avoided choosing Negroes

TABLE 2

ETHNIC GROUPS RANKED FROM HIGH TO LOW ETHNOCENTRISM ON EACH QUESTION

Leadership	*Work*	*Dating*	*Friendship*
Non-Jewish White	Chinese	Chinese	Negro
Negro	Negro	Negro	Japanese
Chinese	Non-Jewish White	Non-Jewish White	Chinese
Japanese	Japanese	Japanese	Jewish
Jewish	Jewish	Jewish	Non-Jewish White

as friends, as will appear below. (See note 13 for an important qualification of the conclusions from Table 1.)

The rank of each ethnic group with respect to their ethnocentrism on each of the four questions is shown in Table 2.

We find that Jews are relatively non-ethnocentric on all questions, and Negroes relatively ethnocentric. The relative position of the other groups varied from question to question—especially that of the non-Jewish Whites, who were the most ethnocentric group in choosing leaders but the least ethnocentric in choosing friends.

Relative friendliness among the ethnic groups is shown in Table 3. For each ethnic group on each question the four out-groups are ranked from most-liked to least-liked, as indicated by the self-preference indices given in parentheses. For example, on leadership the ethnocentrism index of the non-Jewish Whites with respect to Chinese was 18.7; with respect to Japanese 25.3;

TABLE 3

RELATIVE FRIENDLINESS AMONG ETHNIC GROUPS IN CHOOSING LEADERS, WORK PARTNERS, DATES, AND FRIENDS

Ethnic Group of Choosers	Most-Liked	Second Most-Liked	Third Most-Liked	Least Liked
Leadership				
Non-Jewish White	Jewish (6.0)	Negro (6.5)	Chinese (18.7)	Japanese (25.3)
Chinese	Non-Jewish White (2.4)	Negro (6.0)	Jewish (9.6)	Japanese (20.5)
Japanese	Non-Jewish White (2.0)	Chinese (4.4)	Negro (4.5)	Jewish (16.8)
Jewish	Non-Jewish White (0.9)	Negro (5.3)	Chinese (8.9)	Japanese (24.0)
Negro	Non-Jewish White (5.3)	Jewish (26.0)	Chinese (27.3)	Japanese (36.9)
Work				
Non-Jewish White	Jewish (5.9)	Chinese (9.5)	Negro (13.4)	Japanese (18.1)
Chinese	Non-Jewish White (9.5)	Japanese (12.3)	Jewish (40.5)	Negro (87.0)
Japanese	Non-Jewish White (4.9)	Chinese (5.3)	Jewish (14.9)	Negro (34.7)
Jewish	Non-Jewish White (2.7)	Negro (13.4)	Chinese (16.9)	Japanese (34.2)
Negro	Non-Jewish White (7.7)	Jewish (31.1)	Chinese (65.3)	Japanese (66.2)
Dating				
Non-Jewish White	Jewish (6.9)	Chinese (22.9)	Negro (102.6)	Japanese (116.2)
Chinese	Japanese (25.3)	Non-Jewish White (27.7)	Jewish (62.4)	Negro*
Japanese	Non-Jewish White (9.0)	Chinese (9.3)	Jewish (62.0)	Negro*
Jewish	Non-Jewish White (2.6)	Chinese (27.0)	Japanese-Negro*	Negro-Japanese*
Negro	Non-Jewish White (15.4)	Jewish (112.4)	Japanese (136.9)	Chinese*
Friendship				
Non-Jewish White	Jewish (4.3)	Chinese (6.4)	Japanese (11.6)	Negro (12.6)
Chinese	Japanese (33.9)	Jewish (55.7)	Non-Jewish White (57.2)	Negro (179.5)
Japanese	Chinese (22.8)	Non-Jewish White (57.4)	Jewish (76.1)	Negro (81.8)
Jewish	Non-Jewish White (13.5)	Chinese (23.5)	Japanese (57.2)	Negro (126.3)
Negro	Non-Jewish White (61.0)	Jewish (72.8)	Chinese (131.2)	Japanese (132.9)

Table reads: For leadership Non-Jewish Whites prefer, among the minority groups, Jews first, Negroes second, Chinese third, and Japanese least.

* The asterisk indicates that no choices at all were given to that group by the group in stub of table (i.e., the index is infinity).

with respect to Jews 6.0; and with respect to Negroes 6.5. Therefore we can say that non-Jewish Whites like Jews best (or dislike them least), Negroes second, Chinese third, and Japanese least.

Non-Jewish Whites were the most chosen group on leadership, work, and dating, but were chosen only moderately frequently on friendship. Negroes were second highest in choices of leaders but very little chosen on the other three questions. Japanese were also disliked—by all groups on leadership, and by all but the Chinese on other questions.

Non-Jewish Whites and Jews liked each other best (next to themselves) on all questions. Japanese liked Chinese best (next to themselves), as friends and second only to non-Jewish Whites on the other questions, while Chinese liked Japanese best (next to themselves), as friends and dates, second best as work partners, and less than any other out-group as leaders. Racial similarity would seem to account for these friendships. Less easy to explain is the marked antipathy which Japanese and Jews showed each other on all questions; perhaps the fact that both groups value scholastic success and also that they are the two largest minority groups in school make for competition.

The most interesting of the inter-ethnic relations were those between the non-Jewish Whites and each of the minorities.[12] Table 3 shows that in choosing leaders, work-partners, and dates, non-Jewish Whites showed more prejudice toward Japanese, Jews, and Negroes than these minorities showed toward them. But in choosing friends, non-Jewish White prejudice toward the minorities was less than that of the prejudice of the minorities toward the non-Jewish White. (Non-Jewish White prejudice toward Chinese was greater than Chinese prejudice toward non-Jewish White on leadership, equal on work, and less on dating and friendship.)

One possible interpretation of this finding is that the minorities desire more contact with the majority group than is desired in return (as evidenced by the minorities' lower self-preference on the first three hypothetical questions); but in the actual situation—friendship—they do not choose from the majority groups as frequently (relatively) as the majority choose from the minorities. This may be due to over-compensation for rebuffs received when making overtures to the majority in other relations. Extreme ethnocentrism on the part of minorities in the choice of friends may be a sort of defense mechanism from the ethnocentrism of other groups in other relationships.

As regards the choices by specific ethnic groups of members of other ethnic groups, in only a single case did members of an ethnic group prefer a specific out-group to themselves, and then only on the leadership question. This was the case of Jews indicating a small degree of preference (Criswell Index .9, Table 3) for non-Jewish Whites as leaders. All other minority groups chose leaders most frequently from the non-Jewish Whites, next to their own group. Non-Jewish Whites chose leaders from among the Jews most frequently, next to themselves.

The Japanese were proportionally least chosen as leaders by all the groups, perhaps in part because they had been away in relocation centers until three years before the time of the study and in the length of time since their return had not been able to establish themselves in the political life of the school. Every group ranked the Negroes second or third in preference rank in their choice of leaders. These results may be explained, at least in part, by the fact that there were in the school two exceptionally popular Negro boys prominent in school activities.

Comparison of In-Group and Out-Group Choosing

ALL MINORITY groups were least ethnocentric in choosing leaders, but became progressively ethnocentric in choosing work partners, dates, and friends. On the other hand, the non-Jewish White majority were least ethnocentric in choosing friends, showed an increased but equal degree of ethnocentrism in choosing leaders and work partners, and showed their highest degree of ethnocentrism in choosing dates.

One possible explanation of this difference between the majority and the minorities in this respect might be that the majority, feeling secure in its status, can afford the luxury of uninhibited choice of friends, regardless of the minority status of these friends. The minorities, however, do not reciprocate by corresponding freedom in choosing friends from the white majority or from other out-groups. The freedom of choice of friends on the part of the majority group does not extend, however, to the choice of dates, in which relationship they show greater ethnocentrism than Jews and Japanese, but less than the Negroes and the Chinese.

At least part of the explanation of these results may be found in the fact that while the questions regarding leaders, work partners, and dates are hypothetical ("*If* you could have a date with anyone in this school whom would you choose?") whereas the question regarding friends asks for a present fact ("Who *are* your best friends?"). For whatever reason (feelings of insecurity, deliberate cultivation of ethnocentrism, etc.), it remains a significant fact that our data show, for all minorities, a greater ethnocentrism in the choice of friends than is shown by the majority group.

It may be that the mere fact of being consciously a member of a minority causes one to draw together with other numbers of that minority, and that this tendency becomes more pronounced as the minority is smaller in size. That is, ethnocentrism may be a sort of struggle for cultural survival becoming more intense as the survival is threatened.[13]

In spite of the general preference of each ethnic group for leaders, work partners, dates and friends drawn from their own group, each of the ethnic groups chose some of these associates from out-groups. This raises the question: within each ethnic group, how do persons who make out-groups choices differ from those who make only in-group choices? For reasons of space only the most general conclusions are presented in this study.[14]

Characteristics of the Non-Jewish Whites Who Made Out-Group Choices

EIGHTEEN and eight-tenths percent of the non-Jewish White group chose members of some out-group for leaders. Twenty-six percent of these out-group choosers were males, 12.6 percent females (difference significant at .05 level). Similar results, 23 percent and 13.9 percent, were found on the question of work partner. On the dating question, the percentage of out-group choices falls to about 10 percent for both sexes with no significant difference in the percentage of male and female choosers. The lowest ethnocentrism is found among both sexes in choosing friends—males 28.8 percent and females 15 percent—again with a statistically significant difference between the sexes.

Of the twenty-eight factors tested, five were not significantly associated with out-group choosing by either sex, on any of the four questions. These five factors were: church attended, church activities participated in, membership in Masonic organizations, membership in "Y" sponsored organizations, and whether ancestors came only from northwestern Europe or from some other part of the world.

None of the factors was significantly associated with out-group choosing by both sexes on all four questions. The most nearly universally significant factors were membership in a fraternity, sorority, or other exclusive club. Such membership is, among all groups and both sexes, associated with ethnocentrism, with one minor exception, namely, in the case of females choosing leaders. In all other groups and relationships there was a significant positive association between not belonging to fraternal groups and out-group choosing.

A boy was more likely to choose into the out-group on all four questions if he did not belong to a fraternity or to any club at all outside of school and if he lived in a census tract characterized by a high percentage of laborers, persons seeking work, and dwelling units without mechanical refrigeration or central-heating.

None of the twenty-eight factors tested was significantly associated with out-group choosing by the girls on all questions.

The factors chosen for study seemed to function much better in differentiating between boys who chose out-group members and those who chose only non-Jewish Whites than in similarly differentiating between the girls. For the boys a significant association was found in sixty-three of the one hundred chi-square tests made; but for the girls a significant association was found in only fifteen of the one hundred and four similar tests. Even excluding the eighty-eight tests pertaining to characteristics of the census

Selective Association of Ethnic Groups

tract in which a student lived, the ratio is still twenty-four significant factors for the boys and only fourteen for the girls.

The significance of each of the seven principal characteristics here tested for their association with out-group choosing by the non-Jewish Whites may be summarized as follows:

Sex: On all questions but dating, boys were more likely to make out-group choices than the girls were. To explain this phenomenon several hypotheses may be advanced. Perhaps boys were less bound by convention than girls, hence, more likely to disregard taboos against inter-ethnic contact. That is, boys may feel more secure and may not be so fearful of losing their own prestige by choosing persons of lower social status. Again, it may be that boys of high school age are less mature than girls, and it has been shown that the younger (i.e., less mature) students are more likely than older ones to choose from the out-group. Another significant consideration may be the fact that a smaller percentage of boys than of girls belong to organizations outside of school, for it has been shown that ethnocentrism is positively correlated with membership in such clubs.

Age and School-Class: For each sex and question, a chi-square test was applied first to age and then to class, a total of sixteen chi-square tests. In nine of these we found the younger, lower school-class students significantly more likely to make out-group choices than were their older, junior-senior classmates. This finding that ethnocentrism increases with age has already been pretty well established in other ethnic studies. The explanation usually given is that as part of the process of socialization, children become increasingly aware of the cleavages which exist in the adult world and adjust their own behavior to conform.

Nationality: For both sexes on all four questions no significant difference was found between the extent of the out-group choosing by students designating their ancestry as northwestern European as compared with ancestry from some other part of the world.

Membership in Organizations: In twenty-three out of fifty-three tests of significance it was found that membership in organizations made for ethnocentrism—that is, that non-members were more likely to make out-group choices. Excluding the sixteen tests pertaining to church organizations, we find twenty-three out of thirty-seven tests significant. This relationship was especially pronounced in the cases of membership in the more intimate social groups (sororities and fraternities). The data appear to confirm the common sense generalization that membership in an in-group, the essence of which is exclusiveness, must limit freedom of choice in out-groups.

There was one notable exception to this finding. Among girls in choosing leaders, it was the members, not the non-members, of the scholastic honor society who were more likely to make out-group choices. Since membership in the honor society is determined by how well a student does in his studies rather than by his interests or friendships, this finding is not actually an exception to the rule stated above.

Socio-Economic Status: Fifteen different measures of socio-economic status (eleven of them ecological) were tested for each sex on each of the four questions. Of the sixty tests for boys, forty-five showed a significant association between low status and out-group choosing. But of the sixty similar tests for girls, only one was significant. Girls living in census tracts with a high percentage of Negroes were more likely to make out-group choices than those living elsewhere. This seems to indicate that *all* girls are bound by the social proprieties, but only boys of high status tend to be similarly restricted.

There are many possible reasons why high socio-economic status might be correlated with high ethnocentrism: (a) Students living in poorer neighborhoods come into contact with more minority persons; (b) mothers who work outside the home cannot supervise their children's choices of friends as well as housewives can; and (c) students who have jobs themselves do not have time or other resources to join "social" groups, which, as we have seen, operate to restrict frequency of out-group choices.

Residential Propinquity with Minority Students: In choosing work partners, dates, and friends, boys who lived in census tracts which had a high percentage of Negroes or other minorities were less ethnocentric than those living in other areas. But on leadership, the ethnic composition of a boy's neighborhood was not significantly associated with his ethnocentrism. This may be due to the fact that choosing a leader is not based on personal contact with the person chosen; therefore, the amount of contact a person has with the out-group will not influence his leadership choices, but may have a considerable effect on his other choices.

The number of Negroes or members of other minorities living in a girl's neighborhood did not significantly influence her ethnocentrism except in one respect: The percentage of Negroes in the census tract was positively correlated with the tendency of girls to make out-group choices of work partners.

Intelligence-Intellectualism: Results were inconclusive on this subject. Of fifteen tests made, only three showed a significant degree of association. Girls belonging to the scholastic honor society chose out-group leaders significantly more than did non-members, and boys who did not plan to attend college chose out-group co-workers and friends significantly more than did the other boys.

There seems to have been a definite demarcation between leadership and the other three questions. Intelligent or intellectual students seem to be more likely to evaluate leadership qualities without prejudice. However, this does not seem to carry over into the more intimate situations, which, it may be noted, are usually formed on a less intellectual basis.

To summarize: Among the non-Jewish White there was a tendency for groups with the following characteristics to make out-group choices significantly more frequently than was the case in the population as a whole: males, persons under sixteen years of age, freshmen and sophomores, persons not belonging to organizations, and boys—but not girls—with low socio-economic status.

Out-Group Choices by the Minorities

THE CHARACTERISTICS of out-group choosers among the minorities can be best presented in comparison with the findings of the preceding section regarding the characteristics of out-group choosers among the non-Jewish White majority. (All differences noted are significant at the .05 level.)

Sex: Except for the Japanese, boys were less ethnocentric than girls in all the ethnic groups. This was especially marked in the Negro group where they were significantly less ethnocentric than girls on all four questions.

Class: With respect to school class, findings for non-Jewish Whites were in direct contrast with those for the minorities. In the non-Jewish White group it was the freshman and sophomore students rather than juniors and seniors who were more likely to make out-group choices; in the minorities, out-group choices were most often made by upperclassmen. However, this tendency for minority juniors and seniors to make more out-group choices than freshmen and sophomores was true only on the prestige questions—leadership, work, and dating; class and ethnocentrism of minorities were not significantly associated on friendship.

These findings indicate that all students, regardless of whether they belong to the majority or to a minority, give more choices to the majority, on prestige questions, as they advance in school. In other words, as they mature, they acknowledge, and hence reinforce, the prestige of the established leaders.

Age: In general the same tendencies noticed with respect to class were found true for the different age groups. In the majority group, lower school class and younger students were most likely to make out-group choices. In the minority groups, it was the upper school class and older students who made the most out-group choices. The one exception was that "middle-aged" Jews were more likely than either older or younger ones to choose non-Jews as leaders.

Church Attended: This factor was significantly associated with out-group choosing only for the ethnic group which was differentiated on the basis of religion—the Jews. Logically enough, it was the Jews who did not attend church who were least ethnocentric in religion.

Office-Holding: Non-Jewish Whites who did not hold offices were more likely than officers to make out-group choices. There was no significant association between out-group choosing and office holding in the minority groups except that Japanese officers were more likely than non-officers to choose non-Japanese work-partners, which contradicts the findings for the majority group.

Participation in School Activities: Members of school organizations were more ethnocentric than non-members if they were non-Jewish White, Japanese, or Negro, less ethnocentric if they were Chinese, and equally ethnocentric if Jewish.

Plans After Graduation: Non-Jewish White boys who intended to go to college were more ethnocentric than other boys. Chinese who planned to go to college were less ethnocentric than other Chinese. Plans after graduation and out-group choosing were not associated for non-Jewish White girls, Japanese, Jews, and Negroes.

On the basis of the above findings, we can roughly classify our factors into two groups: (1) those which make for ethnocentrism in both the majority and minorities, and (2) those which make for ethnocentrism in one, out-group choosing in the other.

In the first class, we would definitely place sex. Girls were more ethnocentric than boys, in all groups except the Japanese. And, tentatively, we would also place here membership in organizations. Being tied up with an in-group organization—religious in the case of Jews, secular for Japanese, Negroes and non-Jewish Whites—seems to make for less out-group choosing. The exception to this rule was the tendency for Chinese who belonged to school organizations to be less ethnocentric than non-members. This result may be due to the fact that members of the strictly-Chinese Cathay Club (which probably wields strong influence) were classified as non-members.

In the class of factors which make for opposite tendencies with respect to ethnocentrism in the majority and minority groups, we find class and age. The greater the age and class in school, the greater the ethnocentrism of non-Jewish Whites, and the lesser the ethnocentrism of the minorities. Plans after graduation and office-holding may also be placed tentatively in this class. Non-Jewish Whites who planned to go to college and Chinese who did not plan on college tended to be more ethnocentric than their opposites; and non-Jewish White officers, Japanese non-officers also tended to be ethnocentric.

Application of the Findings to Large Populations

THE EXTENT to which the facts and conclusions reported in this study are applicable to other populations in contemporary American society, or, for that matter, to other cultures in other times and places, is of course a matter to be determined by specific studies. To some extent the applicability of the findings of the present study to other populations may be inferred from data in the voluminous literature dealing with different aspects of the subject.[15]

The specific factual findings and conclusions from the present study have been stated in the previous section. The following points may be regarded as partly a restatement of these conclusions, partly a suggestion of hypotheses for further study, and partly some theoretical observations on the subject as a whole.

There probably is no such thing as ethnocentrism or prejudice *in general*. Ethnocentrism or prejudice probably is always an attitude toward *specific relationships* (e.g., the Negro in the South may be *preferred* for certain employment).

Ethnocentrism or prejudice is not confined to the majority or the dominant group. These attitudes are frequently stronger in all the relationships here tested, except leadership, among minority groups toward the majority (e.g., Negro attitudes toward Whites as friends) and toward other minorities (e.g., the attitude of Jews toward Japanese and vice versa).

While the non-Jewish White majority exhibits ethnocentrism of various degrees toward the different minorities, there is reason to believe that this same non-Jewish White group also exhibits similar or higher degrees of exclusion against particular groups or classes within their own non-Jewish White group.[16] For example, a small group of students from an exclusive residential area showed as great ethnocentrism with respect to the rest of the non-Jewish White group as they showed toward some of the minorities.

This raises the interesting and difficult question as to whether civic programs aiming to abolish prejudice against certain minorities should also be directed at equally exclusive or prejudicial behavior within different strata of the majority group. Also, the question may be raised as to the justification of campaigns on behalf of minorities who themselves practice a higher degree of discrimination against the majority group or against other minorities than is practiced against themselves.

It may be, of course, that the discrimination of the minorities against the majority or against each other, even when it is pronounced, is relatively innocuous to the community, as compared with the converse situation. But any comprehensive study of prejudice, discrimination, and ethnocentrism, *per se*, must include both aspects. The question of what should be done, if anything, about the group cleavages and prejudices that are found becomes, then, a practical question of what the standards and attitudes of the community demand.

Unless, therefore, reform organizations make clear, both to themselves and to others, just what specific discriminations they are out to abolish, and what degree of such discrimination they regard as unwarranted, they may be regarded as largely romantic movements dedicated to the abolition of the universal phenomenon of selective association ("discrimination," "prejudice," "unrequited love," etc.,) as suffered by a particular minority.

To the extent, also, that a particular minority is unwilling themselves to abstain from the same types of discrimination as that of which they complain, they merely place themselves in the unfortunate position of seeking special privileges and immunities.

Accordingly, it is suggested that future discussion and action on the general subject of race and inter-ethnic relations had better be guided by more intensive inquiry into the precise nature of the relationships that exist with reference to the norms accepted by all parties. Two questions would appear to be relevant: Is the discrimination complained of greater or more unwarranted than that practiced against other particular classes *within the majority group*? If not, should the proposed reform be equally concerned about these other discriminations?

Is the discrimination in question of a character recognized by the existing laws, mores, and institutions as clearly within the province of personal preference and choice? The denial to a minority for ethnic or racial reasons of the right to vote under the present laws and institutions of the United States, is clearly one thing. Discriminations of various groups against each other in such relationships as have been studied above is equally certainly another matter.

The Abolition of Freedom of Choice

THE TRADITIONAL freedom of choice of associates in these primary group relationships is supposed to be as fully guaranteed by our laws and constitutions as is the right of citizens to vote. Indeed, there is much evidence that free, spontaneous choice of primary group associates is vital both to personal adjustment and to satisfactory group functioning and productivity.

At the same time some fraternal organizations, represented perhaps in their most absurd form by school fraternities and sororities, are probably a nuisance from many community standpoints. As long as such organizations are tolerated, however, and if it can be shown that they practice exactly the same discriminations that become the object of civic attack when practiced by ethnic groups, the ground for singling out the latter for special attention must be clearly indicated.

As for the attempts to reform or abolish the discriminations of fraternal organizations, this is about as absurd as to attempt to abolish the wetness of water or the coldness of ice. Since exclusiveness is the essence of fraternal organizations, as indeed it is inherent in the basic concept of "in-group," attempts to abolish the discriminatory behaviors that constitute exclusiveness and at the same time defend the "freedom" of such associations is self-contradictory and ridiculous.

The first step in a scientific approach to conflicts between in-group and out-groups is to recognize that it is hopelessly contradictory for any group to desire to maintain an exclusive group identity of any kind, and at the same time to expect no differential (discriminatory) behavior toward itself on the basis of precisely the exclusive identity sought. This basic consideration does not abolish either the fact of conflict or the desirability of doing what may be done about it, through education, agitation, legislation, etc. Recognition of the basic nature of the problem, however, affords the only sound basis for action. Action which seeks to advance mutually exclusive values is simply psychopathic.

Thus we are confronted with the unpleasant fact that every gain in the abolition of prejudice may represent a value sacrificed on some other front. The right of a group to exclude from a housing area, from clubs, from employment, from fraternizing, etc., whatever classification of people they wish to exclude, for whatever reason or lack of reason, may be neither "rational," "just," "democratic," or conducive to community peace and good feeling.

Yet, to deny them this right may violate a principle of individual freedom which is still more highly valued by nearly everyone, including most of the minority, the race, the religious or ethnic groups which object to the practice as it operates against themselves. In short, they too, value the principle of freedom to discriminate in these matters and merely want exemption from its operation against themselves.[17]

For it must not be forgotten that these behaviors constitute values to those who practice the behavior. As such, the issues of prejudice and discrimination that have been widely heralded as a special problem turn out to be another case of reconciling or choosing between conflicting values.

The particular respects in which highly ethnocentric personalities differ from the less ethnocentric require more intensive study than the comparison of the twenty-eight factors included in the present study. These factors were selected chiefly because of their objectivity and availability, and consequently their suitability for statistical study. In addition, there is needed intensive study of the pathologically ethnocentric personality by whatever methods promise to throw light on the differences that unquestionably exist in different persons regarding their willingness to choose associates from particular out-groups.

Also, the degree of ethnocentrism which in a given culture at a given time is regarded as a problem needs to be carefully specified, because a certain amount of ethnocentrism is a normal and necessary ingredient of all group life, i.e., it is the basic characteristic that differentiates one group from another and thus is fundamental to social structure.

Ethnocentrism ("discrimination," "prejudice") is, therefore, not in itself necessarily to be regarded as a problem.[18] It is rather a question of determining what degree of it is functional for social survival and satisfaction under given conditions, or at least is not regarded by a society as a problem in the sense of requiring community action. The amount of discrimination that has been shown to exist in the present study, for example, is not incompatible with the peaceful and efficient functioning of the institution in question.

Insofar as the phenomenon of selective association results in community demands for ameliorative action, the facts and the conclusions here reviewed, and many others, need to be taken into consideration. The generality, the degree, or intensity of the discrimination may be crucial aspects.

As J. L. Moreno has observed, members of a "minority" may be accepted by the rest of the community quite readily as long as they do not exceed in number or influence a certain proportion of the total population. Only when the minority threatens to exceed that point does resistance, intolerance, and objectionable discrimination appear. The determination of this "saturation point"[19] in different localities might be a desirable starting point for intelligent ameliorative action.

Notes

[1] For further treatment of this subject see G. A. Lundberg, "Some Neglected Aspects of the "Minorities" Problem," *Mankind Quarterly*, Vol. III, No. 4 (1963), pp. 211–228.

[2] For an example of research in this field, see the report by H. Cantril and L. Free, "Hopes and Fears for Self and Country," *The American Behavioral Scientist*, Vol. VI Supplement, October, 1962. See also S. A. Stouffer, *Communism, Conformity, and Civil Liberties*, Garden City, N.Y., 1955.

[3] "Ethnic" is used throughout this study to include racial and religious classifications as regards the six groups here selected for analysis. "Jewish" was defined as any person who (a) checked "Jewish" in the list of ethnic backgrounds; (b) answered affirmatively the question regarding Jewish church attendance; and (c) belonged to an organization avowedly Jewish.

[4] More detailed figures on the composition of the population may be found in Lenore Dickson, *Social Distance in Two Seattle High Schools*, M.A. Thesis,

unpublished. University of Washington library, 1951. The religious classification was made on the basis of answers to the question, "If you go to church, which church?"

[5] This was followed by a fifth question: "If you think any of the students you listed in question 4 will choose you as one of their best friends, place an X in front of their names." The results of this question are not included in the present paper but will appear in a subsequent article which will also report the results of a question regarding negative choices, i.e., people *disliked*. See G. Lundberg and L. Dickson, "Further Observations of Interethnic Relations in a High School Population," *American Journal of Sociology*, May 1952.

[6] Since choices might include anyone enrolled, regardless of whether he was present or absent on the day of the study, the percentages and computations in subsequent tables are based on the full enrollment (1544) rather than on the 88 percent who completed questionnaires.

A comparison of the personal characteristics of absentees (information supplied by school records) with similar characteristics of students in attendance revealed that the absentees differed to a statistically significant degree (at the .01 level) from students present on the day the questionnaire was given, in the following respects: The absentees were characterized by a higher proportion of (a) non-Jewish Whites and Chinese, (b) males, (c) scholastic honor society, and (f) persons whose parents were not owners, managers, or professional workers. The fact that older students, but not those farther along in school, were more likely to be absent, seems to indicate that being older than one's classmates is a contributing factor toward absenteeism.

On the basis of our finds on factors associated with ethnocentrism, we should predict that absentees—especially the non-Jewish Whites—are less ethnocentric than the average high school student. On the basis of our study at another high school on factors making for unpopularity, it appears that the unpopularity of absentees is due, in part, to certain of their personal and social characteristics. In view of the fact that our sample included 88 percent of the total population, the results could not, of course, be biased by more than 12 percent in any respect. (Actually, about one-third of the "absentees" had dropped out of school, so that only about 8 percent were absent in the usual sense).

[7] Criswell, Joan H., "Sociometric Methods in Measuring Group Preferences," *Sociometry*, 6:398–408, November 1943. This index interprets the actual distribution of choices in relation to the distribution which would occur by chance. This index varies from zero to infinity. A value of 1 indicates that the in-group has no preference one way or another between itself and the out-group. A value of less than 1 indicates that the out-group is preferred, and a value greater than 1 indicates self-preference or ethnocentrism.

For a detailed discussion of the mathematical and logical implications of the Criswell index, see Paul Lazarsfeld, "Some Notes on the Use of Indices in Social Research" (mimeographed, 24 pp., Department of Sociology, University of Washington, Seattle, 1948). "If there were few out-group choices, one more or less makes much difference. If there are already many, the index plays down the adding or subtracting of one more."

[8] Reported in the following M.A. Theses, University of Washington Library: Marilyn Graalfs, *A Sociometric Study of Chinese Students in a Polyethnic High School;* Virginia Hertzler, *A Sociometric Study of Japanese Students in a Polyethnic High School;* Jessie Reichel, *A Sociometric Study of Jewish Students in a Polyethnic High School.*

[9] In the case of the minorities (on account of their relatively small numbers), choices rather than choosers were classified according to the same classifications as

were employed in the majority group. This might result in slightly exaggerating the figures of out-group choices on the part of minorities as compared with the method used for the majority.

[10] The relatively low number of choices of dates is probably attributable to several considerations: (1) The younger group has not yet become involved in this relationship. (2) A number of students indicated they preferred dating with people outside of high school. (3) A number of students indicated loyalty to only one date by refusing to name more than one choice on this question. (4) The dating question was regarded as more personal than the rest and was admittedly more frequently not answered for this reason. Also, since dates are limited to the opposite sex, there is a smaller total to choose from.

[11] From one point of view, dating might be expected to represent a preferred friend. However, the data indicate that this is not necessarily so among high school students of the type included in this study. There is reason to believe that the words "date" and "friend" represent to these high school students at least, rather exclusive categories of different types. For example, friends are chosen predominantly from among persons of the same sex; dates are, by definition, of the other sex.

[12] Of the 786 non-Jewish Whites who filled in questionnaires, 466, or 59.3 percent, did not choose even one minority person on any of the four questions. Since non-Jewish Whites constitute 59 percent of the school enrollment, the probability of one choice going to a non-Jewish White is .59 if chance alone were operating. But the students made an average of 9.2 choices. Therefore, the chance probability of one student choosing only non-Jewish Whites is $(.59)^{9.2}$ or .0039. Multiplying by 786 (the number of non-Jewish Whites who filled out questionnaires) we find that by chance only 3.07 (rather than 466) would have made no out-group choices. The difference between 3 and 466 represents in a sense a measure of the "consciousness of kind" among the non-Jewish White.

[13] This hypothesis is supported by the findings of the study mentioned in note 5. A further qualification to the statement should be made, namely, that the frequent mutual out-group choosing between the two white groups operates to give them relatively low indices of ethnocentrism, which increase if the non-Jewish White and the Jewish groups are combined. For example, the Criswell index for the white group *as a whole* rises to 45 on dating, as against 14.7 and 3.7 (Table 1) for non-Jewish Whites and Jews respectively.

The ethnocentrism index (Criswell) on the other questions is affected only relatively slightly by the combination of the Jewish with the other white group. A combination of the Japanese and Chinese results in reducing their ethnocentrism index on all questions. Of course this does not contradict the findings as reported, but does indicate that the pronounced line of cleavage on dating, at least, is the color line.

[14] The full data comprising some thirty-two tables and two hundred and ten computed chi-squares are available in Lenore Dickson, *op. cit.* To answer the question stated above, the out-group choosers and the in-group choosers of each ethnic group were compared, by sex, on each of twenty-eight categories representing subclasses of the following characteristics: 1. Age and school class; 2. Nationality (Did ancestors come only from northwestern Europe or did they come from some other part of the world?); 3. Membership in organizations (school, church, other organizations outside school); 4. Socio-economic status (Occupation of parents, mother working, student working part-time, living in census tract of known socio-economic status as determined by 11 indices); 5. Propinquity with Negroes and other minorities; 6. Intelligence—intellectualism (Membership in scholastic honor society and plan to attend college).

[15] Robin M. Williams, Jr., *The Reduction of Intergroup Tensions: A Survey of Research on Problems of Ethnic, Racial, and Religious Group Relations*. Social Science Research Council, New York, 1947. (Includes Bibliography of 223 items.) See also Leo Silberman and Betty Spice, *Color and Class in Six Liverpool Schools*, Liverpool, 1950.

[16] Since fraternities and sororities are forbidden in these high schools, the data secured on their membership was unreliable. Nevertheless, Criswell indices for groups admitting membership in sororities and fraternities show definite ethnocentrism. See Orvis Collins, "Ethnic Behavior in Industry" *American Journal of Sociology* (Jan. 1946), 51:293–298, for a striking case of discrimination against a white group. The flagrant discrimination of Irish against "Yankees" reported by Collins is precisely of the same type which when it occurs to certain organized minorities becomes the basis for widespread agitation.

[17] See, for example, the analysis of the conflict of proposed Federal Fair Employment Practices with the Bill of Rights, *Commentary of Donald R. Richberg on S 94* (Pamphlet, To the Senate Committee on Labor and Public Welfare, Oct. 10, 1947).

[18] See Percy Black and Ruth D. Atkins, "Conformity versus Prejudice in White-Negro Populations in the South: Some Methodological Considerations." *Journal of Psychology* (1950), Vol. 30, 109–121.

[19] J. L. Moreno, *Who Shall Survive?* Beacon, N.Y., 1953. Pp. 380–382; 407–409; 560–564.

PART IV
PSYCHOLOGY

BIOGRAPHICAL NOTE

FRIEDRICH KEITER, Ph.D., M.D., *is Professor of Anthropology and Director of the Legal-Anthropological Laboratory at the University of Würzburg, West Germany. Dr. Keiter studied under the noted art historian Professor Josef Strzygowski at the University of Graz, Austria, and studied medicine at the University of Hamburg, Germany. He taught anthropology at both of these universities before going to Würzburg.*

Professor Keiter has investigated the physical anthropology and population genetics of various peoples in Europe and South America and in recent years has taken part in the interdisciplinary studies of the population genetics of the Amerindian population of Brazil.

More than two hundred articles by Dr. Keiter have been published in scientific journals, including papers on morphology and physical anthropology, behavioral, population and human genetics, and art history, to name only a few of the subjects.

He is the author of a number of books, including the classic three-volume work, Rasse und Kultur (Race and Culture), *published during 1938–40. This summarized available knowledge in the field, analyzed methodological problems of the subject, and indicated directions for further research. Dr. Keiter's contribution to this symposium is based on that work. Some of his other works are* Menschenrassen in Vergangenheit und Gegenwart (The Races of Man in Past and Present), *1936;* Rassenpsychologie: eine werdende Wissenschaft (Race Psychology: A Coming Science), *1942; and* Die menschliche Fortpflanzung (The Human Breeding Circle), *1941.*

RACE AND CULTURE

Friedrich Keiter

WOULD THE CULTURAL history of man have taken the same course if population-genetical or racial differences did not exist? Could we conceive that the arbitrary exchange of children in the cradles of diverse peoples and castes would not have an effect on the processes of history?

There are few questions in the realm of human biology, where a strictly scientific answer is as difficult or at least as inconclusive as this one. But somehow an answer to this question should be attempted, since in many ways it is the most important aspect of the study of race. The methodological considerations alone are immensely complicated and manifold.

Race, like sex, age, disease, birth, death, and climate, is a basic anthropological phenomenon of life. It is, therefore, invested with considerable emotion. But it is better to know the true nature of race, which can only be the result of many years of intensive research, than to yield today to pro-racial or anti-racial propaganda, both of which would lead us away from scientific clarification.

The exchange of children experiment mentioned above would doubtless fail immediately since racial differences are visible among the smallest children. Here we encounter the first form of the influence of race upon culture: in the effects which physical racial traits themselves have on human behavior. The outer appearance determines the instinctive physiognomic reactions of man, although he claims to be a "rational animal." Appearance determines social groupings and is one of the essential elements of artistic design. Muscular strength, size, susceptibility to disease, among others, are at the same time racial facts and "guides for cultural behavior."

It should be noted here that we define "culture" in the sense of American "Cultural Anthropology" as all objects created by man and all contents of experience which determine and alter human behavior, as for example the stone in the river determines the eddies which form around it.

We define race in the sense of populations with specific distributions of traits in their gene pool. We may properly speak of taxonomically distinct races, when these differences are so marked that all or almost all individuals of the groups in question are in some way identifiable. There are, however, gene pool differences of all orders of magnitude. This important fundamental insight may now be emphasized for the first time—that races never appear as gene pools *per se*, but always only as "group phenotypes" recognizable in concrete individuals.

Group behavioral phenotypes among human populations, which are culturally created, are also legitimate objects of biological research. With regard to physique alone the same race may appear stunted or advanced, sun-tanned or pale, fat or slender, habitually sympathetic or parasympathetic. In the same manner the men of different cultures are at any rate group phenotypes manifested in various ways either on the basis of the same or on the basis of a different gene pool. How phenotypes develop from genotypes is by all means a biological problem. Indeed the closest cooperation between the historical sciences and the "humanities" is necessary for the solution of such cultural-biological questions.

Racial data can be significant for the history of culture in four ways. First, it is a fact that different races become the bearers of specific cultures simply because these cultures appear in different regions of the world and therefore among racially distinguishable populations. It can become important for the reconstruction of cultural history to know the racial affinity of the bearer of a culture. This, however, does not thereby establish a specific causal relationship between race and culture.

Secondly, the behavioral effects of the morphology of the culture-bearing race upon culture can also be studied. This still does not provide evidence of racially-specific mental and behavioral traits.

Thirdly, races are always manifested as cultural group phenotypes in specific "national characters." The concept of "national character" [*Volkscharakter*] itself contains many problems (Duijker and Frijda, 1960). For us the term "national character" means all behavioral possibilities which are characteristically distinct among the people of different populations. The study of national character is, therefore, closely linked to our problem of the relation between race and culture, since primary race psychological distinctions are realized only in group phenotypes. Of course, they are realized in many different ways depending upon the historical conditions.

Extensive research into national character is the best way of approaching the fourth essential relationship between race and culture—*the population differences in the behavioral-genetic gene pool* which influence culture.

In summary, there are four types of relations between race and culture: (1) the purely factual-historical; (2) the behavioral effects of racial morphology; (3) the differences in national character between racially diverse populations; and (4) the differences in the behavioral-genetic gene pools of those populations.

Physical Appearance and Cultural Historical Processes

IF CULTURE ORIGINATES in different regions of the world, it must necessarily do so among peoples of different physical appearance. This seems obvious. Yet several aspects of this statement are of interest to us.

First of all, the understanding of cultural history will be complete only when the historians can tell us what the people of each particular culture looked like. There are racial diagnostic criteria for many cultural-historical processes. Thus, in later millennia the historical anthropologist will be able to demonstrate that the population of the United States of today, with respect to its racial composition, arrived from the East and not from the West like all the American Indian groups. They will also be able to point out that very different regions of Europe will have to be considered as the place of origin of the American people. But the extent to which racial anthropology in this sense is capable of being an auxiliary science to archaeology cannot be further considered here.

We are much more directly interested in the suggestion that the factual-historical relations between race and culture are necessary relations. We do not view the races of man naked, so to say, but in the "dress" of the culture in which they appear to us. So long as the Chinese wore pigtails, we perhaps did not consider the idea that they could also cut them off. Only after the same race appears in completely different regions of the world—such as the Negroes naked in Africa and as fully-clothed U.S. citizens in America—or, if the same race undergoes drastic historical changes, does this notion become clear. For the European this is best exemplified in the steady change of the "cultural dress" of his forefathers since the early Stone Age.

In certain respects there is only one single cultural history, encompassing in its somewhat developed stages but a few millennia on one planet. For a biologist thinking in terms of the laws of nature, it is worthwhile to keep in mind that the factual history of man was only one among very many possible or conceivable human histories within the limits of the genetic possibilities. The physicist, von Weizsäcker (1949), for example, has emphasized this point not only for the history of culture, but also for the natural history of the earth and even of the cosmos.

If, in spite of this, we wish to consider the history of culture as an experiment of nature in which the behavioral genotypes of racial groups reveal themselves, then we must try to proceed from this historical uniqueness, which is meaningless from the viewpoint of the laws of nature, to the most frequent repetitions, which are independent of one another. Only by this means can we obtain "samples" which can be treated statistically. This has been previously emphasized as "The Principle of Historically Independent Multiple Cases" in the methodology upon which I based my three-volume work *Rasse und Kultur: Eine Kulturbilanz der Menschenrassen* (1938–1940).

Actually, cultural history is divided into so many relatively independent individual histories that an accounting of it can be rendered only to a certain extent. However, the courses of these individual histories are never absolute, but always only relative. A thin thread of historical continuity between the cultural history of the new world versus that of the old world cannot be overlooked. However, it is possible to separate to a certain extent the common heritage from the autonomous development and transformation. The problem is similar to that faced in genetic research, where the existence of an environmental component in the variability does not prevent the calculation of the hereditary component.

In any case the purely factual relations between cultural history and race have common cause in global conditions. Sheer geographical distance leads to differences in race and culture, since the fundamental principle is valid here: the greater the distance, the lesser the chances for similarity. The specific differences in geographical regions of the world are at the same time effective in forming races as well as determining cultures, without one necessarily influencing the other.

It is an extremely difficult task by far to distinguish between geographical and racial effects upon culture, since these effects run parallel.

The Behavioral Effects of Racial Morphology

BEFORE MAN EVER begins to think, he is already influenced by immediate impressions. Thus he is influenced by the looks of his fellow men and of his own.

A beautiful woman because she is beautiful leads a different life than an ugly woman. The "physiognomist" would conclude that external beauty also indicates a beautiful soul. Very probably, however, she does not have any different soul than her unattractive counterpart, for the correlation between morphology and behavioral traits is, as a whole, small. In reality the beautiful woman is merely better suited to suggest a "beautiful soul." A beautiful face then is an obvious representation of a beautiful soul, suits it, and is an effective symbol for it.

We face here a difficult anthropological question. The world of man is built upon the appearances which he sees, and upon the experiences which he makes out of these appearances. Physiognomists, such as Ludwig Klages (1950), believe that appearance reveals the "essence." But, perhaps, it is the reverse. Our concepts of "essence" are oriented toward the physical obviousness of appearance. At least we term that which strikes us as the most evident, tangible, and imperative the "essence" of a thing or person.

No one behaves the same toward a man crippled in war and a healthy man, even though the soul has not been crippled. It takes much critical self-discipline for the crippled individual not to be crushed by the reactions of rejection. This attitude of rejection of the "strange" is the rule among animals. It is found often enough in humans, not only among children but also among adults.

It is a fact that although we are able to determine the character and ability of people astonishingly quickly, we are also very much affected by the suggestions of our impressions. And we believe that people are what they appear. That physique and character should have nothing to do with one another seems unbelievable from the outset, although it has often been demonstrated.

The same effect is without doubt, obtained with respect to racial differences in physical traits. Race psychological differences are instinctively plausible, simply because the notion exists that the different appearances of the people "must have some significance." Some of those racial characteristics which have strong physiognomical power of suggestion are, for example, light and dark color, stockiness and slenderness, tall and short stature, thick lips, and Mongoloid eyelids (all these seen from the viewpoint of Western man). Just as in the case of the beautiful or ugly woman, the differences in outward appearance are transformed into differences in character.

It would also be a mistake to consider these more or less automatic effects of suggestion as the expression of inborn instincts. Inborn roots of impression probably are always present. But it also depends on learned and alterable attitudes whether one abhors black skin or accepts it as a matter of course, loves it or hates it, calls it beautiful or ugly.

In the same way the strongest roots of impression, those based on sex, either can be expressed in an erotic context or can be suppressed in occupational or other contexts. Then one learns to treat women as men, beautiful women the same as ugly women.

The involuntary roots of impression are concerned here. However, they are—as the founder of German behavioral research, von Uexküell (1926) has expressed it—transferred to another function, for example, from the sex function to the function of cooperation. During that process they change their dynamic significance without really becoming nullified.

Without doubt cultures too can shape human nature into very different functions. They are then doing the same as happens everywhere in the animal kingdom, where the animal reacts to changing conditions of treatment and milieu. The instinctive nature of an individual can be made into something different, but not without using this instinctive nature as a starting point.

Allport (1954) contends that direct physiognomic rejection of the Negro is stronger in the Northern States of the United States while in the Southern States the Negroid physiognomy as such is quite accepted but is treated as an inescapable mark of a specific class status. This is an excellent example of the two most important effects of racial physiognomy—the direct effect of suggestion and emotion on the one hand and the significance of racial characteristics as a demarcation of social status on the other.

Social groups are internally unified and integrated almost by necessity through the formation of lines of demarcation with respect to out-groups (Parsons, 1951; Keiter, 1956). Racial distinctions of visible physical characteristics most obviously form such an outer line of demarcation. This constitutes a danger and a problem. But it is historically a very important effect of racial characteristics. Since only those racial groups who have migrated from a great distance are sharply distinguished from the indigenous population, enmity to the alien easily becomes linked to the use of physical traits in the demarcation of groups from outsiders. The "foreigners" need not be recognizable as such individually. Merely the greater opportunity for dissimilar individuals is noted.

Among one's own population the question is not so much a feeling of racial unity but rather of a wide spectrum of very diverse types, whose appearance is familiar because they result from genetic recombination within the gene pool. In addition, this spectrum of types changes with the population. We have asked, for example, subjects in an experimental sample to judge first pairs of north Germans and secondly pairs of one north German and one Portuguese on the basis of photos as "very similar," "similar," "indifferent (do not know)," "dissimilar," "very dissimilar." It should be noted that only physiognomy could be a criterion since color and size could not be judged on the basis of the photos. The results are shown in Table 1. No matter how different

TABLE 1
COMPARISON OF PHYSIOGNOMIC SIMILARITY BETWEEN TWO DIFFERENT NATIONALITIES IN PAIRED PHOTOGRAPHS

Degree of Similarity	North German–North German	North German–Portuguese
Very Similar	6.3%	1.5%
Similar	29.2	20.2
Indifferent	15.5	15.0
Dissimilar	38.8	43.5
Very Dissimilar	10.2	20.0

members of the same group are individually judged to be, they still remain much more frequently similar and less frequently dissimilar compared with the members of other population groups.

Works of Art as a Guide to Race and Culture

ART IS THAT REALM of cultural creativity in which the physiognomical impression itself becomes the criterion. Artistic values do not lie *behind* the phenomena but *in* them. Man is one of the most important objects of art. No matter how far stylistic, expressionistic, and abstract changes may go, racial characteristics as models for artistic form will remain an integral part of the content, the "message" of the works. The classical works of ancient Greece could not have been created in black Africa and vice versa. The history of art—if not the entire history of culture—would have taken a different course had the races been exchanged in the cradle according to the fictional experiment mentioned at the beginning of this article.

To be sure, a precise scientific treatment of the interrelation between racial characteristics and styles in art still has to be written. By the way, one should not speak of "art and race," but of the correlations between artistic formal imagination and some of the morphological types of the specific physiognomic gene pool. In classical Greece, for example, the balanced medium facial line was taken as the artistic standard, while in Byzantine times the much more expressive wide-eyed and large-nosed pointed facial line was preferred. Whether the population had changed in the same way is, however, doubtful.

At any rate, the work of art has the same relation to the total culture as the face of man to his whole being. Just as one thinks primarily of the man's face when a specific person is mentioned, so works of art become the most convincing evidence of a specific culture. It is difficult in both cases to say how far faces and works of art are able to suggest such a connection, because man is an "optical animal" especially dependent upon his visual impressions, and how far the spirit of a time, race, and people can be clearly identified in the works of art or the human soul in the human face. The chapter on "Style" by Meyer Schapiro in Kroeber's *Anthropology Today* (1953) is a good presentation in English of these topics which have been discussed in Germany since Hegel and the Romantic period.

Schultze-Naumburg in his book *Kunst und Rasse* (1928) pointed out long ago that artists tend more or less to depict people very much as self-portrayals. He furnished impressive evidence for this thesis from Lippi, Botticelli, Leonardo, Andrea del Sarto, Dürer, Stuck, and Corinth. Unfortunately, this immensely interesting phenomenon has nowhere been pursued in a detailed fashion. One would also have to consider the reverse connections, that the artists see and depict themselves as they see and depict men in general. It is quite possible that there exists in artists a quasi-instinctive, archetypal (C. Jung, 1923) tendency to project in their depictions of men the image of their own race. Here is room for much fruitful study.

There are excellent illustrations supporting the contention that racially-typical forms of physique and constitution can be recognized in the styles of art. The heavy and static physical style of the Indian and the leptosome and hyper-motoric style of the

Negro find their correspondence in the respective forms of art of these two races. Schwidetzky (1959) summarized Keiter's observations concerning this topic as follows:

"Psycho-physical correlations established by constitutional research may be significant for psychological racial differences, since races differ in body build as well as in the degree of gynadromorphism and in the concurrence of other hormonal factors. In the cultural style of Negroes and Indians and their manner of adaptation to European civilization there is a reflection of traits which can be related to the predominant body type (Keiter, 1938). Some of the schizothymic traits of Negrids, which correspond to their predominantly leptosome physique, include emphasis on form rather than on color with the plastic arts being the distinctive folk art of Negro Africa, and an ability to break up total impressions. Added to this, we find some of the characteristics associated with Basedow's disease or exopthalmic goiter: wide, shining eyes as the physical manifestations and strong and unstable excitability as the psychic manifestation. The physique of the Indianids is predominantly athletic. Those traits which have been noted by experienced observers of Indians and Indian culture fit in well with the portrayal of the sluggish or viscous temperament of the athleticist: emotional tenacity; 'a stoic attitude,' positively manifested as endurance and self-control; stolidity of feeling, 'lack of associative drive'; and relatively crude and monotonous motor activity which among other things finds its expression in music."

Athletic and gracile physique, in still other cases, seem to have a direct correspondence in the cultural picture of the respective peoples. The Germans and Spaniards, Eskimos and Malays, Polynesians and Asiatic Indians are in each case markedly distinct in body build and at the same time show obviously similar behavioral differences. The Neandertal man was a hyperathletic extreme, the Gorilla among human types. The equation which conceives races close to the poles as athletic, and those close to the equator as gracile is without doubt correct in most cases. However, the Polynesians among men and the Gorillas among primates show that this rule does not hold universally, for both reside in tropical regions and are distinctly ungracile-athletic in physique.

TABLE 2
DISTRIBUTION OF THE TWO MAJOR PHYSIOGNOMIC VARIABLES—NASAL SIZE AND FACIAL WIDTH—IN WORKS OF ART IN DIFFERENT RACIAL ZONES*

Nasal Size

Racial Zone	Very Large	Large	Medium	Small	Very Small	Total Number of Art Works
Africa	9.2%	23.5%	23.5%	36.7%	8.2%	98
Melanesia	20.8	43.5	20.8	15.1	—	53
America	37.2	23.0	32.2	10.1	3.7	109
India	11.5	33.3	43.6	11.5	—	78
China	9.4	30.6	43.5	9.4	7.1	85
Ancient Near East	32.9	35.7	26.2	5.5	—	73
Germanic Middle Ages	2.6	27.2	52.9	15.9	1.3	157

Facial Width

Racial Zone	Very Wide	Wide	Medium	Narrow	Very Narrow	Total Number of Art Works
Africa	12.4%	21.7%	16.5%	35.0%	14.4%	97
Melanesia	3.8	15.4	25.0	35.6	21.2	52
America	38.2	25.3	20.7	11.1	4.8	63
India	20.6	38.2	29.4	11.8	—	68
China	14.6	36.6	31.8	17.0	—	71
Ancient Near East	13.1	21.1	36.8	26.3	2.6	38
Germanic Middle Ages	4.5	23.2	38.2	28.6	5.3	112

* Based on the pictorial volumes *Kunst der Welt* and Muhseler's *Deutsche Kunst*.

Table 2 presents works of art of peoples belonging to various racial groups. The works of art are catalogued according to the two most important constitutional characteristics of physiognomy: width of the face and size of the nose. A further division of both variables is possible but is here omitted due to limitations of space.

The distinctions here are considerable and at least in the majority of cases correspond to the actual racial differences. According to their works of art Negroes have smaller noses than Melanesians. Both racial groups appear especially narrow-faced, mostly due to the fact that in both cases masks with long lower face portions were fashioned. According to their works of art the pre-Columbian American Indians are extremely broad-faced, but, at the same time, especially large-nosed. They are exceeded in this respect only by the ancient Near East. In German art, as probably in other more recent European art, a medium-sized nose is dominant. Faces on the average are moderately narrow. The Chinese appear quite large-nosed and moderately broad-faced. The human face in Chinese as well as in Indian and Indonesian art has never been extremely narrow.

It is one important general result of these calculations that the two basic variables of facial form which have been discussed here are reflected in art very much with the same degree of variability which is found in nature. Furthermore, works of different styles are represented in our materials.

We do not plan to investigate here more closely the complicated relations between anthropological and art-historical variations of the human face. It is quite sufficient to state that without any doubt close relations exist between race and art-culture.

The Importance of Social Behavioral Differences of the Sexes

THE PURE DISTINCTION of muscular strength is doubtlessly an important physical presupposition for the almost universal social behavioral differences of the sexes. Men and women certainly are physically very different types even in those characteristics which are not directly related to the sexual role. Consequently, the specific treatment of the two sexes can form an important model for the socio-cultural effects of other biological group distinctions. The approximately 7 percent more growth and on the average about 50 percent more strength of the male, in addition to many other factors, almost necessarily affect the typical cultural behavior of the sexes.

During the last century many authorities suggested that all social differences based on sex were the result of historical accident. This was a healthy counterbalance to the Victorian concept of femininity which stylized the woman more specifically and narrowly than had ever been the case at any other time in history. The discovery that women both academically and in business pursuits could equal and in some cases excel men reduced the Victorian exaggeration to its proper dimension. But whether or not women are better, equal to, or worse than man in many life roles, they are nonetheless always different.

The same achievement can be the result of the employment of entirely different personality factors. This relative independence of achievement with respect to biological personality is manifest in the occupational activity of men and women. A woman as a director of a business is always different from a man as a director, is considered differently, has to defend herself differently, and has other means and weapons available than a man. A woman working at the same machine as a man perhaps has to work harder or less hard than the man to achieve the same result, or is more or less bored than the man and so forth.

The same is true when we deal not with male and female but with other biological differences of type. A large part of the distinctions in personality ultimately is hardly, if at all, recognizable by means of achievement, but by the extraordinarily different interplay of factors which lead to this achievement. Races too can attain the same results by employing different essential traits.

What is hidden, for example, behind the fact that all children finally learn how to read? How varied is the effort, the strategy of learning, the desire for learning, the role which reading is going to play at different ages for different persons?

Here we must pay attention to the view that the biological nature of man is not only expressed in culture, but also suppressed, and directed and coordinated toward a common standard. The more official the cultural activity the less one hears of the person who plays a role in it. Every non-individualistic culture generally does not consider the personality at all but only the ability to fulfill a role.

Differences in adaptation to climate must be especially significant for the processes of culture. According to our present knowledge, the most important causal selective factor in the racial differentiation of mankind is the adaptation to the different degrees of warmth of the earth. Consequently, the behavioral effects of these climatic adaptations should lie at the core of the racial phenomena. An obvious example of this kind of correlation between race and culture is the failure of the Germanic and Slavic North Europeans to survive in the Mediterranean after they had conquered those regions. On the other hand, the Negroes imported to America as slaves have settled firmly from Washington to Rio de Janeiro.

The correlation between climatic zone and man is especially apparent in Peru where from the coastal areas to the Andes all elevations are in close proximity. It is therefore understandable that we owe the most extensive, even though frequently quite hypothetical, presentations concerning the total anthropological effects of climatic differences to the Peruvian scientist, Dr. Valle (1953).

Race and Group Behavioral Phenotypes

RACE CAN ONLY be manifested in populations (Peoples). Studies of national character are, therefore, one of the main prerequisites for clarifying the relation between race and culture.

Duijker and Frijda's (1960) masterful survey of the problem shows that the concept of "national character" is unprecise in many respects. Above all there repeatedly appears a tendency to hypostasize a super-individual total-personality behind the facts of national character. In contrast we consider a consistent statistical, behavioristic, and biological approach adequate for our purposes.

To the national character belong all behavioral differences which mark an individual as being a member of a specific population, precisely because such behavior appears statistically more or less frequently in this population than in others. Since we have to consider here many such behavioral traits, we regard the totality of behavior found in a specific population as collected in its "behavior-pool." The term "behavior-pool" corresponds to the term "gene-pool" which has for a long time proved indispensable in the study of genetics.

In this "behavior-pool" are to be found situational responses, skills, knowledge, manners, habits of thought, which to a certain extent are not specifically characteristic of a particular population, because people everywhere evince many similar patterns of behavior. But they can be, on the other hand, characteristic of a particular population in different degrees. Here a quotient consisting of the frequency of the same behavior in this as compared to other populations is conceivable as a statistical unit of measurement ("critical value"). Single individuals are diagnosed as belonging to the specific population by means of multidimensional—multivariate summation of all behavioral traits under consideration. Accordingly, one does not assume that every German, for example, behaves in such and such a manner, but rather that every German usually manifests some of the totality of characteristic traits from the behavior-pool of his people (Keiter, 1950).

Studies in national character have a proper interest in evaluating the relatively lasting and the structurally significant behavior, rather than arbitrary enumerations of behavior. In other words, such studies should attempt to sort out in some way the frequently occurring in many individual behaviors. This direction of interest is justified by the fact that such a summation of our knowledge has greater significance even in the individual case. In addition it corresponds to the general cognitive tendency to emphasize that which is "essential" in a given appraisal.

To proceed from the "behavior-surface" to the "behavior-core" is a difficult task. It is analogous to the problem of separating the hereditary and racially-specific behavior from general behavior.

With respect to all behavior and therefore also with respect to national character three things have to be considered: (1) the actual situation demanding reactive response and accomplishment; (2) the habitual after-effects of past behavior (experiences, habits, education, attitudes) relating to this situation; and finally (3) the ever-present basic genetic factors. To what extent are national characters actually, habitually, and genetically determined?

Actually determined behavior is variable in order to adequately respond to the conditions of a particular situation. The behavior of a whole nation in many respects is *actual*, determined by prevailing circumstances, and thus typical only as long as the situation lasts. It is a common error to regard such behavior as the permanent national character. Often a foreign people is considered brutal because it is considered only as an enemy in war rather than under normal domestic conditions. It is considered undisciplined because it is known only in time of starvation. It is considered proud because it is viewed only during a period of economic success. Farmers tend to believe that city-dwellers feast every day, because they generally meet them during vacation time, and so forth.

A precise line of demarcation between such forms of behavior conditioned by the actual situation and the permanent national character cannot be drawn. This is because in all actual behavior the habitual and the genetic elements naturally are involved. On the other hand, all actual behavior is habitualized, becomes a habit, and thereby separates itself from the immediate response to the situation.

To study more closely *habitually determined* behavior certainly is the most important task of a fruitful study of national character. Habitual behavior can be further divided:

a) According to its structural significance: whether it determines only single or general, manifold behavioral traits (i.e., the "behavior-core").

b) According to the life-historical position: whether it accompanies long stretches of the process of life beginning perhaps with the first years of childhood, or perhaps constitutes a response to a situation appearing more frequently only in later years.

c) According to the degree of stabilization: whether it can be dissolved and easily changed or, to use an excellent term of W. Hellpach (1953), has become tenaciously "renaturized," i.e., becomes second nature. Here again three elements enter, of which the last one is the most interesting for our genetical problems.

At first a habit (or a "conditioned reflex," to use a term of Pavlov's) establishes itself when the conditioning process has been especially intensive.

Secondly, the more unreasonable it is, the harder it is to extinguish. One holds fast to that which enables him to face the situations of life, to that which he considers still valid or at least not hopelessly incorrect, because he has become accustomed to it. Even religious hope and faith are supported by the argument:

even if not useful, it certainly can do no harm. Man has invested much more reason in his habit formations than is normally conceived to be the case.

Thirdly, harmony and disharmony of behavioral patterns together with the individual genetic structure strongly co-determine the degree of toughness and renaturation. One accepts most readily and surrenders then least readily that which he does ably and therefore quickly and successfully.

Areas of Research in the Study of National Character

THERE CAN HARDLY be too much statistical data in the study of national character. One must separate the three strata of actual, habitual, and genetic behavior, and within the habitual at least the three constituent elements to which we have alluded.

Do such conceptions, which view national character research as fundamentally parallel to population genetics, employing the atomistic-dynamic techniques of statistical analysis of variables, actually do justice to the topic? Do they not distinguish themselves too radically from the viewpoint which considers national characters ultimately as uniform quasi-personal systems?

It must be remembered that gene pools are not arbitrary sums in the sense of Sorokin's Congeries. Gene pools also have marked self-regulatory qualities (Lerner's Genetic Homeostasis). Similarly, there are interrelations, structure and system-formations between the individual gene effects, just as there are between cultural commodities and population-typical forms of action. Gene effects are intelligible and are integrated, since they are the guarantors for the formation of viable organisms.

We recommend an "atomistic" decomposition of the phenomena of national character only because it furthers at the same time the genuine recognition of totalities, patterns, interrelations, and structures. A large part of that which is said concerning races actually concerns the collective or group phenotypes—the national characters—in which the races are manifested. Thus, poor scholastic achievement is undoubtedly part of the group behavioral phenotype of the American Negro. The comparative investigations of the intelligence test performance of Negroes and Whites in the United States constitute by far the most extensive and most manifold experimental-psychological evidence concerning our question of the relation between race and culture.

The uniformity of the results, which have been most extensively presented to the outsider by Shuey (1958; 1966), speaks not of an absolute but at any rate of a persistent negative correlation between Negroes and intelligence test performance. It is especially remarkable that the undoubted improvement in the life of the Negro population in the United States during the last fifty years is not reflected in the test results of Frank McGurk (1951, 1953, 1961).

Even though one tries to avoid a hasty racio-genetic interpretation of these data, we deal at any rate with an apparently universal character trait of the North American Negro population. Whatever the reason, it should be clear that we face here significant behavioral difference between populations within the United States which clearly does not have an actual but rather a habitual character.

A national character trait, which is found over such a wide area among such diverse populations by means of many different tests, must be "perseveringly renaturated." What in general is the structural significance of this characteristic for the life of the Negro? Does it reflect inferior schooling, poverty, suppression, a non-intellectual conception of life, or a different gene pool? A whole series of interpretive possibilities demand consideration. Such an analysis has been in progress for some time.

At what time does the difference in intellectual capacity begin ontogenetically? There are interesting investigations which support the contention that such differences do not appear among infants. However, it must be asked whether the standards set for small children are such that they can be mastered even by those of "Negroid" genetic endowment as well as by those of "White," or whether the positive results with infant Negroes in a portion of these investigations already proves the non-genetic character of the difference in achievement found among adult Negroes?

This example is offered to clarify the nature of the research in national character. First of all, carefully evaluated data is needed as a starting point. In our own time we have but little statistically checked information concerning factual behavioral differences between peoples. Most culture-anthropological research deals only with cultural patterns, rather than concrete practice. How little we have in the way of unequivocal data for even the European nations is evident from the careful reviews of Duijker and Frijda (1960).

Only if we have adequate data with which to commence our inquiry can interpretive effort in the three directions of *structural significance* be undertaken. How much do the given data say concerning the behavior of the population in general—of the ontogenetical, personality-historical significance? Here we may assume a relative lifelong stability of the "folkways," which can become, however, quite misleading. The question of the formative effects of early childhood certainly belong here. The perseverance of renaturation must be considered. What behavior remains constant in the face of altered circumstances?

All these constitute only descriptions of the kind of habitual dependence of the behavioral phenomena concerned. In later parts of this article we shall consider how we can progress from there to a genotypical interpretation.

The methodological situation is not principally different, if the carefully evaluated empirical data consist not of psychological test results as in the case of the comparative distributions of intelligence test performance in the United States, but of direct cultural assessment. These assessments must first be interpreted regarding their psychodynamic and biodynamic significance as actual, habitual, and finally genetical factors of personality and characteristics of population. A comparative cultural assessment on the basis of works of art, which has not been previously published, follows as an example. The author's three-volume work *Rasse and Kultur* (1938–1940) contains many analogous experiments.

Haptic and Optic Historical Works of Art

WE CONSIDER HERE a random sampling of historical works of art illustrating the relative strength of the tendency toward *two-dimensional and three-dimensional* forms in different cultures. Our methodology is based upon the insightful distinction of "haptic" and "optic" forms suggested by the Austrian art-historian Riegl (1900). Haptic-tangible forms are immediate, precisely definable, and subject to motoric grasp. Optic-visible forms, shrunk to two-dimensionality, are distant, affording a grand view, but are relatively undefined, and not subject to control. The fact that some cultures exhibit more haptic art-forms and others more optic might be the consequence of fashion where, so to speak, only the rules and habits are distinguished. But it may indicate fundamental differences in *Weltanschauung* and behavior. It would, therefore, provide tempting possibilities for interpretations of an anthropological and ethnopsychological character.

First of all we have to obtain materials for establishing a point of departure. The following categories of works of art can be distinguished:

> Undecorated art works and architecture.
> Decorated art works and architecture.
> Pictures.
> Semi-plastic and works in relief.
> Full-plastic figures.

Ornament or decoration basically corresponds to our "abstract art." Decoration can be two-dimensional-flat. Then we call it abstract painting. But it also can be three-dimensional, at least a type of relief. Then it belongs to relief in general. That is, it belongs to the flat three-dimensional manner of configuration, or to full plastic figures.

Reliefs in certain ways reflect most literally the reality of our experience, since they present details plastically but imbedded in a larger contextual and optical background. The tangible and visible form together the reality-space of our existence.

On the other hand, the full plastic form loses the total context of the view, and tends towards haptic-isolation. This is particularly evident in the preference for the individual figure, while groups of figures much more readily maintain a total context.

With our methodological example we desire to retain the relatively external characteristics of the two-dimensional, mixed, and figural three-dimensional forms as easily objectifiable, tripartite, measurable variables. Naturally, this method of comparison, which offers the advantage of objectivity, covers only imperfectly the subject matter. Plastic art also might be conceived of as more haptic or more optic. Decoration can consist of fixed, quasi-plastic details or can blend dynamically. However, due to limitations of space we must limit ourselves here to a single variable.

We have classified the art forms of five ethnological areas. Our data are based on the German work *Kunst der Welt*. The differences are marked. For Africa 80 percent of the art works are of full plastic form, while two-dimensional pictures are extremely rare. The other extreme is the Australian aboriginals, for whom two-dimensional pictures are the rule. Melanesians, Polynesians, and Indonesians fit in between these two extremes.

TABLE 3
RATIO OF OPTIC TO HAPTIC WORKS OF ART IN FIVE PRIMITIVE CULTURES*

Primitive Culture	*Optic-Haptic Index*
African Negro	0.126
Australian Aboriginal	11.20
Melanesian	0.74
Polynesian	1.01
Indonesian	2.11

* Based on Lehmann's *Ornamente der Natur- und Halbkulturvölker* (1920).

For purpose of illustration we have calculated an index in which the numerator contains the percentage for decoration, pictures, and half of the relief works, while the denominator contains the other half of the reliefs and the full plastic forms. This "optic-haptic index," which is presented in Table 3, reveals enormous differences between the five cultural regions. The higher the index the stronger is the total tendency toward the two-dimensional-optic form, the lower the index the stronger is the tendency toward the three-dimensional-haptic form.

This raises the following questions: Are the differences in artistic modes among these peoples accidental or are they significant indicators of racial and national character? What is the anthropological and ethno-characteristic structural significance of these different artistic expressions. Similarly, the significance of the verbal group differences demonstrated on psychological tests must be explored.

It is tempting to speak of an incomparable ability in the plastic arts of the Negroes, which in the realm of the haptic-motoric, tangible art forms leads to amazing formal creativity. But, being dry, bound to the immediate environment, and poor in creative phantasy, it has little concern for the optic synthesis. Conversely, the Australians would emphasize the background and be loosely caught up in dreams and pictures.

Is this interpretation poetry or scientific fact? A connection might conceivably be established here between such facts and the limited academic achievement of Negroes in the United States. The Negro because of his manner of perception might somehow be at a disadvantage. Interest in overall associations and total configurations certainly is one of the major characteristics of modern intellectuality. Before this hypothesis can be accepted, it must first of all be shown that the predominance of the haptic over the optic tendency is still found among American Negroes, completely separated as they are from their African background. The most genuine cultural effort of the Negro, jazz, with its preference for the short single-melismas and for improvisation which precludes an extensive structure, at least does not contradict this hypothesis.

Our results certainly show that haptic oriented art forms are not simply "culture-historically primitive," for the Australian aboriginals, who are considered still more "primitive" than the African Negro peoples, show an extreme optic orientation. For the same reason, the "dryness" of Negroid art cannot simply be traced back geographically to the dryness of Africa, since Australia is even dryer.

Finally, the extreme differences between African Negroes and Australian aboriginals show that peripheral or so-called primitive peoples can be differentiated as well as groups with a high culture. The development of different national characters certainly is not a phenomenon of the most recent cultural history.

Prehistoric Cultures Revealed in Art Forms

LET US EXPAND our factual material. In order to make such culture-psychological enumerations meaningful, one needs, as already mentioned, random samples and proportionate series of pictures. This leads us first to the German pictorial work *Die Welt, aus der wir kommen* (Piggott, English edition, 1961). In this volume recognized English specialists present twelve prehistoric cultures without bias or preference with each accorded approximately the same number of illustrations. When we move from the present to prehistory and archaeology the new difficulty arises that accidental preservation or loss of works of art can distort the results. In addition, non-artistic archaeological finds are included, while in the previous example the cultural goods were sorted out according to their artistic character. The basic data are presented in Table 4. These begin only to make sense after the "undecorated" finds are subtracted. The column "full plastic" even then remains relatively small when compared to the first assessment. The haptic-optic indices calculated from this data for the various cultures are presented in Table 5.

Ancient Europe, ancient China, the Aegean cultures of Crete and Mycenaea, and early Anatolia show markedly little haptic-plastic tendencies. In other words, space-penetrating, dynamic, that is, optic decoration is far more frequent than pictorial representation. The Central Asian Nomads show many more pictorial representations in their prehistoric finds. Their optic-haptic index, therefore, declines markedly, yet remains quite high.

Nowhere here is the index as high as among the Australian aboriginals. It is, however, remarkable that the "most primitive," the artists of the Old Stone Age, show a high optic-haptic index. This results not only from the cave pictures but also from the many two-dimensional engravings.

On the other hand, the optic-haptic index nowhere declines to the value found among the African Negroes in our previous cultural assessment. They remain an extreme and a complete exception. Above all, it is not true that the one-sided plastic orientation of the Negro cultures is a survival of the spirit of the ancient Near East. In the cultures of the ancient Near East a two-dimensional optic tendency has always been sufficiently pronounced, with pictorial representations and little dynamic decoration predominating in the art forms of the region. It is a well-known fact that in spite of a strong haptic tendency toward precision, the plastic arts are prominent in the art forms of the ancient Near East and

TABLE 4
DISTRIBUTION OF DIFFERENT TYPES OF TWO- AND THREE-DIMENSIONAL CULTURAL ARTIFACTS IN ARCHAEOLOGICAL FINDS*

Culture	Pictorial Representations	Undecorated Art Works	Decorated Art Works	Relief Art	Full Plastic Art	Architecture	Total Number of Cultural Artifacts
Upper Palaeolithic	22.2%	53.2%	6.7%	4.4%	13.5%	—%	45
Early Southwest Asia	2.9	64.7	11.8	—	13.5	7.1	170
Mesopotamian-Iranian High Cultures	13.5	18.0	16.5	23.3	16.5	12.0	133
Ancient Egypt-Old Empire	24.6	30.7	3.8	5.4	16.1	11.6	130
Phoenicia-Syria	21.3	6.9	14.5	20.4	33.5	3.3	60
Early Anatolia	2.6	14.8	33.1	17.4	10.4	21.7	115
Aegean Cultures	17.2	12.3	31.2	10.6	5.7	22.9	122
Indus Culture	6.0	39.6	23.2	4.8	13.2	13.2	99
Ancient China	9.1	25.0	42.1	7.9	4.5	11.4	88
Southeast Asia	22.1	11.7	13.0	13.0	34.7	15.6	77
Central Asian Nomads	32.2	17.3	12.4	12.4	14.8	11.1	84
Ancient Europe	4.2	21.1	49.5	8.4	5.3	11.6	95
Pre-Columbian America-High Culture	27.8	21.2	11.1	15.6	14.4	10.0	90

* Based on the illustrations in Knaur's *Die Welt aus der wir kommen* (1961).

Egypt. Our optic-haptic index yields medium values for these cultures.

One might at least speculate whether this optic-haptic balance of the perception of reality contributed to the fact that the culture-historical leadership of mankind centered for such a long time in precisely this area. For visual syntheses must be without doubt closely linked to haptic precision, where configurations should result. The African Negroes could be peoples with an overly strong "haptic" orientation. The Germans and Russians

TABLE 5
RATIO OF OPTIC TO HAPTIC WORKS
OF ART IN DIFFERENT CULTURES

Culture	Optic-Haptic Index
Upper Paleolithic	2.04
Early Southwest Asia	1.09
Mesopotamian-Iranian High Cultures	1.48
Ancient Egypt-Old Empire	1.57
Phoenicia-Syria	1.06
Early Anatolia	2.32
Aegean Cultures (Cretan, Mycenean)	4.87
Indus Culture	2.01
Ancient China	6.04
Southeast Asia	1.34
Central Asian Nomads	2.41
Ancient Europe	6.80
Pre-Columbian America-High Cultures	2.12

* Based on the illustrations in Knaur's *Die Welt aus der wir kommen* (1961).

could be peoples with overly strong "optic" orientation. At any rate, the perspectives opened up by the optic-haptic index are probably important in assessments of national character.

Keiter (1938) studied the distribution of ornamental detail characteristics in Negro Africa and Melanesia. The source of his data was Lehmann's *Ornamente der Natur-und Halbkulturvölker* (1920). The ornamental forms of Africa, much more than those of Melanesia, consist of square, separated details, are much more simple geometrically, and on the whole prefer the surface-contrast to working with thin lines. All this has parallels in various individual cultures as a relative regional—and thus racial—constant. The more integrating disposition of the Melanesians and the more atomistic disposition of the black Africans was worked out in detail by the author at that time.

We proceed now to the most modern art and continue with our optic-haptic variable. For this area of cultural activity we have tabulated the number of painters and sculptors listed for individual nations and cultures in the three similarly structured *Lexicons of Modern Art* (1955), *Abstract Painting* (1957), and *Modern Sculpture* (1960), published by Knaur. (See Table 6.) Random sampling again is guaranteed since it is certain that the authors of

TABLE 6
DISTRIBUTION OF MODERN ARTISTS, ABSTRACT PAINTERS, AND MODERN PLASTIC ARTISTS*

Nation or Cultural Region	Modern Art	Abstract Painting	Modern Plastic Art
East Europe	6.8%	6.8%	5.4%
German-Language Regions	26.4	22.4	23.0
Scandinavia	1.2	2.2	2.5
Netherlands	4.4	5.1	4.9
Great Britain	3.9	5.1	5.2
Total North and East Europe	42.5	41.6	41.0
French-Language Regions	36.1	18.4	20.4
Italy	6.8	9.2	12.1
Spain	2.4	1.4	3.2
Israel	—	1.9	3.5
Latin-America	0.8	3.8	7.4
Balkans and Greece	0.8	2.9	3.7
Total Mediterranean Lands	10.8	19.2	29.9
Islamic Lands	—	2.4	0.7
China and Japan	—	1.9	0.3
United States and Canada	3.2	14.3	6.2

* Tabulated from the artists listed in the Knaur *Lexikons of Modern Art* (1955), *Abstract Art* (1957), and *Modern Sculpture* (1960).

these works did not approach their task with our problem in mind.

Here not the works themselves but artistic personalities are counted. This refers us immediately to human beings. Although the contents of the *Lexicon of Modern Art* are more comprehensive, it lists only two hundred and forty-nine artists. The selection is thus more discriminating, as compared to the other two works which enumerate five hundred and eighty-seven abstract painters and four hundred and six modern sculptors. The *Lexicon of Modern Art* begins much earlier. It already includes the Impressionists. This might be the reason for the fact that in this volume the

French and German language areas together comprise the core-region for the development of the "pattern" of modern art. Sixty-two and a half percent of all modern artists come from these two cultural regions, while the proportion of abstract painters has declined to 41.8 percent, and that of modern sculptors to 43.8 percent. This fact might be an expression of the diffusion of the "pattern" of modern art in this period from its original geographi-

TABLE 7
RATIO OF ABSTRACT PAINTERS
TO MODERN PLASTIC ARTISTS*

Nation or Cultural Region	Ratio of Abstract Painters to Plastic Artists
East Europe	1.28
German-Language Regions	0.98
Scandinavia	0.87
Netherlands	1.04
Great Britain	0.99
United States and Canada	2.28
Total Western Culture-Northern Nations	1.24
French-Language Regions	0.95
Italy	0.76
Spain	0.44
Israel	0.54
Latin-America	0.51
Balkans and Greece	0.78
Total Western Culture-Southern Nations	0.66
Islamic Lands	3.44
China and Japan	7.30

* Based on the artists listed in the Knaur *Lexikons of Modern Art* (1955), *Abstract Art* (1957), and *Modern Sculpture* (1960).

cal center toward the periphery. Every successful cultural movement does this, because it becomes "adopted."

Most illuminating for our question is an index based on the ratio of abstract painters to sculptors. The index values for different nations and cultures are presented in Table 7. Again we arrive at a creditable, consistent picture. Everywhere in the northern countries of contemporary Western Culture, that is, in northwest Europe and North America, abstract painting is more frequent—in comparison to modernistic sculpture—than everywhere in the Ibero-Mediterranean area. The optic manner of perception even in contemporary urban art is centered in the north, while the haptic-plastic manner of perception is centered in the south. The French language sphere occupies the same middle position which it also has in geography and history. Contemporary East Asians as well as contemporary Islamic Near Easterners, in so far as they are attracted at all by modern art, are much more active as painters than as plastic artists. This corresponds completely to the traditions of their cultures.

As in all "ornament" or "decoration," so too in the works of modern abstract painting one can distinguish a static-geometric-definite and a dynamic-flowing-indefinite tendency. We have classified the twentieth century abstract paintings of three Eu-

TABLE 8
FREQUENCY OF DIFFERENT TYPES OF
20th CENTURY ABSTRACT PAINTING IN
EUROPEAN CULTURAL GROUPS

Cultural Group	Static-Geometric-Fixed	Medium	Dynamic-Flowing-Indefinite
North Europe, United States and Canada	26.9%	26.2%	46.8%
French-Language Region	29.0	40.1	31.0
South Europe	37.5	43.8	18.7

ropean cultures into three groups: those belonging to either one of the two extremes and a middle group including pictures in which distinct individual figures are present, but show a tendency toward blending. The results are presented in Table 8. The stronger inclination of the Southern European nations toward geometric-static fixity is clearly visible, even though there is in modern abstract painting a whole series of famous "geometrists" from North Europe. These include Malewitsch, Lissitzky, Mondrian, van Doesburg, and Vondemberghe-Gildenwart.

As far as our limited material allows us to come to a conclusion, Southern European abstract pictures are not even half as frequently dynamic-flowing as the Northern European ones. The middle position of the French language region again is quite pronounced. At any rate, this correlation between optic perception and the North and haptic perception and the South presents us with a relative cultural constant, which has persisted thousands of years. We have demonstrated this relationship in the art forms of the oldest prehistoric cultures on the one hand, and in the most recent art history on the other hand. The Austrian art historian, Josef Strzygowsky (1918; 1936), who was probably influenced by Riegl, pointed out the same correlations almost fifty years ago. In 1927 the author studied with Strzygowsky.

Results of Analysis of African and Polynesian Lyric Poetry

THE SAME PHENOMENON of the predominant orientation of the African Negro toward the haptic-tangible and immediate appears in an entirely different context when we make a content-analysis of the nouns found in African and Polynesian lyric poetry. Our date for this comparison are based on the translations in E. von Sydow's anthology *Lyrik der Naturvölker* (1920). African as well as Polynesian lyrics have been translated by many scholars, which should balance out any personal preferences of the translators. A more exhaustive investigation, however, should be based upon the original texts.

We have classified the nouns into eleven categories and have counted their frequency in the poetry of both population groups. The results are presented in Table 9. Only two types of songs are

TABLE 9
COMPARATIVE FREQUENCY OF NOUN
CONTENT FOUND IN AFRICAN NEGRO
AND POLYNESIAN LYRIC POETRY*

Noun Content	Percentage Distribution of 364 African Nouns	Percentage Distribution of 416 Polynesian Nouns
People	27.2%	12.8%
Names	8.2	12.3
Spiritual	9.1	6.5
Actions	7.4	12.5
Temporal Events	5.2	6.5
Parts of the Body	11.8	15.6
Tools	11.5	7.0
Animals	7.4	3.6
Plant	0.3	3.4
Immediate Environment	7.4	3.3
Distant Environment	4.4	21.2

* Based on E. von Sydow's *Lyrik der Naturvölker* (1937).

considered throughout—songs of love and lamentations for the dead. The content of the poetry in both cases is about the same. The greatest difference by far occurs in the last lines, above all the very last line. The inanimate environment, which according to Gestalt psychology is not "emerging figure" but rather "extending ground," is referred to with 11.8 percent of the nouns in the songs of the African Negroes, as compared with 24.5 percent of the nouns in the songs of the Polynesians. The distant, barely visible environment—forest, landscape, sky, clouds, stars—is mentioned with 21.2 percent of the nouns in the Polynesian songs and only 4.4 percent in the Negro songs.

According to their lyrics the Negroes see little into the distant future, little of a general view, but rather more of the tangible, immediate present. When such a basic characteristic is expressed in picture art as well as in lyric poetry, we are then dealing with a style of *Weltanschauung*. At any rate it is a trait which is not limited to the sphere of artistic styles. Since the data in both cases are derived not from one single Negro population but from all the black peoples of Africa, a narrow culture-historical interpretation of such outstanding characteristics is inconceivable.

Without any doubt other lines of our assessment are of psychological interest, even though not as impressive, given our limited reference material. Temporary events and actions are referred to with 12.6 percent of the nouns in Negro poetry, as against 19.0 percent of the nouns in Polynesian poetry. Negro poets mention animals more frequently, while the Polynesians more often mention plants belonging to the fixed experiential background. People appear more than twice as frequently in the songs of the Negroes than in the songs of the Polynesians.

Lehmann's book (1920) is subdivided into several categories of songs. The same Negro traits which we inferred from the statistical analysis of nouns can, to a certain extent, be recognized by their varying contribution to these categories of songs. Thus, six of the fourteen songs about animals originate in Africa, but only one of the twelve songs about nature. Even this one does not contain any depictions of the landscape such as we find in the Polynesian, Eskimo, or Indian songs of nature.

Parenthetically, it might be noted that in the art exhibitions of the 1930's, landscape paintings predominated in North Europe and paintings of figures in the South (Keiter, 1936). This fact again points in the same direction as our other findings.

In the preceding sections we have pointed out directions of rewarding and effective research which are not yet directly oriented toward the behavioral-genetic aspects of our problem. However, these different approaches do concern in a very essential manner the question of the relation between race and culture.

The factual historico-geographical relations between race and culture are not at all as well known as one might legitimately expect after so much racial-anthropological research. Above all, the multivariate population-genetic approach to anthropological population-research is more in its beginning than at its end compared to the older typological-taxonomically inclined research. How can we begin to correlate races and cultures when we are possessed of so few cases in which the racial composition of the populations as well as their cultural behavior can in general be determined with sufficient accuracy?

In addition, it is necessary to enlarge the sphere of empirical data and to extend our knowledge of the behavioral foundations of our subject. These investigations should include the provision of data on constitution and physiognomic morphology, sensory-physiological and neuro-physiological studies (EEG), and research on bio-chemical differences of presumed functional significance, etc. Additional racial-anthropological research of this kind, which is still very necessary, must be accompanied by a cultural research, which conceives culture as the behavior of specific peoples.

Literature

Allport, Gordon W. *The Nature of Prejudice*. Boston: Beacon Press, 1954.

Duijker, Hubertus C. J., and Frijda, N. H., *National Character and National Stereotypes*. Amsterdam, Holland: North Holland Publishing Co., 1960.

Hellpach, Willy. *Kulturpsychologie*. Stuttgart, Germany: Enke, 1953.

Jung, Carl G. *Psychological Types.* London: Routledge & Kegan Paul, 1923.

Keiter, Friedrich. "Zivilisierung als Kulturbiologisches Experiment." *Zeitschrift für Ethnologie.* Vol. 67, pp. 294–317, 1936.
———. "Grundlagen und Hauptaufgaben einer lebensgesetzlichen Kulturlehre." *Archiv für Bevölkerungswissenschaft.* Vol. 6, pp. 316–333, 1936.
———. *Rasse und Kultur.* Vol. I: *Allgemeine Kulturbiologie* (1938). Vol. II: *Vorzeitrassen und Naturvölker* (1939). Vol. III: *Hochkultur und Rasse* (1940). Stuttgart, Germany: Enke.
———. "Volkscharakter und Rassenseele." *Zeitschrift für Rassenkunde.* Vol. 8, pp. 41–53, 1938.
———. "Zwölf Regeln der Sozialgeschichte." *Köln Zeitschrift für Soziologie.* Vol. 2, 1950.
———. "Grundformen gesellschaftlich-kultureller Lebensvorgänge." *Handbuch der Soziologie* (edited by Werner Ziegenfuss). Vol. 2, pp. 716–780. Stuttgart, Germany: Enke, 1956.
Klages, Ludwig. *Die Grundlagen der Charakterkunde.* Bonn, Germany: Bouvier, 1950.
Knaurs Lexikon der moderner Kunst. Munich, Germany: Knaur, 1955.
Knaurs Lexikon der abstrakter Malerei. Munich, Germany: Knaur, 1957.
Knaurs Lexikon der moderner Plastik. Munich, Germany: Knaur, 1960.
Kroeber, Alfred L. (Editor). *Anthropology Today.* Chicago: University of Chicago Press, 1953.

Lehmann, Johannes. *Ornamente der Natur-und Halbkulturvölker.* Frankfurt, Germany: J. Baer, 1920.

McGurk, Frank C. J. *Comparison of the Performance of Negro and White High School Seniors on Cultural and Non-Cultural Psychological Test Questions.* Washington, D.C.: Catholic University of America Press (microcard), 1951.
———. "On White and Negro Test Performance and Socio-Economic Factors." *Journal of Abnormal and Social Psychology.* Vol. 48, pp. 450–454, 1953.
———. "Psychological Test Score Differences and the 'Culture Hypothesis.'" *The Mankind Quarterly.* Vol. 1, pp. 165–175, 1961.

Parsons, Talcott. *The Social System.* New York: Macmillan, 1951.
Piggott, Stuart (Editor). *The Dawn of Civilization.* New York: McGraw-Hill, 1961.

Riegl, Alois. *Stilfragen: Grundlage zu einer Geschichte der Ornamentik.* Berlin, Germany: G. Siemens, 1893.
———. *Die spätrömische Kunstindustrie.* Vienna, Austria: Kaiserlich-Königlichen Hof-und Staatsdruckerei, 1901.

Schapiro, Meyer. "Style," in *Anthropology Today* (Edited by Alfred L. Kroeber). Chicago: University of Chicago Press, 1953.

Schultze-Naumburg, Paul. *Kunst und Rasse.* Munich, Germany: J. F. Lehmann, 1928.
Schwidetzky, Ilse; Heberer, Gerhard; and Kurth, Gottfried. *Anthropologie: A zu Z.* Frankfurt, Germany: Fischer, 1959.
Shuey, Audrey M. *The Testing of Negro Intelligence.* Lynchburg: J. P. Bell, 1958; 2nd ed., New York: Social Science Press, 1966.
Strzygowski, Josef. "Vergleichende Kunstforschung auf geographischer Grundlage." *Mitteilungen der K.K. Geographischen Gessellschaft Wien.* Vol. 61, pp. 20–48, 1918.

———. *Spuren indogermanischen Glaubens in der Bildenden Kunst.* Heidelberg, Germany: Winter, 1936.

———. *Geistige Umkehr.* Heidelberg, Germany: Winter, 1936.

von Sydow, Eckart. *Lyrik der Naturvölker.* Berlin, Germany: Propyläen, 1937.
von Uexküll, Jakob J. *Theoretical Biology.* New York: Harcourt, Brace, 1926.
Valle, Manuel M. *Observaciones sobre Geografía: Geografía Ecológica del Hombre.* Lima, Peru: Editorial Lumen, 1953.

———. *Two Concepts of Race: Human Life Zones.* Lima, Peru: Institute of Human Studies, 1961.

von Weizsäcker, Carl F. *The History of Nature.* Chicago: University of Chicago Press, 1949.

———. *The World View of Physics.* Chicago: University of Chicago Press, 1952.

BIOGRAPHICAL NOTE

FRANK C. J. MCGURK, *M.A., Ph.D., is Associate Professor of Psychology at Alabama College, and before this he held a similar position at Villanova University for six years.*

Professor McGurk has served as a clinical psychologist at the Children's Memorial Clinic in Richmond, Va., and during World War II was an Army psychologist. He has also been a member of the faculties of the University of Pennsylvania, Catholic University, Lehigh University, and was consulting psychologist at the United States Military Academy at West Point for two years.

Dr. McGurk is the author of The Performance of Negro and White High School Seniors on Cultural and Non-Cultural Psychological Test Questions (1951). *Among the journals in which his articles have appeared are the* Journal of Educational Psychology, Journal of Abnormal Social Psychology, Journal of Applied Psychology, Villanova Law Review, U.S. News & World Report, *and* Harvard Educational Review. *He is a member of the American Psychological Association, as well as other professional societies.*

THE CULTURE HYPOTHESIS AND PSYCHOLOGICAL TESTS

Frank C. J. McGurk

Few writers today deny that there are measurable psychological test score differences among racial groups. Most of those presently writing on this subject insist that these differences are not biological differences. They are referred to as cultural differences, and this has given rise to the "culture hypothesis" as the explanation of racial differences. While the culture hypothesis has been expressed in various ways (e.g., Ashley-Montagu, 1945; and Klineberg, 1944) its essence is that what we call observable race differences are really social differences and not biological differences, and that these differences, since they are caused by differences in cultural advantages, will disappear when the differences in cultural advantages disappear.

The culture hypothesis has been invoked particularly in discussions of differences between Negro and White groups. While the advocates of the culture hypothesis have presented strong moral and ethical arguments against biological differences between Negroes and Whites, they have failed to present any factual data in support of their hypothesis.

Ultimately, any hypothesis in science must be tested against the objective phenomena which it attempts to explain. This is the way of science. If the hypothesis is in accord with objective measurment or observation, it gains in stature. If the objective data are out of accord with the hypothesis, the hypothesis must be rejected.

If the culture hypothesis has any meaning, it could be expected that, as cultural differences between Negroes and Whites decreased, the difference between their mean psychological test scores would decrease. The objective measurement of a decrease in mean test score difference would, thus, support the hypothesis. It would not be necessary that the mean racial test score difference should disappear completely. The culture hypothesis would gain in stature if it could be shown empirically that even a small reduction in the mean test score difference between Negroes and Whites accompanied a reduction in the cultural differences between these two racial groups.

Reduction in the cultural differences between Negroes and Whites has occurred in the United States. This paper is interested in showing what measurable psychological test score differences have accompanied the reduction in the racial cultural differences. Does the culture hypothesis have any objective validity?

The Psychological Study of Draftees in World War I

THE MOST convenient place to begin the study of our problem is the World War I period. It was at this time that the first extensive psychological study was done. Tests were administered to very large groups of Negro and White draftees who represented the entire country. The results of this study were carefully recorded and published by Yerkes (1921).

The World War I period was also a period of marked social and economic restriction for the Negro. He was limited in his choice of residence and the choices he had were undesirable by present-day standards. Generally, the Negro was a rural dweller at this time. Schools available to him were poorly equipped, understaffed, and often not accessible. In general, he was limited in his social participation and he was limited economically. There is no question that the World War I period was, when compared with the present, one of great deprivation for him.

During this war period, the psychological test scores of the Negro recruits bore a clearly inferior relationship to the psycho-

The Culture Hypothesis and Psychological Tests 369

logical test scores of the White recruits. For the country as a whole, only about 27 percent of the Negro recruits obtained psychological test scores that equaled or exceeded the mean test score of the White recruits (Garrett, 1945). This is usually referred to as overlapping. It is said that 27 percent of the Negro recruits overlapped the mean of the White recruits. With this degree of overlapping, the Negro mean score is much below the White mean score. This concept of overlapping has nothing to do with range of scores (the difference between the highest and lowest score). The range is notoriously unstable—so much so that it is almost meaningless.

Overlapping, as used here, is concerned only with the relationship between the bulk of Negro scores and the mean White score. Comparisons by the percent of overlap is the simplest method of comparing scores from various psychological tests. Test performance can be compared by comparing measures of central tendency, but this requires elaborate statistical treatment and the product is no more useful than comparisons by means of overlapping.

The World War I period is, then, a basis for testing the culture hypothesis. Here was a period in which 27 percent of Negro recruits equaled or exceeded the mean score of the White recruits when the cultural restrictions for the Negro were marked.

If the inferior test performance of the Negro is truly the result of his cultural restriction, then it follows that, under the cultural hypothesis an improvement in the Negro's cultural status should be accompanied by an improvement in his test performance when compared with Whites. Put otherwise, if the difference between Negro and White mean psychological test performance is the result of differences in cultural opportunities between Negroes and Whites, a decrease in the difference in cultural opportunities must be accompanied by a decrease in the differences in mean test performance.

The cultural position of the Negro has certainly improved since 1918. This improvement has not been sudden, but has been in progress for at least two generations. The Negro has achieved more and more of the social and economic opportunities that were once reserved for the White man, and to say that the cultural status of the Negro has not improved markedly is to deny objective evidence.

What has happened to the relationship between the psychological test scores of Negroes and Whites while this cultural change has been taking place? Has the Negro-White test score difference of the 1918 period reduced in magnitude while the Negro-White cultural differences were being reduced? Do the available data support the cultural hypothesis?

Research Published Between 1935 and 1950

BETWEEN 1935 and 1950 inclusive, about one hundred and forty articles were published in the scientific literature of psychology which dealt with the question of Negro-White test score differences. Only sixty-three of the one hundred and forty articles presented statistical data, and in all sixty-three articles the mean test score of the Negro subjects was lower than the mean test score of the White subjects with whom they were compared. The other seventy-six articles were simply speculative comments about the problem, and almost totally lacking in data.

Of the sixty-three articles which presented data, only six submitted sufficient material to permit comparisons with the World War I period. These six articles are important. They covered a wide range of years, a variety of age groups, different grade groups, and different psychological tests. Because they were spaced over a range of years, they covered a variety of cultural opportunities. Also, they were written by six different investigators.

The Tanser Study—1939

TANSER (1939) is responsible for the earliest of these studies, which was done on a group of Canadian Negroes and Whites. Three standard psychological tests were administered to Negro and White school children enrolled in grades one through eight.

The Culture Hypothesis and Psychological Tests 371

All of the Negro children were described as descendants of slaves who had escaped from the South prior to, and during, the Civil War. According to the author, social and economic opportunities had always been equal for all Negroes and Whites in this area, except for a few minor outbursts of oppression directed towards the Negroes.

Tanser reports that the mean test scores of the Negro children were markedly below the White mean at every age and every grade. Overlapping for the total group (all children of all ages and grades) was between 13 percent and 20 percent, depending on which psychological test was used. In no case did overlap exceed 20 percent. Thus this study, done some twenty-one years after the World War I period, indicated that the gap between Negroes and Whites had not been lessened. It had been increased. In Tanser's study, the Negroes made a much poorer showing relative to Whites, than Negroes did in the World War I study. The cultural advantages of Canadian life did not increase the relative standing of the Negro children to White children, and this study offers no support for the cultural hypothesis.

The Bruce Study—1940

THE SECOND study appeared when Bruce (1940) published her doctoral dissertation. In Bruce's study, three psychological tests were administered to nine- and ten-year-old Negro and White children from an impoverished rural area in Virginia. All children attended segregated rural schools. By administering a socio-economic scale, and pairing children according to score on this scale, the author developed two groups of subjects, one Negro and one White, both of which groups were equivalent for socio-economic factors contained in the scale. All socio-economic scores were very low.

As did Tanser, Bruce found that Negro overlapping varied with the psychological test under consideration, but it never fell below 15 percent and never exceeded 20 percent. Even in these deprived cultural conditions, Bruce's subjects performed almost identically with Tanser's subjects, although the difference in cultural status between Tanser's and Bruce's subjects appears to have been marked. Bruce's findings indicate that equal socio-economic opportunity, even as low as it was, did not change the psychological test score relationship between Negroes and Whites which was shown in World War I. Such evidence does not support the cultural hypothesis.

The Shuey Study—1942

SHUEY (1942) reported the third study. One psychological test, constructed especially for college subjects, was administered to a very highly selected group of students in a New York City college. The subjects ranged in age from eighteen years to thirty-five years, and came from various sections of the country. Negro and White subjects were paired so that, in the opinion of the author, each member of a pair was equivalent in social and economic background. Thus the Negro and White subjects were of the same average age, the same educational background, and generally the same cultural status.

In Shuey's study, Negro overlapping of the White mean was approximately 18 percent. For such a highly selected group of Negroes, this was surprisingly low overlapping, and is quite consistent with Tanser's and Bruce's findings even though the subjects in the latter two studies were considerably lower in cultural status. Moreover, Shuey's findings are markedly below World War I findings and are no indication whatsoever that equal cultural status equalizes or will equalize the Negro's test performance in relation to the White's.

The Brown Study—1944

THE FOURTH study was reported in 1944 (Brown, 1944). An individually-administered psychological test was given to Negro and White kindergarten children in Minneapolis. Brown reports that the average age of each racial group was identical, so we can assume that they were five-year-olds. Unfortunately, Brown made no attempt to equate his racial groups for cultural factors except that all children attended non-segregated schools, and this was assumed to be an equating factor.

Although Brown reported no overlapping data, it was computed that about 31 percent of the Negro children equaled or exceeded the mean White score. While this is better Negro performance than in the previously reported studies, it is no better than the performance recorded by the culturally deprived Negroes of the World War I period. Thus, whatever cultural benefits accrued to the Minneapolis Negro children in 1944, they were not sufficient to change their standing, relative to the White Minneapolis children, when the World War I data are the basis of comparison.

The Rhoads Study—1945

WHILE THE FIFTH study was primarily directed in another direction, interesting psychological data were computed from it (Rhoads, et al., 1945). The subjects were all males, Negro and White, under four years of age, and residents of Philadelphia. An individually-administered psychological test was given to all children when three years old. All children in the study had birthweights of five pounds or over. Each child had been examined physically in a hospital clinic once a month from birth until one year of age, and thereafter every two months until the end of the study. Children of uncooperative parents were dropped from the study before the child was two years old. In addition to the clinical examinations, home visits were made every two weeks by a nurse or social worker in order to keep the experimental conditions as operative as possible. Socio-economic factors were considered to be low, but generally equal for both Negro and White subjects.

Although the psychologist who did the testing reported that the Negro and White mean test scores were not significantly different, this was found to be not the case. The Negro children were significantly lower than the White children. Only 30 percent of the Negro scores overlapped the White mean score. Since these findings are identical with Brown's study described above, the same comments could be repeated. For this paper, it is important to note that whatever cultural differences existed between these Philadelphia three-year-olds in 1945 and the World War I adults and adolescents did not change the relationship between Negro and White test scores.

The McGurk Study—1951

THE LAST STUDY, the sixth, was done by the present writer (McGurk, 1951). A special test was constructed, half the questions of which were rated as depending heavily on cultural background (the cultural questions) while the other half were rated as depending little on cultural background (the non-cultural questions). Each set of questions yielded a score—either a culture score or a non-culture score. Total score was the sum of the cultural and non-cultural scores. These questions were administered to high school seniors in various areas of Pennsylvania and New Jersey. The mean age for each racial group was eighteen years. Negroes and Whites were paired so that the members of each pair—one Negro and one White—were identical or equivalent for fourteen socio-economic factors.

In spite of the socio-economic equivalence, Negro overlapping for total score was only 28 percent—a figure almost identical with that reported for the World War I data. There is no question about the cultural superiority of the Negroes in 1951 over the Negroes in 1918. Yet this did not improve the Negro's test performance at all.

Thus, in the sixteen years between 1935 and 1950, a period of unquestioned cultural advancement for the Negro (compared with World War I period), there can be found no factual evidence to support the claim that equalizing the cultural opportunities of the two races results in equalizing their psychological test scores, or even reducing the racial test score difference. On the basis of the only studies available for this comparison, it must be concluded that the culture hypothesis must be rejected.

The above findings seemed such a clear rejection of the cul-

The Culture Hypothesis and Psychological Tests 375

ture hypothesis that I decided to analyse further the data obtained in the 1951 study (McGurk, 1953a). The social scientists were still persistently announcing (but not supporting) the culture hypothesis as the explanation for the poor Negro test performance. Specifically, I wished to answer this question: If the cultural opportunities were such important factors in causing racial test score differences, what would be found if we compared the difference between Negro and White subjects of very high socio-economic status, on the one hand, with the difference between Negro and White subjects of very low socio-economic status on the other hand? Under the culture-hypothesis the racial test score difference should decrease with an increase in socio-economic status. That is, the racial test score difference between the subjects of very high socio-economic status should have been smaller than the racial test score difference between the subjects of very low socio-economic status.

In order to follow the procedure that was used in answering the above question, it is essential to understand the composition of the socio-economic groups described in the 1951 study (McGurk, 1951). In that study, a White subject was paired with a Negro subject when the White subject was identical or equivalent to the Negro subject in terms of fourteen social and economic factors. There were no White subjects higher in socio-economic status than the highest Negro subject, and there were no Negro subjects lower in socio-economic status than the lowest White subject. Each Negro subject was permanently paired with a White subject so that both subjects were equal or equivalent in terms of each of the fourteen socio-economic factors.

An extremely high socio-economic group was selected by picking out of the entire group of Negro subjects that 25 percent whose socio-economic factors were the highest. This was called the High Negro Group. In picking these Negro subjects, the White subjects who had been permanently paired with them were also picked. This latter group was called the High White Group. There were, then, two groups of subjects, each equivalent in socio-economic status but differing in race.

An extremely low socio-economic group of Negroes was selected by picking from the entire Negro group that 25 percent of

Negro subjects whose socio-economic factors were lowest. These became the Low Negro Group. The White subjects who had been paired with these Negro subjects became the Low White Group. Again, there are two groups of subjects, one Negro and one White, both equivalent in socio-economic status.

In terms of mean test score, the High Negro Group was significantly lower than the High White Group. But when the mean scores of the two low groups were compared, the Low Negro Group was not significantly different from the Low White Group (McGurk, 1953a). The overlapping data indicated the same relationship: only 18 percent of the High Negro Group overlapped the mean of the High White Group, but 41 percent of the Low Negro Group overlapped the mean of the Low White Group (McGurk, 1951).

Thus, in the comparison of the difference between Negroes and Whites of high socio-economic status with the difference between Negroes and Whites of low socio-economic status, the racial test score difference does not decrease with an increase in socio-economic status. The difference between the racial groups was zero when socio-economic status was very low. When socio-economic status was very high, however, the difference between the racial groups was statistically significant, and in favor of the Whites. These data indicate that an increase in the socio-economic status of the Negro *increases* the racial difference. They do not indicate any support for the assumption, under the culture hypothesis, that an increase in the socio-economic status of the Negro decreases the racial test score difference.

Findings Fail to Support Cultural Hypothesis

OTHER ASPECTS of this study (McGurk, 1953a) lead to the rejection of the culture hypothesis. Negroes, highly selected for socio-economic status in 1951, make a poorer showing relative to Whites of similar socio-economic status (Negro overlap was 18 percent) than the Negroes of the culturally restricted World War I period did relative to the Whites of the same time period (Negro overlap was 29 percent). If the culture hypothesis were true, such a finding would be impossible.

The Culture Hypothesis and Psychological Tests

Moreover, when both racial groups were very low in socio-economic status, the Negro mean score was not statistically different from the White mean score—a finding reflected in the overlapping data. This suggests that the only validity possessed by the culture hypothesis is when both racial groups are culturally deprived.

From the finding of this study (McGurk, 1953a) the culture hypothesis could be restated thus: Racial differences in mean psychological test score will disappear when cultural opportunities between the races are equal but extremely low; as cultural opportunities increase for each racial group, mean psychological test score differences increase.

This denial of the culture hypothesis raised still another question. It has been stated as proof of the validity of the culture hypothesis that Negro test score inferiority results from the culturally loaded questions used in most psychological tests, and the inference is that the low cultural status of the Negro was the cause of the Negro's test score inferiority (Klineberg, 1944). Klineberg's assumptions can be verified by comparing the Negro test performance (relative to the White test performance) on both the cultural questions and the non-cultural questions. According to Klineberg's assumption, Negro test performance should be more approximate to White test performance on the non-cultural questions than on the cultural questions.

It must be recalled that the test used in the earlier study contained an equal number of cultural and non-cultural questions. In selecting questions for the test, a cultural question was paired with a non-cultural question when each was of the same approximate empirical difficulty (McGurk, 1951).

Consider first the racial difference with the cultural questions between members of the high socio-economic groups. The mean culture score of the High White Group was significantly greater than the mean culture score of the High Negro Group (McGurk, 1953a). Negro overlapping of the White mean cultural score, for these two High Groups, was 34 percent (McGurk, 1951).

The mean non-culture score of the High White Group was also significantly greater than the mean non-culture score of the High Negro Group (McGurk, 1953a), but the Negro overlapping of the mean White non-culture score was only 25 percent (McGurk,

1951). This does not support Klineberg's assumption. On the basis of the overlapping data, Negroes performed better (relative to the Whites) on the culturally loaded questions than on the less culturally loaded (non-cultural) questions. The racial difference would have been *less* had only *cultural* questions been used. On the basis of their mean scores, however, there was no statistically significant difference between the Negro-White performance on the cultural questions and the Negro-White performance on the non-cultural questions (McGurk, 1953a). Thus, in relation to Whites, Negroes perform as well (or as poorly) on cultural questions as they do on non-cultural questions. Clearly, cultural questions do not penalize the Negro of high socio-economic status.

When the low socio-economic groups were compared, similar findings appeared. For the cultural questions, the mean of the Low Negro Group was actually *higher* than the mean of the Low White Group, but the difference was not statistically significant (McGurk, 1953a). Negro overlapping of the White mean culture score was 53 percent (McGurk, 1951), as was expected from the mean differences. But when performance on the non-cultural questions was compared, the White mean score was significantly higher than the Negro mean (McGurk, 1953a), and Negro overlap was 36 percent (McGurk, 1951). The Negro-White difference on the cultural questions is significantly *lower*, statistically, than the Negro-White difference on the non-cultural questions for these two Low Groups.

Thus, Klineberg's attempted validation of the culture hypothesis by his insistence that culturally loaded test material penalizes the Negro must be rejected.

Cultural Climate and Test-Score Differences

A FURTHER ATTEMPT to validate the culture hypothesis is equally forceless. It has been maintained that increased length of residence in the culturally stimulating environment of New York City causes an increase in the psychological test scores of Negroes, and that this increase is more apparent in the Negro performance on linguistic tests than on performance tests (Klineberg, 1944). This has been interpreted to mean that, with improved cultural status, improvement occurs in Negro performance on culturally loaded test material.

Analysis of the earlier study (McGurk, 1951) does not support Klineberg's (1944) findings. The difference between the mean cultural scores of the High Negro Group and the Low Negro Group was *smaller* than the difference between the mean non-cultural scores of these two groups, although the difference between the two differences was not significant (McGurk, 1953b). The difference in mean cultural score between the High and Low Negro Groups was significant. However, the difference in mean non-culture score between these two Groups was not significant (McGurk, 1951). On the cultural questions, about 39 percent of the Low Negro Group overlapped the mean score of the High Negro Group, and on the non-cultural questions, 36 percent of the Low Negro Group overlapped the mean score of the High Negro Group (McGurk, 1951).

While it may be true that a sample of Negro children who had lived in New York City for ten or more years achieved higher scores on *some* psychological tests than samples of other Negro children who had lived in New York City for shorter periods of time, it is by no means acceptable evidence that the cultural climate of New York City is responsible for the differences in test score. Nor is it acceptable evidence that the cultural climate of New York City increased performance on culturally loaded test questions any more than it increased performance on less culturally loaded test questions. The data presented here are contrary to this assumption as well as they are contrary to the entire culture hypothesis.

Value Judgments and Scientific Evidence

THE VALUES that are attached to the moral and ethical arguments advanced in support of the culture hypothesis should not be confused with scientific evidence that this hypothesis possesses validity. Ethical and moral values are important according to the degree by which they are accepted and believed. Scientific validation, however, is a matter of objective demonstration and should not be confused with beliefs or moral acceptance.

The available objective evidence does not support the culture hypothesis as an explanation for Negro-White differences in psychological test performance. In spite of this, there are many among the social scientists who persist in citing the culture hypothesis as if it were an objectively demonstrated fact.

This places these social scientists in a unique position among scientists. They are in the position of having accepted a hypothesis for which there is not the slightest shred of supporting evidence. Moreover, aside from their speculative argumentation, these social scientists are making no attempt to gather the required evidence.

In science, it is not the usual practice persistently to advance an explanation for observed phenomena without making some effort to obtain empirical support for this explanation. In other sciences, to do such a thing would mean the inevitable loss of status for the scientist attempting it. Among some branches of the social sciences, to insist on validating hypothesis results in loss of status, and in this the social sciences are also unique.

I do not contend that the culture hypothesis is incorrect. I contend that this hypothesis possesses absolutely no factual validity. I further contend that the culture hypothesis, as an explanation for Negro-White psychological test score differences, is contradicted by the available objective evidence. And further, I contend that social science, in making no serious attempt to validate the culture hypothesis, is violating the basic rule of science.

Literature

Ashley-Montagu, M. F. *Man's Most Dangerous Myth: the Fallacy of Race.* New York: Columbia University Press, 1945.

Brown, F. An experimental and critical study of the intelligence of Negro and white kindergarten children. *J. genet. Psychol.*, 65: 161–175, 1944.

Bruce, M. Factors affecting intelligence test performance of whites and Negroes in the rural south. *Arch. Psychol.*, N.Y., No. 252, 1940.

Garrett, H. E. "Facts" and "interpretations" regarding race differences. *Science*, 101: 404–405, 1945.

Klineberg, O. Tests of Negro intelligence. In Otto Klineberg (Ed.), *Characteristics of the American Negro*. New York: Harper Bros., 1944.

McGurk, F. C. J. *Comparison of the Performance of Negro and White High School Seniors on Cultural and Non-Cultural Psychological Test Questions*. Washington, D.C.: Catholic University Press, 1951. (Microcard.)

——. On white and Negro test performance and socio-economic factors. *J. abnorm. soc. Psychol.*, 48: 448–450, 1953a.

——. Socio-economic status and culturally weighted test scores of Negro subjects. *J. appl. Psychol.*, 37: 276–277, 1953b.

Rhoads, T. F., and others. Studies on the growth and development of male children receiving evaporated milk. II. Physical growth, dentition, and intelligence of white and Negro children through the first four years as influenced by vitamin supplements. *J. Pediatrics*, 26: 415–454, 1945.

Shuey, A. M. A comparison of Negro and white college students by means of the ACPE. *J. Psychol.*, 14: 35–52, 1942.

Tanser, H. A. *Kent County Negroes*. Chatham, Ontario: The Sheppherd Publishing Co., 1939.

Yerkes, R. M. Psychological examining in the U.S. Army. *Mem. Natl. Acad. Sci.*, Vol. 15, 1921.

BIOGRAPHICAL NOTE

R. TRAVIS OSBORNE, *M.Sc., Ph.D, is Professor of Psychology and director of the Guidance Center at the University of Georgia. Professor Osborne has been head of the Guidance Center for more than twenty years and active in the field of educational psychology for nearly thirty years.*

He has done extensive research in psychological measurement for educational and vocational guidance and counseling, as well as in the prediction of academic success and in student personnel and selection. In recognition of his work in these fields he was appointed by the Federal Government in 1961 as a psychology consultant of the Veterans Administration and Office of Vocational Rehabilitation.

Dr. Osborne is the author of many articles dealing with psychological testing and measurement which have been published in professional journals. He is a Fellow of the American Psychological Association and a member of the American Association for the Advancement of Science, the South-Eastern Psychology Association and the Southern Society of Philosophy and Psychology, as well as a professional member of the American Personnel and Guidance Association.

RACIAL DIFFERENCES IN MENTAL GROWTH AND SCHOOL ACHIEVEMENT

R. Travis Osborne

O<small>N GROUP</small> achievement tests designed to evaluate the degree of success in learning the basic subjects taught in public schools, the American Negro with rare exception is unable to keep pace with established grade norms. In most subjects the average Negro child falls behind the norm group at the rate of almost one-third of a grade per year, until by the time he graduates from high school he is in some areas four full years below the twelfth grade standard.

It is the purpose of this study to point out some of the practical problems for educators who are forced to balance their schools in terms of factors other than knowledge of and skills in the fundamental school subjects.

In the winter of 1954 the writer was invited to assist in establishing a school testing program in a county in a southeastern state. The program was designed to evaluate pupil progress and to diagnose learning problems of over-achieving and under-achieving children. The first tests were administered in April of 1954. With only slight modifications, the original plan has been repeated each year, 1954–1965 inclusive. From the basic data collected over a twelve-year period, several reports were prepared and published.

In this monograph an attempt will be made to summarize

research completed to date on this project. For the entire published reports, the reader is referred to the original articles. Because of the nature of the various experimental designs, there are slight differences in the number of subjects reported in the base group and the number of subjects shown for the several experiments. These differences are the result of students missing a test or failing to supply information necessary for the experiment.

Basic data resulting from the testing programs are shown in Table 1.[1] It is seen that during the 1954–1965 period the median mental maturity grade placements have remained relatively constant from year to year for both White and Negro children. In terms of mental maturity, eighth graders in 1964 and 1965 seem to be not unlike those of 1954 and 1955.

Due to the increasing emphasis on mathematics and science throughout the entire school system there have been notable gains made in mathematics especially at the high school level. In 1954 the average tenth grade White student was 1.2 grades *below* the norm group in arithmetic. His 1965 counterpart was 1.2 grades *above* the norm for his grade. The 1965 Negro tenth grade student has also shown improvement in arithmetic skills over his 1954 predecessor. However, the average tenth grade Negro student is still three years below his grade norm in arithmetic skills and mathematical reasoning. The arithmetic performance of the Negro student in the tenth grade was more like that of a rising seventh grade pupil than of a second semester tenth grader. Tenth grade reading achievement is about two and one-half years below the norm for the grade.

The instruments used in the testing programs were the California Achievement Tests in Reading and Arithmetic and the California Short-Form Test of Mental Maturity.[2] Appropriate levels of these tests were administered to each group.

One study,[3] using only the 1954 test data, analyzed intelligence

---

[1] Sixth grade testing was discontinued after the 1956 program was completed. All fifth grades were tested beginning February 1957. Special arrangements were made with school officials to examine all graduating seniors of the class of 1960.

[2] *California Achievement Tests; California Short Form Test of Mental Maturity* (*S-Form*). Los Angeles: California Test Bureau.

[3] R. T. Osborne, "School Achievement of White and Negro Children of the Same Mental and Chronological Ages," *The Mankind Quarterly*. Vol. II, No. 1, July–September 1961, pp. 26–29.

TABLE 1
MEDIAN GRADE PLACEMENTS FOR CALIFORNIA ACHIEVEMENT AND MENTAL MATURITY TESTS FOR WHITE AND NEGRO PUPILS IN GRADES 5, 6, 8, AND 10
1954–1965

	WHITE				NEGRO			
	No.	Reading	Arith.	Mental Maturity	No.	Reading	Arith.	Mental Maturity
6th Grade								
1954	1558	5.7	6.1	6.3	932	3.9	4.6	3.9
1955	1603	5.6	6.2	6.5	948	3.9	4.8	4.3
1956	1559	5.6	6.3	6.6	1010	3.6	4.8	4.2
5th Grade								
1957	1901	5.0	5.4	—	1159	3.3	4.3	—
1958	2288	5.6	5.7	5.8	1368	3.4	4.2	3.8
1959	2215	5.7	5.7	6.0	1320	3.7	4.2	4.1
1960	2072	5.9	5.8	6.0	1246	4.1	4.5	4.1
1961	2039	5.9	5.8	6.0	1341	4.2	4.6	4.3
1962	1960	6.0	6.0	6.0	1283	4.2	4.6	4.4
1963	2086	6.1	6.0	6.2	1345	4.5	4.8	4.5
1964	2364	6.2	6.0	6.2	1427	4.5	4.6	4.5
1965	2095	6.2	6.1	6.2	1394	4.7	4.8	4.5
8th Grade								
1954	1206	7.6	7.5	8.1	697	5.6	6.0	6.1
1955	1399	7.7	7.8	8.2	738	5.4	5.9	6.2
1956	1526	7.7	7.9	8.4	830	5.8	5.9	6.2
1957	1544	7.6	7.4	8.2	904	5.7	5.8	6.1
1958	1637	7.5	7.6	8.2	936	5.4	5.8	6.1
1959	1673	7.8	8.2	8.0	888	5.4	6.0	5.6
1960	1850	7.9	8.6	8.4	1001	5.4	6.2	5.7
1961	2074	8.1	8.6	8.3	1140	5.5	6.1	5.9
1962	1952	8.1	8.6	8.3	1180	5.8	6.2	6.0
1963	1896	8.4	8.6	8.3	1111	6.0	6.3	6.0
1964	1982	8.6	8.8	8.5	1184	6.1	6.6	6.2
1965	1918	8.7	8.8	8.5	1178	6.3	6.6	6.2
10th Grade								
1954	919	9.1	8.8	9.4	460	6.5	6.0	6.7
1955	981	9.1	8.7	9.4	486	6.3	5.9	6.4
1956	1015	9.1	8.8	9.5	583	6.6	6.1	6.9
1957	1167	9.7	10.0	10.1	576	6.0	6.0	6.2
1958	1325	9.8	10.2	10.2	712	6.5	6.1	6.8
1959	1445	9.7	9.6	9.8	751	6.3	6.6	6.2
1960	1439	9.6	9.4	9.7	729	6.3	6.7	6.4
1961	1496	9.8	9.4	9.9	672	6.4	6.9	6.6
1962	1657	10.3	10.6	10.3	791	6.9	7.1	7.0
1963	1917	10.3	10.9	10.1	919	6.7	7.1	7.2
1964	1951	10.5	10.9	10.1	1002	6.8	7.1	7.1
1965	1802	10.5	11.2	10.3	916	7.9	7.2	8.1

and achievement test results in an attempt to answer the following question: Do White and Negro children with the same mental ability and the same chronological age achieve at the same level? That is, is there a significant difference in the degree of mastery of reading and arithmetic skills of White and Negro children of the same age and of equal mental test performance?

The subjects used in this study consisted of one thousand three hundred and eighty-eight White and seven hundred and twenty-three Negro sixth grade pupils. These numbers represented all sixth grade pupils in the county for whom complete data were available on the Reading, Arithmetic, and Mental Maturity tests.

It was found that the relationships between mental ability and reading and arithmetic achievement for both groups are within the limits usually found for an ability range restricted to one school grade. The range of achievement-mental ability coefficients of correlation is from .67 to .76. Younger children for both groups tend to be the better achievers. This relationship is less marked for the Negro than for the White group. For the White group the age-achievement correlations are .36 for reading and .29 for arithmetic. For the Negro group the correlations are .22 for reading and .11 for arithmetic. Although the coefficients of correlation are small, the differences are significant at the .01 level.

In this same study the achievement means were adjusted, by the method of analysis of multiple co-variance so as to eliminate the effects of the differences in both mental ability and chronological age on achievement. The co-variance analyses with mental ability and chronological age as control variables yield t-values of 13.42 for reading achievement and 12.05 for arithmetic achievement, indicating significant differences in school achievement between the two racial groups (Tables 2 and 3). That is, after adjusting the groups for individual differences in mental ability and chronological age, the differences in mean arithmetic and reading achievement were so large that they undoubtedly were not caused by sampling accident. Presumably the differences in achievement cannot be accounted for by differences in mental ability and chronological age.

In order to study the mental growth and school achievement patterns of the school children comprising our group, it was determined that a longitudinal approach would be made.

TABLE 2
TEST OF SIGNIFICANCE OF INFLUENCE OF RACE ON READING ACHIEVEMENT OF SIXTH GRADE PUPILS WHEN THE GROUPS ARE ADJUSTED FOR MENTAL AND CHRONOLOGICAL AGE DIFFERENCES

	Sum of Squares	DF	Mean Squares	F
Between Groups	32,430	1	32,430.37	180.06
Within Groups	379,493.01	2107	180.11	
Total	411,923.38	2108		

t = 13.42 significant at .001 level.

TABLE 3
TEST OF SIGNIFICANCE OF INFLUENCE OF RACE ON ARITHMETIC ACHIEVEMENT OF SIXTH GRADE PUPILS WHEN THE GROUPS ARE ADJUSTED FOR MENTAL AND CHRONOLOGICAL AGE DIFFERENCES

	Sum of Squares	DF	Mean Squares	F
Between Groups	24,362.17	1	24,362.17	145.19
Within Groups	353,542.45	2107	167.79	
Total	377,904.62	2108		

t = 12.05 significant at .001 level.

Most previous longitudinal studies have been concerned with very stable and relatively small populations with high-average to superior general ability which, for the most part, have been drawn from high-average socio-economic levels.[4] In addition to the problem of small biased samples the longitudinal design is weakened by selective elimination of subjects through death, ill-

[4] The subjects for Nancy Bayley's well known Berkeley Growth Study were 61 children with a mean Binet I.Q. of over 120. Cf. N. Bayley "On the Growth of Intelligence," *American Psychologist*, Vol. X (1955), pp. 805–823.

At the Child Research Council of the University of Colorado, Hilden used "30 normal children of superior intelligence" for his "Longitudinal Study of Intellectual Development." Cf. A. H. Hilden, "A Longitudinal Study of Intellectual Development," *Journal of Psychology*, Vol. 28 (1949), pp. 187–214.

In describing the mental measurement data for the Fels Institute longitudinal study, Sontag says, "as has been true of most longitudinal studies, our sample mean I.Q. is considerably above the average, and this limits to a large extent many of the kinds of generalizations to be made about the nature of mental growth in all children." Cf. L. W. Sontag, "Mental Growth and Personality Development: A Longitudinal Study," *Child Development*, Vol. 23 (1958), pp. 13–139.

ness, or migration. Poorly articulated achievement tests and mental ability scales of less than perfect reliability may further complicate interpretations made from longitudinal data. However, in spite of these weaknesses the genetic longitudinal approach yields patterns of growth and trends probably more valid than those shown by data based on successive cross sections of development.

The first group selected for a longitudinal analysis included all White and Negro pupils of the system who were tested in the sixth grade in 1954 and the eighth grade in 1956 and the tenth grade in 1958. Students who dropped out, who were retarded, who were accelerated, or who were absent on both the regular and make-up testing dates of any year are not included. That is, the number of cases used represents those pupils who were tested on all three of the test dates. There were eight hundred and fifteen White and four hundred and forty-six Negro children who were tested on all three dates.

Although the principal purpose of the study[5] was to report patterns of intellectual and school achievement growth of White and Negro children over a four-year period, these growth curves will not be discussed in the present paper because a later study extended the growth study through two additional years. These six-year growth curves will be discussed in detail.

In this same report the question of I.Q. consistency or variability is examined by means of group curves of I.Q. changes. Patterns of I.Q. gains and losses are analyzed for superior and retarded portions of the White and Negro groups.

I.Q. Regression

A COMPLIMENTARY phenomenon of special interest was that of regression in intelligence quotients. In the sixth grade the I.Q. range for the White group was from 63 to 149, with a standard deviation of 13.37. In the same grade the I.Q. range for the Negro pupils was from 40 to 118, with a standard deviation of 13.90. Four years later the range for the White group was from 78

---

[5] R. T. Osborne, "Racial Differences in Mental Growth and School Achievement: A Longitudinal Study," *Psychological Reports*, 7, 1960, 233–239.

to 136, with a standard deviation of 8.38, while the tenth grade I.Q. range for Negro pupils was from 50 to 106, with a standard deviation of 9.64. In other words, during the initial four-year period covered by the study, the range of I.Q.s for each group was reduced by approximately 33 percent (Table 4).

This well known but frequently overlooked regression phenomenon has long been recognized by psychologists and is always

TABLE 4
IQ CHANGES WITH AGE FOR WHITE AND NEGRO CHILDREN

IQ	White			Negro		
	Grade 6 1954	Grade 8 1956	Grade 10 1958	Grade 6 1954	Grade 8 1956	Grade 10 1958
140–149	3	1				
130–139	7	4	2			
120–129	47	25	25			
110–119	163	129	100	5	1	
100–109	234	280	379	24	35	6
90– 99	208	257	264	68	92	58
80– 89	106	99	43	120	180	138
70– 79	40	17	2	119	108	164
60– 69	7	3		74	27	72
50– 59				21	3	8
40– 49				15		
N	815	815	815	446	446	446
Mean	101.28	100.58	102.28	78.78	84.35	78.60
SD	13.37	10.73	8.38	13.90	9.93	9.64

present when the correlation between two tests is less than perfect. In order to examine more closely the regression effect in the present data each group was divided into thirds on the basis of the sixth grade I.Q.s. It was hypothesized that on successive testings the deviant individuals in each group would regress toward the mean of the population from which they came and not toward some hypothetical average of eighth or tenth graders in general.

Our finding is shown in Figure 1. As hypothesized, the top third of the White group moved (on the average of 7 I.Q. points) closer to their own mean from the 1954 to 1958 testing period. The below average group of White pupils moved upward 10.35

I.Q. points while the population mean for the total White group remained unchanged over the same four-year period. The Negro group behaved in a similar manner. The bright Negroes lost on an average 9.1 I.Q. points, while the I.Q. of the below average Negroes improved on the average 7.6 points.

From Figure 1 it is seen that although the population means have remained stable throughout the course of the study, the deviant members of each group tend to regress toward the mean of their particular population. Thus by the tenth grade, White and Negro students present two separate distributions with the mean of one almost three standard deviations higher.

In order to provide data for a more comprehensive longitudinal study, the school system agreed to administer the California Battery to the twelfth grade in 1960, although twelfth-grade testing is not a part of their planned program. This study[6] reports patterns of test intelligence and school achievement growth over a six-year period for more than eight hundred White and Negro children. Growth curves are described in an effort to determine what generalizations may be made concerning patterns of mental development and learning progress of an unselected population of public school children.

The subjects used in this study were five hundred and thirty-nine White and two hundred and seventy-three Negro children. This represents the total number of children who were tested in the sixth grade in 1954, in the eighth grade in 1956, in the tenth grade in 1958, and in the twelfth grade in 1960. That is, the number of cases used represents those pupils who were tested on all four test dates.

Of the one thousand four hundred and sixty-seven White and eight hundred and seventy-six Negro children who were tested in April of 1954, five hundred and thirty-nine White and two hundred and seventy-three Negro pupils remained in the school system, were promoted each year, and were retested in 1956, 1958, and 1960. The attrition rate over the six-year period was 63 percent for the White students and 69 percent for the Negro students.

At the time of initial testing the mean age of the White children

[6] R. T. Osborne, "Racial Differences in School Achievement," *Mankind Monographs III*, November, 1962, 18 pp.

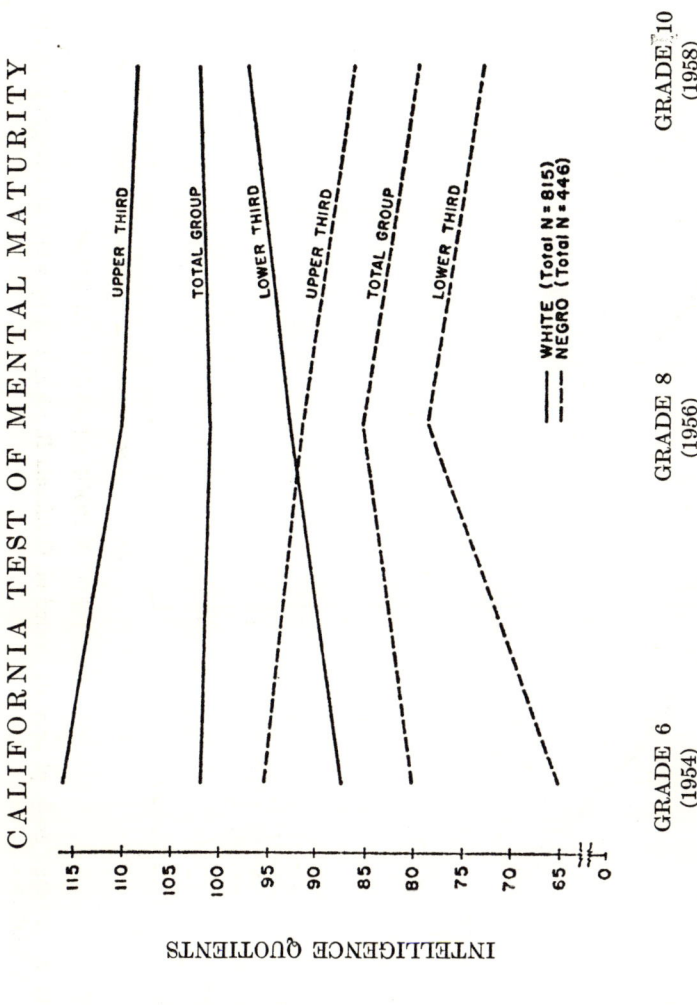

Fig. 1 Changes in IQ with age for different ability levels of white and Negro children

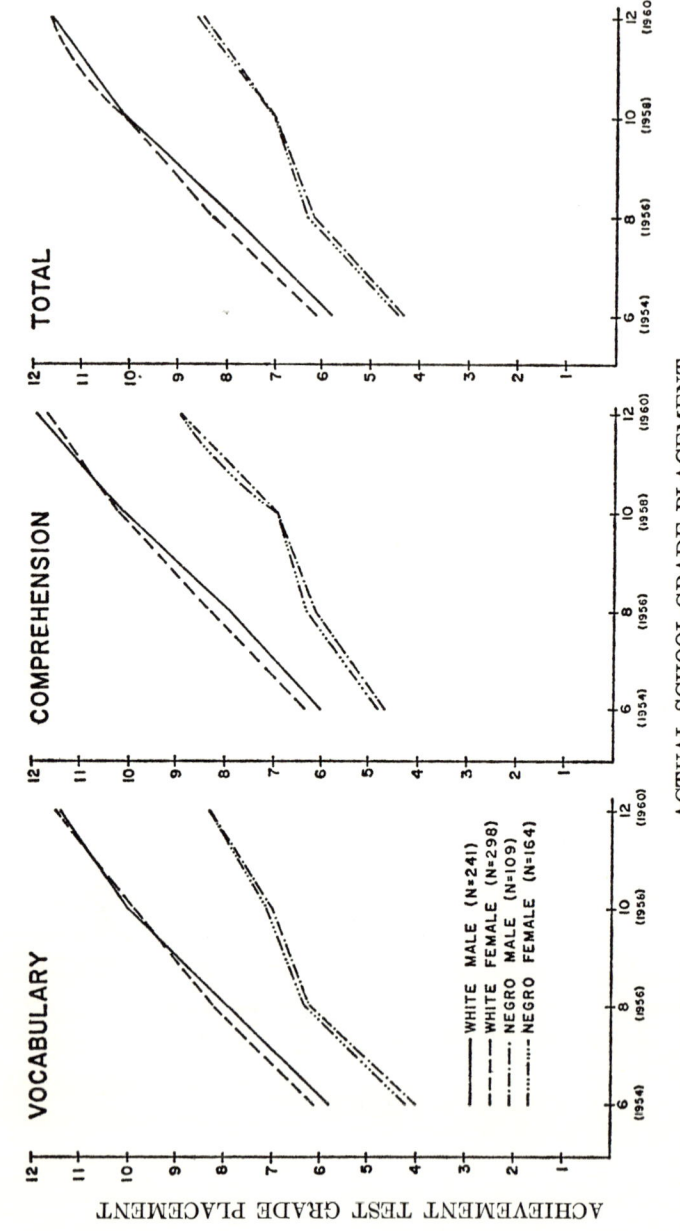

Fig. 2. Average grade placements earned on California Reading Test by white and Negro pupils tested in grades 6, 8, 10, and 12.

was eleven years nine months with a standard deviation of five months. The mean age for the Negro group was eleven years ten months with a standard deviation of eight months. The Negro children on the average were one month older than the White boys and girls.

Results obtained from repeated testings over the six-year period are shown in Figures 2, 3, and 4. Reading test results are shown in Figure 2. Here it is seen that the Negro-White achievement differences of almost two years at grade six increased steadily until at grade twelve the difference in reading level was over three school grades. This widening gap in achievement between the two groups is apparent on both the vocabulary and comprehension subtests as well as for the total reading scale.

The pattern in arithmetic (Figure 3) is the same as for reading. In the sixth grade White-Negro differences were just over one grade for the areas covered by the California Arithmetic Test. In the eighth grade the two groups maintained their relative positions in arithmetic reasoning but on the tests of arithmetic fundamentals the Negro group was now nearly two grades behind the White pupils. Six years after the first test when both groups were examined during the second semester of the twelfth school year there was a difference in arithmetic achievement of almost four grades between the two groups. The arithmetic grade placement of the average Negro twelfth grade pupil was below the eighth grade national norms while the White group tested above the eleventh trade on the same norm group.

In other words, in terms of arithmetic skills, especially fundamental operations involving only numbers, White children in the eighth grade were not only significantly above the eighth grade Negro group, but they were also superior in arithmetic skills to tenth and twelfth grade Negro pupils.

Growth patterns of mental ability grade placement for the two groups are seen in Figure 4. The difference in mental maturity of over two years at the sixth grade (1954) was slightly attenuated at the eighth grade testing (1956). But by the second semester of the tenth grade (1958) the means of the two groups are separated by over three years. The same relative position of the two curves was maintained through the last testing period of the experi-

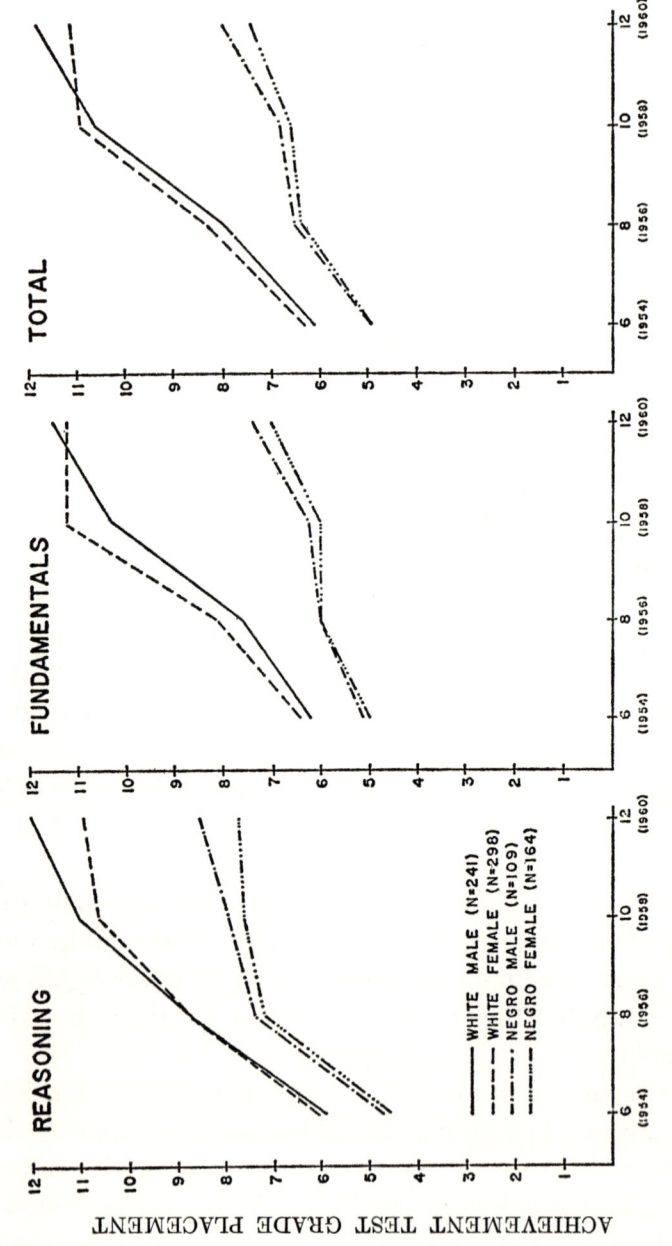

Fig. 3 Average grade placements earned on California Arithmetic Test by white and Negro pupils tested in grades 6, 8, 10, and 12.

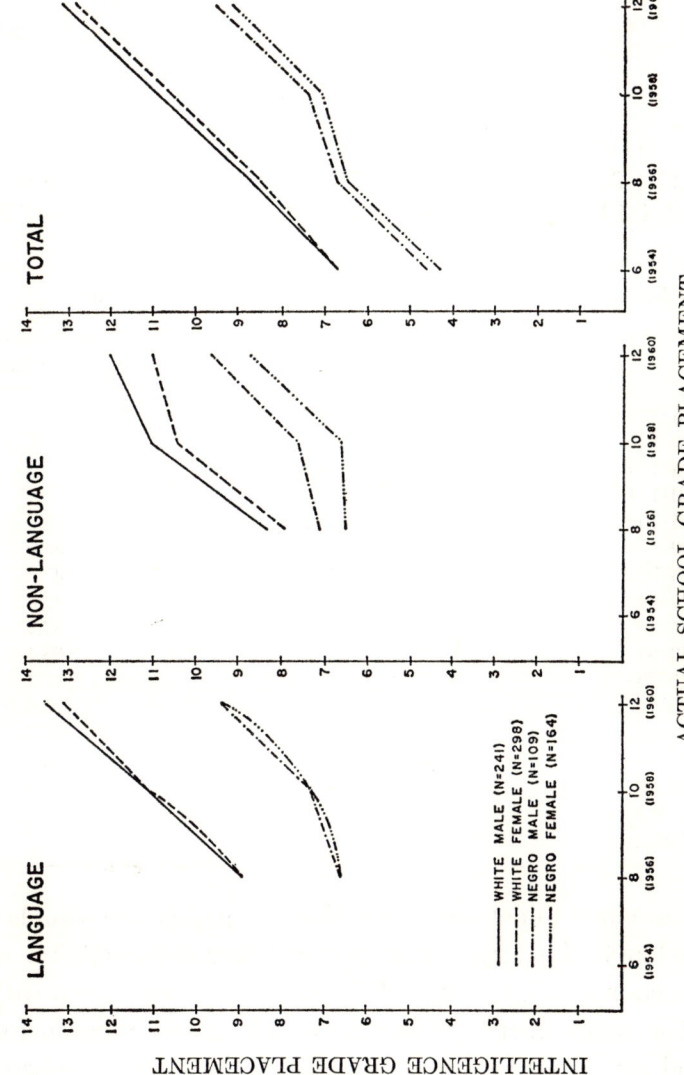

FIG. 4 Average intelligence grade placements earned on California Mental Maturity Test by white and Negro pupils tested in grades 6, 8, 10, and 12.

ment—the twelfth grade (1960). By the time the students were examined at the tenth grade there was practically no overlap in I.Q. That is, only one tenth grade child in the White group earned an I.Q. below the median I.Q. of the Negro children in the same grade. At the tenth grade only 1 percent of the Negro pupils equaled or exceeded the median I.Q. of the Whites (Table 5).

TABLE 5

DISTRIBUTION OF INTELLIGENCE QUOTIENTS EARNED BY TENTH GRADE PUPILS IN A SOUTH-EASTERN COUNTY IN 1958

I.Q.	White		Negro	
	Frequency	Cumulative Per Cent	Frequency	Cumulative Per Cent
125–129	11	99.9		
120–124	6	98.0		
115–119	27	96.8		
110–114	51	91.8		
105–109	119	82.4	1	99.9
100–104	150	60.3	5	99.6
95–99	104	32.5	15	97.8
90–94	49	13.2	28	92.3
85–89	19	4.1	38	82.1
80–84	2	.6	63	68.1
75–79	1	.2	53	45.1
70–74			38	25.6
65–69			26	11.7
60–64			5	2.2
55–59			1	.4
N =	539		273	
Median =	103		81	

In an effort to determine whether the population sample used in the longitudinal study was representative of the children in the entire county, achievement of the sample was compared with the median achievement grade placements for all children for the period 1954–1965 (Table 1). Because of the weakness inherent in the longitudinal design, all children remaining in the longitudinal group read better and have a better understanding of the fundamentals of arithmetic than do their age mates in the same school grade. The longitudinal group represents those boys and girls of

Racial Differences in Mental Growth

both races who have made normal school progress. Selective elimination of "drop outs," "repeaters," and "school leavers" tends to raise the median achievement grade placement of the remaining students of both groups. Thus it is seen from Table 1 that group achievement differences are somewhat greater when all children are considered than when only the longitudinal samples are compared.

Races and Sexes Paired

IN A FURTHER effort to understand school achievement variations, two groups of White and Negro sixth grade children were experimentally matched in 1954 for intelligence and sex. The White and Negro male groups and the White and Negro female groups were homogeneous and homoscedastic with respect to chronological age. For the White males the mean age was 141.2 months with a standard deviation of 6.9 months; for the Negro males, 141.0 and 6.1; for the White females, 140.3 and 6.0; and for the Negro females 140.2 and 6.3. Fifty-nine matched pairs of boys and eighty-one matched pairs of girls remained in the school system, made normal progress in their respective schools, and were retested in 1956, 1958, and 1960. In order to match the one hundred and forty pairs of students it was necessary to select the majority of the children from opposite ends of the two distributions. The White children in the equated group were considerably below the average of their White classmates, while a majority of the Negro children were above the 75th percentile of their group.

Mental ability growth curves for the two matched groups are seen in Figure 5. Here we have represented the records of two groups of sixth grade children of the same age, same sex, and of equal initial mental test performance. When these children were re-examined two years later, differences were slight but apparent. When all members of the group were again tested in the tenth and twelfth grades, the White-Negro differences in mental test performance ranged from one to two grade placement years.

When White and Negro children were initially equated for sex, mental ability, and school grade placement, and later examined at

CALIFORNIA TEST OF MENTAL MATURITY

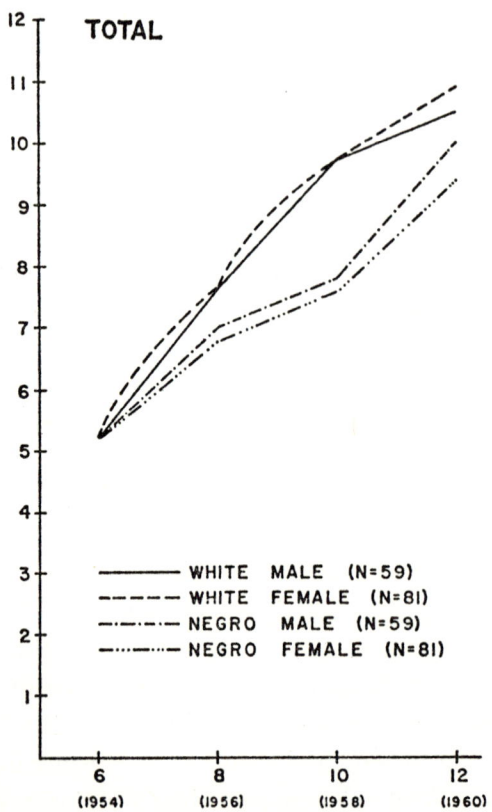

FIG. 5 Average intelligence grade placements earned on California Mental Maturity Test by groups of white and Negro pupils equated on the basis of intelligence quotients earned at the sixth grade level.

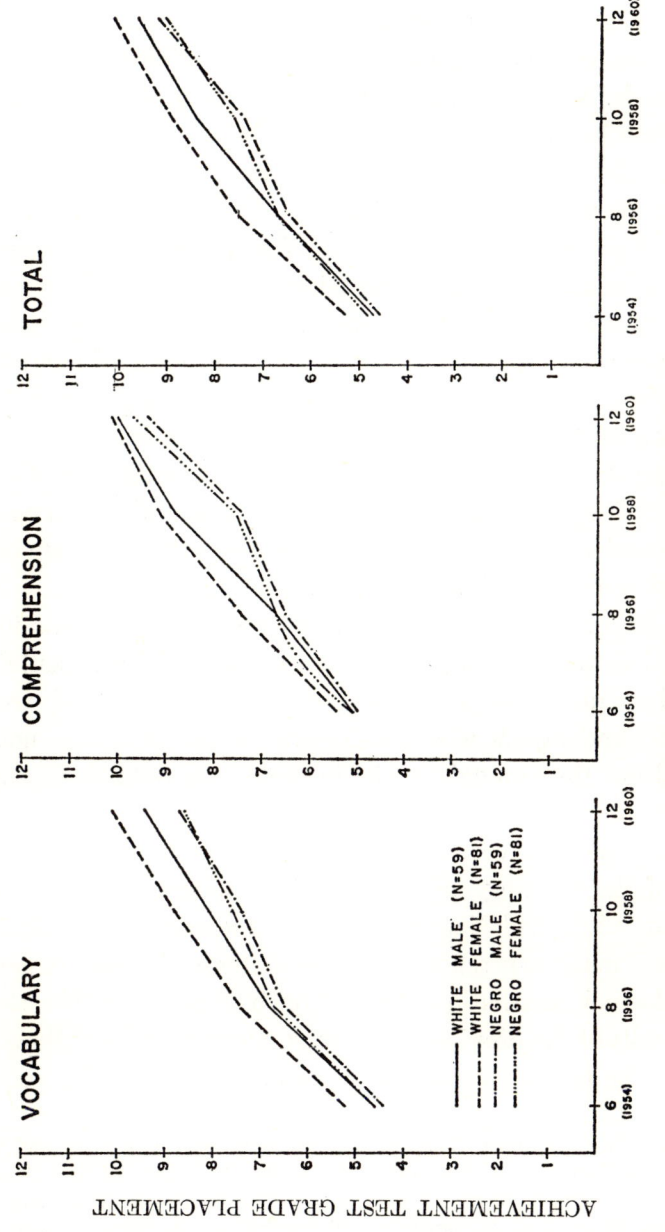

Fig. 6 Average grade placements earned on California Reading Test by groups of white and Negro pupils equated on the basis of intelligence quotients earned at the sixth grade level.

regular intervals of their school history, reading achievement differences (Figure 6) were not as great as mental ability differences. The Negro child seems to be weakest on the vocabulary section of the California Reading Test. Comprehension and total reading are within one grade of the matched White group at most test periods. As is the usual case, girls in both groups tend to read better than boys.

It is in the area of arithmetic achievement that the Negro child seems to be most deficient (Figure 7). Negro children of mental age grade placement equal to that of White children are unable to learn mathematical skills at the same rate as their White experimental partners. The Negro children, a majority of whom were selected from the top fourth of their group in terms of mental age grade placement, are unable to keep pace with the group of White children, most of whom were drawn from the lowest fourth of their class. Over the six-year period of the study the rate of learning new arithmetic skills for Negro children was about 50 percent of the standard norm rate and about 68 percent of the rate of the equated White experimental group.

This finding of higher achievement for Negro students in the so-called culturally weighted areas than in the fundamental numerical operations of arithmetic corroborates the careful work of McGurk[7] and others who consistently report that it is not the cultural but the non-cultural items which are difficult for Negro pupils to learn.

During the early years of the present experiment a comparative study of the training and qualifications of the more than eight hundred White and Negro teachers of the county in which this study was made was reported by the writer at the 1957 American Psychological Association Convention in New York. The significant results of the previous study were summarized as follows:

Six of the ten interracial differences in training and experience

[7] F. C. J. McGurk, 1951, *Comparison of the Performance of Negro and White High School Seniors on Cultural and Non-Cultural Psychological Test Questions*, Catholic University of America Press (microcard), Washington, D.C.; 1953, "On White and Negro Test Performance and Socio-Economic Factors," *Journal of Abnormal and Social Psychology*, Vol. XLVIII, p. 450; 1961, "Psychological Test Score Differences and the 'Culture Hypothesis,'" *The Mankind Quarterly*, Vol. I, No. 3, pp. 165–175.

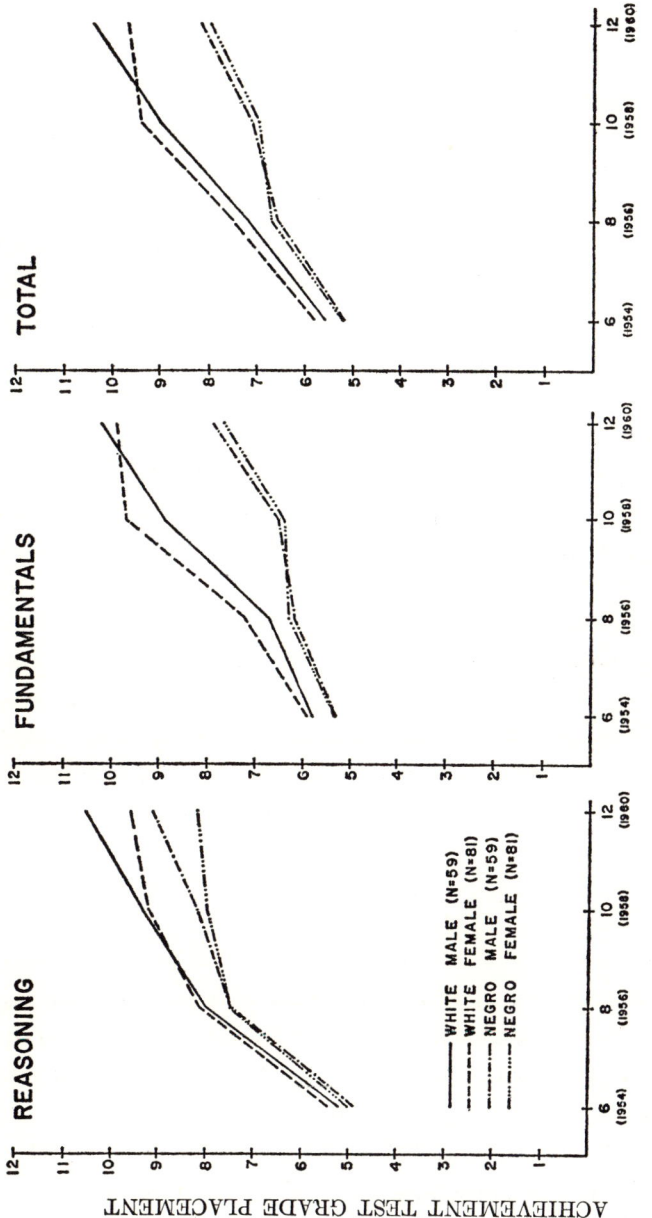

FIG. 7 Average grade placements earned on California Arithmetic Test by groups of white and Negro pupils equated on the basis of intelligence quotients earned at the sixth grade level.

background were statistically significant. These differences indicate that:

1. The Negro teachers had completed a greater number of years of college training than the White teachers.

2. Negro teachers had completed college course work more recently than had the White teachers.

3. The mean yearly salary of Negro teachers markedly exceeded that of the White teachers.

4. Negro principals assigned relatively lower competence ratings to the Negro teachers under their supervision than the White principals assigned to the White teachers under their supervision.

5. A higher proportion of Negro teachers than of White teachers held master's degrees.

6. A higher proportion of Negro teachers than of White teachers held five-year teaching certificates.

It should be pointed out that all teachers in the school system were used for the teacher comparative study whereas only successive sixth, eighth, tenth, and twelfth grade students were examined for the longitudinal study. It should also be noted that at the time of the teacher study (1957) there was only a limited number of integrated universities in the Southeast offering graduate work in professional education. Most Negro teachers in the study had received their training at the better colleges of the North, East and Midwest. The White teachers usually attended their state university or a local teacher training college.

Problem for Educators

THE FINDINGS reported here are part of a comprehensive study of ethnic differences in mental growth and school achievement. The populations were unselected and represented a broad cross section of sociological and economic aspects of a large county in the southeastern United States. Our group was unlike those used in most previous longitudinal studies where populations were relatively small and considerably above average in intelligence.

The findings of this study reinforce the well-known fact that on most school achievement and intelligence type tests Negro children as a group do not do as well as White boys and girls in the same school grades. These significant and persistent differences between White and Negro children in school achievement have been attributed to limitations of experiences, lack of practice, inadequate motivation, and the cultural bias of test items. It would not be unreasonable to attribute reading (verbal achievement) differences at least in part to these factors. However, this leaves unexplained the equally large and significant differences in non-verbal achievement (arithmetic) where it is claimed that Negro children have more experience than White children in dealing with practical non-verbal problems encountered on the street and in the play-ground.

The results, then, support McGurk's[8] thesis that, contrary to the position held by the environmentalist, racial differences are greater in non-cultural areas than in cultural areas. At the tenth and twelfth grade levels, median scores on vocabulary, reading comprehension, and arithmetic reasoning subtests were significantly above the mean for arithmetic fundamentals. On the culturally weighted verbal tests Negro children held their own but on non-verbal items involving only number combinations the overlap between the two groups was virtually eliminated at the last testing.

When Negro children were experimentally matched with White children in terms of intelligence, sex, and school grade placement, significant achievement differences were apparent in the basic school subjects. Even for the group matched in terms of mental ability it is in the non-cultural areas that the Negro child lags behind.

The finding of lower I.Q.s among Negro than among White children has also been attributed to poor early environment and limited educational opportunities. The environmental interpretation, however, leaves unexplained the reason both Negro and White groups of the lowest initial intelligence earn higher I.Q.s at later ages while the bright children of both races tend to earn lower scores on subsequent testings. Even those who argue most

---

[8] Op. cit.

strongly for the environmental interpretation of test differences would concede that the bright children of both groups would not likely be from low income, non-stimulating homes. Nor would one expect to find most dull children of both races in stimulating, high income homes. The parsimonious explanation of the apparent change in I.Q.s from the 1954 to the 1958 testing seems to be the normal decrease in variability between ages twelve and sixteen[9] and the regression phenomenon of tests of less than perfect reliability.

The above findings seem to lessen the importance of the so-called cultural bias of test items and differential educational opportunities as explanations for the racial differences in test performance and to suggest the need for research designed to explore developmental and motivational factors which may be related to I.Q. and achievement test differences between White and Negro children.

The issue of the equality of school achievement of White and Negro children of equal intelligence and the same age was a principal point investigated in one phase of the study. By analysis of multiple-co-variance, achievement means were adjusted so as to eliminate the effects of both mental maturity and chronological age on achievement. The co-variance analysis with mental ability and chronological age as control variables yielded significant t-values for arithmetic and reading achievement, indicating significant overall between-group differences in these skills.

It was hypothesized that pupils who earn equal scores on intelligence tests, which have been validated by checking each item in terms of the relative school success of pupils who answer the item correctly, should achieve in school at the same level. This was not our finding. After making necessary adjustments for the mental ability and chronological age differentials, Negro pupils significantly under-achieve White boys and girls in the same school grade.

These significant racial differences in school achievement exist in a county where a higher proportion of Negro teachers than of White held master's degrees and five-year level teaching certifi-

---

[9] L. M. Terman and M. A. Merrill, *Measuring Intelligence*, Cambridge, Mass. The Riverside Press, 1937.

Racial Differences in Mental Growth 405

cates. Negro teachers had also completed college course work more recently than had the White teachers. As a result of higher professional training and more teaching experience the mean yearly salary of Negro teachers markedly exceeded that of the White teachers.

This report of racial differences in school achievement is not presented in the way of new evidence but rather to point out a practical educational problem heretofore ignored by those who demand that schools be balanced in terms of factors other than mastery of basic educational objectives. The school administrator who is charged with the responsibility of providing meaningful educational experiences for all children in his district is not too concerned with Klineberg's[10] explanation that significant racial differences in mental ability and school achievement can be attributed to cultural and environmental factors. Nor is it likely to be of much comfort for the school leader to know that some psychologists believe achievement variations are the result of genetically conditioned experience producing "drives." What the administrator needs to know is how to assimilate into White school systems Negro children who in spite of better trained and higher paid teachers still learn at a rate only one-half to three-fourths of that of the White children in the same school district.

If public schools are ordered to integrate en masse there appear to be three possible courses of action:

1. Lower the educational standards and level of instruction in the White schools to the present passing level in the Negro schools. The net result of this would be to maintain for Negro pupils standards now existing in their schools, but lower expectations for the White children two to four years below their present grade norm. If this plan were adopted, there would be few if any failures or repeaters among the White children because they would almost never do so poorly as to fail by present Negro standards. Thus, it goes without saying that no reasonable citizen would sanction such a plan to lower our educational standards at a time when there is a world-wide attempt to strengthen teaching and up-grade education at all levels.

[10] Otto Klineberg, *Social Psychology*, New York, Henry Holt & Co., 1940, pp. 282–316; *Race and Psychology*, Unesco, Paris, 1951.

2. Raise educational standards required of the Negro child to those required of White children and maintain the present level of instruction and rate of failures. This alternative would result in a 40 to 60 percent Negro failure rate in intermediate grades. At the high school level where achievement differences are of the magnitude of three to four years, failure rate for the Negro student would be 80 to 90 percent with larger and larger numbers of Negro children piling up in the lower grades.

3. The final alternative would be to maintain the two existing levels of instruction and to apply differential marking and evaluation systems to the two groups. This alternative would result in *de facto* segregation because for teaching efficiency learners within each school are grouped according to achievement and learning ability.

None of the proposed alternatives represents a real solution to the problem and each would result in educational chaos and confusion and bring about an overall weakening of the educational system. The school administrator who has the responsibility of providing meaningful educational experiences for all children must have an instructional program that will provide realistic educational goals for all boys and girls regardless of race.

In regions of the United States where the Negro population is relatively small there may be no problem of balancing the schools in terms of race. However, in the southeastern United States where upwards of 30 percent of the population is Negro, racial differences in school achievement can no longer be ignored. Attempts to explain the reasons for the differences on the basis of environmental or genetic conditioning will not solve the problem. Regardless of etiology, racial differences in school achievement do exist and must be reckoned with.

BIOGRAPHICAL NOTE

STANLEY D. PORTEUS, *D.Sc., is Professor Emeritus of Clinical Psychology at the University of Hawaii and former director of the university's Psychological Research Center.*

Professor Porteus is the inventor of the famous Porteus Maze Test, a pioneer work in the development of intelligence tests for use with primitive and non-literate peoples. He has made many original contributions to the science of race psychology. His research on the various racial and national groups in Hawaii, which combined the approaches of physical anthropology, comparative anatomy, psychology, sociology and history, was one of the first interdisciplinary studies of racial differences in intelligence and temperament. The results of this study were published in his classic work, Temperament and Race (1926).

Dr. Porteus is a member of the American Psychological Association, the Association of Consulting Psychologists, and a Fellow of the International Institute of Arts and Literature. He is the author of more than eighty articles and monographs and fourteen books.

Among his books are Studies in Mental Deviation (1923), The Psychology of a Primitive People: A Study of the Australian Aborigine (1931), Primitive Intelligence and Environment (1937), The Practice of Clinical Psychology (1941), Calabashes and Kings (1945), And Blow Not the Trumpet (1947), The Restless Voyage (1949), Some Have Greatness (1962), *not to mention several volumes dealing with the Maze Test published between 1950 and 1960.*

ETHNIC GROUPS AND THE MAZE TEST

S. D. Porteus

THERE ARE several considerations that must be taken into account in any attempt at the measurement of mental differences between ethnic groups, especially when primitive peoples are concerned. The first is that the nature of the test should be affected as little as possible by cultural backgrounds. The second is motivational in character. The task set by the test should be acceptable as a worthwhile challenge to the interest and effort of individuals regardless of their background. The third desideratum is that the results of the test will be of proven significance as regards the mental adjustments which any individual is likely to be called upon to make during his ordinary life experiences.

Admittedly, it is impossible to discover a measure which is completely culture-free, which is inherently interesting to all people and the results of which are basically significant. However, there is evidence that the Porteus Maze Test, through its apparent universal applicability and interest, especially to primitive subjects, comes nearest to fulfilling two of these requirements. As to the relevancy of its results, the proof may be necessarily indirect but nevertheless convincing. Hence, comparison of the performances of various ethnic groups by its use should be illuminating.

At the outset we disclaim any intention of defining race as the term is applied to the divisions of mankind. Hence there will be little or no attempt to classify racially the groups examined, or to deal with their physical differences. All that we shall concern ourselves with is the results of various applications of the Maze Test to more or less primitive groups, who by geographical distribution, language, or other isolating factors are grouped together anthropologically and termed: Bushmen, Ainu, Santals, Chamorros, Australian aborigines, Mchopi, Sakai, etc.

If samples from all their subdivisions or tribes could be examined, these results might finally be assembled and then compared on the basis of any broad division of races upon which anthropologists might agree. But that goal is very far from attainment either from the standpoint of scope of psychological inquiry or anthropological concurrence. Therefore, only certain facts are being presented here in detail, leaving their final interpretation for the future.

Undeniably, however, on the basis of what has already been done, some implications as to comparative status seem to be quite reasonable. If this is true, then the work provides at least the best answer at present possible to the vexed questions of ethnic mental differences. At the least it demonstrates that inequalities in mental equipment do exist.

Fortunately the first two criteria of the suitability of a test for this type of inquiry, namely, understanding of the test problem as not being entirely outside the subject's cultural experience and acceptability of the task as a worthwhile challenge are both related to motivation. If the problem has features which fit into his cultural experience, the primitive subject will attack it with zest and even enjoyment.

The Response of Aborigines

THIS POINT OF interest and consequent "worthwhileness" cannot be determined except through actual examination experience. The present writer (1931) took with him into the Australian interior the Thurstone Hand Test, line drawings of hands with the fingers in varied positions, the problem being to sort the drawings into left and right hands. As many aborigines employ a manual sign language, it was thought that this test would be usable, only to find that the natives after sorting the first simple drawings correctly, apparently decided that it was child's play and unworthy of serious effort.

They similarly rejected the imitation of set patterns with colored blocks, such as the Kohs Block Design Test. They were not *their* colors nor designs. On the other hand, the form of the Maze designs was possibly suggestive of some of their totemic representations. In any case, finding their way through the Maze by avoiding traps seemed to appeal to them as it did to the Bushmen of the Kalahari, with whom the digging of game pits is traditional.

The reasons for aboriginal ready acceptance of the Maze Test are not clear, but there is no doubt as to their most eager motivation. The writer very early in his testing experience found that if he wished to retain the goodwill of the Lombadinian group he dared not exclude from examination even the most unlikely subjects.

At Lombadina, a branch of the Beagle Bay (Catholic) Mission, which was situated in a place most difficult of access on the scarcely inhabited coast between Broome and Derby, Northwest Australia, I had omitted to test an old, half-blind aboriginal, who was, however, one of the most influential members of the tribe. One of the rare winter rains was threatening and I was hastily packing to depart, for even less than an inch of rain would have made passage across a black soil plain impracticable for several weeks.

But since I hoped to return later and film night dances, I had to unpack and apply the tests. When I stopped with the simpler mazes, my unwelcome subject complained that I had given him only "the baby plays." Moreover, he resented any assistance. Hence I had to wait for over an hour while old Gregory Nangin painfully traversed the whole series. Of this experience, I wrote in 1933:

"Anyone who is wont to ascribe to the untutored savage impulsiveness or childish instability of interest has certainly never seen an old aboriginal at work on a Maze Test" (Porteus, 1933).

Two South Australian medical men, Drs. Fry and Pulleine (1931), both of whom had had considerable experience with aborigines, examined a group of Iliaura natives in Central Australia and reported their results. Among other measures they applied the Porteus Maze. They wrote:

"Tests with the mazes 'caught on' more sucessfully than any other performance test. . . . The aborigine is totally unacquainted with geometrical, mathematical, grammatical, pictorial or mechanical problems, such as form the usual basis of systems for testing intelligence. Also it is hard to interest him sufficiently to make any real attempt at any such problems. The Porteus Mazes have proved to be the most interesting of the normal tests . . . but the task is abnormally hard for the natives. While watching a native at work on these problems, one can almost feel the intensity of the mental strain involved."

Kilton Stewart (1935) applied the Maze to the Sakai, a people living in the Perak-Kelanton mountains in the Malayan Peninsula. An earlier visitor to this region, Evans (1919) noted that "it is difficult to find a Sakai who will, or can fix his attentions on any one subject for more than a few minutes at a time. . . . To question an aboriginal, especially a member of one of the wilder tribes, minutely and elaborately, usually only results in the visible distress and confusion of the savage."

On the other hand, Stewart, who on three trips accompanied Dr. H. D. Noone, then ethnographer to the Perak Museum, was able to test fifty-six males. His comment was: "They seemed to comprehend the test readily and showed great interest in making a good score. When they asked what it was for, they were told it was a white man's game and that it had been brought along to entertain them." Stewart added that they had a number of puzzles and games of their own which are somewhat comparable to the Maze situation.

Stewart also applied the test to Formosa aboriginals' children. He said: "They seemed to get great fun out of playing this American game."

Drs. Alice Joseph and Veronica F. Murray (1951) examined Chamorros and Carolinians on the island of Saipan. Their evidence was that "for the most part the children were remarkable in their ability to ignore disturbing surroundings. They were very solemn and seldom smiled during the test, though they often made grunts of satisfaction and even laughed when they solved a maze, evidently their favorite among the tests."

Dr. Cora DuBois (1944) spent fifteen months on the island of Alor, just north of Timor, and applied the Maze there. In a private communication she stated that she always knew when the test became difficult by the increase of the examinee's body odor. Any test which will make an Australian aboriginal strain his attention to a painful degree, or will make an Alorese sweat, or a Saipanese grunt with satisfaction over his success, is certainly acceptable.

Bushmen Show Keen Interest

ONE MORE instance on this important point of native interest in the test is more significant because it occurred among a group who showed inferior performance. The writer threw some test blanks on a camp fire in the Kalahari, when a sudden updraft of air scattered them over the veldt. Seven Bushmen who had been lying near the fire sprang to their feet and ran about retrieving the test blanks. I made signs that I did not need the papers but they soon showed they had another purpose in mind.

Each man took a charred twig from the fire and in a moment all were lying on their stomachs, heads to the fire radiating like the spokes of a wheel, earnestly tracing courses through the mazes. Seeing their interest, I distributed some more test blanks, most of which they had worked through during the day (Porteus, 1937).

One old man showed such disinterest that I wished to see whether his indifference was not too obvious to be genuine. I offered him three or four of the easier designs. Immediately, he pushed a couple of the young men aside and soon was working as busily as the rest. Because of his poor eyesight I had not examined him previously. Then, like my Australian friend, he complained to the interpreter, "I am not a child. The teacher has given me only a simple writing paper." When all had finished, they asked if they could take the papers home to their village—not to test their women but to show the latter how clever they were.

Considering these happenings among widely separated peoples, there cannot be any uncertainty regarding the appeal of the test to primitive people. These instances effectively dispose of the suggestion that lower scores, when observable, can be ascribed to perfunctory attention to, and lack of effort in a test quite outside their familiar cultural experience.

On the other hand, the inferior response of primitive women is quite striking. They seemed to the examiner to regard the test as something belonging in the male sphere of activity rather than their own. Their apparent stupidity might easily have been assumed. Should a woman do very well in the test and the fact become known, she might come into disfavor as trespassing on a masculine province. Aboriginal women, evidently, know their place.

Indirect, but striking proof of the acceptability of the Maze tests is provided by the high scores attained by certain groups. The disparity in performance is so great that it could hardly be explained except on the basis of differences in ability. Stewart (1935), for example, reported comparatively high averages of illiterate Tamils of India, Ainu of north Japan, illiterate Peiping coolies, and Chinese Poor House inmates, and the latter scored twelve years, about the same as the Arunta in Central Australia.

This raises the interesting question as to what happens among less educated individuals reared in a civilized environment. Does inferior educational interest and experience affect their scores adversely, a deficiency certainly well marked with regard to verbal tests? This point is important in the interpretation of Maze scores as indicating the industrial trainability of a native group in relation to their adaptability to civilization.

Results of Test in an Air Force Unit

FORTUNATELY, answers to possible questions on this score are provided by the work of Jensen (1961) in screening individuals for Air Force basic training at San Antonio, Texas, during the Korean War.

In 1952 Colonel Jensen became impressed with the large number of failures in the Airman Cluster Battery (AC-1B) and the Air Force Qualifying Test (AFQT), two lengthy tests devised by psychologists for screening purposes. This screening process seemed to him a great loss in potential manpower, especially as those failures clustered most thickly among men from Southern states where educational opportunities seemed inferior. Many such failures were on the part of Negroes. Retesting these failures by non-verbal tests, particularly the Porteus Maze, he found that the average test quotient of six hundred thirty-four of these men was 112 as against 78 by the AC-1B and 77 by the AFQT. Their mean by the Ammons Picture Vocabulary Test was 97. Jensen attributed these disparities in score between verbal and non-verbal tests to be mainly due to poor motivation.

Out of this group of retested men, Jensen decided to admit four hundred and thirty-two to basic training regardless of their failure in the Air Force tests. Results were at first given in mimeographed form but have now (1961) been published in a journal article in which he said: "Broadly interpreted, the basic training records of the retested airmen were nearly as satisfactory as were those of the airmen who did not fail the group tests. The percentages of the groups retained in service (98.3 and 96.1) are not significantly different." After tactical training in Air Flights, 82 percent of those who passed the psychological test were promoted as against 72 percent of the retested men.

Thus it would seem that ability as measured by the Maze Test is clearly related to mechanical trainability, a conclusion that would be important in considering the comparatively high scores attained by some primitive groups. It should be said, however, that the "retested" men of Jensen's subjects were mainly Whites from Southern states with poor educational records, and some Negroes. In the case of primitive peoples, educational opportunities were almost entirely lacking. Jensen's retested men were not so much distinguished by lack of opportunity as by disinclination for schooling. This attitude doubtless extended to performance in the Air Force tests, which together constituted a six and one-half hour examination.

The above experience as a whole led Jensen to the following conclusion:

"The non-verbal test scores, particularly those of the Porteus Mazes, and the basic training records of those clinically examined who were retained in service after failure in the group test led to the conclusion that, outside the academic field, most of them were not inferior—'low level'—and that many of them were truly superior. . . . In the clinical situation every individual scoring high on the Porteus test presents qualitative evidence of power to plan ahead, to execute with precision, and to adapt readily to tasks of increasing complexity."

In the writer's opinion, the same conclusion would be justified with regard to primitive subjects whose scores in the Maze run above twelve and one-half years of age, a test quotient of 90 or above. It should be remembered that these potentialities lie "outside the academic field." The Maze test, though it correlates about .6 with general intelligence tests, is not an adequate measure of scholastic brightness. Adaptation to all the requirements of our kind of life undoubtedly calls also for verbal intelligence. The fact that may primitive peoples have such limited experience with tools and gadgets throws their good performance in the Maze into higher relief.

Test Performance of American Indians

THE GREAT VARIETY of performances among primitive peoples indicates that cultural inequalities can hardly be appealed to as explaining differences in ethnic group performance. As an outstanding example, we may cite the results with Plains and Southwest American Indian tribes as found by Havighurst and Hilkevitch (1944). Their subjects were six hundred and seventy Navaho, Hopi, Zuni, Zen, Papagos, and Sioux children, who were examined by the Arthur Performance Scale, which includes a Porteus Maze series.

It should be noted, however, that the seven examiners had had training for varying periods only from four days to three weeks in applying the tests, and that none was a psychologist. Inexperienced examiners often are not strict enough in the application of the testing rules, so that their scores tend to be somewhat too high.

The obtained results show that in eight out of ten age groups

Indian children were above White norms. They found the Maze and the Mare and Foal tests to be the easiest in the scale, but that is easily understood with regard to the latter test. In this test there are seven cut-out portions of a picture of a mare and foal in a field, and the time taken to replace them in position is the basis of the score.

Indian children are, of course, familiar with the animals depicted. But the score, except for young children, depends on simple space perception and mechanical dexterity, more than on any cognitive factor. It is scored on speed of reaction and is a poor test of intelligence. This criticism does not apply to the Maze, in which the average test quotient for ten age groups from six and one-half to fifteen and one-half years was 107. Grouping the cases above thirteen years of age did not lower the average test quotient, a rather unusual result. Their test age was fourteen and four-tenths years, only about two thirds of a year below that of boys of similar age, mainly Japanese, attending high school in Honolulu.

It is interesting to note that another study of American Indians also resulted in relatively high Maze scores. Sparling (1941), in dealing with Indian cases who were referred to the Mental Health Clinic (evidently for mental diagnosis) at London, Ontario, observed that some scholastically backward cases frequently obtained good scores on the Porteus Maze, while at the same time they achieved poor records on the Stanford-Binet scale.

To investigate this disparity, thirty-two "representative" Indian children from the Mount Elgin residential school in the Muncey Reserve were examined. There were seventeen girls and fifteen boys ranging in age from eight to seventeen years. Again it was demonstrated that scores derived from non-verbal tests differed markedly from those obtained by the Stanford-Binet. The mean test quotient* for the Porteus Maze was 108 (S.D. = 16), while that for the Binet was 75 (S.D. = 13.5), a difference of thirty-three points. Sparling states that "the standard error of this differ-

---

* The present writer has for many years deprecated the use of the term intelligence quotient (I.Q.) on the ground that no scale of tests is an adequate measure of general ability. Hence the only justifiable term for the relation of mental to actual age is test quotient (T.Q.).

ence is 5.2 points. Such a difference is extremely unlikely to be due to chance sampling."

In this instance the use of a standard test based on facility in English is grossly unfair. The investigator was evidently fully seized with this injustice, for she remarks that thirteen of the children had quotients below 70. By the standards of diagnosis commonly accepted in 1941 (but now happily discarded by competent psychologists), these cases would have been "rated as morons, although their average Porteus T.Q. was 102."

Thus Sparling's results are very similar to those obtained by Jensen and fully support her conclusion that "entirely different standards must be used for White children." It is only now that clinicians have realized that those standards were unjust to Whites also. It should be remembered that most of Jensen's six hundred and thirty-two cases could also have been judged mentally deficient, yet four hundred of them were able to complete basic training, no task suitable for a "moron."

Recalculating Sparling's data gives for subjects over twelve years of age a mean T.Q. of 103 and for younger children a mean of 109. The restricted upper range of the Maze Test (the highest age attainable is seventeen years) means that it is easier for young children to obtain higher quotients. However, this has now been corrected in the revised scoring (Porteus, 1959).

Results Among Various Asiatic Groups

OUTSTANDING among records attained by non-European subjects are those presented by two medical investigators, Drs. Murray and Joseph (1951), who worked for some time with Chamorros and Carolinians on the island of Saipan. The mean Maze T.Q. for fifty Carolinian boys was 113 and for fifty girls 99.5. Fifty Chamorro boys averaged 103.5 T.Q. points, while the same number of girls averaged 92.5 T.Q. points. As described by the authors, the conditions for examination were not ideal, but this would hardly account for such high records.

For comparative purposes we may quote Honolulu results obtained by Leiter, Piddington, and Stewart in 1933. Japanese

(N = 809) averaged 98, Chinese (N = 881) 95, and Part-Hawaiians (N = 463) 96. As regards verbal tests, the relative position of the Chinese and Japanese are reversed, the former being slightly above the Japanese.

Obviously it would be ridiculous to invoke cultural advantages, superior motivation or educational opportunity as explaining the excellent performance of these Saipanese as compared with Whites. Yet those who put so much emphasis on environmental advantages do not hesitate to explain the difference between Whites and primitive subjects in exactly those terms.

Similarly, the people of Alor, an island fifty miles long and thirty miles wide, just north of Timor in the East Indies, also manifested a good performance. The examiner was an experienced anthropologist, Dr. Cora DuBois (1944), who stayed long enough to acquire sufficient ability in Alorese to be able to communicate with the natives directly. She found that the level of performance by twenty-eight men was suprisingly high, the Maze test quotient being 91. This is equivalent to a mental age of 12.76 years. The women's performance was, as is usual in primitive peoples, considerably lower, an average age of 9.43 years and a T.Q. of 67. In a note appearing in Dr. DuBois' book, I suggested that native women are unwilling to attempt a task that seems to them to lie outside the feminine province. This, however, only partially accounts for female deficiency, as almost every study of natives, regardless of racial origin, shows males to be slightly superior to females, and the more primitive the subjects the greater the discrepancy.

In a study of tenth grade Honululu high school students (1955), one hundred and fifty boys excelled one hundred and fifty girls by .31 of a year in test age when the original (Vineland Revision) was applied, and in the Maze Extension series the boys excelled girls by .69 of a year. Porteus and Bassett (1919) reported that in a study of six hundred and eighty-two high school children in New Jersey, U.S.A., the boys excelled girls both in Maze Test accuracy and speed. Sex differences are, however, merely incidental to this present discussion of Maze performance of native peoples.

It is now possible to summarize in tabular form the average

TABLE 1
LOW PERFORMANCE

Group	Number	Locality	Mean	S.D.	Examiner
Bushmen	25	Kalahari, South Africa	7.56	2.17	Porteus
Sakai Jeram	29	Coastal Malaya	7.88	2.49	Stewart
Mchopi	28	Portugese East Africa	8.34	2.45	Porteus
Negrito	22	Zambali Mts., Philippines	8.86	2.76	Stewart
Shangaans	25	Portuguese East Africa	9.30	2.66	Porteus
Bengali	36	Berhampore, India	9.42	2.44	Vicary
Galla Negroes	19	St. Helena, South Carolina, U.S.A.	9.42	—	Peterson & Telford
Santals	59	North Bengal, India	9.52	—	Vicary

TABLE 2
MEDIUM PERFORMANCE

Group	Number	Locality	Mean	S.D.	Examiner
Senoi	56	Perak-Kalanton Mts., Malaya	10.43	2.70	Stewart
Keidja-Nyul	56	Kimberley, Northwest Australia	10.48	2.30	Porteus
Karadjeri	24	Kimberley, Northwest Australia	10.52	2.60	Piddington
Chinese (illiterates)	27	Peiping, China	10.52	2.67	Stewart
Bajou	22	North Borneo	10.61	2.56	Stewart
Amaxosa	25	South Africa	10.72	2.76	Porteus
Iliaura	10	Central Australia	10.72	2.76	Fry & Pulleine
Gurkhas	21	Nepal	11.33	2.70	Stewart
Ndau	43	Southern Rhodesia	11.41	2.20	Porteus
Wakaranga	32	Southern Rhodesia	11.57	2.17	Porteus
Chinese Coolies (illiterates)	50	Peiping, China	11.68	2.74	Stewart
Bathonga	29	Northwest Transvaal, South Africa	11.72	2.22	Porteus

TABLE 3
GOOD PERFORMANCE

Group	Number	Locality	Mean	S.D.	Examiner
Chinese (literates)	40	Poor House, Peiping, China	12.01	3.00	Stewart
Arunta	25	Central Australia	12.08	2.10	Porteus
Alorese	28	Alor, Indonesia	12.76	—	DuBois
Ainu	51	Northern Japan	13.00	2.13	Stewart
Tamils	20	Southern India	13.18	2.32	Stewart
North American Indians	269	Southwest & Plains, USA	14.30	—	Havighurst-Hilkevitch
North American Indians	18	Ontario, Canada	14.40	—	Sparling
Chamorros	14	Saipan	14.50	2.54	Joseph-Murray
Carolinians	12	Saipan	15.60	2.28	Joseph-Murray

Ethnic Groups and the Maze Test

scores of the ethnic groups which have been mentioned. For purposes of comparison, results have been collected in three tables. Table 1 presents by ethnic groups and habitats those who scored below ten years on the Maze. Table 2 groups together those between ten and thirteen years. Table 3 presents all results which were above thirteen years. The first grouping includes those with low, the second those with medium, while the third category lists those with relatively good performance.

Differences in Test Achievement

INSPECTION of these tables reveals marked inequalities in Maze performance. As has already been indicated, the difference between results for the Australian aborigines and for the Kalahari Bushmen cannot be explained on the grounds of inferior motivation on the part of the last named. The Arunta natives, because of their long and intimate contact with the Herrmannsburg Mission—contact increased by topographical isolation—might for the present be omitted from comparison.

However, the Keidja-Nyul examined by me, the Karakjeri tested by Piddington, and the Iliaura seen by Fry and Pulleine, though possessing little more than casual contact with Whites, resembled very closely in way of life the Kalahari Bushmen, the men being the hunters, the women the gathers. The three Australian groups, their habitats separated at the extremes by about one thousand miles, when examined by three different examiners, averaged 10.5 years of test age, with only .22 of a year separating the extremes in mean score. On the other hand, the Bushmen averaged only 7.56, almost three years lower.

From the standpoint of difficulty of human survival, it is possible to compare though not to equate environments. From extensive personal experience in both regions, the writer would judge that actual subsistence is much more difficult in the interior of Australia than in the Kalahari region of South Africa. In regard to dearth of surface water, both Bushmen and Australian aborigines are under tremendous disadvantages, though conditions are entirely different.

Central Australia is subject to prolonged intense droughts, so that permanent springs and waterholes may be as much as a hundred miles apart. In much of the Kalahari there is no surface water but scattered thunderstorms occur in summer, and as a consequence soakages are known to and drawn upon by the Bushmen. But the salvation of both wild game and people is assured by the tsama melons, which provide both food and drink, the latter being stored in ostrich egg shells. There are no edible melons in the Australian desert and the natives camp within reach of water so that receptacles for storing water are unnecessary.

But as to food supplies, the Bushmen have a great advantage. During a four months' sojourn in the Kalahari the writer saw twenty kinds of big game that could be hunted and killed by Bushmen with poisoned arrows, excluding elephants, hippos, and rhinos, found only near water.

In Australia the only large animals are those of the kangaroo species which are hunted with the spear. Stalking is more difficult there on account of the sparsity of low cover, while its common appearance in the Kalahari makes approach relatively easy for the small Bushmen. The aborigines must supplement their food with grubs, ants, lizards, and snakes, while their women must often range twenty miles to gather enough plant food for a meal. *Veldt Kos,* mainly of vegetable type, is not rare in the Kalahari.

The Bushmen move their camps in accordance with the thunderstorm patterns. Along the Fitzroy River in the Kimberley region of Northwest Australia there is a concentration of game, but this occurs only during the height of the dry season when the river becomes a chain of waterholes. Fifty miles away from the stream bed even aborigines could die of thirst.

In actual hunting, mental alertness is, I believe, necessary to a higher degree in Australia, and this is probably reflected in higher Maze Test scores. Aborigines, however, are in no danger from carnivorous animals. Both peoples are superlative trackers. But once again the softer surface of the Kalahari makes following the "spoor" of game much easier than in the flinty ranges and stony plains of the Australian interior. These problems were explored in great detail in my books *Primitive Intelligence and Environment* (1937).

The Question of Mental Alertness

IF, AS SEEMS most probable, mental alertness is a function of the reticular system in the lower brain, then there is provided a structural development subject to hereditary factors. Over the generations it could be expected that natural selection would operate towards survival of those who are by nature better equipped to exercise constant watchfulness. Prolonged sensory acuity and keen attention constitute what we call being wide-awake.

There is evidence to show that in a debilitated state due to vitamin-B deficiency, or under constant medication by tranquilizing drugs, this awareness as shown in the Maze Test performance is blunted. Furthermore, this dulling of sensitiveness to surroundings may well be at the root of the lessened excitability and emotional disturbance which follows psychosurgery. One could postulate also lessened activity of the reticular formation in people living in coastal plains as compared with mountain dwellers, where subsistence would demand more alert activity.

If this is so, then we can easily understand the difference in Maze scores of the Sakai Jeram, who live in the steamy coastal regions of Malaya, and their near neighbors, the mountain-dwelling Senoi, where survival depends on the exercise of keener alertness. There was a difference of two and one-half years in Maze test age in favor of the latter, whose mean score was almost the same as Australian "bush" natives. The Sakai Jeram were at a cultural level similar to the South African Bushmen.

None of the peoples discussed can be considered warlike, and warding off or avoiding hostile action must make very exceptional demands on mental alertness. If this awareness is correlated highly, as we should expect, with good Maze performance, then the high scores of the North American Indians are also explicable. Planfulness in a part-agricultural, part-hunting and frequently warring people would certainly be necessary to survival. This would account for the rather remarkably high Maze scores attained by these Indian tribes.

Moreover, tribes over a thousand miles apart in habitat exhibit the same type of proficiency. It should be noted that this theoretical explanation does not make environmental demands the crucial factor except when they tend to fixate specific abilities through heredity. It is only when natural selection has time to work that we should expect the occurrence of such ethnic group differences.

The very high scores of the Chamorros and Carolinians are difficult to understand, unless, like the Polynesians, the spirit of nautical adventure, which to be successful must depend on constant sensory awareness, becomes part of the mental make-up. A sea-going people certainly requires a high state of awareness kept at a peak over long periods of time. It is not surprising to find that Hawaiians score relatively high on the Maze, but not as high as the Saipanese. Looking at a map of the Pacific could mislead one into the belief that "island-hopping" by canoes would be relatively easy. But the vast distances to be covered put a high premium on constant wakefulness, which physiological studies indicate is dependent on adequate functioning of the reticular formation.

Investigations of maze performance in relation to tranquilizing drugs has already demonstrated declines. But the behavioral effect of stimulating drugs, such as caffeine, might lie in the opposite direction. This calls for additional study. If a relation between Maze performance and specific adaptions to varying environments can be proved, then it would support the author's suggestion that the Porteus Maze is a better measure of man the doer, than man the thinker, and possibly a better index of the mental equipment which he shares with his fellow animals. Add planfulness to mental alertness and we have a very superior animal. These ideas may be speculative, but may finally issue in very fruitful experimentation.

Of potential relevancy also are deficiencies that result from induced vitamin-B deficiency, as demonstrated by the work of O'Shea, Elsom and Higbe (1942). A relation between diet and capacity for planfulness might thus be important from the standpoint either of mental decline of peoples or failure to progress towards civilization.

Man the Animal and Man the Thinker

IF THE PORTEUS Maze does relate to more fundamental traits than the ability to compute, to use language, to reason abstractly; in short, if it is a better measure of man the animal than man the thinker, then it must be validated on a different level to the tests of scholastic ability. And this has been demonstrated. Fortunately, the evidence for the test as a measure of human adaptability at the level of self-management and self-support seems unequivocal. For almost fifty years the Maze has been recognized as a reliable indicator of social sufficiency and has its greatest usefulness in relation to border-line cases or suspected mental deficiency.

More spectacular still is the work of the past twenty years on the mental effects of frontal lobe operations undertaken for the relief or care of certain psychotic symptoms. On the basis of three large studies by the Columbia-Greystone Associates (1949, 1951, 1956) in New York, as well as by other investigators, it has been generally concluded that the Maze Test is the most consistently sensitive to brain damage, and much more so than any other standard test, including the so-called general intelligence tests.

Moreover, a similar finding has been reached by Brown, French, Ogle and Jahnson (1956) with regard to operations on the temporal lobe of the brain. An eight-year follow-up study by Smith (1959) of operated patients in Rockland State Hospital, New York, confirms the sensitivity of the Maze. Sixteen out of seventeen patients (93 percent) who suffered topectomy in the superior frontal regions showed marked deficits. Porteus and Diamond (1961), analyzing the same data, have shown that patients with optical ablations of the frontal cortex also suffer similar losses.

It seems quite safe to assume that the forebrains of native individuals carry out the same functions as do the frontal regions of Europeans and that similar operations on their brains would have similar results. There is every reason to suppose that Maze scores have great significance regardless of the ethnic origin of the subjects of examination.

Finally there remains the important question of the significance of comparative maze test performance. There is one vital consideration that has, I believe, been much underestimated in the discussion of differences between ethnic or racial groups in intelligence. If we define group intelligence, as we do its individual appearance, in terms of adaptability to environment, then we have no right to regard primitive peoples as unintelligent, or to assume that a great gulf exists between peoples of low and high intelligence. The simple fact is that these primitive folk are our contemporaries. In other words, they are still here, and in many cases are maintaining themselves against pressure and competition from "superior" peoples.

Hence, any test that relates the divisions of mankind closer together must be, generally speaking, the best measure. The Maze results do rank the peoples of earth much closer together than do tests of the Binet type. But if this fact be admitted and that value maintained, then surely it is obvious that the inter-ethnic differences which the Maze reveals must be real and significant. In my opinion, this would settle the vexed question of the existence of those differences.

Literature

Brown, Ian A., Drench, Lyle A., Ogle, William S., and Jahnson, Shirley, Temporal lobe epilepsy: its clinical manifestations and surgical treatment. *Medicine*, 35: 425–459, 1956.

Columbia-Greystone Associates, *Selective Partial Ablation of the Frontal Cortex* (Edited by Mettler). New York, 1949.

———, *Psychosurgical Problems* (Edited by Mettler). Philadelphia, 1952.

DuBois, Cora, *The People of Alor*. Minneapolis, 1944.

Evans, Ivor H. N., Some Sakai beliefs and customs. *J. Roy. Anthrop. Inst.*, 18, 1918.

Fry, H. K. and Pulleine, R. H., The mentality of the Australian aborigine. *Austral. J. Exper. Biol. and Med. Sci.*, 8: 153–167, 1931.

Havighurst, Robert J. and Hilkevitch, Rhea R., The intelligence of Indian children as measured by a performance scale. *J. Abn. and Soc. Psychol.*, 39: 419–433, 1944.

Jensen, Milton B., *Basic airmen who fail to meet minimum mental standards for retention in the Air Force*. (Mimeographed) Lackland Air Force Base, 1952.

Jensen, Milton B., The "low-level" airman in retesting and basic training: A sociological study. *J. Soc. Psychol.*, 55: 177–190, 1961.

Joseph, Alice and Murray, Veronica F., *Chamorros and Carolinians of Saipan.* Cambridge, Mass., 1951.

Leiter, R. G., Piddington, R., and Stewart, K. S., The standardization of the Porteus Maze Test (Unpublished report, cited by Porteus). *Tabulae Biologicae*, 18: 66–75, 1939.

Lewis, N. D. S., Landis, C., and King, H. E. (Editors), *Studies in Topectomy.* New York, 1956.

O'Shea, Harriet E., Elsom, K., and Higbe, R., Studies of the B-vitamins in the human subject. *Amer. J. Med. Sciences*, 203: 388–397, 1942.

Piddington, R., Report of field work in Northwestern Australia. *Oceania*, 2: 342–358, 1932.

Porteus, S. D., *Psychology of a Primitive People.* London, 1931.

———, *The Maze Test and Mental Differences.* Vineland, N.J., 1933.

———, *Primitive Intelligence and Environment.* New York, 1937.

———, *The Maze Test—Recent Advances.* Palo Alto, Calif., 1955.

———, Maze Test reactions after chlorpromazine. *J. Consult. Psychol.*, 21: 15–21, 1957 (a).

———, *The Maze Test and Clinical Psychology.* Palo Alto, Calif., 1959.

———, and Barclay, John E., A further note on chlorpromazine: Maze reactions. *J. Consult. Psychol.*, 21: 297–299, 1957 (b).

———, and Bassett, Dorothy, Sex differences on Porteus Maze Test performance. *Training School Bulletin*, Vineland, N.J., Nov. 1920.

———, and Diamond, L., Porteus Maze changes after psychosurgery. *J. Ment. Sci.*, 110, 1962.

Smith, Aaron, Changes in Porteus Maze scores of brain-operated schizophrenics after an eight-year interval. *J. Ment. Sci.*, 106: 967–978, 1960.

Sparling, Margaret E., Intelligence of Indian children—the relationship between Binet and Porteus Scores. *Amer. J. Ment. Defic.*

Stewart, Kilton, A report on Porteus Maze Test results from some of the racial groups of Southeast Asia and the peripheral islands. (Unpublished study cited in Porteus, *Primitive Intelligence and Environment*, 1935.)

INDEX

ABO blood groups. *See* blood groups
Abel, Wolfgang, 108, 134
abortion, 247
Abyssinia. *See* Ethiopia
Achewa tribes, 87
adaptation to environment, 8, 13, 16, 19–22, 69, 74–76, 124, 152, 182–84, 189–91, 199, 216–17, 277, 229–30, 238, 246, 272–74, 289, 342, 345–46, 421–24, 426; capacity for, 73, 74, 216–17, 228
adrenal glands, 210
Adriatic race, 44, 45
Adriatic Sea, 7
Aegean cultures, 355
Africa, 6–7, 19, 76–90, 113, 182, 227, 229, 235, 236, 242, 243, 244, 245; central, 190, 213; east, 17, 78, 213, 420; north, 10, 11, 73, 110, 124, 149, 152, 240, 241, 249–50; south, 17, 69–92, 150, 154, 226, 229, 234, 420; South West, 76, 78, 124; west, 213
Africans, north, 11
agriculture, 243, 244–45, 248–50, 256; origins of, 230–32
Ainu, 14, 15, 214, 268, 410, 414, 420
Air Force Qualifying Test, 414–15
Aird, I., 186
Airman Cluster Battery (AC-1B), 414–15
albinism, 152
albumin, 203–204, 208
Alexander the Great, 251
Algerians, 202
Allen, A. C., xxii, 180
"Allen's Rule," 20

Allison, C. A., 182
Allport, Gordon W., 339
Alorese people, 413, 419, 420
Alpine race, 9, 10, 45, 54, 126, 269
Alps, Swiss, 7, 230
Altai Mountains, 6, 13
altitude, effects of, 152, 423–24
Amenemhet III, 111
America. *See* Western Hemisphere
American Indians. *See* Indians, American
American Psychological Association, 400
Americans (U.S.), 203, 414–16, 419; Caucasian, 146, 147, 202, 203, 209–210, 212, 263, 305, 322, 350, 367–80, 383–406, 415–16, 417; Jewish Caucasian, 307–308, 310–21, 322; non-Jewish Caucasian, 307–308, 310–21, 322; Filipino, 307; Hawaiian, 307; Indian, American, 15, 202–203, 307, 416–18, 420, 423; Mongoloid, 201, 206; Chinese, 307, 310–21, Japanese, 307, 310–21, 322; Negro, 125, 154, 204, 206, 212, 263, 295, 305, 307, 310–21, 322, 339, 349–50, 354, 367–80, 383–406, 415–16, 420
Ammon, Otto, 96
Ammons Picture Vocabulary Test, 415
anemia, 89, 145, 152, 212–13, 214
Anatolia, 250, 355
Andes Mountains, 152, 346
Angel, J. L., 103
Anglo-Saxons, 267, 269
Angoni tribes, Nyasaland, 87
Annamites, 134

ii *Index*

anthropogeography, 3–22; literature survey, 22–26
Anthropological Congress (Wrocław, Poland, 1952), 46
anthropological structures, stability of, 63
anthropological theories of history, 95–98
anthropological types, mutual relationship between, 39
Anthropologie der Badener, 96–97
anthropology and race, 3–22; literature survey, 23–26
anthropology, biochemical, 197–22; objections to, 198
anthropology, cultural, 334
anthropology, physical: and race, 283–85; and racial history, 102–105
Anthropology Today, 341
Arabia, 190, 235, 240, 241, 242, 244; *felix*, 241; Inner, 7
Arabs, 11, 166, 242, 245, 250, 263
Aramaic tribes, 112
archeology, 24, 25, 26, 336
Armenia, 10
Armenians, 10
Armenoid race, 9, 10, 12, 38, 43, 44, 45, 55, 78
Armenoid-Nordic hybrid form, 45
art: as guide to race and culture, 340–44; haptic vs. optic historical works, 351–54; prehistoric cultures revealed in, 354–61
arthritis: gouty, 211–12; rheumatoid, 215
Arthur Performance Scale, 416–18
Aryans, 12, 241, 242, 243, 244, 245, 250, 252; pre-, 269
Ashley-Montagu, M. F., xvii, 155
Asia, 6–8, 9, 13–14, 74, 149, 157, 216, 227, 230, 242, 243; central, 240; east, 157, 227; south, 10; southeast, 17, 213; southwest, 227, 231, west, 10
Asia Minor, 10, 73, 149
Asians, 111, 148–49, 210, 215
Asiatic type, western, 78
Assyria, 107, 250, 253
Assyrians, 104, 105, 112, 244, 250
Athens, ancient, 239, 250
Atlantic Ocean, 242
Atlas Mountains, 11

Augustus, 108, 113
Australia, 229, 230, 267, 410–12, 420–22
Australian aborigines. *See* Australoid race.
Australoid race, 5, 16, 18, 19, 144, 149, 151, 176, 205, 206, 207, 410–13, 414, 420, 421–22

Babylonia, 112, 261
Babylonians, 104, 105, 254
Balkan Peninsula, 103
Balkan peoples, 10
Baltic Sea, 7, 9, 10
Bantu, 206, 209, 211, 234, 242, 262; ethnogenesis and ethnology, 80–82; geographic distribution, 77–78; opportunity for study of genetic drift, 88–90; physical anthropology, 84–88; racial origins, 77–80; racial traits, 78–80; social organization, 83–84
Basques, 176, 216
Basutoland, 80–81
Bechuanaland, 80–81, 85
Beckman, L., 133, 176, 177
behavior, human (*See also* ethnocentrism; group behavioral phenotypes; social selection): and disease, 225; and ethnocentrism, 279–81; and genes, 335; and population density, 245–48; difference between men and women, 344–46; effects of racial morphology, 337–40
Belgium, 267
Bentall, H. H., 186
Bergmann, C., xxii
"Bergmann's Rule," 20
Bering Strait, 15, 153, 205, 229
Bettleheim, Bruno, 280
Bhaca tribes, 86
Biasutti, R., 44
biochemical anthropology, 197–222; and further study of races, 216–17; cholesterol, 202–203, 215; hemoglobins, 213–14; methods and techniques, 199–200; miscellaneous factors, 214–16; nutritional substances, 200–201; salivary amylase and uric acid, 211–13; serum electrolytes and

Index

biochemical anthropology—(continued)
 pepsinogen, 210–11; serum proteins, 203–207
biochemical genetics, 193
biological catastrophes, 73–74
biological concept of race. *See* race, concepts of
biological history of peoples, 95–119
biology, racial. *See* racial biology
Birdsell, J. B., 152
Birth control. *See* population control
black race. *See* Negro race
blood composition: and disease, 109, 145, 151–52, 157, 186–89, 190–91, 210–14, 229–30; and phonetic divergence, 243–44; and sex-linked genes, 177; and social homogeneity, 239
blood groups: ABO, 4, 7, 15, 16, 38, 144, 146–47, 150–51, 156–58, 186–88, 190–91, 211, 215–16, 230; MN, 176, 187; Rh, 176, 180, 187–88, 215–16
blood groups, distribution of: American Indians, 157, 176, 211, 215, (Peruvian, 144, 146, 150–51); Arabians, 190; Asians, East, 157; Australian aborigines, 144, 176; Bantu, 86, 87; Basques, 176, 216; Bushmen, 76, 86–87; Caucasians, 176 (U.S., 146; U.S. Catholics, Jews and Protestants, 157); Chinese, 146, 214; Congo pygmies, 149; Eskimos, 176; Europeans, 214; Greeks, 214; Hottentots, 86–87; Indians, East, 190, 214; Israelis, 156–57; Italians, 152; Koranas, 86–87; Liberians, 214; Malays, 214; Mediterranean peoples, 190; Mongoloids, 215; Nepalese, 214; Negritos, Philippine, 149; Negroes, 145, 152, 176, 190, 213; Swedes, 176–77, Tasmanians, 76
blood pressure, 76
Blumenbach, J. F., 28
Blutsgemeinschaften, 283
Boas, Franz, 61, 270
Boers, 85
bone density, comparison of Caucasian, Caucasian-Chinese, Mongoloid and Negro, 201

Borneo, 14, 420
Bos indicus, 165
Bos taurus, 165
Bowman, B. H., 182
Boyd, W. C., 75, 124, 150
brachycephaly. *See* crania
Brahmaputra River, 10
brain damage, 425
Brazil, 208, 209, 267, 293
breeding systems, human (*See also* endogamy; exogamy; homogamy; homonoia; hybridization; marriage; panmixia; sexual selection; social selection), 227–29, 244–45, 247–48, 251, 253, 255–57, 286–88, 297
Brenci, G., 128
British Commonwealth, 264, 275
British Isles, 74, 230, 241, 264, 268–69; England, 73, 240, 267, 269; Wales, 269
Broca, Paul, 32, 33
Bronze Age, 237–38, 242, 243–45, 253
Brown, F., Study (1944), 372–73
Brown, Ian A., 425
"brown" peoples. *See* Hamites
brown race. *See* Malay race
Bruce, M., Study (1940), 371–72
Buckwalter, J. A., 187
Buddhism, 262
Burmese, 154
Burt, Cyril, 74
Bushmen, 17–18, 72, 76–82, 85–88, 150, 151, 152, 205, 206, 207, 211, 410–11, 413–14, 420, 421–22
Buxton, *See* "Thomson-Buxton Rule," 20
Byzantium, 341

CDE blood groups. *See* blood groups, Rh.
Caesar, 110
California Achievement Tests in Reading and Arithmetic, 384–86
California Short-Form Test of Mental Maturity, 384–86
Canaanites, 111
Canada, 200, 264, 267, 370–71, 417, 420
Canary Islands, 11
cancer, 61; skin, 152, stomach, 157, 186–87

"Cape Coloreds," 154, 209
Cape of Good Hope, 85
cardiovascular disease, 202, 203
Caribbean Sea countries, 191
Carib Indians, 207
Caribs, Black, 190–91
Carolinians, 412, 418–19, 420, 424
Carothers, J. C., 89
Carr-Saunders, A. M., 246
Carthage, 249–50
Caspian people, 105
caste (*See also* social classes; social selection), 70, 113, 239, 251, 253, 254, 256; and migration, 249–50; genesis of, 235–37
Caucasus, 7
Caucasian-Mongoloid mixture, 201
Caucasian race, 3–427 *passim*; physical traits, 3, 6–12, 21, 39, 44, 49, 50, 52, 53, 56–59, 97, 128–33, 135–37, 143, 144, 146–48, 152, 156–57, 176, 177, 190, 200–17 *passim*; psychical traits, 340–41, 343–44, 349, 355–61, 363, 367–80, 383–406, 414–16
Celts, 9, 105, 241, 269
Central America, 17, 125, 231; racial distribution, 126
cephalic indices, 4, 6, 16, 38, 39, 48, 55, 59, 64, 78, 86, 104, 126, 127, 265; divergence of observed and theoretically calculated mean values in European races, 53
cerebral cortex, 155
Ceylonese, 204
chamaecephaly. *See* crania
Chamberlain, H. S., 96
Chaldeans, 112
Chamorros, 410, 412, 418–19, 420, 424
chemistry, human, 199
Childe, Gordon, 231, 234
Chilean Indians, 205
chimpanzee, 230
China, 14, 19, 205, 234, 236, 242, 354, 420
Chinese 14, 16, 105, 143, 146, 147, 201, 205, 206, 207, 209, 212, 214, 414, 419
Chinese Wall, 14
Chnumhoteps II, 111
cholera, 73–74
cholesterol, 202–203, 215

Chopi tribes, 86, 87
Christianity, 247, 248, 254–55, 262, 264
chromosomal theory, 69
chromosomes, human, 141–42
Churitic names, 112
circumcision, 254
city, the: characteristics of, 70, 128; inhabitants' racial traits, 97; origins, 237–40
civilization (*See also* culture): carrying, 250; decline, 275; decline and race mixture, 108–112; effects on natural selection, 60, 189–91, 248; effects on primitive peoples, 76; origins, 236
civilized societies, race consciousness in, 263–64
Clark, K. B., 294
classification of races. *See* races, classification of
climate, 8, 13, 16, 19–22, 74, 75, 152, 229, 342, 345–46, 421–24
colonialism and hybridization, 125
Columbia-Greystone Associates, 425
Comas, Juan, xvii
Communists, 295
Congo, the, 145
Congo pygmies, 17–19, 87, 145, 149, 150, 205, 215, 227
Congolese, Negro, 205
Congress of German Anthropologists (Lindau, 1899), 32
"consciousness of kind," 288–90, 291
contraception, 74
Cooley's anemia, 152
Coon, Carleton S., xvii, xxii, 74, 99, 152, 227, 285
copper race. *See* American Indians.
Copts, 166
Corso di Sociologia, 71–72
crania: brachycephalic, 7, 8, 10, 39, 45, 55, 78, 104, 126; chamaecephalic, 6, 7, 11, 13, 15, 16, 17; dolichocephalic, 7–8, 10, 12, 15, 40, 78, 85, 97, 127; hypsicephalic, 6, 7, 10, 11, 13, 15, 16; mesocephalic, 39; morphological relation of ancient skulls, 36
cranial characteristics, comparative: American Indian, 15; Bantu, 78; Bushman-Hottentot, 79; Cauca-

cranial characteristics—(*continued*)
 sian, 6–11; Eskimo, 15–16; Hamite, 79; Mongoloid, 13; Negro, 17, 79; Tasmanian, 76
cranial development, level of: Bushman-Hottentot, 76, 79–80; Hamite, 79; Negro, 78–79
cranial indices, height-length, 13
cranial indices, breadth-length. *See* cephalic indices
cranial types, geographic distribution of: Armenoid, 78; Asiatic, western, 78; European, western, 78; Nordic, 78; Nordic-Iranian, 103
Cretans, 249
Crete, 244, 250, 355
Crimea, the, 249
Criswell self-preference index, 308, 309, 314
Cro-Magnoids, 11, 55
cross-breeding. *See* hybridization
Crusades, The, 264
cultural barriers (*See also* social selection), 154–59, 172, 222, 274–75; influence of, 156–59
cultural historical processes and physical appearance, 335–37
culture (*See also* civilization): art as guide, 340–44; prehistoric, revealed in art forms, 354–61; decline, 236; growth, 236; growth and population structure, 105–108; racial influences, 333–63
culture concept of race. *See* race, concepts of
culture formation (*See also* ethnogenesis; race formation), 106, 154–56, 226–27, 240, 252–53, 256–57, 333–35; demographic factors, 106–116; religious and racial factors, 253–56
Cummins Pattern Index, 87
Cuvier, Georges, 28
Cyclades, the, 250
Cyrus the Great, 251
Czechoslovakia, 41, 264
Czekanowski, Jan, 27, 44

DNA. *See* deoxyribonucleic acid
da Gama, Vasco, 78
Danes, 204, 269
Danube River, 7; valley, 240, 241, 242

Darius I, 251
Darlington, C. D., xvii, xxii, 88, 285
Dart, R. A., 77, 78, 79, 80, 85, 86, 107, 226
Darwin, Charles, 229, 246, 247, 248, 290
Davenport, C. B., 59
de Coulanges, Fustel, 245
Dee River, 241
de Gobineau, Comte, 95, 96, 97, 98
demography, 106–116
Deniker, Joseph, 5, 33, 34, 44, 45, 54, 56
Denmark, 8
de Saxe, H., 85
deoxyribonucleic acid, 142
dermatoglyphics, 87, 150, 157; Australian aborigines, 151; Bantu, 88; Bushmen, 87–88, 151; Congo pygmies, 87–88; Israelis, 157; U.S. Caucasian Catholics, Jews and Protestants, 157
"developmental identification," 290–92
diabetes, 216
Diamond, L., 425
dimorphism, 97
Dinaric race, 10, 55; hybrid-form, 44
Diocletian, 252
discrimination. *See* ethnocentrism, social selection
disease, 8, 73–74, 89, 138, 144–45, 152, 186–88, 190–91, 202, 203, 208, 210, 243, 342; albinism, 152; anemia, 89, 145, 151–52, 190–91, 212–14, 229–30; arthritis and gout, 211–12, 215; bubonic plague, 8, 230; cancer, 61, 152, 157, 186–87; cardiovascular, 202–203; cholera, 73–74; diabetes, 216; erythroblastosis, 188; goiter, 217, 342; kuru, 144; malaria, 89, 152, 190–91, 213, 214, 229–30; rheumatic fever, 187; smallpox, 230; tuberculosis, 108, 203, 214; ulcers, peptic, 157, 187, 210
Dobzhansky, T., 180, 183
dolichocephaly. *See* crania
domestication of animals, 233–34
dominance, phenomena of, 37–41, 54, 56–59, 64
Don River, 241

Drosophila, 70, 72, 171, 173–76, 179–83, 185–86, 191
drugs, tranquilizing and stimulating, 424
Du Bois, Cora, 413, 419
Duijker, Hubertus C. J., 346, 351
Dunn, L. C., 180
Dutch, 75, 204
Dutch Guiana, 75
dwarfism, 18, 20
Dyakids, 14
dysgenic breeding, 74, 138

early man, 226–27
East, E., 124
East Baltic race, 10
East-European race, 56
East Mediterraneans (*See also* Mediterranean Sea), 10, 11, 12
Eastern Hemisphere, 124
ecology, human, 216
education: problems of racial integration, 383, 402–406; racial differences in achievement at school, 383–406
ego development and ethnocentrism, 290–92, 296–98
Egypt, 6, 11, 104, 111, 114, 234, 236, 239, 241, 249–50, 253, 261
Egyptians, 250; ancient, 104, 166, 238, 244; modern, 11, 166
Elsdon-Dew, R., 87
Elsom, K., 424
emigration. *See* migration.
empires, downfall of, 254
England. *See* British Isles.
English, 205, 268–69
endogamy (*See also* breeding systems, human; social selection), 75–76, 88, 128–33, 227–29, 235, 237, 253, 285–86
environment (*See also* adaptation to environment): and human survival, 421–22; and culture formation, 154–56; artificiality created by man, 60, 189–91, 248; selective forces, 216–17
epicanthus, 14, 144, 150
epigamia. *See* hybridization
erythroblastosis, 188
Eskimos, 15–17, 152, 176, 201, 203, 205, 206, 210, 215, 216, 229, 262, 342, 362

Ethiopia, 241, 243
Ethiopians, ancient, 111
ethnic groups. *See* populations
ethnic mixture. *See* hybridization
ethnocentrism (*See also* social selection), 166–67, 261–64, 270–72, 279–98, 308, 322–26, 337–39; Gumplowicz theory, 281–83; human behavior, 279–81; increased variability of adult response, 294–96; role in race formation, 270–72; social animals, 279–80
ethnogenesis (*See also* culture formation; race formation), 235–37
ethnographic concept of race. *See* race, concepts of
Etruria, 9, 244, 249, 269
Etruscans, 251
"Eurafricans," 125
Euphrates River, 105; valley, 237, 244
Eurasia, 6
Europe, 6–8, 9–11, 30, 33, 41, 44, 45, 51, 54, 56, 74, 100, 105, 149, 177, 216, 227, 230, 234, 235, 236, 240, 241, 243, 252, 254, 284; central, 38, 45, 264; eastern, 33; northeastern, 45; southern, 152; western, 157
Europeans, 42, 44, 45, 51, 60, 64, 65, 76, 126, 134–37, 148–49, 202, 205, 214, 263, 265, 269, 351; cephalic indices, 53; racial classifications, 9–11, 45, 51, 56, 78, 103
Europids. *See* Caucasian race
europrosopy, 55
Evans, Ivor H. N., 412
evolution (*See also* hybridization; isolation; mutation; selection), 60–61, 71–72, 124, 189–91, 226–37; effects of ethnocentrism, 274–75; effects of disease, dysgenic breeding and war, 73–74; psychical traits, 256–57; theories, 277–303
exogamy (*See also* breeding systems; social selection), 88, 227–29, 253, 286, 288
eyelid fold. *See* epicanthus

facial characteristics, 5, 41, 343–44; epicanthus, 14, 144, 150; euro-

facial characteristics (*continued*)
  prosopy and leptoprosopy, 55; indices, 48
facial descriptions: Alpine race, 9; Arabs, 11, Armenoid race, 10; Bantu, 85–86, Bushman-Hottentot, 76, 80, 150; Dinaric race, 10; East Baltic race, 10; Hamites, 79; Mongoloids, 15, 21, 152; Negroes, 21, 79; Tasmanian, 76; Veddids, 11
family size: relation of class level, 69; relation of intelligence, 74
fat, body: Jamaicans and Japanese, 201
Fertile Crescent, 231, 241, 249
fertility, human, 75, 69, 189, 238, 242, 247
feudalism, 236
Filipinos, 205, 211, 212, 217
Fingerprints. *See* dermatoglyphics
Fingo tribes, 86
Finnish tribes, 9
Fischer, Eugen, xvii, xxiv, 124
Fischer-Saller scale, 49
Fisher, Ronald, xvii, xxiv
flouride levels: East Indians, Eskimos, Iranians, Pakistanis, 200–201
Folkways, 281
fontanelle, 76
Fore tribe, 144
France, 7, 33, 249, 264
Franklin, Benjamin, 60
Fraser-Roberts, J. A., 124
freedom of association (*See also* social selection), 324–26
freedom vs. security, 237
French, 269
French, Lyle A., 425
Frijda, N. H., 346, 351
Fry, H. K., 411, 421

Galacia, 241
Galicia, 241
Galton, Francis, 35
Ganzheitsschau, 21
Garn, S. M., 152
Garrett, Henry E., xvii
Gates, R. Ruggles, xviii, 124, 134, 285
Gaul, 113, 249
Gear, J. H., 85
Gedda, L., 128, 134, 137

Gegenbauer, Karl, 61
genes and ability, 73–77, 226, 255, 345, 349–50, 423–24
genes and culture formation, 154–56
genes and disease, 89, 144, 145, 180, 184–89
genes and fertility, 69
genes and population differences, 145–48, 158, 335
genes and population relationship, 150–54
genes and race formation, 69–72, 238, 265–66
genes and race mixture, 98–102
genes, different, among similar phenotypes, 181–82
genes, effects of interaction of, 186–89
genes, knowledge needed of, 191–93
genetic drift, 4, 88–90, 154, 157–58, 288
genetic unbalance and pleiotropism, 184–86
Genghis Khan, 14
genic constitution, study of, 176–78
genic diversity, 142–44, 178–81, 238, 285, 290; origins of, 178–81
Genna, Guiseppa, xvii, xxiv
geographic concept of race. *See* race, concepts of
German National Socialism, 96, 263, 270–71
Germanic tribes, 9, 105, 269
Germans, 62, 63, 75, 211, 269, 342, 346, 357
Germany, 8, 134, 241
Gestalt psychology, 362
Ghana, 213
gibbon, 226
Gibowski, M., 63
Gibraltar skull, 32, 36
Giddings, Franklin, 288
Gilgamesh, epic of, 240
Gini, Corrado, 71–72, 279, 282, 287
Gittler, J. B., 294
Glacial Age, 6, 8, 13, 15, 230
Glass, H. B., 124
globulins, 203–209, 215
Gloger, C. L., xxii
"Gloger-Görnitz's Rule," 20
Gmelin, J. F., 28
Gobi Desert, 13

goiter, 217, 342
Goodman, M. E., 293
gorilla, 342
Görnitz. See "Gloger-Görnitz's Rule"
Goths, 241
Gout. See arthritis
Grant, Madison, 96
Greece, ancient, 103, 109, 110–11, 113–15, 249, 250, 269; city states, 240, 251; Classical Period, 103; Golden Age of, 107–108; Middle Helladic Period, 103; Mycaean Period, 103
Greeks: ancient, 95, 101, 103–104, 110, 244, 245, 249, 251, 254, 261; contemporary, 212, 214
Green, K. C., 179, 183
Green, M. M., 179
Greenland, 229
Gregor, A. James, xvii, 71
group behavioral phenotypes and race, 346–49
Guenther, Hans F. K., 96
Guinea, 17
Gumplowicz, Ludwig, 278–279, 285, 287, 297–98; development of Gumplowicz Theory, 281–83
Gypsies, 12; Romany-speaking, 235

habitat destruction and subsequent migration, 248–50
hair structure, 146, 148, 150, 152–53; spiral, 76, 78, 143, 144, 146, 148; "peppercorns," 76, 79, 150; straight, 143, 144, 146, 148; wavy, 79
hair structure of: Bushmen-Hottentots, 76, 79, 150; Caucasians, 144; Hamites, 79; Mongoloids, 143, 144, 146, 148; Negroes, 78, 143, 144, 146, 148; Tasmanians, 76
Haldane, J. B. S., 229
Hamites, 77–79, 241, 243, 244; physical characteristics, 79, 85
Hamitic-Bushman mixture, 77
Hannibal, 250
haptoglobins, 204–206, 215
hauptrassen, 28, 30
Havighurst, Robert J., 416–18
Hawaii, 293, 418–19
Hawaiians, 154, 202, 419, 424

head and face descriptions: African Negro, 78–79; Bushman-Hottentot, 76, 78, 79–80; Hamite, 79
Hebrew religion. See Judaism
Hegel, Georg W. F., 341
height, 18, 20, 63, 197, 239; Andaman Islands Negritos, 18; Bantu, 78–80; Bushmen, 18, 150; Bushmen-Hottentots, 76, 79; Chinese, 14; Congo pygmies, 17, 145, 147; Dinaric race, 10; Japanese, 145, 147; Lapps, 3; Malay Peninsula Negritos, 18; Mediterranean race, 10; Mongoloids, 21; Negroes, 78; New Guinea Negritos, 18; Nordic race, 9; Philippine Islands Negritos, 18, 149; Swedes, 3, 133, 147
Hellas. See Greece, ancient
Hellenes. See Greeks, ancient
Hellpach, Willy, 348
hemoglobin mutants, 145, 151, 152, 181–82, 190–91, 213–14, 216, 217, 229
hemoglobins, 213–14
hemolytic anemia, 212–13, 214
Herder, J. G., 95–96
heredity. See genes; population; race
heterosis. See hybrid vigor
Heuse, Georges A., xvii
Heyerdahl, Thor, 19
Higbe, R., 424
Hilkevitch, Rhea R., 416–18
Hinduism, 239, 247; Brahminism, 253, 254
Hindus (See also Indians, East), 10, 239, 253
history: and genetics, 225; anthropological theories of, 95–98; biological, of peoples, 95–119; racial, and physical anthropology, 102–105
Hittites, 244, 245, 250
Hoernle, A. W., 83, 84
Hogben, L., 124
homeostasis, 199, 349
Homo albus. See Caucasian race
Homo badius. See Mongoloid race
Homo cupreus. See American Indians
Homo fuscus. See Malay race
Homo niger. See Negroes
Homo vistulensis, 56

homogamy, 64
homonoia, 251, 255
homosexuality, 247
Hong Kong, 212
Hopi Indians, 416–18, 420–23
Horowitz, E. L., 294
horse economy, 8, 13–14, 242–43
Hottentots, 18, 76–77, 81, 86, 87, 206
Hottentot-Bushman mixture, 77
Howells, W., 152, 171, 183, 192, 193
Huguenots, 255
Hungary, 9
Huns, 7, 14
Huxley Lecture (1904), 34
hybrid vigor, 133, 134, 161–67, 274
hybridization, animal, 162–66
hybridization, human, 11, 44, 45, 95–98, 99, 106, 123–39, 154, 173, 175–76, 237, 239–40, 251, 256–57; abstention from, 166–67; 253–54; barriers to, 96, 154–59, 172, 222, 227, 235–36, 251, 274–75, 282–83; Caucasians with the other major races, 159–60; colonialism and, 125; and decline of civilizations, 108–112, 253–56; dysgenic, 74, 138; Europeans with Moroccans and Annamites, 134; examples of, 103–105; 108–115; genetics of, 98–102, 124, 161–66; Germans with U.S. Negroes, 134; increase in, 124–25, 137–38; Italians with Negroes, East Indians, etc., 134–37; Japanese with U.S. Caucasians and Negroes, 134; results of, 100, 101, 159–67; slavery and, 125; of subsidiary races, 125–33; war and, 133–37
hybridization, plant, 162–66
Hyksos people, 238
hypsicephaly. *See* crania

I.Q. regression, 388–97
Ice Ages. *See* Glacial Ages
Icelanders, 166–67
Ichheiser, G., 292
Illyrians, 110
immigration. *See* migration
inbreeding. *See* endogamy
Inca bone, 76

India, 6, 10, 19, 125, 149, 167, 190, 234, 235, 245, 253, 420; racial composition, 11–13
Indian epidemic (19th century), 73–74
Indian Ocean, 242
Indians, American, 4–427 *passim*; physical traits, 15–17, 21, 144, 146, 150–51, 157, 176, 200–217 *passim*; psychical traits, 21, 341–42, 343–44, 356–57, 416–18, 420
Indians, East, 11–13, 16, 134–37, 200–201, 204, 210, 212, 214, 342; Aboriginal tribes, 214; Dravidians, 210
Indids, 125
Indo-Europeans, 10, 12, 13, 103, 105; blonde tribes, 8–9, 269
Indonesia, 420
Indonesians, 242
Indus River valley, 238, 244
infanticide, 246, 247
Ingram, V. M., 181, 182
intelligence (*See also* physical traits, over-all; psychological testing): and adaptability, 74, 100; ethnic-group differences, 409–426; evolutionary development of, 226–27; and family size, 74; and genes, 69, 73–77; I.Q. regression, 388–97; racial differences, 349–50, 367–81, 383–406, 426; and social selection, 156; types of, 425–26
interbreeding. *See* hybridization
interfertility of man, 165
invasions. *See* migrations
inventions and ethnogenesis, 235–37
Inyambane tribes, 87
Ionians, 250
Ipuwer, 111
Iran, 10
Iranians, 10, 201, 205
Irish, 9, 210–11
Iron Age, 242, 245
Islam (*See also* Muslims), 247, 248, 255, 262
Isocrates, 111
isolation, geographic, 153–54, 172, 174, 176, 192–93, 230, 251, 268, 272–74, 288, 335
isolation, ecological, 172, 174, 229–30

isolation, social (*See also* cultural barriers; ethnocentrism; social selection), 63, 285–88
isoniazid, 214–15
Israel, 156
Israelis, 156, 295
Italian Committee for the Study of Population Problems, 266
Italians, 125, 134–37, 205, 211, 269, 272
Italy (*See also* Etruria, Rome, Roman Empire), 7, 126–32, 152, 241, 249, 251
Ivory Coast, 204

Jahnson, Shirley, 425
Jahoda, Marie, xvii
Jamaica, 75
Jamaicans, 201
Japan, 134, 205, 209, 236, 244, 420
Japanese, 14, 134, 145, 147, 201, 205, 263, 268, 417, 418–19
jazz, 354
Jensen, Milton B., 414–16, 418
Jericho, 231
Jews (*See also* Israelis), 11, 156–57, 166, 211, 239, 245, 253–55, 261, 264, 271, 295; U.S., 307–308, 310–21, 322; Oriental, 212
Jones, D. F., 124
Joseph, Alice, 412, 418
Judaism, 156, 239, 247, 248, 255
Juvenal, 113

Kaffirs, 17
Kalahari Desert, 76, 78, 85, 150, 421–22
Kassitic names, 112
Keeble, F., 163
Keiter, Friedrich, 357
Keith, Arthur, 273, 279, 282
Kemp, Tage, xvii, xxvii
Khoisan peoples, 77–78
Klages, Ludwig, 338
Klemm, Gustav, 97
Klineberg, Otto, 377, 378, 379, 405, xvii
Kluckhohn, Clyde, 284
Kóčka, W., 45, 56
Kohs Block Design Test, 411
Kola Peninsula, 14

Kollman, Julius, 30, 31, 32, 43, 44
Korana tribes, 86, 87
Kretschmer, E., 100, 101
Kroeber, Alfred L., 341
Kulturleistungen der Menschheit, Die, 98
Kunst der Welt, 353
Kunst und Rasse, 341
Kurgan people, 33
kuru, 144

labor, division of, 106
Lake Albert, 77
Lake Victoria, 77
Lamarck, Jean de, 151
Landauer, Walter, xvii, xxvi–xxvii
Landsteiner, K., 174
language (*See also* linguistic expansions), 227, 243; destruction of, 243; diversity, 227; phonetic divergence and blood groups, 243–44; splits, 243–44
languages: Arabic, 11; Aryan, 243, 244; Basque, 244; Bushman, 81; Celtic, 241, 243, 244; Greek, 103, 241; Hebrew, 11; Hittite, 241; Indo-European, 8; Latin, 241, 243, 244; Nguni, 81; Paleolithic Age, 243; Persian, 241; Sanskrit, 241; Slavic, 243; Teutonic, 243
Lapouge, V., 96
Lapponoid race, 38, 43, 45, 48, 54, 56, 57
Lapps, 3, 9
Lapp-Swedish mixture, 108
Lasker, B., 292
Latin peoples, 270
Laurence-Moon-Bardet-Biedl syndrome, 185
"Law of Ammon," 97
"Law of Ancestral Heredity," 37
"Law of Dominance," 36
"Law of Frequency of Types," 38, 41, 42, 43, 45, 46, 55, 56, 57, 65
"Law of Segregation," 31
"Law of the Anthropological Mean Value of the Cranial Index," 40, 46, 51
"Law of the Cultural Pyramid," 106, 107
"Law of the Mean Value of the Cephalic Index," 40–41, 48
Lebanese, 157

Lehmann, Johannes, 357, 362
Leiter, R. G., 418
Lemba tribe, 82
Lenz, Fritz, xvii, xxiv–xxv
leptoprosopy, 55
Lerner's Genetic Homeostasis, 349
Lewis, E. B., 179
lex Papia Poppea, 113
Liberians, 204, 205, 206, 214
Libya, 250
Libyans, ancient, 111
linguistic concept of race. See race, concepts of
linguistic expansions, 240–43, 267
linguistic geography, 26
Linnaeus, Carolus, xxiv, 28, 96
Lissitzky, E., 360
literacy (*See also* psychological test results), 70
Lithuania, 241
"Litoral race," 55
Little Antilles, 75
Livingstone, F. B., 190
Livy, 240
longevity, Bushman, 76
Lundborg, H., 108
Lydia, 244
Lydians, 249
Lyrik der Naturvölker, 361

McGurk, Frank C. J., 350, 400, 403
McGurk, Frank C. J., Study (1951), 374–78
MN blood groups. See blood groups
Macedonian Empire, 244
Mackey, G. P., 89
Madagascans, 210
Maghreb (*See also* Africa, north), 241
malaria, 89, 152, 190–91, 213, 214, 229–30
Malay Archipelago, 149
Malay race, 28–427 *passim*; physical traits, 14, 79, 200–217 *passim*; psychical traits, 343–44, 353, 361–62, 418–20
Malaya, 204, 206, 412, 420, 423
Malayans, 14, 205, 214, 342
Malewitsch, K., 360
Malthus, Thomas R., 248
Mamelukes, 250
Mantegazza, P., 284

Maoris, 212, 217, 234
Mare and Foal Test, 417
marriage (*See also* breeding systems): abstention from interracial, 166–67; customs, 70, 83, 84, 87, 124; laws, 113
marsupials, 18
Martin, Rudolf, 35
Martin Scale, 49, 56
Mather, K. xvii, xxv
Mayan Empire, 107
Mayr, Ernst, 124
maze tests, 409–427
Mchopi people, 410
Mediterranean race, 10, 11, 38, 43, 48, 55, 103, 105, 127, 145, 269
Mediterranean Sea, 230, 249; surrounding lands, 7, 10, 110, 114, 190, 212, 214, 250, 346
Meiners, Cristoph, 95, 96
Melanesians, 16; in New Guinea, 144, 204, 205, 206
Mendel, Gregor, 31, 151, 273
Mendel Institute, Gregor, 128
Mendelian laws, 36, 37
Mendelian patterns, 134, 187
mental ability. See intelligence
mental alertness (*See also* intelligence), 423–24
mental illness, 61
Mercuri, A., 134, 137
mesocephaly. See crania
Mesopatamia, 103, 111–12
mestizos, 125, 211
"Method of Approximation" (Adam Wanke), 46–54, 55, 56
Mexicans, 211
Mexico, 105, 267
Michalski, I., 55
Micronesians, 210
Middle Ages, 7, 12, 54, 240, 255
Migration, 6–8, 9, 20, 97, 103, 104, 110–11, 112–16, 127–28, 172, 175, 190, 232–35, 240–45, 250–51, 252; to cities, 97, 127–28, 62; domestic, and subracial hybridization, 127–28, 133; following habitat destruction, 248–50; and interpopulation differences, 153–54; restrictive legislation, 264, 270; and racial types, 62–65

Minoans, 249, 250
miscegenation. *See* hybridization
Miszkiewicz, Bruno, 43
Mitanni, Indo-European, 105
Mithraism, 247
Mondrian, 360
Mongoloid-Caucasian mixture, 201
Mongoloid race, 4–427 *passim*; physical traits, 13–17 *passim*, 20–21, 50, 143–48 *passim*, 152, 157, 176, 200–217 *passim*; psychical traits, 20–21, 343–44, 355–60, 414, 418–20
Mongols, 7, 8, 9, 12, 14
monomorphism, 76
monovalent-divalent ion ratio, 199
Moravia. *See* Czechoslovakia
Moreland, J. H., 182
Moroccans, 134
Morocco, 7, 11
morphological concept of race. *See* race, concepts of
Morselli, 284
Mosca, Gaetano, 278–79, 282
Mosjesj, Chief, 81
Mourant, A. E., 177
Mozambique, 82
Mpondo tribes, 86, 87
Muller, H. J., xvii, xxvi
Murray, Veronica F., 412, 418
Muslim expansion, 242
Muslims (*See also* Islam), 264
mutation, 19, 64, 142–43, 151–52, 155, 161, 173–75, 176, 178–80, 181–82, 229–30, 246
Mycenaeans, 250
Mydlarski, Jan, 63

Nahua people, 105
nasal index, 48
nation, the: influence of social customs, 69–72; origins, 237–40; as race in formation; difference from race or people, 266–67
"national character," 335, 346–49; areas of research in, 349–51
nationhood, 253
Navajo Indians, 202–203, 207, 208, 416–18
Ndebele tribes, 80–81
Neandertal man, 32, 35, 342
Near East, 7, 10, 104, 109, 110, 261
nebenrassen, 33

Negritos, 229; Andaman Islands, 18, 262; Malay Peninsula, 18; New Guinea, 18; Philippine Islands, 18, 149, 420
Negro race, 5–427 *passim*; physical traits, 11–19 *passim*, 21, 72, 75, 76, 78–80, 84–88 *passim*, 135–37, 143, 144–52 *passim*, 176, 190, 200–217 *passim*; psychical traits, 21, 340–44, 349–50, 353–55, 357, 361–62, 367–80, 383–406, 413–16, 420–23
Neolithic Age, 61, 103, 237, 244, 245, 247
Neolithic expansion, 232–35, 240
Neolithic peoples, 234, 241, 244, 245
"Neolithic Revolution," 231
Nepal, 420
Nepalese, 214
Netherland Antilles, 208
neurocranium, 41
neuropathological disease, 144
New Guinea, 18–19, 144, 230
New World, 229, 231, 233–34, 243, 256
New Zealand, 234, 267
New Zealanders; Caucasian, 212; Maoris, 212, 217, 234,
Nguni ethnic group, 80–82, 84, 88
Niceforo, Alfredo, 282, 288
Nietzsche, Friedrich, W., 97, 98
Niger River, 213
Nigeria, 77, 208
Nigerians, 202, 204, 205
Nile River, 241; valley, 237, 244
Nilotic Negroes, 143–44
Ninevah, 261
Noone, H. D., 412
Nordic race, 9, 10, 12, 38, 43, 48, 56, 57, 58, 62, 75, 78, 269
Nordic-Iranian cranial type, 103
Norman Conquest, 95, 240
Normans, 269
North Atlantic race, 9
North Sea, 7, 9
Norwegians, 205
Nubia, 11, 240, 241
Nubians, 111, 244
nutrition, 18, 63, 89, 147, 200–201, 233, 245–46, 423–24
Oceanic peoples, 17–19
Ogle, William S., 425

Old World, 229, 231, 233–34, 243, 256
Oliver, C. P., 183
"Oriental" race, 45, 55
Orientals, 270
Ornamente der Natur-und Halbkulturvölker, 357
O'Shea, Harriet E., 424
outbreeding. *See* exogamy
over-specialization (*See also* adaptation to environment), 69

Pakistanis, 201, 204
"Paleo-Europid race," 45, 56
Paleolithic Age, 229, 237, 243
Paleolithic culture, 76, 228, 237, 247
Paleolithic expansion, last, 229–30
Paleolithic peoples, 234, 238, 241, 243, 244, 245
Palestine, 156, 249, 263
Palestinians, ancient, 104
palmprints. *See* dermatoglyphics
panmixia, 69, 77, 89, 128, 138
Papagos Indians, 416–18, 420–23
Papuans, 206
parasite-borne diseases, effects of, 89
Parsis, 166–67
Patterson, J. T., 183
Pavelčik, Jan, 41, 42
Pavlov, Ivan P., 348
Pearson, Karl, 30, 35, 37, 47; Biometric School, 35
Pellew, C., 163
pelvis, Tasmanian, 76
Penrose, L. S., 184, 189
people, distinction between race, nation and, 266–67
"peppercorns" hair, 76, 79, 150
pepsinogen, 210–11, 217
Persia, 167, 250, 253
Persian Empire, 244
Persians, ancient, 104, 244, 245, 251
Peru, 346
Peruvian Indians, 144, 146, 147, 150, 205
Philippine Islands, 14, 149
Phoenicia, 250
Phoenicians, 249
phosphoarginine, 199
phosphocreatine, 199

physical appearance: behavioral reaction to, 337–40; and cultural historical processes, 335–37
physical racial traits. *See* racial traits
physique, 20–21; American Indians, 21; Bantu, 78–79; Bushmen, 79; Caucasians, 21; Hamites, 79; Mongoloids, 13, 20–21; Negritos, 18; Negroes, 21, 78; Veddids, 11–12
Piddington, R., 418, 421
pigmentation, 8, 41, 45, 46, 56, 74–76, 152, 229; albinism, 152; and cancer, 61; and race classification, 29
pigmentation, eye, 41, 48, 56–59, 145, 148; dominance, 57–58
pigmentation, hair, 48, 55, 145; Hamites, 79; Indo-Europeans, 8–9, 269; Italians, 128–29, Negroes, 78, Tasmanians, 76
pigmentation, skin, 148–49, 197; Bantu, 86; Bushmen, 17, 76, 79, 86, 150; Bushmen-Hottentots, 76; Caucasian, 143, 148; Chinese, 143, 144; Congo pygmies, 17; Germans, rural vs. urban, 97; Hamites, 79; Indo-Europeans, 12; Italians, 128–30; Mongoloids, 148; Negritos, 18, Negroes, 75, 78, 143, 144, 148; Veddids, 12
Pithecanthropus, 35
Plague, the Great, 8
pleiotropism and genetic unbalance, 184–86
Pleistocene Epoch, 78
Po River valley, 152
poetry, African and Polynesian, 361–63
Poland, 43
Poles, 43, 45, 62, 64, 205
Polish racial anthropology, 54, 55, 61, 62
politics and race study, 123, 322–24
polyandry. *See* breeding systems, human
Polybius, 114
polygamy. *See* breeding systems, human
polygyny. *See* breeding systems, human

polymorphism, 70, 72, 73, 74, 75, 77, 85, 88–89, 100, 174–76
Polynesia, 230
Polynesians, 19, 205, 342, 361–62, 424
population control, 69, 74, 84, 113, 238, 245–48
population differences (*See also* racial differences, racial traits), 145–59, 154–56, 282–83, 287; among units, 174–76; within a unit, 173–74; in art and poetry 351–63; biochemical, 200–217; in Porteus Maze Test scores, 409–427; genetic factors, 145–48
population explosion, 247
population genetics, 142–44, 150–54, 176–77, 189–91, 192, 215, 282–93, 297, 349; and formation of races, 69–72
population relationship, genetic factors in, 150–54
population structure and cultural growth, 105–108
populationship concept of race. *See* race, concepts of
Porteus Maze Test. *See* maze tests.
Portuguese, 85
potassium, blood, 210; hyperpotassemia, 210
preferential breeding. *See* selection, sexual; selection, social
prehistoric cultures revealed in art forms, 354–61
prejudice. *See* ethnocentrism; social selection
primates, non-human, 205, 206, chimpanzee, 230; gibbon, 226, gorilla, 342
primitive peoples, 228, 262–63, 409–426
"Principle of Self-Exaggeration," 226–27, 231–32
Prussia, 255
psychological tests, standard, results of American Indians in, 417–18
psychological tests, standard, results of U.S. Caucasians and Negroes in: tests performed (1939–53), 370–79; tests performed (1954–65), 384–402 World War I draftees, 368–70; Korean War Air Force unit (1952), 414–16;

psychological tests—(*continued*) research published (1935–50), 370; the "culture hypothesis," 367–68, 376–80
psychological tests, non-verbal: considerations in devising, 409–410; efficacy compared to standard tests, 425–26
psychological tests, non-verbal, results of: aboriginal response to different varieties, 410–13; differences between the sexes, 414, 419; relation of mental alertness to high achievement, 423–24; wide differences in achievement, 421–22; various Asiatic peoples, 414, 418–21, 423–24; Australian aborigines, 414, 420, 421–23; American Indians, 416–18, 420, 423; Bushmen, 413–14, 420, 421–22, 423; Negritos, 420; U.S. Air Force unit, 414–16; variety of U.S. children, 419
Puerto Ricans, 212
Pulleine, R. H., 411, 421
Punic Wars, 109
pygmies, Congo. *See* Congo pygmies
pygmies in Andaman Islands, Malay Peninsula, New Guinea, Philippine Islands. *See* Negritos

Quetelet, A., 284

race: and anthropology, 3–26; art as a guide, 340–44; consciousness of, in civilized societies, 363–64; relation of culture and religion to, 253–56; and group behavioral phenotypes, 346–49; distinction between people, nation, and, 266–67; and physical anthropology, 283–85; "purity," 264–66, 270; and society, 277–303; and sociology, 261–75
Race and Psychology (Unesco), xvii
Race and Science (Unesco), xvi
Race Concept: Results of an Inquiry, the (Unesco), xvi, xxii–xxvii
race, concepts of (*See also* races, classification of), 29–34, 64–65, 101, 123, 131–33, 151–52, 161,

Index

race—(continued)
 282, 285–87, 297, 367–81, 403–404, 424, 426
race, definitions of, 3–4, 54–59, 148–50, 171–72, 176, 266–67, 334; analysis of definitions, 54–59
Race Relations and Mental Health (Unesco), xvii
races, classification of (See also races, concepts of), 4–6, 29–67, 142, 197–98, 199, 284; comparison of systems used in classifying Europeans, 44, 56; criticism of morphological approach, 54–59; Deniker's system compared to Polish system, 55; ethnographic-linguistic, 29, 30; geographic, 29, 33, 34, 35; morphological, 33–67, 176; morphological-linguistic, 33; pigmentation of skin, 29; 5, 33; typological analysis of the living, 41–45
races, formation of (See also culture formation; ethnogenesis; evolution), 19–22, 34–41, 57, 59, 69–72, 95–11, 180, 192–93, 216–17, 225–27, 231, 233–34, 250–51, 255, 272–73, 283, 286, 287–88, 345; geographic factors, 272–74; effect of group sentiment, 270–72
races, primary, 5, 29–30, 33
races, subsidiary, 5, 33
racial composition of: the Bantu, 77–80; Central and South America, 126; France, Germany, Italy, and ancient Greece, Etruria and Rome, 269; Great Britain, 268–69; India, 11–13; Japan, 268; modern Europe, 9–11
racial differences (See also population differences; racial traits): anthropological aspects, 3–26; biochemical, 200–217; effect of, on culture formation, 333–37; evidence in art and poetry, 351–63; evidence contradicting the "culture hypothesis," 30, 31, 34–41, 56–57, 59, 367, 374–75, 376–78, 410, 426; knowledge needed, 191–93; psychological test results and school achievement, 367–81, 383–406; and the structure of so-

racial differences—(continued)
 ciety, 237–40; value judgments vs. scientific evidence, 379–80
racial history and physical anthropology, 102–105
racial integration in schools, 402–406
racial mixture. See hybridization
Racial Myths (Unesco), xvii
racial traits, nature of, 72, 161, 190, 267–88
racial traits, physical (See also biochemical anthropology; blood groups; crania; cranial characteristics; cranial development; dermatoglyphics; disease; facial characteristics; hair structure; over-all head characteristics; height; pelvis; physique; pigmentation; respiratory systems; sex organs; steatopygia; sweat glands; voice), 4–6, 134–37, 333–35, 342
racial traits, psychical (See also intelligence; psychological tests; temperament): revealed in art and poetry, 340–62; and culture formation, 154–56; and evolution, 256–57; evolutionary development of, 19–22, 226–27; and genes, 158–59; and race mixture, 100–102
racism. See ethnocentrism; social selection
Rasse und Kultur, 351
Rassenkampf, Der, 281
Rechtsstaat und Socialismus, 282
"Regression Law" (Galton), 35–36
Rehebother Bastaards, 124
religion: and civilization, 251, 252; as cultural barrier; 156, 261; relation of, to culture and race, 253–56; and male vs. female dominance, 244–45; and population control, 247–48; and social selection, 307, 320
religions: Buddhism, 262; Christianity, 247, 248, 254–55, 262, 264; Hinduism, 239, 247; Islam, 247, 248; Judaism, 156, 239, 247, 248, 255; Mithraism, 247
respiratory systems, specialized: American Indians, South, 152; Negro, 75

Rhesus blood groups. *See* blood groups, Rh
rheumatic fever, 187
Rhoads, T. F., Study (1945), 373-74
Rhodesia, 78, 420
Riegl, Alois, 352, 361
Rife, David C., 124
Ripley, W. Z., 33, 34, 44, 45
"rivalry of intolerances," 295
Roberts, D. F., 187
Roman Empire, 98, 108, 109-110, 113-15, 244, 252, 255, 269, 275
Romans, ancient, 104, 105, 109-110, 113, 245, 251, 254, 261
Rome, ancient, 239, 250
Rosinski, Boleslaw, 56
Ruge, George, 60
"Rules of Climate," 20
rural dwellers, racial traits of, 97
Russia, 9, 10, 242, 274; Asian Russia, 73; Great Russia, 33; steppes, 242; Soviet Russia, 267, 295
Russians, 357

Saba Island, 75
sacrifice, human, 247
Sahara Desert, 11, 77-78
Saipan, 412, 418, 420
Sakai Jeram people, 410, 412, 420, 423
salivary amylase, 211-13
Saller, Karl, xvii, xxv
Santa Gertrudes, 164-66
Santals, 410, 420
Sardinians, 212
Saxons, 269
Scandinavia, 145, 152, 241, 265
Scandinavians, 166
Schapiro, Meyer, 341
Scheidt, Walter, xvii, xxv
Schlaginhaufen, Otto, 44, 54, 56
Schneider, H., 98, 99, 107
Schneider, R. G., 182
Schultze-Naumburg, Paul, 341
Schweitzer, B., 101
Schwidetzky, Ilse, 342
Scythians, 242
segregation. *See* social selection
selection, "disruptive," 235-36, 256
selection, natural, 16, 19, 61, 63, 124, 146, 151-52, 157-58, 161, 167, 182-84, 189-91, 226,

selection, natural—(*continued*) 231-33, 246, 248, 285, 290, 423; interruption of, 161-66, 189
selection, sexual (*see also* breeding systems, human), 64, 69, 71, 72, 73, 124, 184, 229, 253, 282-83, 286-88, 290
selection, social (*see also* cultural barriers; ethnocentrism), 64, 69, 237, 238-40, 251, 253, 285-86, 288-90, 296-98; of ethnic groups, 305-329; and evolution, 256-57; and freedom of choice, 324-26; and similarity, 292-94
Semites, 82, 95, 241, 242, 243, 244, 245, 250; Akkadian, 105
"Semitic smile," 11
Senoi people, 420, 423
serfdom, 236
Serio, A., 134, 137
serological incompatability, 109
serum electrolytes, 210-11
serum proteins, 203-207
Severus, Lucius Septimius, 110
sex organs, atypical, 76
sexes, differences between the: in psychological-test scores, 414, 419; in social behavior, 316, 317, 318, 320, 321, 344-46
sexual activity, 226
Shaka, Chief, 81, 85
Shangaan tribes, 87
Shangana-Tsonga tribes, 82
Shuey, Audrey M., 350
Shuey, Audrey M., Study (1942), 372
Siberians, 152
Sicily, 249
sicklaemia, 89
sickle-cell anaemia, 89, 145, 151-52, 213
Sieg, R., 134
Simpson, G. G., 124
Singapore, 212
Sioux Indians, 211, 416-18
skulls. *See* crania
slavery, 19, 21, 109-111, 125, 236, 247, 251, 252
Slavs, 9, 105, 241, 252, 270, 346
social classes (See also culture formation; castes; social selection), 70, 74, 113, 239, 251, 253, 256

social customs and rules, influence on races and nations of, 69–72
"social suggestion," 297
social systems: of the Bantu, 83–84; and evolution, 256–57; immigration factor in, 112–16; male vs. female dominance, 244–45
sociology: and race, 261–75; developmental level, 277–29
sodium, blood, 210
soil erosion, 248–50
Solomon Islands, 19
Somaliland, 124
Sorokin, P., 256
Sorokin's Congeries, 349
Sotho ethnic group, 81–82, 84, 85, 86, 88
Sotho tribes (*See also* Tswana tribes), 81–82, 87
South Africa, Republic of, 80–82, 209
South America, 17, 125, 230, 267, 274; racial distribution, 126
Spain, 7, 11, 113, 263–64, 267
Spaini, P., 128
Spaniards, 267, 342
Sparling, Margaret E., 417–18
Sparta, ancient, 239
species: definitions, 171–72; formation, 69
speech. *See* language
splanchnocranium, 41
Stanford-Binet test, 417–18, 426
"Statement on the Nature of Race and Race Differences" (Unesco), xvi, xxii–xxvii
Stember, C. H., 294
steatopygia, 76, 150, 152
Stewart, Kilton, 412, 414, 418
Stolyhwo, K., 64
Stone, W. S., 183
Stone Age, 14, 354, 355
Strzygowsky, Josef, 361
Sturtevant, A. H., xvii, xxvi
subracial mixture. *See* hybridization
Sudan, 17
Sudanese, 154, 166
Sumer, 107, 244, 249–50, 253
Sumerians, 104, 105, 241
Sumner, William Graham, 279, 280, 281, 297
Sunda Islands, 19

Surowiecki, W., 30, 33, 42, 44
Swazi tribes, 80–81, 86, 87
Swaziland, 80–81
sweat glands, specialized, 21, 75
Sweden, 133
Swedes, 3, 133, 147, 177–78, 204
Swiss, 47–59 *passim*, 63
Switzerland, 241, 267
Syria, 10, 11, 114, 249, 250
Syrians, 104, 110, 157
Szmyt, Jacek, 61

Taiwan, 14, 205, 206, 412
Tamerlane, 14
Tamils, 414, 420
Tana River, 77
Tanser, H. A., Study (1939), 370–71
Tasmanians, 76
Tatars, 14
temperament (*See also* psychical traits, over-all): American Indians, 21; Caucasians, 21; Mongoloids, 20–21; Negroes, 21
Teotihuacan people, 105
Teutons, 252
Thais, 205, 206, 215
thalassemia, 214
"Thomson-Buxton Rule," 20
Thracians, 10
Thurstone Hand Test, 410
Tierra del Fuego, 15
Tigris River, 105
Tobias, P. V., 72, 76, 87
Tocher, J. F., 61
tool-making skill, 227
trade, effects of, 234–35
Trajan, 110
transferrins, 206–208, 215
Trevor, J. C., 124
tribes, genesis of, 235–37, 285
tropical peoples, 230
Tschepurkowsky, Ethyme, 33
Tsonga ethnic group, 82, 86
Tswana tribes, 81–82, 86, 87
tuberculosis, 108, 203, 214
Turkestan, 10
Turkic peoples, 14
Tweed, G. V., 187

Ukraine, the, 241
ulcers, peptic, 157, 187, 210
Unesco, xvi–xxvii *passim*

United States, 96, 125, 149, 182, 200, 205, 264, 267, 270, 275, 295, 349–50, 351, 372–79
urban. *See* city
uric acid, 211–13

Valle, Manuel, 346
van Doesburg, T., 360
Veddids, 11, 12, 14, 19, 125
Venda ethnic group, 82, 84, 88
Venezuela, 229
Venezuelan Indians, 205, 207, 217
Venice, ancient, 239
Verknüpfung, 40, 59
Vespasian, 110
Victoria Falls, 78
Vikings, 241
Virchow, Rudolf, 30, 35; contribution to morphological classification of race, 32–34
Vistulienne race, 44
Voelker, 30
voice, Bushmen's, 76
Vondemberghe-Gildenwart, 360
von Eickstedt, Egon, 5, 44, 95, 99
von Sydow, Eckart, 361
von Uexküell, Jakob J., 339
von Weizsäcker, Carl F., 336

Wanke, Adam, 41, 55, 56; "Method of Approximation," 46–54
war, effects of, 8, 74, 81–82, 85, 109, 124, 133–37, 231, 248

War Mulattoes, 124
Weinert, Hans, xvii, xxv
Welt, aus der wir Kommen, Die, 355
weltanschauung, 352, 362
Western Civilization, 113, 342, 358–61
Western Hemisphere, 6, 15–17, 21, 104, 152, 205, 229, 230, 346
white race. *See* Caucasian race
White Sea, 14
Williams, Roger J., 198
Wokroj, F., 63
Woltmann, L., 96
World War I, 134
World War II, 127, 134–35

Xhosa tribes, 80–81, 86, 87

Yamato people, 268
yellow race. *See* Mongoloid race
Yellow River valley, 242
Yemen, 241
Yerkes, R. M., 368
Yupa tribe, 207

Zambesi River, 85, 213
Zen Indians, 416–18, 420, 423
Zoroastrians, 167
Zulu tribes, 80–82, 85, 86, 87, 205, 206
Zulu Wars, 81–82, 85
Zuni Indians, 416–18, 420–23